# THE ITALIAN ECONOMY AT THE DAWN OF THE 21ST CENTURY

*To Patrizia and Flora*

# The Italian Economy at the Dawn of the 21st Century

*Edited by*
**MASSIMO DI MATTEO**
*Università di Siena*

**PAOLO PIACENTINI**
*Università La Sapienza, Roma*

LONDON AND NEW YORK

First published 2003 by Ashgate Publishing

Reissued 2018 by Routledge
2 Park Square, Milton Park, Abingdon, Oxon OX14 4RN
711 Third Avenue, New York, NY 10017, USA

*Routledge is an imprint of the Taylor & Francis Group, an informa business*

Copyright © Massimo Di Matteo and Paolo Piacentini 2003

The editors have asserted their moral right under the Copyright, Designs and Patents Act, 1988, to be identified as the editors of this work.

All rights reserved. No part of this book may be reprinted or reproduced or utilised in any form or by any electronic, mechanical, or other means, now known or hereafter invented, including photocopying and recording, or in any information storage or retrieval system, without permission in writing from the publishers.

Notice:
Product or corporate names may be trademarks or registered trademarks, and are used only for identification and explanation without intent to infringe.

Publisher's Note
The publisher has gone to great lengths to ensure the quality of this reprint but points out that some imperfections in the original copies may be apparent.

Disclaimer
The publisher has made every effort to trace copyright holders and welcomes correspondence from those they have been unable to contact.

A Library of Congress record exists under LC control number: 2002043967

ISBN 13: 978-1-138-71455-7 (hbk)
ISBN 13: 978-1-138-71453-3 (pbk)
ISBN 13: 978-1-315-19785-2 (ebk)

# Contents

List of Contributors *viii*
Preface *x*

## PART I: GROWTH PATTERNS AND STRUCTURAL FEATURES

1   Italy's First Phase of Postwar Development: The Role of
    Aggregate Demand                                                    3
    *Massimo Di Matteo*
    Comment                                                            11
    *Hiroshi Yoshikawa*

2   The Italian Economy after the Bretton Woods Era (1971-2001)        13
    *Alessandro Vercelli and Luciano Fiordoni*

3   The Italian Labour Market and Production System:
    Structural Features and Main Developments                          38
    *Carlo De Gregorio, Andrea de Panizza, Roberto Monducci
    and Leonello Tronti*
    Comment                                                            76
    *Kenichi Sakai*

## PART II: ASPECTS OF A DUAL ECONOMY

4   Old and New Dualisms in the Italian Labour Market                  81
    *Roberto Schiattarella and Paolo Piacentini*
    Comment                                                           100
    *Sumi Iwamoto*

5   Development Policies in the Italian Mezzogiorno:
    Lessons from the Past                                             104
    *Maurizio Franzini*

6   Rethinking Development Policies in Italy                          129
    *Fabrizio Barca*

| | | |
|---|---|---|
| 7 | Evolution of Production Structure in the Italian Regions<br>*Carlo Andrea Bollino and Marcello Signorelli*<br>Comment<br>*Micaela Notarangelo and Giovanni Russo* | 150<br><br>172 |

## PART III: CORPORATE GOVERNANCE AND INDUSTRIAL ORGANIZATION

| | | |
|---|---|---|
| 8 | Continuity and Change in Italian Corporate Governance:<br>The Institutional Stability of One Variety of Capitalism<br>*Ugo Pagano and Sandro Trento* | 177 |
| 9 | Production Outsourcing in Italian Manufacturing Industry<br>*Alessandro Innocenti*<br>Comment<br>*Katsuhito Iwai* | 212<br><br>233 |
| 10 | Italian Districts in the International Economy<br>*Rodolfo Helg*<br>Comment<br>*Yoshiyuki Okamoto* | 236<br><br>246 |
| 11 | Banking System and the Dualistic Development of<br>the Italian Economy<br>*Cesare Imbriani*<br>Comment<br>*Osamu Ito* | <br>248<br><br>256 |

## PART IV: SOCIAL INSTITUTIONS AND NETWORKS

| | | |
|---|---|---|
| 12 | The Fiscal Decentralization and the Autonomy of<br>the Local Government<br>*Carlo Filippini and Giampaolo Arachi*<br>Comment<br>*Hiroko Kudo* | <br>261<br><br>287 |
| 13 | The Italian Third Sector: An Overview at the Beginning<br>of the Century<br>*Marco Demarie and Stefano Cima*<br>Comment<br>*Yousuke Mamiya* | <br>292<br><br>311 |

| 14 | The Family and Social Networks in the Socio-Economic Development of Italy | 313 |
|---|---|---|
| | *Andrea Toma* | |
| | Comment | 331 |
| | *Masao Kotani* | |
| 15 | The Italian Welfare System Between the European Unification and the Globalization Processes: A Suggested Interpretation | 334 |
| | *Paolo Calza Bini* | |
| | Comment | 351 |
| | *Nobuhiro Hiwatari* | |

*Index* 355

# List of Contributors

Massimo Di Matteo, Università di Siena
Hiroshi Yoshikawa, University of Tokyo
Alessandro Vercelli, Università di Siena
Luciano Fiordoni, Banca Monte dei Paschi di Siena
Carlo De Gregorio, ISTAT, Roma
Andrea de Panizza, ISTAT, Roma
Roberto Monducci, ISTAT, Roma
Leonello Tronti, ISTAT, Roma
Kenichi Sakai, Tokyo Keizai University
Roberto Schiattarella, Università di Camerino
Paolo Piacentini, Università La Sapienza, Roma
Sumi Iwamoto, Bunkyo University
Maurizio Franzini, Università La Sapienza, Roma
Fabrizio Barca, Ministero dell' Economia, Roma
Carlo Andrea Bollino, Università di Perugia and LUISS Guido Carli, Roma
Marcello Signorelli, Università di Perugia
Micaela Notarangelo, Hokkaido University and Utrecht University
Giovanni Russo, Utrecht University
Ugo Pagano, Università di Siena
Sandro Trento, Banca d' Italia, Roma
Alessandro Innocenti, Università di Siena
Katsuhito Iwai, University of Tokyo
Rodolfo Helg, Università Carlo Cattaneo, Castellanza and Università Commerciale
      Luigi Bocconi, Milano
Yoshiyuki Okamoto, Hosei University, Tokyo
Cesare Imbriani, Università La Sapienza, Roma
Osamu Ito, Saitama University

# List of Contributors

Carlo Filippini, Università Commerciale Luigi Bocconi, Milano

Giampaolo Arachi, Università di Lecce and Università Commerciale Luigi Bocconi, Milano

Hiroko Kudo, Waseda University, Tokyo

Marco Demarie, Fondazione Giovanni Agnelli, Torino

Stefano Cima, Istituto per la Ricerca Sociale, Milano

Yousuke Mamiya, University of Kyoto

Andrea Toma, Fondazione CENSIS, Roma

Masao Kotani, Ochanomizu University, Tokyo

Paolo Calza Bini, Università La Sapienza, Roma

Nobuhiro Hiwatari, University of Tokyo

# Preface

1. Most of the essays collected in this volume are the result of the reports presented at the conference on "Enterprises, Labour Markets, and Institutions in Italy facing the Challenges of the XXI Century (University of Tokyo, 23-4 October 2001), organised as part of the initiatives of "Italy in Japan, 2001".

The editors wish to express their deep gratitude to the Institutions and individuals, who have, first, supported the initiative of the conference, and then encouraged the publication of the present volume: The Italy in Japan 2001 Foundation, The Italian Ministry of Foreign Affairs, The Italian Chamber of Commerce in Tokyo, the Italian Ministry of Higher Education and Research and the University of Tokyo.

The original aim pursued in the occasion of the conference, was that of presenting an overview of the "state" of present-day Italy through reports on a selected range of economic and social topics. We hoped, through concise presentations, to draw the attention of Japanese scholars, who, in their professional or academic activities, had an interest in comparative socio-economic analysis. To this end the reports actually presented were discussed by scholars from various Japanese Universities. However a few essays could not be discussed in Tokyo because the authors could not attend the meeting.

2. On reflecting on the aftermath of the conference we felt that the papers could be developed in order to address a wider audience.

Japan and Italy, nothwithstanding their enormous geographical distance and extremely different historical backgrounds, are both, we believe, representative of mature manufacturing economies with strong interdependences with their regional, European and Asian, contexts. They have often shared similar patterns of development, with years of high growth after a phase of reconstruction from a lost war. Nowadays, they are confronted with a broad range of structural problems, in the face of slackening growth and in the context of the international process of financial and real integration.

We did not however intend to publish a collection of essays centred on the comparison between Italy and Japan, as this has already been the object of another volume edited quite recently [*Comparing Economic Systems. Italy and Japan*, Boltho, A., Vercelli, A., Yoshikawa, H., eds, Palgrave 2001].

We wished, in fact, to introduce, and discuss, the peculiarities, and sometimes the uniqueness, of the Italian "mode" of organizing the productive and social framework. Standard country-studies, as those occasionally drafted by the research staff of international organisations, are often limited to a survey of the so called macroeconomic fundamentals and trends. These are not sufficiently informative, we believe, of the condition of a country which cannot be represented by its national averages, given the wide range of territorial differentiation in terms of income and productivity, conditions in the labour market, development of the industrial structure, and unemployment rates.

Looking back at the evolution of the Italian economy and society in the past 50 years or so, we cannot help remembering how exceptional the period between 1950 and 1970 actually was. Late comers like Italy (and Japan as well) in a few, exciting years jumped from the situation of a semi-developed and mainly agricultural society to that of a modern industrialized nation: the shift in value added and employment from agriculture to industry, the dramatic fall in unemployment, the intense urbanization process, the changing pattern of consumption are typical of those aspects that Kuznets described in an unsurpassed way.

The period of high growth ended around 1970 and the GDP growth rates never reached the previous levels again. A steady process of growth would have probably made Italy more and more similar to her partners in Europe, completing her modernization process.

In absence of such conditions the country remained, so to speak, at half way: the gap between an advanced North and a backward South (which was a feature well known to development economists and economic historians since its emergence at the birth of a unified national State in the late XIX century) did not close and even widened. Features of the growth process and aspects of this unresolved dualism are documented in the I and II Parts of the book.

Other contributions in the book (mainly in the III Part) are dedicated to another structural aspect of the Italian economy which has been paid a lot of attention by specialists in comparative industrial organisation.

Italy is characterized by an extreme fragmentation of its productive texture, with average size of plants, share of employment in the smaller enterprises, number of independent, artisan workers, which show "abnormal" levels if confronted with the figures found in other modern, industrialized economies.

The persistence of this structure over time has led to questioning the solidity of the arguments that tend to associate growth with economies of scale and increasing returns. The competitive effectiveness of this Italian industrial model, and in particular of the local networks of small enterprises ("industrial districts"), is an actual point of interest within a wider discussion on the prospects of the persistence of a plurality of "national models" of capitalism, in the face of global competition.

Successes and shortfalls in the macroeconomic and microeconomic performances, must finally be understood in the wider context of a social framework, where the conditions for the reproduction of a community and its welfare are mediated by a set of fundamental institutions of a modern society. These are not working in the same way in each country and in addition their respective role evolves over time in response to ever changing economic conditions as is witnessed by the roles performed by the family and the recent development of other non profit organizations.

Again here it can be noted that in Italy the family seems to be engaged in a wider range of activities (of economic as well as of social support, if not substitution, with respect to the State and the Market) than in other countries. Is this a peculiar feature of Italy that, as some historian has recently claimed, has marked the country over a large part of her history, making it a genetic characteristic? Could it not be that the insufficient development of other institutions called for the persistence of a relevant role of the family?

Although the majority of the contributors to the volume belongs to the economist field, in the last Part we have included essays by sociologists, working within Research Foundations, with a long standing experience in the drafting of authoritative reports on the state and evolution of the social conditions of the country. The family, the welfare system, and the so-called "third sector" are the objects of specialized contributions.

It seems to us the structure of the book reflects in a fairly good way the peculiarities of Italy as we have summarily reported, a country that, despite belonging to the G8 group, should be considered in many aspects as an outlier.

3. The ordered list of contributions intentionally follows an ideal sequence from introductive and more general presentations to more dedicated essays for specialised topics.

In the opening Part, we first include two papers aimed at presenting a historical introduction, summarizing characteristics, phases, "push' factors and limiting constraints, influencing the quantitative growth and structural changes of the Italian economy since world war II. The two papers are organized in a chronological sequence, with the first essay by Di Matteo covering the years of high growth, after the economic reconstruction and industrial take-off, broadly from 1950 to the end of the sixties while the second, by Vercelli and Fiordoni, describes the difficult path of the Italian macroeconomic developments and policies from the two oil shocks, through the years of high inflation, up to the phase of stabilisation which has culminated with a successful convergence towards the parameters and conditions of the Maastricht Treaty, in order to gain access to the EMU at its onset.

The third contribution, elaborated by Tronti et al. within the research department of the Central Institute of Statistics (ISTAT), is, on the other hand, meant to provide the reader with an essential, quantitative survey of the Italian economic structure and labour market conditions, at the onset of the XXI Century. Attention is given to the "anomalies" of the Italian case vis-a-vis comparative figures for other industrialised countries. This paper concentrates on the bulk of tables and figures for the "essential statistics" of the country, with the purpose, also, of avoiding excesses of quantitative reference to general data in the topical essays which follow.

Part II opens with the contribution by Schiattarella and Piacentini, prepared at the Fondazione Brodolini, a think tank on labour problems. According to a widespread view, that, with reference to Italy, dates back to V.Lutz's analysis, the origin and causes of a dualistic industrial structure are mainly to be found in the features and working of the labour market: segmentation and lack of flexibility resulting from a supply-side behaviour of workers are considered to be at the root of a large share of the unemployment problem and an extension of irregular jobs. The picture appears, in fact, less simple and more complex to interpret. A dualistic frame, in any case, appears to be essential in describing the structural features of the Italian labour market, not only in the sense of the traditional, territorial divide between the North and the South, but more in general, between a segment of legally and contractually protected jobs, and another segment, including the various typologies of more precarious work conditions.

As is well known the "*questione meridionale*" [The Southern question] has always been at the centre of the policy debate ever since the birth of Italy in 1861. Because of the evolving economic situation and the changing orientations of the policy makers (following Keynes' final remarks in the *General Theory*) the actions actually implemented in the attempt to solve the "*questione meridionale*" have dramatically varied over time. Franzini offers a brief description and an interpretation of such attempts over the postwar period, so that the reader can appreciate why recently a shift in the orientation of economic policy for the less developed areas has occurred. The emphasis is now centered on local, endogenous development; its policy background is briefly reviewed, within the context of a process of internal differentiation that is taking place in the South itself, between regions persistently trapped in underdevolopment and areas showing appreciable growth rates.

In the subsequent contribution, written by Barca, Director of the Department for Development and Social Cohesion Policies at the Italian Treasury, a full exposition of the targets and articulations of the new policy to be implemented in Italy, is provided. Since this approach involves the cooperation between different structures of public administration at the central and local level and private actors (firms, banks, etc), particular attention is devoted to an analysis of the institutional mechanisms designed to overcome the difficulties implicit in agreeing on contractual engagements which are necessarily set within the context of uncertainty and incomplete information.

No policy action however can be fully appreciated unless estimates, imperfect as they may be, of its quantitative effects are provided. Bollino (presently an advisor to the Ministry of Productive Activities) and Signorelli, applying a flexible production function model with spillover effects, compute the likely effects of alternative policy measures, for a disaggregated analysis of regional data.

The III part opens with an essay by Pagano and Trento who describe and interpret (on the basis of a well articulated theoretical vision) the evolution of the Italian system of corporate governance over an extended period of time. They examine the actual institutional shocks that have diversified the Italian corporate governance system from that prevailing in other capitalistic economies. In the midst of the several changes that have occurred over the past years the strong presence of families in the governance of big firms has been an important aspect of systemic continuity. This feature has not been demolished by an extensive privatization process that took place in the 1990s.

This has been paralled, as already noticed, by a widespread growth of the number of smaller firms that, although with differential patterns across the sectors, represent by now the bulk of the industrial texture of the country. The persistence of a large share of smaller firms in many areas, cannot be accounted for only by cyclical factors, but needs to be explained within a deeper understanding of the institutional and structural factors. The changing role of information and knowledge transmission among firms, central to this new phase of goods and services production and exchange, following demand evolutions of industrialized countries, lies at the heart of the interpretation put forward by Innocenti in his paper.

How successful on the international markets is this way of organizing production? Helg in his contribution concentrates on a relevant subset of the smaller firms' universe, namely, that of the "industrial districts". He carefully shows that the latter typology of industrial organization is still a driving force in the Italian export performance and contributes to a large extent to the shapening of the competitive advantage of the Italian productive system.

A process of privatization of the banking system and a dramatic increase in its concentration, has taken place in the last decade and is far from being completed. As banks still play a central role, especially for the financing of small firms, due to the relatively small importance of the Stock Market (and other pro growth financial institutions), inefficiency and propensity to discriminate are particularly damaging for firms of the South, as documented by Imbriani in his essay.

The existence of such a differentiated situation over different areas of the country, as emphasized, is probably at the root of the powerful drive towards devolution (or outright federalism) that has developed in Italy, in particular from the past decade onwards. The push towards devolution of power to local authorities is justified, by its proponents, on efficiency considerations: the control of the administration by the citizens is more effectively exercised within local communities and this makes public administrators more easily accountable. Devolution of power, if it has to be effective, entails the power of raising funds, taxation in the first place, at local level, and the autonomy in deciding the criteria of its allocation.

However owing to the very existence of differentiated growth and conditions across regions, devolution of powers could end up reinforcing a tendency towards an enlargement of the gap between richer and poorer regions, with severe consequences not only for economic growth but also for social cohesion. All this is documented at length by Filippini and Arachi in their contribution, where proposals and formulae for a system of fiscal transfers equalizing the satisfaction of a common standard of basic needs over the whole country are presented.

The central and local public authorities are increasingly confronted by expenditure constraints, also because of the clauses of the Stability Pact of the European Union and the prevailing political opinion that considers any increase in the share of public expenditure on national income to be potentially harmful as it implies a reduction in the disposable income and choice opportunities by the households. On the other hand social expenditures, given the demographic trends and other factors, can hardly be cut. In this situation, there is room for the development of the so-called Third Sector. The latter, in addition to supplementing the provision of social services, would give employment opportunities to many people willing to be engaged in activities of social utility. De Marie (Director of the Fondazione Agnelli, a think tank on economic and social problems) and Cima give a wide ranging review of the various aspects and typologies of actors within the Third Sector, from a legal, economic and social viewpoint.

The complementarity, or substitutability, of the functions performed by the family with that of other non profit institutions (the Welfare State and the Third

Sector) is one of the central themes in the multifaceted discussion, at sociological level, concerning the relevance of the family context in Italian society. These roles can be viewed from different aspects, as the family is, at the same time, a solidarity network for providing services not available on the market, a support for its old and/or sick members, a source for supplementing the income of the unemployed and for establishing connections useful for social insertion and finding job opportunities, in a segmented labour market. In his paper Toma (at Censis, a Foundation for the study of social problems) documents all these aspects.

Finally, in addition to the family and/or non profit organizations, among the institutions that shape the context within which the economic and social welfare of a country is developing, the role of the public sector cannot be overlooked. Sociologists have perhaps been among the first to declare the crisis of the Welfare State, looking at the contradictions that its function and extention have brought over the years.

Italy, again, is a peculiar case, as the Welfare State did not take a well settled form, from the point of view of coverage of functions and definition of the institutional structure, before the end of the 1970s (or even later than that). Calza Bini (former Director of IRIDISS, an Institute for the Research on the Welfare State) analyzes the range of possible contradictions between people' expectations, the changing economic environment and the constraints brought about by the process of globalization.

4. In concluding this brief outline of the volume, the editors wish to remind the reader of the general orientation followed in the selection of the topics and the tasks assigned to the contributors. Although each author obviously has his own orientation, and reference to a different "school" of economic or sociological thought, effort was requested and, we believe, was substantially maintained, in presenting informative facts and comments, seeking to reduce, as far as possible, partisan value judgements or undocumented opinions.

Of course, pure objectivity, even if it could be attained, might result in unattractive description. It is natural, therefore, that orientation of thought and models of reference might be guessed from the lay-out of the diverse essays. The careful, and patient, reader would appreciate, then, that the group which has taken part to the initiative of the conference and then contributed to the volume, is not homogeneous from the point of view of allegiance to some common "school" of thought, or more simply, in terms of personal inclination towards more optimistic or pessimistic points of view of the state of their own country. Some of the contributors hold operative or consulting positions within the present circumstances of the political scene in Italy; others have had similar tasks in a previous legislature, when the coalition, now in opposition, was in office.

Notwithstanding this heterogeneity, the editors have found an appreciable collaboration from the authors, in their effort to conform to the principal aim of the publication, that, of providing an informative and fact-centered survey of Italy to the foreign reader. In a period of a harshening political and social climate in the country, the editors wish to express their appreciation of this point.

# PART I
# GROWTH PATTERNS AND STRUCTURAL FEATURES

# Chapter 1

# Italy's First Phase of Postwar Development: The Role of Aggregate Demand[1]

Massimo Di Matteo

**Introduction**

The aim of the paper is to offer a framework for analyzing the first two decades of postwar economic growth in Italy. The emphasis is on the role played by aggregate demand and its components in shaping the extremely fast process of economic growth that occurred in Italy during the fifties and sixties. This was accompanied by a profound process of structural change that will briefly be dealt with.

Generally the process of growth is understood as a purely supply side phenomenon along the path of Solow's model or (more recently) the new (endogenous) growth approach. I follow a different approach that merges Lewis' emphasis on the "unlimited" supply of labour with the Keynesian argument that what constrains output is effective demand. The link between the two is the existence of a wide dispersion of labour productivity across sectors of the economy: in such a situation aggregate demand drives real output. The process of growth can then be best described as a process in which labour moves from low to high productivity sectors resulting in a change in the structure of the economy.

The possibility that growth depends on demand is not wholly discarded by Solow (1997) himself, although he maintains that this possibility is uncommon:

'A more interesting question is whether a major episode in the growth of potential output can be driven from the demand side. Can demand create its own supply? The magnitudes suggest that it would be awfully difficult for a surge of aggregate demand to generate enough investment to provide the capacity necessary to accommodate it. In special circumstances it might be done, say, in an economy that has a pool of labour (rural, foreign) that it can mobilize. It might also work if strong aggregate demand can induce a rise in total factor productivity (TFP). This may be less far-fetched than it sounds, if we recognize that a large part of TFP originates not in the research laboratory, but on the shop floor, as production workers figure out how to gain a little efficiency here and a little there. The demand driven growth story sounds quite implausible to me under current conditions; but it is an example of the kind of question that needs to be asked.'

Di Matteo & Yoshikawa (2001) showed that at least in post war Italy and Japan demand driven growth was not so special. The framework that we used can be thought of as a threefold generalization of Lewis' approach. First, it is not necessary that (marginal) productivity in agriculture (the backward sector) be zero, but it can be positive. Secondly, there is a whole range of (marginal) productivities in the various branches of the secondary sector. These productivities can be ranked from the lowest to the highest. In such a situation there is therefore disguised unemployment, because if workers could be moved from low to high productivity sectors, GDP would increase: the latter is not constrained by lack of resources. Thirdly, reinvesting the profits of the industrial sector depends on the (expected) growth of demand and it cannot be assumed to be an automatic process.

Here I will concern myself with applying the demand driven "story" to the case of Italy in the period between (roughly) 1950 and 1970. This is the period when Italy grew faster than in any other period of her history, namely 5.6% on average.

This chronology may cause some uneasiness as it is commonly held in Italy that 1963 was the last year of the "economic miracle" and that a period of depression followed. On my reading of the facts (for an earlier view consistent with the present one, however, see Vaciago 1970) I disagree with the common interpretation, though of course the discussion is open as to which periodization is the most fruitful.

The paper is organized as follows. In the next section reasons are given that enable one to apply the Lewis framework to the Italian economy in the period under consideration. In the third section the pattern and evolution of aggregate demand in the period under consideration are elucidated. In the last section the turning point of Italian development in the late 1960s is interpreted.

## The background

At the beginning of the fifties the Italian economy could be described (Kindleberger 1967) as a backward economy with "unlimited" supplies of labour: the large amount of population in agriculture did contribute very little to the level of output so that their productivity could be considered extremely low and well below that prevailing in other sectors of the economy (e.g. Orlando 1978).

A few data will suffice to illustrate the point. It is derived from three sources: an estimate of average (which can be considered proportional to marginal) productivity in the primary with respect to the secondary sector, unemployment figures, and migration flows. For example we observe that in the early fifties average labour productivity in "ferrous metal production" and "furniture and wood" was three and two times the corresponding value in agriculture, respectively. In line with the general point that disguised unemployment is linked to differences in marginal productivities across sectors, there was indeed huge dispersion of marginal productivity values, a fact which is contrary to the received doctrine.

It is difficult to have reliable data on migration within the country, due to intermittent revising and updating of statistical records. However we can measure the difference between two population censuses for resident population in the Centre-North and South (after eliminating the natural increase). This provides an estimate of internal migration as it is assumed that people moved from the South to the Centre North, but it is a rough one as people also moved within these large areas, e.g. from inland to coastal areas. However, in their detailed analysis, Padoa Schioppa and Attanasio (1991) rely upon this measure:

|  | Outflows(-) Inflows (+) 1951-1960 | Outflows(-) Inflows (+) 1960-1972 |
|---|---|---|
| South | -1,566,000 | -2,365,000 |
| Centre North | +657,500 | +1,601,000 |

Source: Padoa Schioppa and Attanasio (1991, p.312)

The difference between the two figures in each decade is migration abroad. On the basis of different estimates, Graziani (2000, p.73) argues that one million people moved to the North in the fifties from other parts of Italy.

Over the period 1954-1970, the unemployment rate fluctuated between 10.4% and 5% except in 1963-4 when it hit a minimum of about 4%. Unemployment figures should always be taken with care as they depend heavily on how the the survey (the first Italian survey was in 1954) is actually conducted. Before then data is available on registered unemployed and has been used and discussed by Hildebrand (1965, p.157ff) to whom we refer the interested reader.

One further element to be added to the overall picture is the share of agricultural employment, that fell continuously from 43.1% in 1951 to 20% in 1969. This indicates that about 5 million people left country areas up to 1970. This is again consistent with the existence of a large pool of labour in the primary sector that could be "mobilized", as Solow (1997) states in the passage quoted above.

All the evidence reported so far boils down to a situation of widespread disguised unemployment in Italy at least during the 1951-1970 period. The heuristic value of the concept of disguised unemployment, also in the context of recent evolution of the Italian economy, was recently reaffirmed by Graziani (2000, pp.200-1).

At the same time, northern Italy had a limited industrial sector with a bias towards heavy industries, a legacy from the fascist period. The ruling wage in industry could be interpreted as a conventional wage, somewhat higher than the "subsistence" wage (i.e. the wage received or the income earned by people on the land) to account for the cost of moving out of agriculture. In the industrial sector, where capitalistic conditions prevailed, workers were hired as long as their productivity was higher than this wage.

Here, however, comes a major difference with Lewis' original formulation: he argues that in the above conditions, a self propelled process of growth sets in, owing to reinvestment of profits generated in the industrial sector. Can one take for granted, as Lewis did, that, in the context of a backward economy, all profits (or most of them) are reinvested? In fact profits (in excess of capital replacement) could be spent on consumer goods and the equilibrium could be perpetuated without any growth occurring (although this type of equilibrium could be associated with balance of payments problems). *If* profits were reinvested, accumulation could certainly go on without any fall in profit margins as long as money wages increased at a rate lower than (or equal to) labour productivity.

The main argument put forward by Lewis consists in showing that in the process of growth, there will be a shift in the distribution of income towards higher saving groups: the process of growth does emanate from this pure supply side phenomenon. There are two points to this. First, as far as Italy is concerned, the share of labour income in GDP did not fall in the fifties but increased slightly from 37% in 1951 to 40% in 1961 and this can be taken as an empirical refutation of Lewis' hypothesis if, as is commonly held, wage earners have a lower propensity to save than profit receivers and secondly, it is more sensible to assume that the (share of) profits reinvested depend on the amount of demand firms expect for their products.

I think that the start of the process of growth and its continuation depend on the expectation of good prospects for aggregate demand. And indeed conditions of excess supply prevailed in Italy for many decades, as is well documented, without any prolonged growth process ever taking place: supply considerations alone can hardly be the whole story.

## The dynamics of aggregate demand

One is therefore led to enquire which components of aggregate demand were actually the most dynamic in the period under consideration. Consumption was not a major dynamic force as its share in income fell continuously: it regained the 1952 figure only in 1964.

Investments and exports were the components of demand with by far the highest growth rates. Let us take them in turn.

Total investments grew faster than GDP until 1963, reaching a share of almost 30% and then stabilized at an average share of 27% for the next ten years until 1973. The pioneering analysis by Ackley (1962) stresses the role of *autonomous* investments in the agriculture and housing sectors, affected by government policy in a variety of ways (e.g. the Tupini public works bill and the Fanfani public housing plan), and in the communications and transport sectors.

As for the need of investment in residential construction, it is obvious that people relocating from South to North needed new houses. One can have a rough estimate of the number of new families by looking at the number of marriages that were 6.9 (per 1000 inhabitants) in 1951 and increased to 7.9 in 1961, levelling off at 7.5 in 1971. This information can be supplemented with the index of first nuptiality which is also a close approximation of the number of first marriages for women between 16 and 49: it has two peaks, one in 1963 and another in the early seventies and then fell continuously. This meant an increasing number of new families which, coupled with population movements, indicate an increasing demand for houses that contributed to aggregate demand evolution. The latter was also stimulated by the total increase in population that was 0.64% in the fifties and 0.42% in the sixties and declined to 0.11% in the seventies (these rates are corrected for migration).

Another indirect source of labour mobility, and therefore housing needs, is the shift of employed workers away from the agriculture sector and towards the industrial and the service sectors as mentioned above. As workers employed in agriculture were concentrated in the South and workers in the industrial sector in the Centre-North, the above is a rough indication of the population moving towards urban areas and away from rural areas. Not surprisingly, this is reflected in the pattern of residential construction (as a share of GDP) which grew very fast in the period and peaked in 1969. A similar story can be told for non-residential construction investment that also started to decrease (as a share of GDP) around 1967.

Before turning to the discussion of the pattern of foreign demand in the next paragraph, we have to remember that in this context, among the exogenous factors, we can include state-owned firms that were very active. During this period governments did not pursue a liberistic policy domestically: IRI (a state owned holding company and a legacy of the fascist period), was not dismantled but rather empowered, ENI (the national oil company) was created in 1953, an agency for infrastructure investment in the South was established in 1950 (Cassa per il Mezzogiorno) and investment projects in electricity power, steel production, telephone network, and other basic sectors were carried out (Ciocca, Filosa & Rey 1975). This reduced the possibility of bottlenecks in basic sectors that could have choked off the process and hinder a demand led growth path without at the same time directly fostering the development of Southern firms.

Following the process of external liberalization that initiated very early and was conducted very vigorously, exports too grew faster than GDP moving from an initial 5% share in GDP to 15% in 1970. However I maintain that the external component, in quantitative terms, was not the driving force of growth except for a very few years following the formation of the European Common Market in 1957. More in particular, while it is true that on average exports grew faster than any other component of aggregate demand, this however is not tremendously significant as, at that time, exports (as just remembered) were only a tiny fraction of aggregate demand. In addition net exports were consistently negative for the whole postwar period with a few exceptions (1978, 1993, 1994). And also the analysis of relative contribution to income shows that on average the value gained by exports is smaller than that got by investment.

These statements do not contradict the recognition that the external liberalisation policy (elimination of quotas, participation in OECE, etc.) was a milestone in the Italian post-war economic policy. The policy of opening up the Italian economy to foreign competition appears to have been more important in providing the right incentives to the firms than in being directly the major impulse to growth. Indeed the main effects were that of forcing firms to be more competitive on the domestic as well as foreign markets, to invest for their survival, to take advantage of being late comers by adopting the newest technology. This pattern did not spread to all sectors in an even degree: what the liberalisation policy actually did was to reinforce the preexisting dualistic structure of the Italian economy.

The Italian industrial structure was actually divided into two sectors, one characterised by more modern techniques and relatively high wages and in a position to compete with foreign firms; the other in a sheltered position with low wages and low productivity growth, mainly oriented to the sections of the domestic market immune from foreign competition. To this a territorial dualism between North (advanced) and South (backward) correspond.

Indeed it was only in a few years that exports became a relatively important factor of growth, namely after the European Common Market was established in 1957 (from that date until 1963 one could talk, if ever, of export-led growth). Then a virtuous circle set in linking exports and investments as the favourable conditions of the labour market helped maintaining competitiveness of the Italian firms which were thus motivated to increase investments (and hence productivity). Although the pace of productivity was extremely high between the birth of the Common Market and 1963, it remained on good levels for the whole period under consideration in our analysis: this performance will never be attained by the Italian economy in the following years.

Viewed in this perspective it might be then too emphatic to refer to the period immediately preceding 1963 as the "economic miracle" (as it is commonly called). It is perhaps easier to understand the reasons for the end of the period of sustained growth that however I see happening at the end of the 1960s. Those who favour 1963 as a watershed year blamed the end of the fast growth on the exhaustion of surplus labour, but this is not wholly convincing as still in 1963 there was a gross flow of migrants to other European countries of almost 100.000 workers and it has been estimated a number of 200,000 net migrants from the South to Centre North for the same year. Vaciago (1970) remarked that the 1963 episode (marked by a balance of payments crisis and a delayed but severe credit squeeze by the Central Bank) could be seen as an episode of cyclical nature, though a very important one, characterized by an outburst of workers' militancy. In any case after the 1963-4 crisis the rate of growth of GDP was still rather high (in comparison with the previous as well as the following years) and in a long term analysis is sensible to include the rest of the 1960s in the first period characterised by high growth.

Finally I briefly recollect some of the reasons why Italian entrepreneurs could have been optimist at the end of the 1940s. First the international setting: the economic policy of the USA was expansive (maybe in order to counter the communist menace) as witnessed, inter alia, by the ERP (although at first the funds were piled up to increase Central Bank reserves); there were extensive developments in multilateral exchanges within Europe; the Korean war was a favourable external shock. As for the internal environment, one recalls: the moderate policy of the communist party (accused of being too soft in defending workers' rights) whose aim was to let the country grow as only in this way the contradictions of capitalism could develop; the splitting in 1947 of the trade union movement that weakenend the workers' bargaining power within and outside the factories (to this contributed in the same year also the severe credit squeeze operated by the Central Bank to fight inflation); the giving up of the "change of currency" (with its related taxation of war profits) that reassured the country that no punitive measures would have been taken.

Secondly around 1949-50 the leading Cristian Democrats party shifted its policy emphasis away from a liberistic approach towards a social approach (concern for the satisfaction of basic needs) with emphasis on growth and employment as guiding lines for the conduct of economic policy.

Finally some entrepreneurs themselves, like Valletta (general manager of FIAT), were entusiastic about future development because they clearly saw a niche for Italian firms and products in the US dominated western economy. In my opinion all these elements established a favourable climate to the big developments that came afterwards.

## Conclusions

I argue then that the process of growth could have continued provided certain favourable conditions had been maintained. This was not the case, however. In the post 1963 period looking at the surplus in the trade balance growth could have been faster (the same conclusion derives from observing the low level of capacity utilisation): the main difference with the "economic miracle" was the relatively restrictive nature of both fiscal and monetary policies and the reduction in public expenditure (as a share of GDP), in particular of the state owned firms (Sylos Labini 1974). In this context foreign demand and domestic demand went into a relation of substitution rather than complementarity and this marked a huge difference with the virtuous circle period (especially from 1958 to 1963): because of the insufficient level of domestic demand, firms were stimulated to look abroad for selling their products.

I am arguing however that the process of dualistic growth that I have recalled could have continued, provided that the modern sector had been developing so fast as to reproduce on a large scale the differential productivity and that policy had continued to be permissive. It is true that increased production in the industrial sector *for a given productivity level* tends to absorb workers and reduce the unemployed pool; at the same time however *for a given output level* in the industrial sector the increased productivity that takes place over time expels workers that go to the unemployed pool. There is a possibility that these two contrasting forces produce a situation where money wages will not increase more than productivity in the industrial sector and this gives a macroeconomic condition for stability in the growth process: in this environment unemployment can well be reduced without necessarily impairing the continuation of growth. This situation can either be spontaneously attained or reached through political consensus.

I think that a process of growth is best described by the search and implementation of new methods of production (and/or new products) that enable firms to move workers from less to more productive sectors. This process is easier when you can take advantage of being a backward country and adopting already existing techniques: it becomes more difficult but certainly not impossible when this stage is over. It is interesting to note, in this connection, that by 1970 the level of Italian GDP per capita approached that of the USA in 1950 (Maddison 1995) and the share of investment will never recover the share in GDP reached then.

To explain what actually happened in the period following the 1963-4 crisis De Cecco (1972) has a brilliant analogy by stating that firms treated different workers as different types of land and restructured labour force by concentrating demand on those who were considered to be more productive (male, experienced, etc.) and discarding others (women, very young and old workers, etc.). So it was a process of rationalization and restructuring on a very short term perspective. Here Italy missed the occasion of developing a modern economy centred on high income elastic sectors: this would have required appropriate long term policies (in education, investment in R&D, etc.) that in the 1960s were intensively talked about but not implemented (For an early lucid diagnosis and therapy, see Fuà 1965).

The end of the first period could be symbolically associated with the "hot autumn" (1969) when there was an unprecedented burst of workers' unrest and consequent wage explosion and price inflation: this was the result of both economic factors (concentration of labour demand) and political ones (reaction to the "strike of investments" and lack of structural reforms).

However the slowing down of growth was due to the end of those features of the process that I have highlighted, mainly end of reallocation process and migration with a consequent fall in the residential and non residential share of investment not compensated for by other items of aggregate investments.

## Note

[1] All the statiscal data quoted in the paper without mentioning the source have been computed by the author using the data bank set up by Prometeia.

## References

Ackley, G. (1962), 'An Econometric Model of Italian Postwar Growth', MS.
Ciocca, P.L., Filosa, R. and Rey, G.M. (1975), 'Integration and Development of the Italian Economy', *Banca Nazionale del Lavoro Quarterly Review*, 28, 114, pp. 284-320.
De Cecco, M. (1972), 'Un' interpretazione ricardiana della dinamica della forza lavoro in Italia nel decennio 1959-69', *Note Economiche*.
Fua', G. (1965), Notes on Italian Economic Growth 1861-1964, Giuffre'.
Graziani, A. (2000), Lo sviluppo dell' economia italiana. Dalla ricostruzione alla moneta europea, Bollati Boringhieri.
Hildebrand, G. (1965), *Growth and Structure in the Economy of Modern Italy*, Harvard UP.
Kindleberger, C.P. (1967), *Europe's Postwar Growth*, Oxford UP.
Maddison, A. (1995), *Monitoring the World Economy*, OECD.
Orlando, G. (1978), 'Progressi e difficoltà nell' agricoltura', in G. Fua' (ed), *Lo sviluppo economico in Italia, vol.III*, F.Angeli.

Padoa Schioppa, F. and Attanasio, O. (1991), 'Regional Inequalities, Migration, and Mismatch', in F. Padoa Schioppa (ed), *Mismatch and Labour Mobility*, Cambridge UP.
Solow, R.M. (1997), 'Is there a core of usable macroeconomics that we should all believe in?', *American Economic Review P&P*, 87, 2, pp. 230-2.
Sylos Labini, P. (1974), *Trade Unions, Inflation, and Productivity*, Lexington Books.
Vaciago, G. (1970), 'Theories of Economic Growth and the Italian Case', *Banca Nazionale del Lavoro Quarterly Review*, 23, 93, pp. 180-211.

# Comment

Hiroshi Yoshikawa

1. Growth theory has gained renewed interest in macroeconomics in the past fifteen years. Theoretically, a contest between Solow's old growth model and the new endogenous growth theory has been the main battle field. Empirically, many (too many!?) cross – country regressions based on the World Bank data has been carried out.

A vast amount of literature in the field has, however, curiously left an important question untouched, namely the role of aggregate demand in the process of economic growth. This may not be surprising because in the past twenty years, the profession has minimized the role of demand even in the theory of short – run fluctuations with the Real Business Cycle theory as the culmination. I believe that this situation is very unfortunate, and that demand plays a central role not only in the short – run fluctuations but also in the long – run economic growth. It is actually not an easy task to present a theoretical growth model in which demand plays a central role, however. Aoki and Yoshikawa (2002) is such an example. There, we argue that demand – creating innovations which overcome demand – saturation is an engine of economic growth.

2. As pointed out by professor Di Matteo, demand – led growth presumes inequality of productivity among sectors / firms. Historically, the most important productivity differential lay (or lie still today in developing countries such as China) between agriculture and modern manufacturing industry. As is well known, the process of economic growth in this dual economy was analyzed by Lewis (1954). The Lewis model takes it for granted that the modern industrial sector enjoys high profitability as long as the surplus labour in the traditional sector prevents the real wages from rising, and that it keeps high investment which leads to high economic growth. However, how and what demand assures high profitability in the manufacturing sector? Where does high demand come from? Since the Lewis model actually applies not only to developing countries but also to well developed nations as Kindleberger (1967) argues, it is an important agenda to

supplement the Lewis model by demand factors. Toward this goal, the most promising approach is a careful case study.

Yoshikawa (1995, Chapter 2) showed that postwar Japanese economic growth during the 1950s and 1960s was well explained by the modified Lewis model, and that demand played a crucial role in growth. Professor Di Matteo now persuasively shows that the similar mechanism worked also in the Italian growth. I believe that this kind of historical case study is much more productive than often lousy cross – country analyses.

## References

Aoki, Masanao and Yoshikawa, Hiroshi (2002), 'Demand Saturation-Creation and Economic Growth', *Journal of Economic Behavior and Organization* Vol.48 (2002) pp.127-154.

Kindleberger, C. (1967), *Europe's Postwar Growth*, Cambridge, Mass Harvard: University Press.

Lewis, W. Arthur (1954), 'Economic Development with Unlimited Supplies of Labour', *Manchester School of Economic and Social Sutudies, May*.

Yoshikawa, Hiroshi (1995), *Macroeconomics and the Japanese Economy*, Oxford: Oxford University Press.

# Chapter 2

# The Italian Economy after the Bretton Woods Era (1971-2001)

Alessandro Vercelli
Luciano Fiordoni

## Introduction

This work aims to analyze briefly the macroeconomic evolution of the Italian economy during the final three decades of the twentieth century by adopting a cyclical-growth approach that provides a few suggestive links with the co-evolution of some of the economy's structural features. Since the latter are analyzed in further detail in the following chapters, we intend to limit the analysis here to a cursory look at their interaction with the development of the economy without any attempt to provide an in-depth analysis of their determinants.

This chapter is structured as follows. A definition of periods for the Italian economy in the post-war era is given in section 2. The changes in the economy are briefly described thereafter in the following three sections dedicated to **Stagflation (1971-1980)**, **Disinflation (1980-1993)** and **Integration in the Eurozone (1993-2001)**. Section 6 takes a look at the origins, main features and implications of the budget instability during the eighties and of the successful fiscal consolidation of the nineties. The interaction between structural changes and macroeconomic evolution in the economy is briefly analyzed in section 7 for the whole period considered in this paper. The work ends with a few concluding remarks.

## Definition of periods

It is impossible to analyze the evolution of a specific economy over three decades without providing a basic diachronic structure by means of some sort of sensible definition of periods. As usual, the definition of periods suggested here is conventional and thus risks exaggerating the principal discontinuities in the changes described. However, we believe that in this case the discontinuities so emphasized are much less arbitrary than they are normally in economics, since the structural changes of the Italian economy in the post-war period were characterized by a few relatively well-defined turning points. Such turning points may be identified by focusing on the changes in the average values of a few key macroeconomic variables throughout the succession of business cycles during the historical period considered. Therefore, we need to adopt a definition of business cycles for the second part of the last century. To this end we use the official definition of business cycles suggested by the most reliable official sources in Italy: ISCO and ISAE/BDI (see Table 1).

**Table 1 – Definition of Periods**

| Phases | Initial Minimum | Maximum | Final Minimum | Phases (in months) | | |
|---|---|---|---|---|---|---|
| | | | | Expansion | Recession | Total Cycle |
| I | May - 52 | Sept - 57 | Aug - 58 | 64 | 11 | 75 |
| II | Aug - 58 | Oct - 63 | Jan - 65 | 62 | 15 | 77 |
| III | Jan - 65 | Oct - 70 | Oct - 71 | 69 | 12 | 81 |
| IV | Oct - 71 | Jun - 74 | May - 75 | 32 | 11 | 43 |
| V | May - 75 | Feb - 77 | Dec - 77 | 21 | 10 | 31 |
| VI | Dec - 77 | Mar - 80 | Mar - 83 | 27 | 36 | 63 |
| VII | Mar - 83 | Mar - 92 | Jul - 93 | 108 | 16 | 124 |
| VIII | Jul - 93 | Nov - 95 | Nov - 96 | 28 | 12 | 40 |
| IX | Nov - 96 | Apr - 98 | Jan - 99 | 17 | 9 | 26 |
| X | Jan - 99 | Dec - 00 | Dec - 01 | 23 | 12 | 35 |

(*) Cycle based on industrial production index (cycle-trend, 1995=100)

*Source*: ISCO and ISAE/BDI

In the post-war era the Italian economy never managed to avoid simultaneously monetary and real instability, apart from a very short period between the late fifties and the early sixties. Therefore the macroeconomic environment and the ensuing entrepreneurial decisions and economic policies have always been dominated by at least one of these two concerns, and often by both (particularly in the seventies). The change in the mix of these two basic types of macroeconomic instability strongly influenced the trend of all principal macroeconomic variables and the trend of economic policy, thereby suggesting well-defined criteria for the definition of periods.

Plotting the average value of unemployment and inflation for each business cycle (see Chart 1), we can identify four periods for the post-war Italian economic development:

*Economic Miracle* (1952-1971), a period of decreasing unemployment and absence of serious inflationary pressures;

*Stagflation* (1971-1980), a period marked by a rapid increase in inflation and a moderate growth in unemployment;

*Disinflation* (1980-1993), a period of deceleration of inflation and progressive increase in unemployment;

*Integration in the Eurozone* (1993-2001), a period of rapid consolidation of macroeconomic stability in all its basic dimensions, and resurgence, after a 20-year period, of a trend of reduction of unemployment which however turned out to be very slow and fragile.

The boundaries between these periods coincide with those between the relevant underlying business cycles, with the only exception being the boundary between *Stagflation* and *Disinflation* (1980) that coincides with the peak of the cycle 1977-1983. In fact, from a long-term perspective, the year of 1980 happens to be the most appropriate conventional boundary between *Stagflation* and *Disinflation* since it was also the peak of the "long cycle" depicted by Chart 1.[1]

**Chart 1 – The Long Cycle**

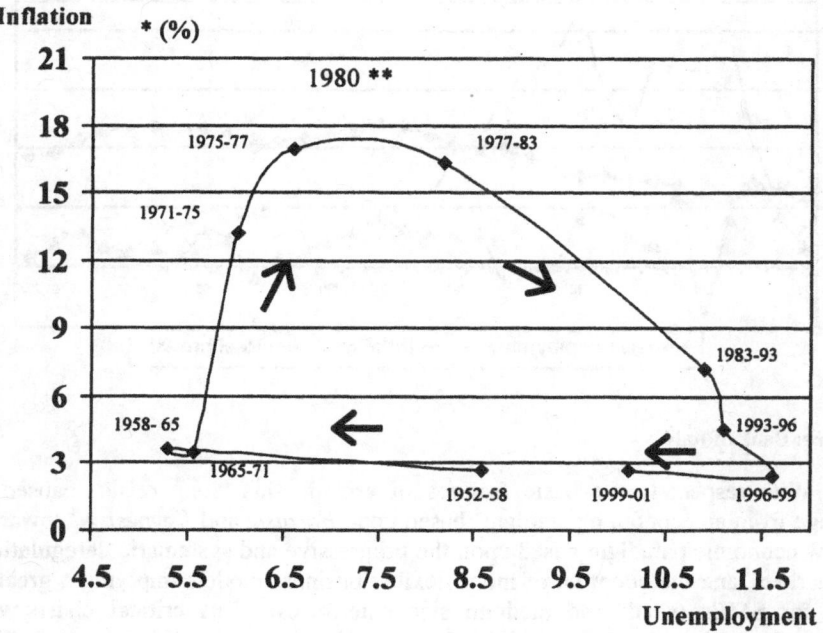

(*) *average values for each cycle period*
(**) *average values for the year*

Source: Elaboration of the Authors based on ISCO-ISAE data

Since the first period was already analyzed in the preceding chapter, the analysis here focuses on the last three periods only.

## Stagflation (1971-1980)

This period was marked by what might be called a "long crisis" (see Charts 1 and 2). Unlike a typical crisis of few quarters during a normal business cycle which usually paves the way to a new period of expansion without implying profound structural changes, economic instability was a dominant theme of this entire period and caused a radical structural change in the main features of economic growth.[2] It is suggestive to think of this long crisis as the crucial critical phase of the "long cycle" depicted in Chart 1.[3]

**Chart 2 – Macroeconomic Evolution**

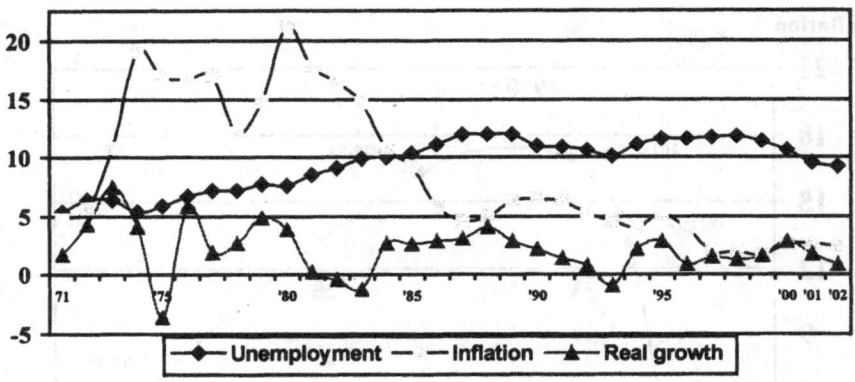

*Source*: Bank of Italy

With respect to the basic features of growth, this "long crisis" caused a change from an economic paradigm[4] based upon *Fordism* and *Keynesism*[5] towards a new economic paradigm based upon the progressive and systematic deregulation of markets, and the adoption of more flexible business models implying a greater role for SMEs (small and medium size enterprises). This critical phase was triggered, and initially dominated, by the intensification of the distributive conflict and by the ensuing hardening in the use of the labor force. This increased the structural uncertainty[6] of the Italian economy, contributing to the obsolescence of the economic paradigm that had presided over the so-called "economic miracle" of the fifties and sixties (further comments on these structural issues will be developed in section 7). The macroeconomic developments were profoundly affected by the structural changes mentioned above. Real growth exhibited a fluctuating pattern deeply influenced by stop-and-go economic policies (Vercelli, 1977).

The trough of 1971 was heavily affected by (i) the industrial stoppages of 1968 and 1969 (culminating in the so-called "hot autumn" of 1969 with a loss of 302 million of working hours) and (ii) the ensuing restrictive policies reacting to the inflationary pressures exerted by rapid wage rises. The easing of tensions on the labor front favored by the approval of a "workers statute",[7] and the growth of domestic consumption driven by wage increases triggered a strong recovery during 1971 and 1972. The rate of growth plummeted after the first oil shock of 1973 and then bottomed out in 1975. As a reaction public spending increased very rapidly reaching 47% of GDP by 1977 (vis-à-vis 30% of 20 years before) mainly due to the growth in current expenditures (interest payments and social expenditures[8]) rather than in capital account. After a vigorous but brief recovery in the late 1975 and early 1976, there was a new setback between late 1976 and early 1977, and then a new milder, but steadier, recovery through 1979 (see Chart 2). These sharp but short recoveries were insufficient to stop the trend towards increasingly higher unemployment, while the sharp declines in the growth rate managed to steer inflation somewhat lower from the high peak recorded in 1974 (19.1%), but not to a single-digit level. Inflation reached a new higher peak in 1980 (21.2%), after the second oil shock, convincing the authorities that a much more restrictive policy had to be introduced.

**Chart 3 – Balance of Payments**

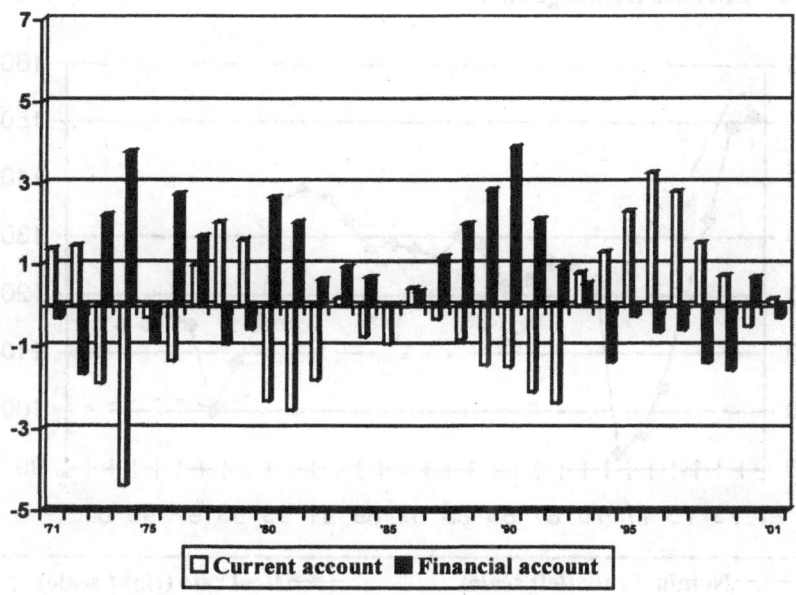

Balances as a percentage of GDP

*Source*: International Financial Statistics, IMF

Notwithstanding the increase in exports, in response to the expansion of the global cycle,[9] which propelled the expansionary phases of 1973 and 1976, the weight of the external constraint became increasingly evident in this period (see Chart 3) as a result of Italy's structural deficit in the energy field (due to the lack of energy sources in the country) and in the agricultural and food sectors (due to the geological and climatic features of the country). Therefore the manufacturing sector was entrusted with the difficult task of re-equilibrating the trade balance. In the seventies, this role was mainly played by light industry (textiles, fashion, shoes, ceramics, etc.) which managed to offset the growing deficits in heavy and high-tech manufacturing (for example chemicals, metallurgy, and electronics). However this peculiar model of specialization became increasingly unsustainable because of the growing contradiction between the structure of demand (which was progressively converging towards the structure of most industrialized countries) and the structure of exports (which was progressively moving away from that structure).[10] The foreign exchange policy was used as a counter-cyclical mechanism to offset the loss of competitiveness due to higher inflation, a significant degree of wage and salary indexation (because of the specific clauses contained in collective bargaining agreements), and a growing technological gap (see section 7).

**Chart 4 – Effective Exchange Rates**

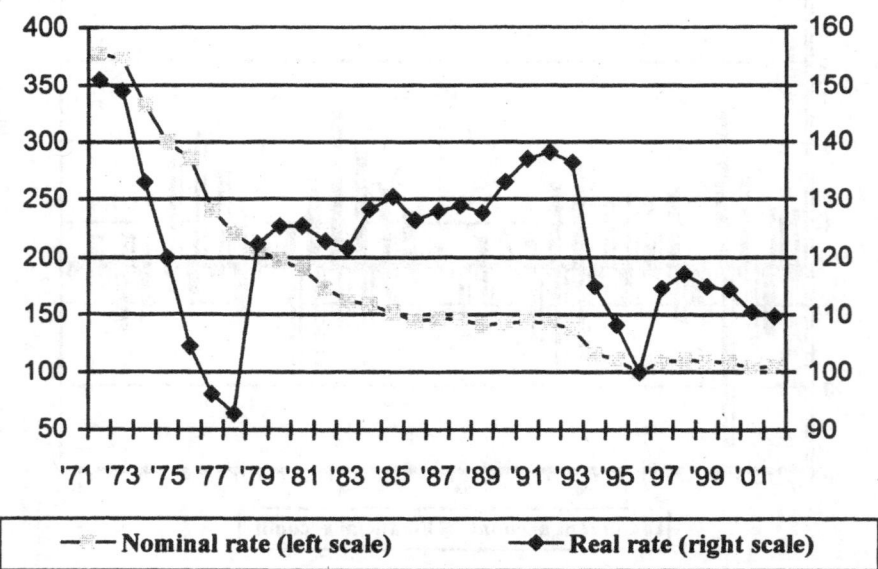

— — Nominal rate (left scale)   —♦— Real rate (right scale)

Index Numbers (1995=100)

*Source*: International Financial Statistics, IMF

The Lira exchange rate was cleverly maneuvered in order to obtain a slow but progressive depreciation vis-à-vis the German Mark, the currency of the main market for Italian exports, while avoiding a depreciation vis-à-vis the US dollar, i.e. the currency of most Italian imports. This helped to keep substantial equilibrium in the balance of payments since an increase in the price of imports was immediately apparent in that balance, while an improved competitiveness of exports had a lagged impact. In addition, the combination of such exchange rate policy with a restrictive budgetary policy, especially after the 1976 cyclical rebound, succeeded in reducing the inflationary pressures and produced a current account surplus for the period 1977 until the second oil shock in 1979.

During this period, real interest rates were negative (see Chart 5) with long-term rates falling to -10% in 1974, when inflation reached one of its peaks. A new minimum was reached in 1980 (-5%) as a consequence of imported inflation following the second oil shock. However the new restrictive policies inaugurated with Italy's joining the EMS in 1979 (though within a larger band[11]) not only caused a progressive increase in real interest rates, that ended up having a considerable impact in the subsequent period, and a tendential appreciation of the lira (see Chart 4) but also led to a long period of disinflation.

**Chart 5 – Real Interest Rates**

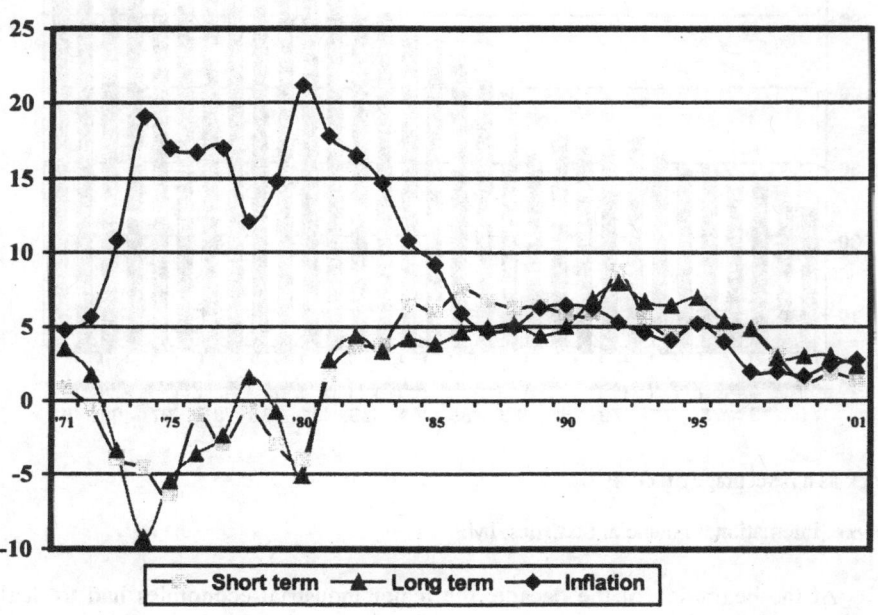

*Source*: International Financial Statistics, IMF

## Disinflation (1980-1993)

This period was marked by the ongoing deceleration of inflation accompanied by a progressive increase in unemployment (see Charts 1 and 2). The disinflationary effects of a very restrictive monetary policy were somewhat offset by a permissive policy of deficit spending. This was reflected in the simultaneous increase in real interest rates (see Chart 5) and public debt (see Chart 6).

### Chart 6 – Public Debt

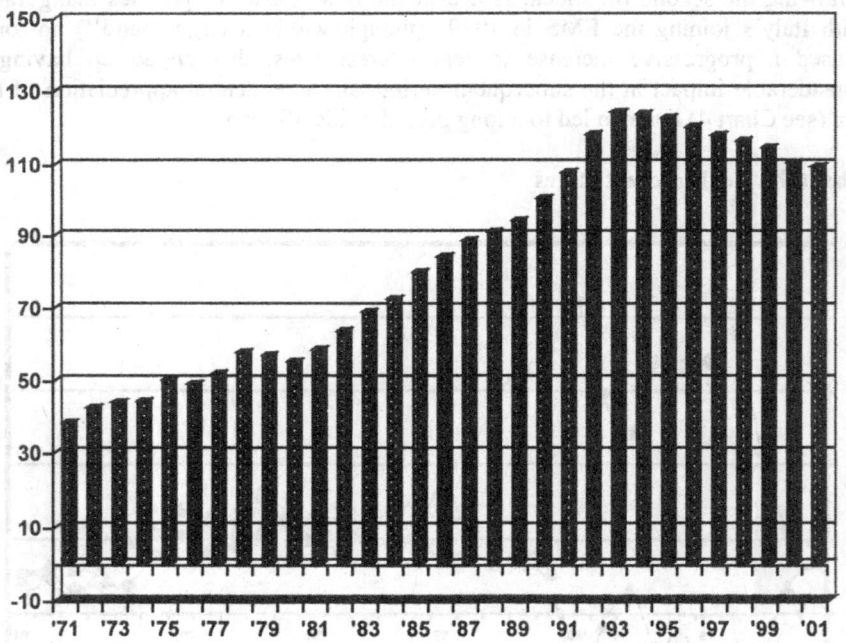

Stock as a percentage of GDP

*Source*: International Financial Statistics, IMF

At the beginning of the decade, the major industrial economies had to deal with the effects of the second oil shock. The reaction of the Western economies was mostly unilateral and uncoordinated: some countries stimulated the inflow of petrodollars (this was the case in the UK), others tried to increase the exports by devaluating their currencies (Japan) or to reduce the imports of oil (Germany). In most countries, including the U.S., interest rates were raised to attract foreign capital. Such action eventually led to the debt crisis of emerging countries and the U.S. stock exchange crash of 1987.

In Italy, the restrictive monetary policy and the ensuing appreciation of the lira caused a profound structural change in the economy and in particular in the manufacturing sector. The organizational, technological and financial structure of the firms was re-engineered in order to assure a higher level of flexibility. The same drive towards flexibility happened in the industrial relations and in the management of the labor force. Domestic prices were affected to a lesser extent by imported inflation, deficit spending, the growing cost of capital, and the increase in the price of public services, while the effect of the indexing mechanism was progressively weakened.[12] The accumulation of productive capital slowed but the economic efficiency of investment increased in consequence of a shift towards more flexible forms of investment. This process was consistent with innovation in the productive process but was inconsistent with product innovation, especially in the high-tech sector which needs long-term investment in R&D and in new plants, and this eventually enhanced the technological gap between Italy and other industrialized countries.

At the same time, the financial system embarked on a process of change that decentralized a few crucial categories of financial decisions giving more weight to competition and redistributing in a more efficient manner the financial risks, but increasing the fragility of the financial system.[13] In addition a reduction in inflation was accompanied by an increase in the budgetary instability (see Chart 6 and section 7).

The fall in growth, which hit a low in 1983, pushed unemployment over the 10% level. By 1987, the disinflationary process had succeeded for the first time in steering the inflation rate under the threshold of 5% although only at the cost of a more than 12% level of unemployment (Chart 2). The last part of the period (1988-1991) was marked by a moderate expansion that succeeded in cutting the unemployment rate at the cost of a limited rebound in inflation. However the real rate of growth, after hitting almost 5% in 1988, kept decelerating until it turned negative in 1993. These figures may be reconciled by taking into account the strong increase of the unofficial economy during this period; this increase reduced the rate of effective unemployment but was obviously not reflected in the official statistics.

Through 1987, there were various realignments in the lira central parity within the EMS; such realignments tended to make up for the progressive loss of Italy's competitiveness abroad and favored the containment of the current account deficit. From 1987 to 1992, the lira was realigned only once (in 1990) when it entered the smaller band of fluctuation. On the whole, the Italian lira appreciated in real terms during the period (see Chart 4). The growing external deficit from 1987 to 1992 (Chart 3) forced the authorities to further increase the interest rates up to 1992 (Chart 5). The downside effects were the creation of huge internal and external deficits. Considering the policy of deficit spending together with the restrictive monetary stance and resulting high interest rates, the sustainability of public debt was increasingly jeopardized. In the eighties, the public deficit expanded at an annual average rate exceeding 10% of GDP. Also alarming was the ensuing increase in the foreign debt that went from a negligible value of 1979 to 15% of GDP ten years later (see section 6).

## Integration in the Eurozone (1993-2001)

In the last period considered herein, the successful process of *Integration in the Eurozone*, Italy's economic policy obtained remarkable, and to some extent unexpected, results in the direction of a complete stabilization of the economy from the viewpoint of both monetary and budgetary equilibrium.

Following the crisis of the EMS in 1992 and the ensuing progressive depreciation of the Italian lira (from September 1992 to the middle of 1995), the process of integration was pushed by the acceleration of monetary and economic unification of European countries. In fact Italy reacted to the severe disequilibria caused by the currency crisis with strict monetary and budgetary policies designed to force prompt convergence of the Italian macroeconomic parameters towards the Maastricht parameters.[14] The average fiscal burden in Italy went from 31% of GDP in 1980 to 40% in 1990, exceeding 43% in 1999. The stock of debt that had continuously increased in the *Stagflation* period from about 50% of GDP to more than 120% in 1993, started to decrease as of 1994 and continued declining throughout the period (see Chart 6, and the next section for further details).

Since October 1992 the real interest rates began to drop, in consequence of falling inflation accompanied by a sharp increase in primary surplus, inducing a considerable fall in interest payments by the Government (see Chart 7).

**Chart 7 – General Government Revenue, Expenditure and Primary Surplus**

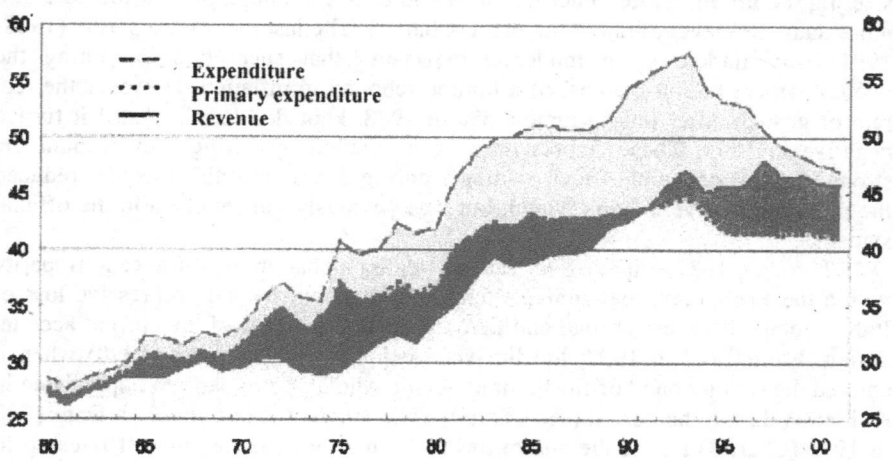

As a percentage of GDP

*Source*: Balassone et al. (2002)

The rigorous policy of stabilization implied strong sacrifices from the point of view of disposable income and employment opportunities, but these sacrifices were justified by the desire of public authorities to get Italy promptly back into the "club" of countries leading the process of European economic integration.

This stabilization effort contributed to the fairly low average rates of growth throughout the period (see Chart 2). In fact, the growth of output, after a reasonable performance in 1994-95, driven by foreign demand revived by the depreciation of the currency[15] in a framework of complacent incomes policies, shrank to an average of 1-1.5% afterwards, until 2000. As a consequence, the foreign trade balance, that had been increasingly negative in the *Deflation* period, became strongly positive (see Chart 3).[16] The unemployment rate rose further until 1998, while inflation remained at values close to 5% until 1995 because of the influence of imported inflation after the devaluation (see Chart 2). Eventually in 1997 the inflation rate fell to values substantially consistent with the Maastricht parameters. As of 1998, unemployment started to fall again, while inflation increased only marginally. Thus, there was hope that a stable economy could get back on a track of rapid growth. However the rate of growth remained disappointingly low (2.9% in 2000 and 1.8% in 2001[17]).

Being unemployment partly mitigated by the presence of unofficial economy, particularly intense in the northeast and southern regions,[18] the big loop described by the Italian economy after the second world war was almost closed (see Chart 1). At this point, the main challenge was that of repeating the first part of the loop to recover full employment in a framework of macroeconomic stability.

**The fiscal consolidation of the nineties: the "second economic miracle"**

It is usual to call "economic miracle" an economic event (or process) that occurs (is triggered) abruptly although it was completely unexpected, or almost so. The rapid and steady process of growth initiated in the early fifties and continuing to the late sixties received the name of "economic miracle" because it was unexpected by both the public and experts after a long destructive war and two decades of Fascist rule (see Di Matteo in this volume).

By the same token, the extremely rapid process of fiscal consolidation occurring in the 1993-1997 period which allowed the adoption of Euro with the first group of European countries could merit the name of the "second economic miracle". This is because the final part of the process (1993-1997, and in particular the crucial final leap of 1997) took place extremely rapidly while its success was generally unexpected by the public and experts only a few months before the goal was attained (see Spaventa-Chiorazzo, 1999). However, economic miracles, though unexpected ex ante, have rational explanations ex post. In this section we intend to summarize some of the crucial determinants of this success. To this end we have to reconstruct the origins of a problem that cuts across the periods considered in this paper (see Chart 7).

The economic miracle of the fifties and sixties was marked by a high degree of macroeconomic stability. Mild primary deficits appeared in the sixties in consequence of the downturn of 1963 and to counter the first signs of structural difficulties in the late sixties. However the deficits became sizable and systematic only in the seventies when an expansionary fiscal policy was adopted in order to slow the progressive increase in unemployment. The ensuing expansion in public debt increased the interest payments (ibidem). This increase accelerated very much in the eighties in consequence of the sharp increase of the rate of interest caused by a restrictive monetary policy. Consolidation policies started only in the second half of the eighties, but, at that point, they were not courageous enough to be successful. The way out could only be found by producing consistent, persistent and growing primary surpluses. The first primary surplus in 30 years was achieved in 1991 (see Chart 7); other primary surpluses were reported in the years thereafter under the pressure of serious external shocks (in particular the currency crisis of 1992) and the persistent increase of public debt. Interest payments that had doubled in the eighties to 10.5 % of GDP, in the years 1991-1993, rose further by 2.5% of GDP exceeding not only the mild improvement in the primary balance in the late eighties but even the sizeable surpluses of the early nineties. Only in 1994 did the cost of debt start to shrink and this was due to lower inflation (notwithstanding the imported inflation arising from the depreciation of the Italian lira in 1993 and 1994) and a progressive reduction of the risk premium on public debt due to an increasing confidence in the efforts to redress Italy's public finances.

However, these improvements were considered too slow to permit full compliance with the Maastricht parameters by the end of 1997. Given the situation, the government decided to make an all-out effort to ensure Italy's participation in the third phase of EMU, and thus embraced a sort of shock therapy to facilitate a final leap to the finishing line. This occurred with a 1997 primary surplus of no less than 7% of GDP (about the double of the sizeable surpluses of the last two years). Though this result was implemented mainly through temporary and accounting measures, the determination of the government and the strong personal credibility of the Treasury Minister Carlo Azeglio Ciampi (formerly highly esteemed governor of the Bank of Italy, and now Italy's President since 1998) and of the Prime Minister Romano Prodi (elected in 1999 as President of the European Commission) made possible a typical case of self-fulfilling prophecy by dramatically reducing the risk premium on public debt.

However, we have to underline that, if the goal was reached just in time by the extraordinary final leap of 1997, this success was made possible by a longer process of stabilization which began to take shape in the late eighties and which was implemented with vigor in the early nineties. This process appears ex post more temporarily consistent and structurally solid than it looked to most observers at the time (see Chart 7). No doubt there were an excess of within-year corrections that greatly reduced the credibility of the adjustment process and increased its cost. However, in the meantime, the main structural problems were not ignored. In particular, the crucial problem of pension expenditure was tackled in two successive rounds in 1992 and 1995. This problem (that affects all the developed countries) is especially serious in Italy because the fertility rate is particularly low (1.2 children per woman in childbearing age) while the ratio of the elderly to the working age population is expected to increase from 21% in 1990 to about 30% in 2010 and 48% in 2030 (see Balassone, et al., 2002). As a result of these demographic trends, the Italian Pension System became unsustainable at least since the early eighties. Pension expenditures increased from 5.0% of GDP in 1960 to 10.2% in 1980 and 14.9% in 1992, far exceeding the growth of the other items of social spending (ibidem) as well as the growth of social contributions.

Structural measures were also taken in order to contain public health expenditures.[19] As a consequence, there was a progressive contraction of public expenditures to total health expenditures. During the nineties, Italy was not only one of a few OECD members to cut health care budgets, but it showed one of the lowest contributions of public expenditure to overall NHS expenditures. During the 1990-1999 period, the national health expenditure grew in nominal terms from ITL 80,262 billion to ITL 120,380 billion, but in real terms the annual rate of growth was only 0.5%. The ratio of health care expenditures to GDP decreased from a maximum of 6.5% in 1991 to 5.7% in the late nineties. The trend of public health care expenditures in other European countries was less favorable, notwithstanding better demographics.[20] However, as a consequence of these reforms, the percentage of Italian households health expenditure over their total expenditure soared by 11 percentage points from 15.5% in 1990 to 26.8% in 1999, mainly because individuals had to bear a greater portion of the cost of certain services and some free services were completely eliminated.

Another courageous structural adjustment carried out in the nineties, mainly in the second half of the decade, was a systematic program of privatization. Not only did this process strongly contribute to fiscal consolidation by keeping the stock-flow adjustment broadly neutral, but it also helped to curtail an excessively bureaucratic system, while enhancing the outlook for the country's financial markets and private entrepreneurship.

The Italian privatization process began relatively late, in 1992. At that time, state companies, classified on the basis of their economic activity, were under the control of four public bodies (IRI, EFIM, ENI and ENEL). In 1992, these bodies were converted into public limited-liability companies and their investments were transferred to the Treasury. They not only changed the legal status, but also their mission, going from bodies operating in the general public interest to market-oriented companies.

The divestiture of public assets was the result of financial emergency and pressures for deregulation from the European Commission. The main goal, as described by the government at the time, was an increase in efficiency and the improvement of competition in the industrial sector and in the stock market. However the most successful objective attained so far was a massive flow of revenues that played a crucial role in the sharp reduction of the public debt.

Even though only a minor portion of the assets sold were actually removed from state control, the process was nevertheless important in terms of volumes.[21] The proceeds of the privatizations in Italy as a percentage of GDP were second only to those realized in the United Kingdom, but were realized in much shorter time (US$ 121.1 billion between 1993 and year-end 2000 of which 66% recorded after 1996: see Table 2).

## Table 2 – Incomes from Privatization in Europe

| Countries | Years | Billion of US$ | % of GDP (*) |
|---|---|---|---|
| UK | 1984-99 | 118.9 | 23 |
| Italy | 1993-00 | 121.1 | 13.4 |
| France | 1986-99 | 65.8 | 7.2 |
| Germany | 1986-99 | 48.0 | 4.0 |
| Spain | 1993-99 | 44.1 | 10.4 |

(*) incomes as % of GDP in the first year of privatizatio

*Source*: Confindustria, Sept. 2000

The "second economic miracle" was not only a successful episode of fiscal consolidation but the completion of a long process of macroeconomic "detoxification". As we have seen, the Italian economic policy reacted to the shocks of the seventies with a rather lax monetary policy that drove inflation to unsustainable levels, while in the eighties monetary stabilization was somehow offset by a lax budgetary policy. Throughout the seventies and eighties the priority of economic policy was the defense of employment. When the fiscal "methadone" showed its disruptive negative effects after the monetary addiction, it became clear that complete macroeconomic stabilization could no longer be eluded or postponed. The final stage of detoxification in the second half of the nineties was particularly difficult because, by adopting the euro as national currency, the Italian policy makers had to commit to give up the devaluation of the national currency, the last resort drug which the Italian economy all too often had relied upon in the past, even during the recent 1992-1994 period. Therefore the focus of economic policy had to shift to structural issues.

Detoxification is a necessary condition for good sustainable performance but the hangover may be long while the structural weaknesses are fully made explicit, including a persisting risk of relapse that would have devastating effects within the euro framework, even in the short period. In particular, real growth in the nineties was no more than 1.5%, sizably lower than in the preceding decades but also lower than in the other developed countries. However this performance of the real economy was considerable in the light of the severely restrictive budgetary policy. This was made possible by a very responsible attitude of Trade Unions that accepted a severe income policy. On this basis a gradual reduction of the fiscal pressure, made possible by the fiscal consolidation, was expected to sustain domestic consumption and investment. However the mild relaxation of the fiscal policy after 1998 has thus far not produced any sizeable positive effects on the real economy. This may depend in part on some negative structural implications of the stabilization policy pursued in the nineties; in particular, the strong reduction of public-sector capital spending caused further deterioration of the country's infrastructures (see Balassone et al.,1992). In addition, the mediocre performance of the real economy at the turn of the millennium is also related to the peculiarities of the industrial structure, and in particular, its specialization in the traditional manufacturing sector (see Spaventa-Chiorazzo, 1999).

## Interaction with the structural evolution

In the post-war era, the Italian economy was marked by a long economic cycle that started at the end of the post-war reconstruction (1945-51) from a high level of unemployment (above 9%) and a low level of inflation (less than 3%) and was somehow "closed" by the end of the Millennium with similar values of inflation and unemployment. After a virtuous circle featuring diminishing unemployment and substantial monetary stability that lasted about 20 years (the so-called *Economic Miracle*), we distinguished three successive periods all characterized by economic instability: *Stagflation* (1971-1980), *Disinflation* (1980-1993) and *Integration in the Eurozone* (1993-2001). During the first of these periods the growth model at the root of the *Economic Miracle* imploded and opened a Pandora's box of macroeconomic instabilities: increasing unemployment, inflation, public debt, deficits of the public budget, trade accounts and balance of payments, etc. However the mix of the most important macroeconomic disequilibria and stabilization policies changed in each period. In the *Stagflation* period, slowly growing unemployment was accompanied by accelerating inflation while fairly permissive monetary and budgetary policies were adopted to stabilize unemployment. In particular, the macroeconomic policy reacted to the growing tension in industrial relations by allowing some acceleration of inflation that could ease the distributional conflict. In the period of *Disinflation* more rapid growth of unemployment was accompanied by slowly decelerating inflation, while the policy priority shifted to monetary stabilization. In this period, macroeconomic policy had to curb the excess of inflation undermining the competitiveness of the Italian industry, while the disruptive implications for unemployment were mitigated by a fairly lax budgetary policy. Finally in the third period of *Integration in the Eurozone* both monetary and budget stability were considered urgent policy priorities as both were required by the Maastricht parameters. The consensus on the economic sacrifices involved by an all-encompassing macroeconomic rigor was based on the widespread conviction that the first train to Europe could not be missed by one of the founding members of the European Community.

The change of focus of macroeconomic policy depended on the change of domestic and international scenarios and on the relative urgency of macroeconomic disequilibria. In particular, the change of the mix of macroeconomic imbalances depended, with a quite long and variable lag (having an order of magnitude of a few years), on the macroeconomic policy pursued in the recent past and depended on the evolution of the structural features of the economy.

The *Economic Miracle* of the 1950s and 1960s may be interpreted as a structural catching-up. While the industrialized democratic countries managed to get out of the *Great Depression* of the 1930s by restructuring their economies according to the principles of *Fordism* and *Keynesism* (see footnote 5), in Italy this evolution was slowed down, and to some extent limited, by the Fascist Regime in the 1930s and by the war in the 1940s (because of the war economy until 1945 and the reconstruction afterwards). The Fascist Regime sustained the economy through public expenditures even before most other industrialized market economies resorted to such policy. However the isolationism of Italy's economic policy and the corporatism brought by the fascist regime increased a pre-existing technological gap by slowing down the structural updating of the economy and delaying growth. The structural reforms introduced during the *Reconstruction*, meant to establish a free-market economy in a Parliamentary Democracy, triggered a process of convergence towards the economic structure of the other industrialized market economies. The technological gap partially mitigated, while the economy was put in the position of exploiting the opportunities offered by international trade. This process of structural catching up propelled a sustained process of growth that characterized the so-called "economic miracle" of the fifties and sixties, i.e. the unexpected superior macroeconomic performance of the Italian economy, as compared with that of the other industrialized countries (see Di Matteo, in this volume, for more details).

However, at the end of the sixties the economic model based on *Fordism* and *Keynesism* began to crumble in industrialized countries for similar reasons, albeit with timing and conditions which varied. The main problem was the inconsistency between persistent full employment (reached by most industrialized countries by the early sixties) and the rigidities of the labor market. In the industrial sector this was related to the hierarchical organization of big firms and the inflexible Fordist technologies, while the growing size of the welfare state and the public bureaucracy were also important causes. In Italy, the problems were aggravated by institutional peculiarities including a high percentage of union membership within the labor force and the periodic concentration of contract renewals approximately every 3 years (see Vercelli 1977). This produced periodic industrial conflicts, strikes, work stoppages, and sharp increases in the cost of labor.

The ensuing inflationary tensions creeping into all of the economies of industrialized countries after the late sixties (though with different intensity and timing) caused the collapse of the Bretton Woods system based on fixed exchange rates. The new regime based on flexible exchange rates soon proved to be inconsistent with the rigidities of *Fordism* and *Keynesism*. The new scenario affected by sharp inflationary upsurges and the new external scenario based on flexible exchange rates introduced a degree of systemic uncertainty which was much more intense than in the two previous decades. The ensuing search for flexibility produced the collapse of the hierarchical and centralized model of the organization of economic activity typical of the preceding economic model. This paved the way for a decentralization of economic activity and managerial decisions within the firms (flatter organization and *intra*preneurship) and between firms (outsourcing and subcontracting).

The new scenario encouraged an unexpected revival of SMEs. While in the preceding decades the role of these companies had continuously declined, in the seventies this decline ceased and started to reverse. In particular, the number of people employed by SMEs that had continuously contracted in the preceding decades started to increase, slowly but steadily, and has continued to date (see Chart 8).

## Chart 8 – Distribution of Labour Force

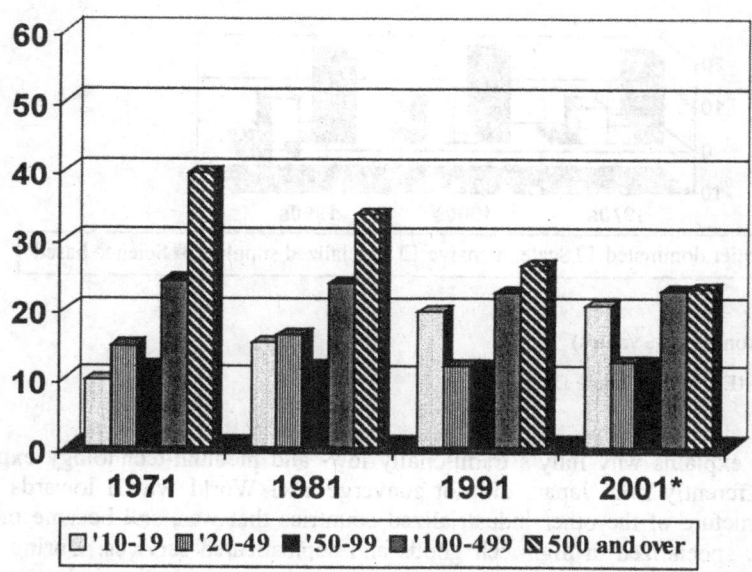

Firms of Manufacturing Sector Classified by Number of Workers (% quota)
* Provisional data

*Source*: Istat

In the early eighties the UK and US markets recorded a systematic process of privatization and deregulation. The Italian economy participated in this broad-based process of re-directing structural change, albeit with its own peculiarities. The shift of weight in favor of SMEs was particularly pronounced, and its impact particularly remarkable, also because in absolute terms their weight was much more crucial (more than 60% of the labor force vis-à-vis 20-30% of the other industrialized countries with the only partial exception of Japan). The increasing weight of SMEs that assured a high level of flexibility to the Italian industry was reinforced by the successful adoption of an original model of local agglomeration of SMEs (industrial districts), that proved to be able to exploit the external economies of proximity and interaction. While the crisis of heavy industry and standardized manufactured goods was particularly strong, the complex network of SMEs and industrial districts, particularly concentrated in the northeastern and central regions of Italy, as well as along the Adriatic rim, proved particularly successful in the so-called "made-in-Italy sectors" of household goods, textiles and apparel, and the typical Italian food industry.

**Chart 9 - Contribution to Trade Balance**

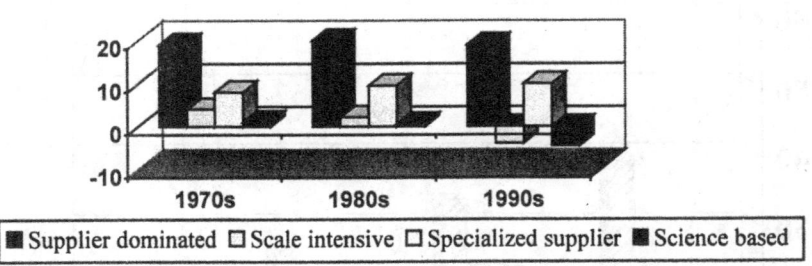

Pavitt taxonomy (% values)

*Source*: SIE – World Trade Data Base

This explains why Italy's traditionally low- and medium-technology export goods, differently from Japan, did not converge after World War II towards the typical structure of the other industrialized countries that was, and became more and more, specialized in high-tech goods and sophisticated services. During the last three decades the contribution of different categories of Italian industries to trade balance, based on Pavitt's taxonomy,[22] records a progressive contraction of scale intensive and science based sectors, to become negative during the nineties (see Chart 9).

These peculiarities in the industrial structure implied that the technological gap, widened in the inter-war period, was only partially mitigated in the second half of the century. This is confirmed by a series of indicators such as the percentage of aggregate expenditure in R&D which remained much lower than that for other industrialized countries (see Chart 10) and the structural deficit of the technological balance of payments (see Chart 11). The gap in development between the northern and southern regions of the country started to close in the late sixties and early seventies as a result of systematic subsidies, public infrastructure expenditure, and the creation of industrial development poles based on the construction by state bodies (IRI, ENI) of big plants in heavy industry (steelworks in Bagnoli and Taranto, oil refineries, chemical plants). Unfortunately, the heavy industry crisis in the seventies (which tended to materialize in most industrialized countries) stopped the process of convergence, and started a trend of further gradual deterioration of the gap between development in the northern regions and development in the southern regions of the country (see Chart 12).

## Chart 10 - R & D Expenditure

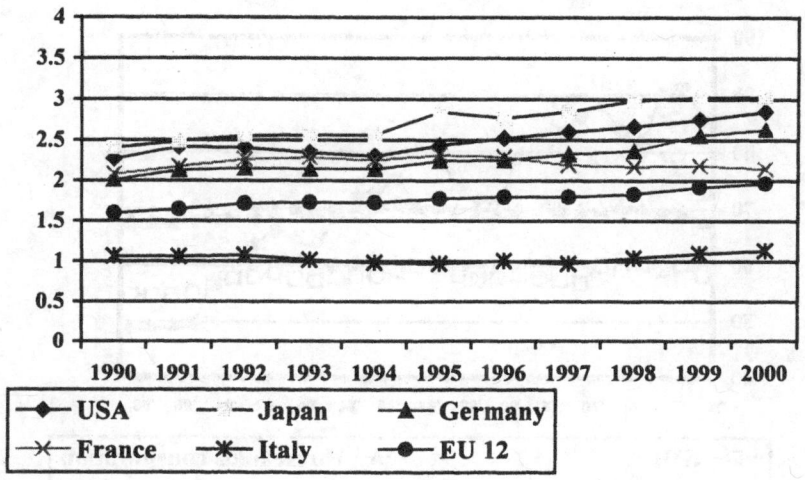

As a percentage of GDP

*Source*: Main Science and Technology Indicators, OECD May 2000

## Chart 11 - Technological Balance of Payments

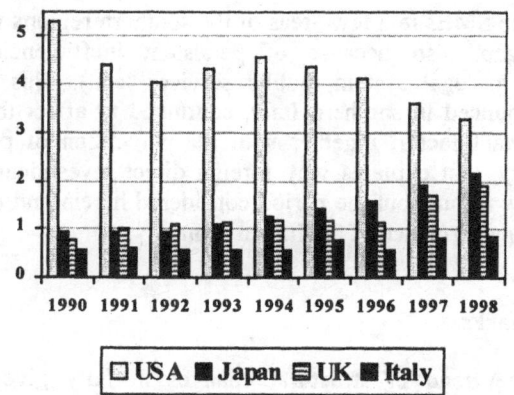

High-Tech Sectors Cover (Export/Import)

*Source*: Main Science and Technology Indicators, OECD May 2000

**Chart 12 - North – South Divide**

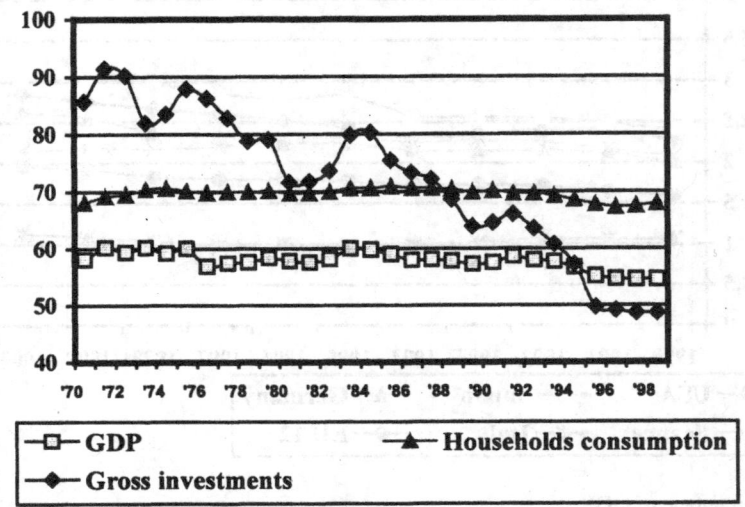

Values per inhabitant
Southern as % of Central – Northern Regions

*Source*: Svimez

The strength of the SMEs in a few areas of the southern regions was not sufficient to reduce the gap, also because of persistent inefficiencies in intangible infrastructures (e.g. legal system, public services, etc.). This problem, though particularly pronounced in southern Italy, continued to affect the entire country. This is an important factor, together with the perception of potentially greater political instability, that explains why foreign direct investment continued to be comparatively low throughout the period considered herein and contributed to the mediocre growth performance of the Italian economy.

**Concluding Remarks**

Understanding the trend of structural changes in Italy gives insight on the determinants of its macroeconomic evolution. The monetary instability in the seventies emerged as a way to give flexibility to the economy, first relieving the industrial conflict and then triggering the profound redirection of structural change in industry. The cost-push inflation of the *Stagflation* period (1971-1980) was triggered by loose monetary policy (as shown by negative real interest rates throughout the seventies) and systematically transmitted by a strong indexation system throughout the whole economy.

By the end of the seventies, with industrial relations having improved and a more flexible industrial structure, the participation in the EMS offered the occasion for a dramatic changeover to rigorous monetary policy characterized by high real interest rates. In the *Deflation* period (1980-1993), the disruptive welfare implication of the progressive increase in unemployment was somehow kept under control by a fairly lax budgetary policy heavily affected by redundancy payments and social transfers (pensions, health, education, subsidies to the less developed areas of the countries, etc.). The ensuing collapse of public accounts and the temporary withdrawal from the exchange rate mechanism of the EMS as a result of the currency crisis of 1992 led to a new phase characterized by a consistent, and fairly successful, attempt to promptly resume the process of *Integration in the Eurozone* (1993-2001) by adopting a rigorous policy of stabilization of all the aspects of macroeconomic policy with the help of a massive process of privatization of state-owned industries, and the introduction of some degree of deregulation of the markets.

It is not the purpose of this paper to evaluate whether the macroeconomic policies pursued throughout the period considered were the only possible, or the best, choice given the circumstances. The tentative reconstruction of what happened is only meant to clarify some plausible motivations underlying the adoption of the various policies in each phase of the long cycle and the impact thereof on the structural changes within the Italian economy. Generally speaking we may say that, though the policies adopted helped solving what was believed to be the salient instability in each period, thus contributing to defuse its disruptive potential, typically these results were achieved only at the cost of heavy 'side effects' which generated various phases of macroeconomic instability. Only in the second part of the nineties was a fairly consistent macroeconomic policy pursued under the pressure of economic integration in the Eurozone and this brought about a full stabilization of the Italian economy. The process of fiscal consolidation was so rapid and its successful completion so unexpected that it could merit the name of the "second economic miracle", also because its negative impact on the growth rate of the period was less disruptive than it was expected ex ante.

In any case, regardless of the influence of economic policy in assuring a minimum standard of macroeconomic stability, we have to acknowledge that it was unable to solve the main structural problems that prevented, and still jeopardize, a healthy path of sustainable growth: namely a persistent technological gap with other industrialized countries, a widening divide between economic development in the northern and southern regions of the country, and a chronic low quality of infrastructures (including a poor legal framework and fairly unreliable bureaucratic apparatus). As long as these structural problems persist, there will be danger of new bouts of macroeconomic instability at any time.

## Notes

[1] Another possibility could be the year 1979 when two important events – the second oil crisis and Italy's joining the EMS – exerted a major impact on the change of direction of the main macroeconomic time series (see Chart 2). However the impact of these events on

the time series only became fully apparent in the registered empirical evidence with the usual lag of a few months, and therefore was fully reflected only during 1980.

[2] Therefore, in this case, the term "crisis" means a "sharp structural change", close to the meaning suggested by its Ancient Greek etymology. As is well known, the term assumed in business cycle theory the broader meaning of the process that accompanies or fosters a change of state (e.g. from expansion to depression) without necessarily implying a crucial structural change.

[3] In this work we have not delved into the subject of whether this long cycle may be interpreted as a Kondratief long wave. In any case, a reference to literature on long waves may be useful to interpret the main features and the underlying causes of the "long cycle" described in this work (see Vercelli, 1989). However this does not imply any built-in tendency to the regular repetition of this sort of "long" cycle.

[4] As is well known, the school of Freeman introduced the notion of technological paradigm (see Dosi, 1984) building upon the notion of a scientific paradigm introduced by Kuhn (1970). We use the concept of economic paradigm in order to extend the concept beyond the technological aspects and to incorporate the organizational and institutional aspects of the mode of production and distribution of goods and services.

[5] By Fordism we mean the organization of production based on the standardization of goods and systematic application of Taylorism, while by Keynesism we mean a policy of systematic intervention of the State in the economy, not only to stabilize growth by means of anti-cyclical measures but also to consolidate and extend the so called "welfare state". Fordism increased the productivity of labour and therefore the volume of aggregate supply, while Keynesism sustained effective demand in order to absorb the maximum potential production and assure full employment. The genesis, rise and breakdown of the economic paradigm based on Fordism and Keynesism are analysed in Vercelli (86b, 88, 89).

[6] The higher degree of systemic uncertainty spurred the search for greater flexibility in the use of productive factors and for more liquid financial positions, but brought about lower productive investments (see Vercelli 1986b).

[7] The "workers statute", approved in 1970, introduced a new regulatory framework for the industrial relations imposing precise terms and conditions safeguarding workers' rights within the companies.

[8] Outlays for government pensions rose to 12% of GDP in 1977, while in 1978 health care expenditures were 5% of GDP (see section 6 for further details and comments).

[9] The early seventies were marked by an unusual synchronization of the upward part of the business cycle in industrial countries. This produced a "growing ascending semi-wave of a worldwide cycle that for its amplitude and international diffusion may be considered the most marked of the post war period" (ISCO, 1973).

[10] As is well known (Conti 1978; Pierelli 1983), the Italian economy is the only industrialized country in the post-war period to have kept, if not increased, a pattern of specialization of its exports in the traditional sectors rather than in the high-tech sector. This sort of specialization in sectors where the world demand was less dynamic and the more challenging competition from developing countries urged a continuous upgrading of the quality of products and of productive processes.

[11] The Italian Authorities required and obtained a special status within the EMS with the lira allowed to fluctuate within a band of +/-6% vis-à-vis central parity, compared with +/-2.75% for the currencies of the other countries. The same special status was later given to the UK and Spain when they entered the EMS.

[12] New collective bargaining agreements finalized in July 1992 and July 1993 marked the end of wage indexation with the removal of the escalator clauses (so called "scala

mobile"). The question of inflation was left up to national negotiations while other wages adjustments were left up to individual firms.

[13] The Italian banking system was at the time an oligopolistic market highly segmented on the basis of the functional distinction between retail banking and long-term financing. The systematic bailout of banks in critical situation succeeded in preventing potential financial crises but only at the cost of encouraging less accountability for individuals behavior because of the moral hazard involved.

[14] The Treaty of Maastricht was signed in February 1992 and confirmed by the Treaty of Amsterdam of June 1997 that fixed the Pact of Stability and Development. The Maastricht parameters allow for a public debt of less than 60% of GDP, a public deficit of no more than 3% of GDP, an inflation rate of no more than 1.5 % (the rate of most stable countries), and interest rates of no more than 2 % higher than the average of the countries with the lowest inflation.

[15] About 40% vis-à-vis the dollar from the beginning of 1993 to the end of 1995.

[16] However there was a growing flight to quality of Italian capital abroad following the deregulation of capital movement and the reduced confidence in the country (in 1993 S&P downgraded Italy's public debt).

[17] In 2002 the rate of growth is expected to be lower than 1% (see e.g. the Prometeia forecast of July 2002).

[18] Recent estimates (Censis 2001) suggest that unofficial workers in 1999 reached a figure of 3.5 mio (exceeding 14% of overall workforce). In terms of volumes unofficial economy is estimated to approximate 20% of GDP.

[19] The Italian National Health System (NHS) was set up in 1978 with a share of public health expenditure on GDP of around 5%. Since 1987, total health expenditures have steadily grown, and public health expenditures followed a similar pattern until 1991. As of 1992, public health expenditures began to decline and stabilized at around 5.5% of GDP (69.9% of total expenditures in 1997).

[20] During the eighties in UK, under the Thatcher government, the NHS expenditure grew from 5.1% to 5.9% of GDP, in Germany from 6.7% to 8.3% of GDP, and in France from 6.6% to 7.1% of GDP.

[21] The Italian privatization process is far from being concluded; the State still plays a major role in many economic sectors so that, considering the average value of capitalization during the first months of year 2000, the residual value of the holdings to be sold amounts to around USD 60 billion, or about 50% of the amount generated with the 1993-00 divestitures. Including the unquoted state companies, the residual value is probably actually higher than the value of privatizations already completed.

[22] Pavitt describes sector diversity in innovative behaviour by identifying four categories of industries with different technological trajectories, i.e cost cutting, product design or mixed. He uses data collected on about 2000 significant innovations in Britain between 1945 and 1979. The different technological trajectories are in turn explained by sector differences in the source of technology, type of user, and means of appropriation, etc. The four categories in Pavitt taxonomy are 1) supplier dominated: usually small, with weak in-house R&D and engineering capabilities, and largely non-technical means of appropriation. Technological trajectories are therefore defined in terms of cutting costs, with suppliers as a source of new technology, mostly in production; 2) innovating scale intensive firms: relatively big and with a large contribution to the innovations; 3) specialized suppliers: relatively small firms focusing on product innovation for use in other sectors; 4) science based firms: the main sources of technology are the R&D activities of firms in the sector, based on rapid development of the underlying sciences.

These firms are relatively big and produce a relatively high proportion of process as well product innovations in their sector of activity.

## References

Altissimo, F., Marchetti, D.J. and Oneto, G.P. (1999), 'The Italian Business Cycle: New Coincident and Leading Indicators and some Stylised Facts', *ISA documents*, n.8.
Conti, G. (1978), 'La posizione dell'Italia nella divisione internazionale del lavoro', in Alessandrini, ed., *Specializzazione e competitività internazionale dell'Italia*, Il Mulino, Bologna.
Balassone,F., Franco, D., Momigliano, S., and D.Monacelli (2002), *Italy: Fiscal Consolidation and its Legacy*, paper presented at the Workshop on 'Fiscal Impact', Bank of Italy, Perugia 21-23 March 2002, forthcoming in the Proceedings of the Conference.
Censis (Nov. 2001), Report, Rome.
Confindustria (Sept. 2000), Report: Privatizzazioni, Liberalizzazioni, Competitività, Rome.
Dosi, G. (1984), 'Technological pardigms and Technological Trajectories', in Freeman, ed., *Long waves in the World Economy*, Pinter, London.
Graziani, A (1998), *Lo sviluppo dell'economia Italiana*, Bollati Boringhieri, Torino.
EIU, Data Base (December 2001).
IMF, International Financial Statistics, Washington.
ISAE (Jan. 2002), Quarterly Report, Rome.
ISCO (Nov. 1973), Report to CNEL, Rome.
ISTAT (Oct. 2001), 8° Censimento generale dell'industria e dei servizi, Rome.
Kuhn, T.S. (1970), *The Structure of Scientific Revolutions*, 2nd edn, Chicago University Press, Chicago.
Pierelli, F. (1983), 'I mutamenti nella struttura degli scambi mondiali e la "posizione italiana"', in *Temi di Discussione*, Banca d'italia, Rome.
OECD (2000), Main Science and Technology Indicators, Paris.
Prometeia (2002), Rapporto di previsone, Bologna.
SIE, World Trade database, New York.
Spaventa, L., and Chiorazzo, V. (1999), 'The Prodigal Son or a Confidence Trickster? How Italy got into EMU', in D. Cobham and G. Zis, eds., 1999, *From EMS to EMU*, London, Macmillan.
SVIMEZ (2001), Rapporto 2000 sull'economia del Mezzogiorno, Roma.
Vercelli, A. (1977), 'The Phillips dilemma: a new suggested approach', *Economic Notes*, n.1.
Vercelli, A. (1986a), 'Stagflation and the recent revival of Schumpeterian entrepreneurship', in H. Frisch and B. Gahlen (eds.), *Causes of Contemporary Stagnation*, Springer, New York.
Vercelli, A. (1986b), 'La "lunga crisi": interpretazioni e prospettive', in Ente Einaudi (ed.), 1986, *Oltre la crisi. Le prospettive di sviluppo dell'economia italiana e il contributo del sistema finanziario*, Il Mulino, Bologna.
Vercelli, A. (1988), 'Technological flexibility, financial fragility and the recent revival of Schumpeterian entrepreneurship', *Recherches Economiques de Louvain*, 54 (1).
Vercelli, A. (1989), 'Uncertainty, Technological Flexibility and Long Term Fluctuations', in Di Matteo, M., Goodwin and R., Vercelli, A. (eds.), 1989, *Technological and Social Factors in Long Term Fluctuations*, Springer, New York.

Vercelli, A. (1994), 'Structural changes in the post-war Italian economy', in B. Boehm and L.F. Punzo (eds.), *Economic Performance: a look at Austria and Italy*, Springer Verlag, Berlin.

Vercelli, A. (2000), 'Small Firms and Employment in manufacturing: Japan and Italy (1980-1995)', in A Boltho, H.Yoshikawa and A.Vercelli (eds), *Comparing the Japanese and the Italian Economies*, Macmillan, London.

Chapter 3

# The Italian Labour Market and Production System: Structural Features and Main Developments

Carlo De Gregorio, Andrea de Panizza,
Roberto Monducci and Leonello Tronti

## Introduction

Italy is a mid-sized country in the world context, and one of the largest in the European Union. It has nearly the same population as France and the UK – about 15% of the European Union and 45% of Japan – but also one of the lowest birth rates in the world. Indeed, the natural rate of population growth is negative, and total growth remains positive only through a rather strong net migratory inflow (Table 1). Consequently, the Italian population is rapidly ageing. In 2000, the ratio of the elderly (65 years or more) to the very young (0-14) was 1.21, well above the Japanese (1.10) and the Spanish ratios (1.07).

Table 1 – Key demographic indicators – 1999 and 2000

|  | Total population[a] (2000, millions) | Yearly rate of increase (1999, per thousand) | | | Age structure[a] (65+/0-14) |
|---|---|---|---|---|---|
|  |  | Total | *Natural* | *Migratory* |  |
| USA | 276.8 | 9.0 | *5.5* | *3.5* | 0.59 |
| EU (15) | 377.0 | 2.8 | *1.0* | *1.8* | 0.95 |
| Japan | 126.7 | 1.7 | *1.8* | *-0.1* | 1.10 |
| **Italy** | **57.8** | **2.8** | ***-0.3*** | ***3.1*** | **1.21** |
| Germany | 82.2 | 0.4 | *-0.9* | *1.3* | 1.01 |
| France | 59.4 | 5.0 | *4.1* | *0.9* | 0.83 |
| UK | 59.7 | 3.5 | *1.2* | *2.3* | 0.82 |
| Spain | 39.5 | 1.2 | *0.7* | *0.5* | 1.07 |

(a) Year average.
*Source*: Eurostat

Besides population ageing, other macro characters and patterns of structural change, common to many advanced economies, include the high and growing role of services in employment and value added, and the rise of new activities, often induced by technology, within both services and manufacturing.

**Table 2 – Growth and employment – 1995-2000** *(Decomposition of per capita GDP; EU15=100; GDP and productivity in purchasing power parities)*

| | Per capita GDP (Pps) | = Avg. Hourly productivity (Pps) | X Avg. Working Time | x Employment Rate | x Working-age population as a % of total population |
|---|---|---|---|---|---|
| | [GDP/Pop.] | = [GDP/Hours worked] | X [Hours/Employment] | x [Emp/Wap (15-64)] | x [Wap/Pop] |

| | 2000 | 1995 | 2000 | 1995 | 2000 | 1995 | 2000 | 1995 | 2000 | 1995 |
|---|---|---|---|---|---|---|---|---|---|---|
| USA | 155 | 148 | 119 | 109 | 117 | 119 | 117 | 122 | 96 | 94 |
| EU15 | 100 | 100 | 100 | 100 | 100 | 100 | 100 | 100 | 100 | 100 |
| Japan | 112 | 119 | 81 | 81 | 114 | 114 | 109 | 116 | 110 | 110 |
| Italy | 102 | 104 | 112 | 115 | 102 | 99 | 85 | 84 | 106 | 107 |
| Germany | 105 | 110 | 106 | 106 | 92 | 95 | 103 | 108 | 104 | 102 |
| France | 99 | 104 | 111 | 114 | 97 | 98 | 98 | 99 | 94 | 93 |
| UK | 104 | 96 | 92 | 84 | 106 | 106 | 113 | 114 | 95 | 94 |
| Spain | 81 | 78 | 79 | 85 | 112 | 110 | 87 | 77 | 105 | 109 |

*Source*: Eurostat, OECD for Japan and US employment rates

Italy, France, the UK and Germany – the four European members of G7 (EU-4) – also present very close levels of per capita GDP, when adjusted for differences in purchasing power (Table 2). Furthermore, EU-4 economies have multiple and deep reciprocal linkages, both in the financial and in the manufacturing sector. More open than Japan and the US because of their smaller domestic markets, for all of them intra-EU trade amounts to more than 50% of total foreign trade, and is equivalent to a share of between 10 and 16% of GDP.[1] Supra-national EU policies and the development of the single market have reinforced the integration tendencies among all European economies while, as of January 1st, 2002, the euro has become the legal tender in Italy, France, Germany, and eight other countries. However, when the structural features of employment and production are considered, the Italian economy still presents striking differences with the other advanced economies of the G7, differences that are at the heart of the long-debated "Italian puzzle".

In a nutshell, one side of the puzzle is that while income levels are similar to the other EU-4 countries, activity and employment rates of working age population are considerably lower. In other words, Italian labour productivity is, on average, higher (Table 2). The other side is that such evidence, though influenced by statistical issues and economic *caveats*,[2] appears clearly at odds with the persistence of somewhat "backward" technological, organisational, and territorial characteristics of the production system. Indeed, in the Italian economy:

"Traditional" sectors, although exposed to growing cost competition, are still very important in the specialisation pattern, while the share of hi-tech products in merchandise exports continues to be about half the EU average (Table 3);

The R&D expenditure rate is about half the level of the other G7 economies (Table 3), and both the employment share of knowledge-intensive activities and the mean educational attainment of workers are the lowest amongst EU-4 (Table 8);

**Table 3 – Key technological indicators. Most recent year**

|  | Share of hi-tech products (% of total goods exports) [a] | | Research and Development Expenditure (% of GDP, 1999) [b] | | Patents per million inhabitants [c] |
|---|---|---|---|---|---|
|  | 2000 | 2000-95 | Total | *Business sector* | 1999 |
| USA | 30.0 | 4.2 | 2.6 | 2 | 93.3 |
| EU 15 | 19.8 | 4.5 | 1.9 | 1.2 | 111.2 |
| **Japan** | 25.1 | -0.2 | 3.0 | 2.2 | 116.0 |
| **Italy** | 8.4 | 1.0 | 1.0 | 0.6 | 52.2 |
| Germany | 15.5 | 3.9 | 2.4 | 1.6 | 221.7 |
| France | 25.5 | 6.2 | 2.2 | 1.4 | 105.7 |
| UK | 25.0 | 4.1 | 1.8 | 1.2 | 69.7 |
| Spain | 6.1 | 0.5 | 0.9 | 0.5 | 12.1 |

(a) USA and Japan, 1999.
(b) Japan, France, and UK, 1998
(c) Applications addressed at the European and the US Patent Offices (EPO and USPTO), per country of origin, 1999

*Source*: Eurostat

In nearly all sectors, there is an uncommonly high number of enterprises, with a much smaller mean size than the EU average (3.9 workers vs. 6.1), while self-employment is the highest amongst G7 countries and even greater than in Spain (Table 8).

Last but not least, Italy is characterised by persistent regional disparities (among the widest in the European context) in the levels of income and employment (see par. 2 below), as well as in trade openness and in production specialisation.

Explanations of the "Italian puzzle" point mainly to an intrinsic widespread flexibility of the production system (in products, enterprises and labour usage) and to systemic advantages acquired in "traditional sectors", often based on local economies and relational networks (Putnam, 1993; Tronti and Toma, 1997), peculiar to the "industrial districts". This paper will not address such issues directly, as enquiring into the relative efficiency and "sustainability" of the Italian pattern of development goes far beyond its scope, but it aims at an introductory presentation of the main issues at stake.

The paper's analytical path is as follows: the first paragraph provides a brief presentation of the general features of the economy and its growth pattern, emphasising its heavy dependence on the manufacturing sector and on what we call the "life-style system". These two factors, while accounting for about 90% of Italian exports and being characterised by effective forms of integration and high productivity levels, impress to the whole economy a low-tech and labour-intensive feature, that contrasts with the comparatively intensive use of production automation and product innovation in other countries.

The second paragraph illustrates the main features of the labour market (its limited extension as well as its recent growth), while paragraph 3 briefly discusses the characteristics of labour supply, paragraph 4 those of labour demand, and paragraph 5 concentrates upon some crucial aspects of the Italian labour market policy and industrial relations scenario. In particular, the paper analyses the short-time working institution of *Cassa Integrazione Guadagni* and the wage-setting system implemented through the tripartite agreement of July 23, 1993. The first has proved a successful policy instrument to adjust employment to cyclical downturns and to ease firm and industry restructuring and reorganisation; the second has succeeded in cooling down wage growth on a long-term basis, thus helping the Italian economy to control inflation and preserve at least part of its competitiveness.

Paragraphs 6 to 9 present the main features of the Italian productive system. Paragraph 6 evidences the industrial structure of the Italian economy and its bias toward the small dimension, while paragraph 7 illustrates the recent performance of Italian firms and the role of innovation. Paragraph 8 synthesises the main empirical aspects of the debated role of industrial districts in Italian manufacturing, while paragraph 9 presents an outline of recent industrial policies and regulatory reforms.

The last paragraph contains the concluding remarks, focussing on the aspects presented in the paper that can throw some light on the "Italian puzzle", and discussing their robustness in face of present and prospective technological changes.

## General features of the Italian economy

In a way, the Italian growth path is similar to that of Germany and Japan, in that all these three *latecomers* in development still have a relatively important industrial sector, in contrast with the more service oriented economies of France, the UK and the US (Graph 1). It is interesting to note that a more developed specialisation in services seems to have positively influenced the growth performance of G7 countries during the last decade (Graph 2), while the well known direct relationship between the expansion of services shares and the employment elasticity of growth has been confirmed (Graph 3) (Istat, 2001).

**Graph 1 – Service shares in employment and value added: G7 countries. 1970-2000**

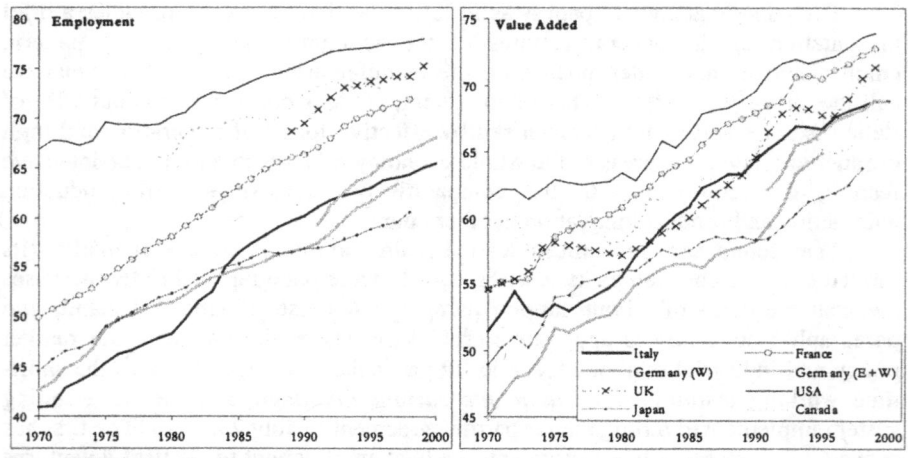

*Source*: European Commission

**Graph 2 – Services shares in employment and value added and economic growth** (Service percentage shares in 1990 – Germany, 1991; x axes – and index numbers of GDP in 2000 – y axes

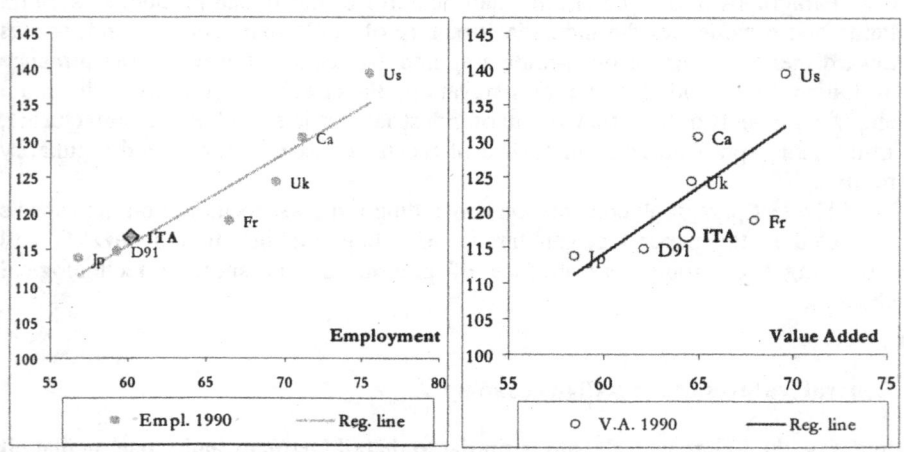

*Source*: own calculations on OECD National Accounts data

**Graph 3 – Employment elasticity of GDP Growth: Italy, France, Germany and the UK, 1962-2000**

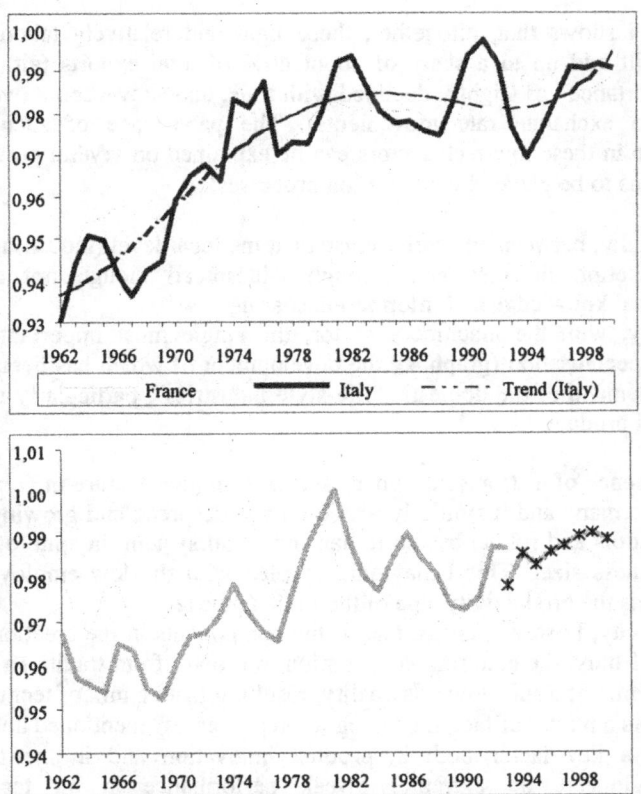

*Source*: Authors' calculations on European Commission, *Macroeconomic database*

Within manufacturing, the Italian pattern of specialisation relies heavily on light and relatively labour-intensive industries, in what could be defined as the "life-style system". This includes:

- a *fashion sub-system*, made up of textiles, clothing and apparel, leather and shoes, glasses, jewels, perfumes, etc.;

- a *house* (and office) *sub-system*, made up of any sort of home equipment (from concrete to tiling and marble, tools for lightning, sitting, resting, storing clothes, objects and food, heating, cooking, refrigerating, eating, tapping water and washing clothes, dishes, etc.) plus many related service activities (design, architecture and engineering, etc.);

- a *quality food sub-system*, which is gaining importance, although Italy traditionally has a heavy deficit on agricultural products.

Graph 4 shows that, altogether, these light and relatively labour-intensive industries still add up to a share of about 40% of total exports (although their relative importance has slightly declined with time, and shows some over-reacting behaviour to exchange rate movements). The persistence of such a strong specialisation in these low-tech sectors can be explained on several grounds, but a key role seems to be played by integration processes:

- horizontally, between enterprise clusters at the local level (industrial districts), in production linkages and through widespread though not necessarily intentional knowledge and information sharing;
- vertically, with the machinery sector, the single most important sector of Italian specialisation (graph 4), the development of which has been enhanced by the demand of the domestic "life-style industries", particularly in terms of "tailored products".

The presence of a strong machinery sector is another feature in common with Japan and Germany and it similarly results in a widespread and growing adoption of machine tools and robots by the Italian industrial system, in spite of the small average business size.[3] This behaviour, coupled with the low employment rate, partly explains the productivity side of the Italian puzzle.

Productivity, however, is just one of the components in the creation of value. In the case of Italy, the enduring contribution to growth from traditional sectors is also the outcome of a shift towards quality, resulting from a mix of technology and innovation. As a matter of fact, the "integration processes" mentioned above can be regarded as a key factor both in product innovation and in the transfer of technology. Indeed, an extremely weak performance in all technological benchmarking measurements notwithstanding, the innovation drive of Italian enterprises is the highest among EU-4 countries, with new products accounting for 13.5% of turnover, against an EU average of 6.5%. In addition, the "life-style system" firms have had an increasing role in innovating their products, often incorporating technological devices whose single components were conceived for other purposes.

**Graph 4** – **Export shares and contributions to goods trade-balance: manufacturing and other activities, 2000**

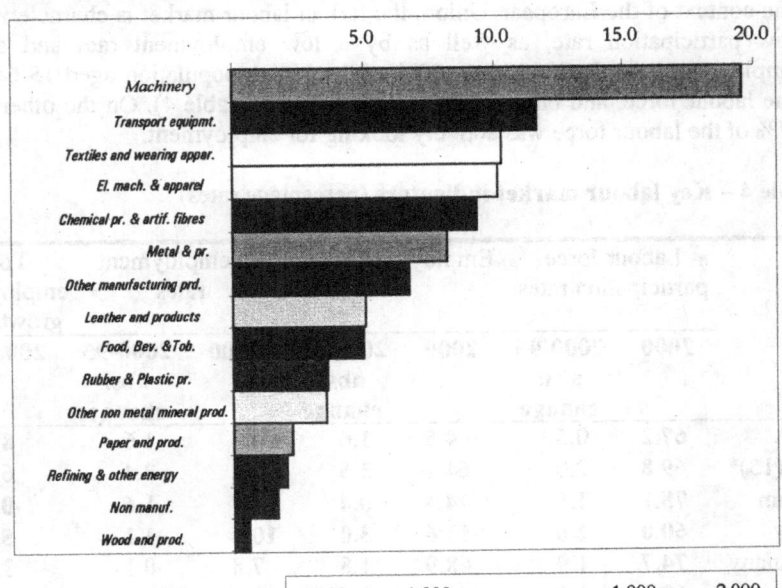

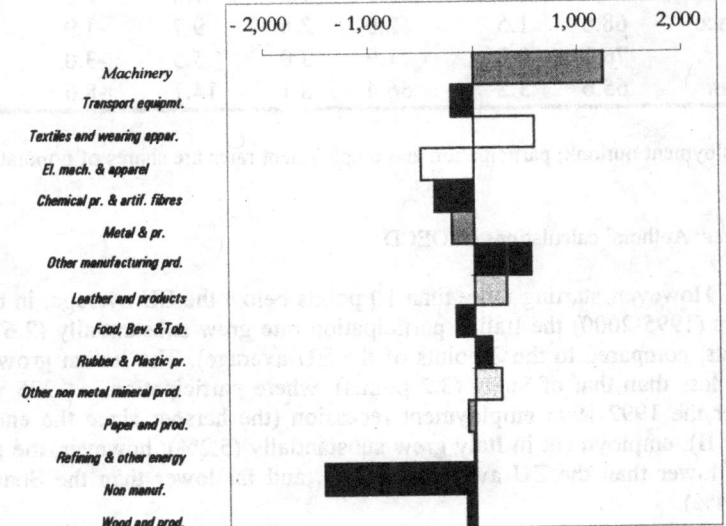

*Source*: Own calculations on Istat external trade data

## General features of the labour market

In the context of the European Union, the Italian labour market is characterised by a low participation rate, as well as by a low employment rate and a high unemployment rate. In 2000, only 60% of the Italian population aged 15-64 were in the labour force, and only 53.6% were employed (Table 4). On the other hand, 10.7% of the labour force was actively looking for employment.

**Table 4 – Key labour market indicators** (percentage rates)

|  | Labour force participation rates | | Employment rates | | Unemployment rates | | Total employment growth (%) |
|---|---|---|---|---|---|---|---|
|  | 2000 | 2000-95 abs. change | 2000 | 2000-95 abs. change | 2000 | 2000-95 abs. change | 2000/95 |
| USA | 67.2 | 0.5 | 64.5 | 1.6 | 4.0 | -1.6 | 8.3 |
| EU (15)* | 69.8 | 2.0 | 64.1 | 3.5 | 8.2 | -2.4 | 6.8 |
| Japan | 78.1 | 1.6 | 74.4 | 0.4 | 4.7 | 1.6 | -0.2 |
| Italy | 60.0 | 2.6 | 53.6 | 3.0 | 10.7 | -1.1 | 5.2 |
| Germany | 74.7 | 1.9 | 68.9 | 1.8 | 7.8 | -0.1 | 3.1 |
| France | 68.6 | 1.5 | 62.0 | 2.6 | 9.7 | -1.9 | 6.0 |
| UK | 76.1 | 0.8 | 71.9 | 3.0 | 5.5 | -3.0 | 6.7 |
| Spain | 65.6 | 3.2 | 56.4 | 8.1 | 14.1 | -8.6 | 18.4 |

Employment outlook; participation and employment rates are shares of population aged 15-64.

*Source*: Authors' calculations on OECD

However, starting more than 10 points below the EU average, in the last five years (1995-2000) the Italian participation rate grew substantially (2.6 percentage points, compared to the 2 points of the EU average). The Italian growth, though, was less than that of Spain (3.2 points), where participation in 1995 was higher. After the 1992-1995 employment recession (the harsher since the end of World War II), employment in Italy grew substantially (5.2%); however, the growth rate was lower than the EU average (6.8%), and far lower than the Spanish record (18.4%).

Such an employment growth, combined with a low growth in working-age population, led to a 3-point increase in the employment rate; but here again the change was less substantial than both the EU and the Spanish ones. Consequently, the unemployment rate fell only by 1.1 percentage points, against a 2.4 fall in the EU average and an 8.6 fall in the Spanish record.

As we have already mentioned, in Italy the labour market is characterised by a high degree of regional disparity – a feature that is particularly evident with respect to unemployment in general and, in particular, to female and youth unemployment, and intertwined with the regional disparities in income levels mentioned above.

## Labour supply

The key Italian labour supply peculiarity is the low participation of women, particularly evident in the Mezzogiorno (southern) regions, but felt also in many areas of the Centre and the North. In a European perspective, the participation rate of Italian women (46.6%) is almost 14 percentage points lower than the EU average, and consistently lower than not only the other EU-4 economies, but also than the laggard Spain, that shows a 4-point advantage over Italy (Table 5).

This peculiarity is partly due to cultural causes, in connection with the traditional (and only slowly changing) Mediterranean model for the division of labour within the family, which results in a relevant proportion of the time and effort of Italian women being spent within the house walls. A further and related cause is the relatively small size of the labour market, as evidenced by the low employment rate. If the Italian economic system can accommodate into employment barely more than one working-age person over two, this person would predominantly be a male (63%), and possibly a prime-age male if not a father. Both labour market institutions and employers' behaviour have traditionally favoured the employment of family heads and such preference, in the face of a small employment pie, has correspondingly reduced the opportunities for female and young people (Tronti, 1996).

Thus, the Italian employment gap is explained by a female employment rate below 40% – 14.4 points lower than the EU average, 18.5 points lower than the German rate and 15.3 points lower than the French rate. Conversely, the female unemployment rate in Italy is particularly high (14.8%), although still lower than in Spain (20.4%). A further characteristic of Italian unemployment is duration (Table 6). Labour supply of women has been rapidly increasing in the last decades, but the selection mechanism described above, traditionally favouring the employment of prime-age males, has been keeping women and young people in unemployment for relatively long periods. Long-term unemployment (over 12 months) is, in Italy, a bigger share of total unemployment than in the rest of the EU (61% against 45% in the average, 51% in Germany, and 42% in Spain), and it makes up a bigger share of the labour force (6.4% against 3.6% in the average, 4% in Germany, and 5,9% in Spain,). The selection mechanisms are particularly unfavourable to young people, whose long-term unemployment rate, though sensibly declining, is still above 17%.

## Table 5 – Key indicators of the female labour market – 1995-2000

|  | UE (15) | | Italy | | Germany | | France | | Spain | |
|---|---|---|---|---|---|---|---|---|---|---|
|  | Thousands | Percentage yearly growth | Thousands | Percentage yearly growth | Thousands | Percentage yearly growth | Thousands | Percentage yearly growth | Thousands | Percentage yearly growth |
| Employment | 67,443 | 1.9 | 7,707 | 1.7 | 15,901 | 1.0 | 10,484 | 1.4 | 5,390 | 5.4 |
| - Agriculture | 2,255 | -3.8 | 335 | -8.9 | 336 | -6.0 | 301 | -3.8 | 269 | -2.7 |
| - Industry | 10,346 | 0.1 | 1,583 | 0.7 | 2,912 | -1.0 | 1,480 | 0.0 | 780 | 6.1 |
| - Services | 54,842 | 2.5 | 5,789 | 2.9 | 12,653 | 1.8 | 8,703 | 1.9 | 4,341 | 5.9 |
| Unemployment | 7,367 | -2.1 | 1,340 | 1.0 | 1,433 | -0.7 | 1,460 | -1.4 | 1,382 | -4.6 |
| Labour force | 74,810 | 1.5 | 9,047 | 1.6 | 17,334 | 0.9 | 11,944 | 1.1 | 6,772 | 2.8 |
|  | % Values | Differences in % points | % Values | Differences in % points | % Values | Differences in % points | % Values | Differences in % points | % Values | Differences in % points |
| Employment rate | 54.4 | 4.3 | 39.7 | 3.7 | 58.2 | 2.4 | 55.0 | 2.8 | 40.6 | 9.0 |
| Unemployment rate | 9.8 | -1.9 | 14.8 | -0.5 | 8.3 | -0.7 | 12.2 | -1.6 | 20.4 | -9.2 |
| Participation rate | 60.3 | 3.6 | 46.6 | 4.1 | 63.4 | 2.2 | 62.6 | 2.1 | 51.0 | 6.0 |

Source: Eurostat, *Labour Force Survey*

## Table 6 – Long-term unemployment rates – 1995-2000

|  | all ages | | | | | <25 years | | | |
|---|---|---|---|---|---|---|---|---|---|
|  | Total | | | Females | | Total | | Females | |
|  | 2000 | (% of Total Unempl.) | Abs. change 2000-1995 | 2000 | Abs. change 2000-1995 | 2000 | Abs. change 2000-1995 | 2000 | Abs. change 2000-1995 |
| EU (15) | 3.6 | (45.1) | -1.6 | 4.4 | -1.8 | 4.8 | -3.7 | 5.6 | -3.9 |
| Italy | 6.4 | (61.0) | -1.0 | 8.8 | -1.7 | 17.4 | -4.0 | 20.2 | -4.9 |
| Germany | 4.0 | (50.6) | 0.1 | 4.3 | -0.6 | 2.0 | -0.4 | 1.7 | -0.8 |
| France | 3.8 | (40.0) | -0.8 | 4.7 | -1 | 4.3 | -1.9 | 5 | -2.7 |
| UK | 1.5 | (27.3) | -2.2 | 0.9 | -1.3 | 1.6 | -2.7 | 1.1 | -1.7 |
| Spain | 5.9 | (41.8) | -6.5 | 9.5 | -8.8 | 7.7 | -11.6 | 10.8 | -13.8 |

Source: Eurostat, *Labour Force Survey*

In the last five years, however, the labour market has been rapidly expanding in the whole European Union: as a growing share of new jobs has been opening to women and young people, employment has been growing and unemployment declining for them almost in every country. In Italy, female employment growth has been substantial (1.7% per year in 1995-2000, against 0.5% for males), resulting in an increase of their employment rate by 3.7 percentage points. For the time being, however, this favourable evolution has affected the unemployment pool only marginally, reducing the unemployment rate by only 0.5 points.

## Employment and labour demand

The sectoral employment structure of the Italian economy is still rather traditional. The share of agriculture in total employment is high (almost one point above the EU average), and even more so is that of the industrial sector (almost 3 points above the EU average). Consequently, one can consider the Italian economy as a case of "undertertiarisation"; this is particularly evident in the case of services to persons and families (almost 4 points below the EU average) and services to business (almost 2 points below).

**Table 7 – Sectoral employment as a share of working-age population – 2000** (percentage shares)

|  | UE (15) | Italy | Germany | France | Spain |
|---|---|---|---|---|---|
| Agriculture | 2.7 | 2.8 | 1.7 | 2.6 | 3.8 |
| Industry | 18.5 | 17.2 | 22.1 | 16.3 | 17.0 |
| Services | 42.7 | 34.1 | 42.1 | 43.1 | 34.4 |
| - Business services | 7.7 | 5.6 | 7.7 | 7.7 | 5.4 |
| - Distributive services | 13.4 | 11.7 | 13.0 | 12.3 | 12.3 |
| - Services to persons and families | 16.7 | 12.1 | 16.0 | 17.4 | 13.2 |
| - Government | 4.9 | 4.8 | 5.4 | 5.7 | 3.5 |

*Source*: Eurostat, *Labour Force Survey*

This situation is even more evident if we look to employment shares in working age population (Table 7), instead of total employment, thus taking into account which sectors are responsible for the differences in the overall employment rate. In this case, both agricultural and industrial employment appear to be in line with the average shares, while the service gap widens to more than 8.5 percentage points. The service employment gap is then explained by personal and family services (4.5 points), business services (2.1 points) and distributive services (1.7 points). The Italian employment gap in personal services concentrates in recreation and amusement, domestic, health and other personal services.

Further to its peculiarities in sectoral and gender distribution, Italian employment shows a comparatively low share of high-level educated workers (Table 8). The share of workers with a university degree is exactly one half of the EU average, and the share of workers with an upper secondary or university degree is only 78% of the EU average. The higher education gap is partially due to the peculiar organisation of Italian universities, that up to a few years ago did not offer degrees obtainable through two or three-years courses, but only longer ones (from 4 to 7 years).

**Table 8 – Key features of the employment structure** (percentage shares)

|  | Female employment as a % of total employment | | Self-employment as a % of total employment | | Educated employment as a % of total employment (2000) | |
| --- | --- | --- | --- | --- | --- | --- |
|  | 2000 | 2000-91 differences | 2000 | 2000-91 differences | Upper secondary + university | university |
| US | 46.5 | 1.1 | 7.4 | -1.6 | n.a. | n.a. |
| EU (15) | 42.6 | 1.7 | 14.8 | -0.8 | 72.0 | 26.0 |
| **Japan** | **40.8** | *0.1* | 16.9 | *-4.5* | n.a. | n.a. |
| **Italy** | **37.2** | *1.9* | 33.8 | *-0.9* | 55.8 | 13.0 |
| Germany | 43.9 | 1.8 | 10.2 | 0.9 | 86.4 | 28.2 |
| France | 45.2 | 1.9 | 9.0 | -2.2 | 70.0 | 25.8 |
| UK | 45.0 | 0.1 | 11.7 | -1.7 | 87.1 | 32.2 |
| Spain | 37.2 | 4.9 | 17.4 | -2.4 | 47.4 | 29.0 |

*Sources*: Female employment, self-employment: OECD (LFS, EO69); educated employment: Eurostat.

Another peculiarity is the very high percentage of self-employment, accounting for a share in total employment more than double that of the EU, and almost double the once large share of Japan. This characteristic is strongly linked to the very high number of micro and small enterprises in the Italian productive system (see paragraphs 6 and 7 below).

However, self-employment and the service sector have long been the traditional valve for adjusting the Italian labour market to cyclical downturns and providing the appropriate degree of labour flexibility. In Italy, many jobs that elsewhere would have been regulated by wage-employment relationships have been organised in a self-employment form, and this is often still the case.

For this reason, some traditional forms of non-standard labour arrangements have developed only recently, and Italy is still lagging behind partner economies in terms of part-time and temporary employment.

## Some key aspects of labour market policies and industrial relations

*Short-time earnings compensation: the Italian way to hoard industrial labour*

The Italian labour market is characterised by many peculiar institutions but, probably, its more outstanding divergence in the area of labour policies is the intense use of the short-time working compensation fund (*Cassa integrazione guadagni*). The purpose of this fund is to guarantee industrial workers' earnings in case of lay-offs or a reduction in the company's activity due to temporary events not attributable to the employer or the employees, or caused by the economic cycle. The fund operates through two different instruments:

1) *Regular short-time earnings compensation (Cassa integrazione guadagni ordinaria – Cig)*, aimed at helping industrial businesses to hoard labour, and industrial workers to retain employment, during cyclical downturns;[4]
2) *Special short-time earnings compensation (Cassa integrazione guadagni straordinaria – Cigs)*, aimed at helping industrial businesses and labour to weather long-term restructuring programmes.[5]

**Graph 5 – Hoarding industrial labour: Short-time earnings compensation fund – 1970-2000** (full-time equivalents financed by the fund as a share of total industrial employees)

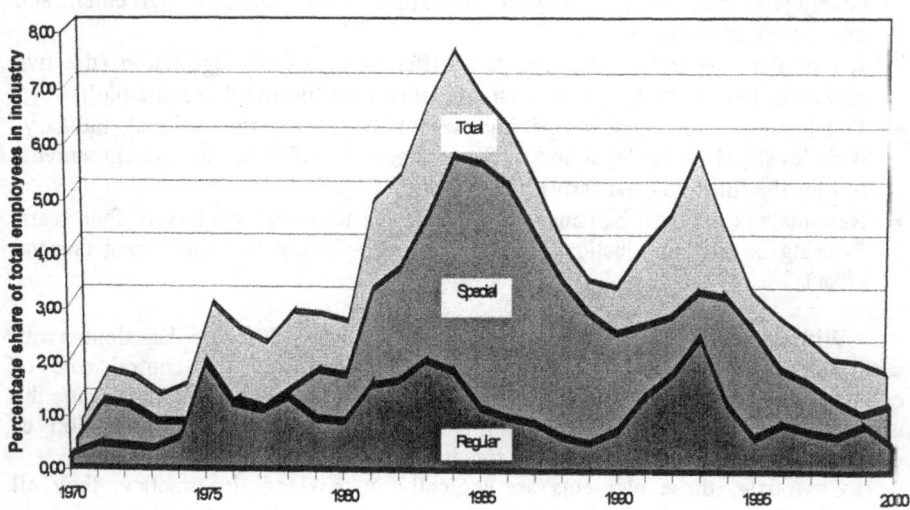

*Source*: Own calculations based on the national social security agency (INPS) and Istat data

In the recession of the 1980s, *Cassa integrazione guadagni* came to finance the hoarding of about 8% of total industrial workforce (Graph 5). The progressively decreasing use of special compensation, a result not only of the end of the recession but also of a restrictive law reform in 1992 and of the gradual exhaustion of the eligibility period, entails a corresponding increase in the Mobility rolls (see footnote 5). This is because the shift from employed status (granted to workers on short-time compensation) to that of unemployed status requires an interim period on the Mobility rolls. The latter has thus expanded for some years, as many workers at zero working hours were passing from Cigs to Mobility rolls. More recently, the need for the short-time working compensation fund has been further reduced by the rapid growth of temporary work arrangements and the possibility to shift full-time workers to part-time regimes.

## *The 1993 wage-setting system and its effects*

On 23 July, 1993, after a long period of wage-pushed inflation, trade unions, employers associations and the Government signed a tripartite pact that enacted a new, general framework for wage negotiation in Italy. The most important changes embodied in the new system were:

- An agreement in principle on income policy;
- The definitive abrogation of the *scala mobile* (the automatic mechanism of wage-indexation to inflation) and the introduction of partial cost-of-living coverage during intervals between the expiry of one collective agreement and the signing of the next;
- A complete separation between two different levels of negotiation (the two pillars of the new wage-setting system), ruled by a 'no-overlap principle';
- The institution of wage bargaining every two years at the national, industry-wide level (while the legal and work rules portions of the collective agreements run for the full four-year term) (first pillar);
- New matters for local bargaining at company or territorial level every four years, focusing on the introduction of forms of profit-sharing or gain-sharing (second pillar).

With regard to bargaining arrangements, the July 1993 pact has done away with automatic indexation, and has formally recognised the central role of collective bargaining – if not compulsory (which it is not) it has at least become the normal mode of wage determination – and the consequent normalisation of collective agreement negotiation and renewal procedures.

Obviously, these elements are logically intertwined. In practice, they all respond to the need to simplify wage rules and avoid overlapping and summing-up of bargaining levels.

A significant provision is the new, staggered negotiation schedule, with regulatory provisions revised every four years and the economic clauses renegotiated every two years. This should relieve the normative portion of labour agreements of the excessive load of bargaining issues and tensions that has marked Italian practices in this sphere until now (Treu, 1993).

This is the standpoint from which to examine the relationship between national and decentralised bargaining levels (first and second pillars). Essentially, there are two mechanisms by which the higher level might dominate the lower level: a *referral clause*, restricting decentralised agreements to matters within the limits specified by the national agreement; and the *specialisation principle*, by which local bargaining can only deal with matters not settled at the central level. The solution enacted with the 1993 pact combines the two. It establishes that the items provided for in decentralised agreements must be different, not repetitive of national agreement items, and it further specifies that company-level wage items must be related to productivity and the economic performance of the firm.

A particularly interesting feature is the new relationship between wages and inflation. First-level bargaining takes as its point of reference the government's inflation target, with a clause permitting to recoup, after two years, any differential between actual and target inflation. Second-level bargaining is conducted at the company or district level, with reference to local productivity or profits. For this reason, given the no-overlap clause, if productivity improves, total earnings (first-plus second-level) remain tied to company performance, eliminating the inflationary potential of wage increases. This advantage is reinforced by the fact that this way of determining wages helps to limit the distribution of productivity gains between dynamic and stagnant companies, producing better balanced growth, as between industries exposed to international competition and those sheltered from it (Tronti and Tanda, 1997).

As a consequence of the 1993 pact, wage growth slowed down significantly in subsequent years (Graph 6). In some sectors (Agriculture, Transport and Banking) real wage growth was even negative or null – at least during the period of intense international realignment that prepared the Italian entry into the Euro club (1993-97).

**Graph 6 – Total wages by sector – 1993-2000** (Real wages of full-time workers; 1993=100; 3-ts. m.a.)

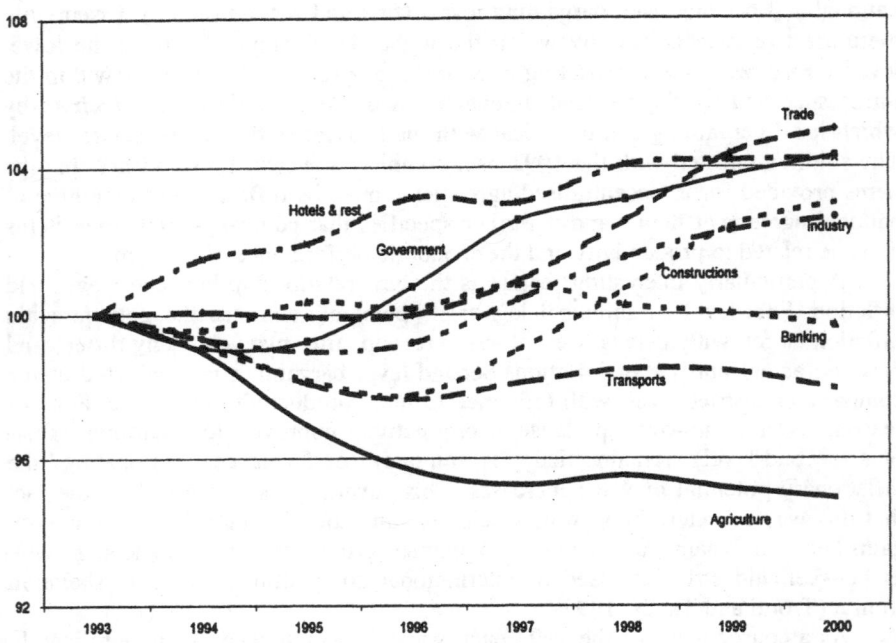

*Source*: calculations by the Bank of Italy and by the authors, based on Istat data

Wage moderation, in turn, contributed to a substantial slowdown in unit labour cost after 1993 (Graph 7.A), as well as to the simultaneous decline of the labour share in added value (Graph 7.B). Both changes restored the traditionally low profitability of Italian firms. In particular, the decline in the labour share, that reached almost five percentage points for the whole economy, was even heavier in agriculture and in the private services, allowing for intense sectoral restructuring.

**Graph 7 – Unit labour cost by sector and the share of labour into value added – 1980-2000** (1980=100, 3-term m.a.)

A) Unit labour cost

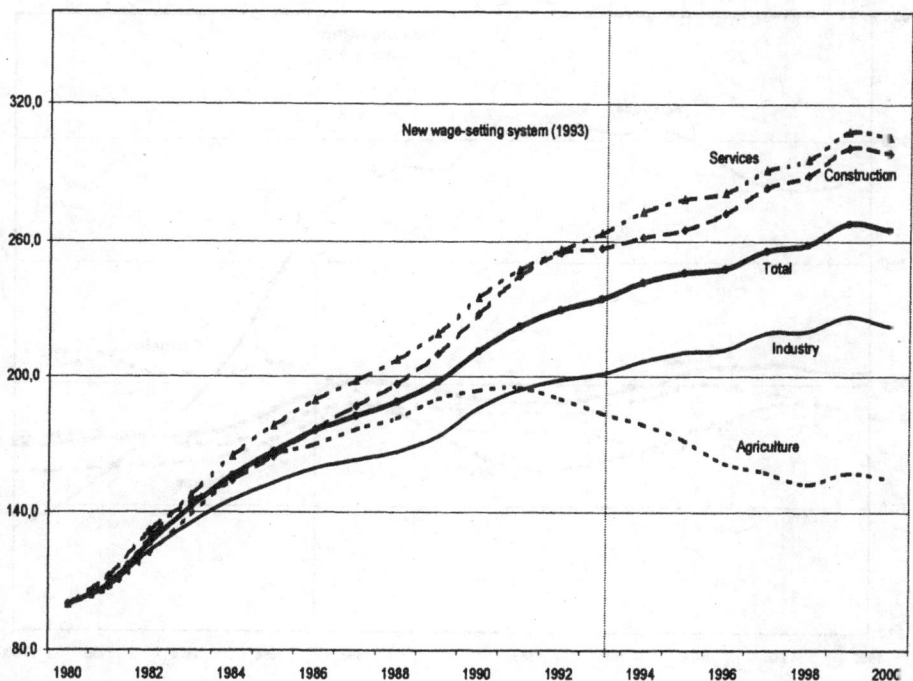

*Source*: calculations by the Bank of Italy and by the authors, based on Istat data

*B) Percentage share of labour in value added*

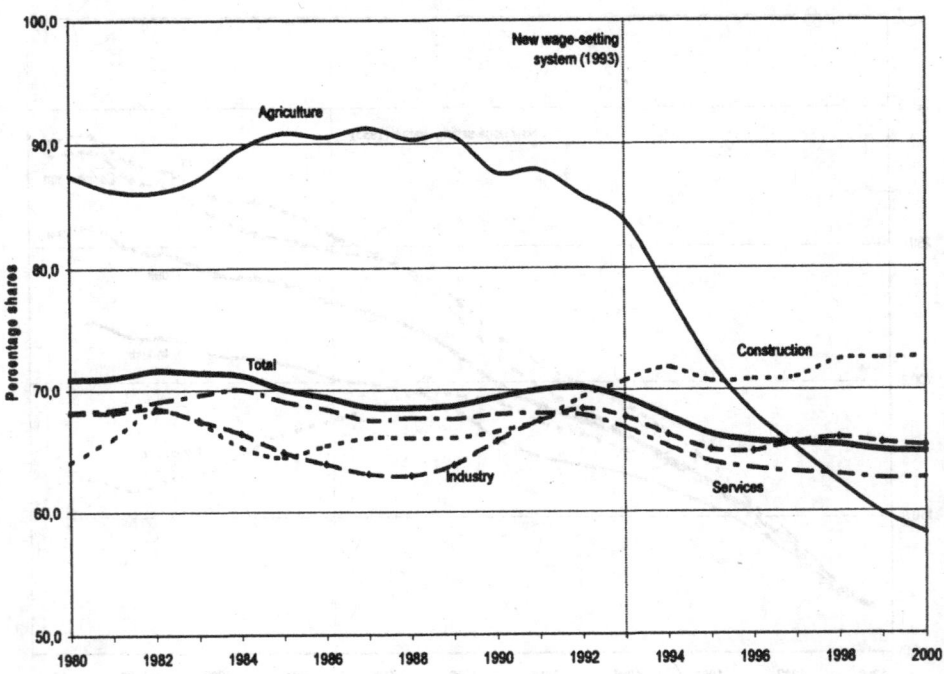

Source: calculations by the Bank of Italy and by the authors, based on Istat data

## Sectoral and dimensional aspects of the Italian production system

*The firm size question*

Most analyses of the Italian economic system from the post-war period to day emphasise the specificity of the Italian economic structure vis-à-vis the main developed western countries. This specificity fundamentally lies in the widespread presence of small and medium firms in most sectors and areas of the country. Small units prevail in the market services sectors, and especially in the retail trade, where they outnumber the partners; insofar as industry is concerned, a great number of sectors is characterised by an important presence of highly integrated small and medium-sized enterprises (SMEs).

With reference to manufacturing firms, there is a large body of literature dedicated to the factors determining the coexistence of such a wide range of firm sizes within the same sectors. In particular, the presence of small firms in northern regions has been interpreted as a new industrial pattern based on flexible specialisation, with positive influences on the systemic efficiency, as well as on the social consequences of industrial development. At least until the early 1970s, however, this had been negatively evaluated, as a sign of the Italian economic structure's inadequacy and of the incapacity of firms to establish sound patterns of growth and to exploit scale economies, to use more advanced technologies and to obtain stable shares in foreign markets. In recent years, however, the good performance of SMEs and the crisis of large industrial enterprises have spurred a wider debate, underlining different aspects: the good performance of small firms and their role in the job-creation process; the coherence between the remarkable existence of small-sized units and the characteristics of labour markets; the factors determining the success of small firms in specific areas.

In the services sectors, in turn, the large presence of small enterprises shows not only their limits (a "structural" inflationary trend, slow growth in productivity and the supply quality), but also their "qualities" (extraordinary growth in employment, a positive response to demand pressures). The too large distribution sector, business fragmentation, poor fiscal accountability, the persistence of professional regulations, the questionable model of urban development and the inefficiency of public services explain many of the limits referred to above, but they also significantly explain the reasons associated with the expansion of service businesses.

## Business structure and firm size

In the following pages, we outline some structural aspects of the Italian production system. In particular, the question is whether the Italian firm size reflects an efficient segmentation of the production system in terms of productivity and profitability, or simply reflects the predominance of industry, territorial and market factors over firms' economic and financial arrangements.

Structural information from the General Census of Industry and Services of 1996 has been processed in order to identify some characteristics of firm size structure in every economic sector and to classify them in terms of prevailing "market size". As regards the measurement of the economic performance and the competitiveness of the Italian firms, we use the Structural Business Statistics database referred to 1998.

As outlined above, the structure of Italian business sectors is quite peculiar, with respect to both the other EU countries and the other major industrial countries. The most distinguishing features involve the number and size of Italian firms on one hand, and the sectoral distribution of firms and employment on the other.

According to the results of the last enterprise census (1996), in the Italian industrial and service sectors there are more than 3.5 million enterprises, employing around 14 million persons. Services account for more than 70% of Italian firms, although their share in terms of persons employed is much lower (for details, see Appendix table 1). Manufacturing activities involve less than 30% of total employment, while the construction sector represents 10%. Most of the Italian service firms operate in the industries related to trade, hotels and restaurants, which represent more than 40% of Italian firms but less than 30% of total employment, averaging less than three persons employed per firm.

Italian firms represent more than one fifth of the 17 million EU firms, but less than one seventh of its 102 million persons employed (Table A.1). The average size of the Italian firm is thus significantly smaller than that of the EU.[6] This only partially depends on differences in the sectoral distribution of firms: in fact industrial firms average 9 persons employed, as compared to 16 in the EU; service firms average 3 persons employed, as compared to 5 in the EU.

In some sectors, like wood and paper processing, other manufacturing industries, wholesale and commission trade and other business activities, the average size of Italian firms is less then half the size of EU firms. A much lower business size than the EU average is often accompanied by a smaller weight in the economy too. And this can be regarded as a factor of weakness: in most such sectors, indeed, the opening up of the domestic market during the 1990s has resulted in a growing penetration and control by foreign (mostly EU) firms, while Italian firms have rarely managed to expand abroad.

In some manufacturing sectors, namely textile industry, clothing and leather, Italy shows a noticeable degree of specialisation, with a relatively more consistent presence of firms and persons employed. Moreover, the relative weight of service sectors seems quite low with respect to the rest of the EU and to the other major industrialised countries, while industry and energy sectors represent a share of total employment still significantly above that of the EU.

The peculiarity of the Italian business structure becomes even more evident if we examine the degree of concentration of firms and employment according to the firm size. Almost one half of total employment is accounted for by firms with less than 10 employees: these firms represent more than 95% of Italian firms, but less then one third of total turnover. Also in the EU, smaller firms (with less than 10 employees) represent more than the 90% of the total, but their share in employment and turnover is much smaller (respectively one third and one sixth).

As a consequence, in Italy larger firms (with more than 250 employees) account for only slightly more than one fifth of total employment, and less than one third of total turnover. Their weight on the business sector is then much lower than in the EU average, where larger firms account for slightly less then one half of total turnover. Financial intermediation, transport, and communication are the only sectors where larger firms represent at least one half of sector employment and turnover.

Another distinguishing feature of the Italian business structure is the strong presence of smaller firms with no employees and of unincorporated firms. Zero-employee firms represent on average more than one half of Italian firms: in industry and in the energy sectors their weight is much lower, representing slightly more than one third of total firms. These firms account for 13.2% of employment and 6.5% of turnover. Their share on total employment, however, is higher than 20% in the trade, hotel and restaurant industries, in other business activities and in other services. These kinds of firms are also very important in construction, where they account for more than 10% of total turnover. In industry and in the energy sectors, on the other hand, zero-employee firms represent lower shares of turnover and employment. Moreover, 65% of Italian firms are unincorporated, accounting for 28% of total employment: the average size of these firms is 1.6 persons employed and it is larger in manufacturing sectors (nearly 4).[7]

If we look at the concentration ratio in the manufacturing sector, while in aggregate terms it shows a value slightly lower than 15%, meaningful differences emerge among sectors, with the highest values in the motor vehicle industry and in the chemicals, rubber and plastics industry.[8]

These data show that most of Italian manufacturing firms are concentrated in sectors with prevailingly small sizes of employment and turnover. In any case, in a large part of manufacturing activities, small firms and large firms coexist. It is possible to regard this in two ways: on one hand, it may be argued that the Italian firm structure reflects a somewhat efficient co-ordination between small and large firms, also in sectors characterised by a strong homogeneity in the goods produced; on the other hand, this coexistence may be viewed as the result of a difficult transition of small firms to larger dimensions.

## The recent performance of Italian firms

### Main performance indicators

In 1998, Italian industry and service firms (excluding banking and financial services) employed 14.1 million persons (of which 9 million were employees), with a total value added of 495 billion euro. Smaller firms (with less than 20 persons employed) had a share of 60% in total employment (but of only 38.8 in employees), and slightly more than 40% in added value and turnover, with strong sectoral differences (table A.2).[9] The presence of small firms is associated with a higher share of independent workers and, correspondingly, with a higher share of individual entrepreneurs.[10]

In 1998, Italian firms' per capita value added averaged 352 thousands euro. Taking this as a measure of nominal labour productivity, there emerges that the sector distribution of productivity is highly irregular: in fact, in industry and in the energy sectors per capita productivity amounts to 426 thousands euro, while in construction and in the services it amounts, respectively, to 252 and 321 thousands euro. This heterogeneity depends heavily on sectoral differences, concerning especially capital intensity and the characteristics of the production processes. In any case, it is possible to identify effects induced by differences in efficiency standards and innovative behaviours and effects associated with differences in the average firm size.

Productivity levels, in particular, seem positively correlated with firm size. In small firms, per capita value added shows average values nearly one half those of larger firms. This disparity between small and medium-large firms is certainly not surprising, being justified by fundamental technological, organisational and market differences. This notwithstanding, productivity differentials among size classes are very large, especially if compared with those of the other European Union economies.

This disadvantage of smaller firms in terms of labour productivity occurs despite the fact that smaller firms are characterised by a more intensive use of labour. In fact, in small firms the hours worked per employee are 6.1% higher than in larger firms (with more than 249 persons employed): this discrepancy takes place in all sectors of economic activity. On the other hand, total remuneration of employees reflects in a substantial way the productivity levels of sectors and size classes: the labour cost per hour worked of small firms is about one half that of larger firms.

If we look at gross profits, gross operating surplus (once corrected by the remuneration of independent workers) represents a 31.7% share of total value added (Table A.2). Industry and energy show higher shares (on average 37.7%) than services (28.4%) and construction (16.6%). Moreover, in all the three sectors considered, profit margins grow with firm size, reaching their highest value among firms with more than 19 and less than 100 persons employed.

In 1998, the north-western regions accounted for 39.1% of total value added, the north-eastern regions 24.9%, the central regions 20.3% and the southern regions 15.7%. More in detail, examining macro-regional value added shares by sector and size classes, there emerges a "specialisation" of the north-western regions in large sized industry sectors. The north-eastern regions are more specialised in small-sized industry sectors and in large-sized construction sectors, while the central regions are specialised in medium-/large-sized service sectors and the southern regions in construction and small-sized service sectors.

Labour cost and productivity data confirm the existence of strong regional differences, which go beyond the effects of the different sector specialisation and firm size. In particular, the productivity of southern firms' is much lower than that of businesses in the rest of Italy (especially if we consider smaller firms), while for labour costs the difference is not as wide.[11]

*Propensity to export of manufacturing firms*

Italian manufacturing sectors are characterised by a remarkable openness toward foreign markets: in 1998, exporting firms accounted for 58.7% of total manufacturing employment and for 70.1% of total value added. In aggregate terms, the propensity to export of manufacturing firms (as measured by the export/turnover ratio) was 25.9%, but small firms with less than 20 persons employed exported only 11.8% of their turnover, while firms with at least 20 persons employed exported 29.8%.[12] Average export propensity, which is 11.8% in small firms, grows with firm size, and is higher than 30% among firms with 100 or more persons employed.

In terms of employment, exporting firms represent 27.2% among small firms with less than 20 persons employed. This share increases with size classes and reaches 90% of employment among the largest size class. Average exporting firms' size is 28.9 persons employed (Table A.3), a size much higher than the manufacturing firms average (8.6). This suggests the existence of a sort of "threshold size" necessary to manage direct exporting activities and to deal with the economic and organisational burdens implied by the presence on foreign markets.

Exporting firms show higher productivity levels among small and medium-sized firms than non-exporting ones. This difference is particularly evident among smaller firms,[13] while productivity differentials decrease as long as we pass to higher size classes.

Among firms with less than 100 persons employed, exporting firms are also characterised by higher levels of per capita investments and labour costs. This happens in all the sectors, and shows that the competitive performance of exporting firms has to do with productivity levels and not with labour costs.[14]

## Research & development and innovation

The meaningfulness of indicators of the Italian presence in high-tech areas is related to the definition of "high-tech" adopted. In the OECD definition, focusing on R&D-intensive sectors, statistical data on the share of "high-tech" sectors' value added and employment (from ISTAT and EUROSTAT Structural Business Statistics, SBS) confirm a structural weakness of Italy, compared to other developed countries, in terms of share of high-tech activities relative to total employment or value added (Table 9).

However, we should look also at the results of the European Community Innovation Survey (CIS) about the introduction of technological innovations in the so-called "traditional industries". The main finding is an increase in the overall percentage of innovators, which has grown from 33.1% in 1990-1992 to 48% in 1994-1996 (Table 10).

If we look at data aggregated through a Pavitt-like taxonomy, there emerges that "traditional industries" experienced the highest growth (+19.2%) in innovation intensity, followed by "specialised suppliers" (13%). In a context of growing propensity to innovate, some industries – namely the "traditional industries" – have performed much more effectively than others, in terms of both process and product innovation. Thus, a catching-up effect has taken place, with an increasing adoption of new process technologies in traditional industries, as well as with the insertion of new technologies in "traditional" products.

**Table 9 – Employment in high technology sectors: percentage of selected groups of NACE sectors relative to total employment**

|  | YEAR | | | | |
|---|---|---|---|---|---|
|  | 1995 | 1996 | 1997 | 1998 | 1999 |
| | Total high technology: NACE Rev.1 24, 29 to 35, 64, 72 and 73 | | | | |
| European Union (15) | n.a. | 45.9 | 45.7 | 46.6 | 46.2 |
| Germany | n.a. | 59.5 | 58.8 | 58.7 | 58.9 |
| United Kingdom | n.a. | 47.3 | 47.5 | 49.1 | 51.4 |
| France | 47.7 | 45.3 | 46.3 | 45.5 | 46.3 |
| Italy | 43.8 | 43.5 | 43.4 | 43.0 | 44.0 |
| Spain | 29.7 | 31.9 | 30.1 | 32.0 | 33.0 |
| | High tech manufacturing sectors: NACE Rev.1 24 and 29 to 35. | | | | |
| European Union (15) | n.a. | 34.2 | 33.6 | 34.2 | 34.8 |
| Germany | n.a. | 46.2 | 47.4 | 46.1 | 47.7 |
| United Kingdom | n.a. | 35.0 | 33.9 | 34.4 | 33.7 |
| France | 30.6 | 31.6 | 29.9 | 31.8 | 30.8 |
| Italy | 32.4 | 30.8 | 30.8 | 33.5 | 33.5 |
| Spain | 22.7 | 21.8 | 23.8 | 24.5 | 24.0 |
| | Higher tech manufacturing: NACE Rev.1 30 and 32. | | | | |
| European Union (15) | n.a. | 6.0 | 5.9 | 6.0 | 5.9 |
| Germany | n.a. | 4.4 | 4.2 | 4.4 | 4.2 |
| United Kingdom | n.a. | 4.9 | 5.1 | 5.1 | 4.9 |
| France | 5.6 | 5.4 | 5.6 | 5.8 | 5.4 |
| Italy | 5.8 | 5.1 | 5.0 | 4.4 | 4.0 |
| Spain | 2.8 | 2.3 | 2.6 | 2.8 | 2.7 |

*Source*: EUROSTAT's New Cronos database

**Table 10 – Innovation intensity in selected "traditional industries", 1990-92 and 1994-96 (\*)**

| SECTOR | Percentage of innovators | |
|---|---|---|
| | 1990-92 | 1994-96 |
| **Total** | **33.1** | **48.0** |
| Traditional industries | 25.2 | 44.4 |
| High R&D intensive industry | 55.3 | 57.3 |
| Scale-intensive industries | 37.5 | 47.6 |
| Specialised suppliers | 45.4 | 58.1 |
| **Selected industries** | | |
| Wearing apparel | 11.3 | 30.4 |
| Leather and footwear | 18.8 | 27.9 |
| Textile | 28.1 | 37.4 |
| Wood (furniture excluded) | 28.8 | 41.1 |

Source: ISTAT – CIS1, CIS2

(\*) The comparison between CIS1 and CIS2 data has to be considered as partially affected by methodological differences in the collection process. The two surveys mainly differ about their nature: census survey for CIS1 and sample survey for CIS 2.

## Industrial districts and the geographical distribution of manufacturing activities

One of the most peculiar aspects of the Italian business structure involves the localisation of productive activities. Here, Italian industrial districts deserve some deeper consideration. Industrial districts are defined as aggregations of municipalities, each characterised by two distinguishing features: a strong homogeneity of local labour markets, and a strong specialisation in manufacturing activities.[15] The 1996 census data allow for the identification of 199 industrial districts: they represent almost one half of total export of manufacturing products (Table 11), in most cases through products which traditionally characterise Italian export (the so called *Made in Italy*). More specifically, industrial districts' share of total exports is particularly high in textiles, leather and leather products, footwear, furniture and other manufactured goods. In other sectors, such as food products, their export share is relatively low, but still represents a very significant contribution, since it is one of the most important sectors of *Made in Italy*.

**Table 11 – Industrial districts' share of total Italian exports of manufacturing goods, Year 1996**

| PRODUCTS | SHARE |
| --- | --- |
| Food products & beverages | 34.7 |
| Tobacco products | 17.0 |
| Textiles | 72.1 |
| Wearing apparel; furs | 56.2 |
| Leather and leather products | 66.9 |
| Wood & products of wood & cork (except furniture); articles of straw & plaiting materials | 55.8 |
| Pulp, paper & paper products | 47.3 |
| Printed matter & recorded media | 30.9 |
| Coke, refined petroleum products & nuclear fuel | 0.9 |
| Chemicals, chemical products & man-made fibres | 26.4 |
| Rubber & plastic products | 41.3 |
| Other non metallic mineral products | 60.4 |
| Basic metals | 42.7 |
| Fabricated metal products, except machinery & equipment | 59.4 |
| Machinery & equipment n.e.c. | 51.6 |
| Office machinery & computers | 9.7 |
| Electrical machinery & apparatus n.e.c. | 47.8 |
| Radio, television & communication equipment & apparatus | 8.7 |
| Medical, precision & optical instruments; watches & clocks | 35.5 |
| Motor vehicles, trailers & semi-trailers | 23.1 |
| Other transport equipment | 21.1 |
| Furniture; other manufactured goods n.e.c. | 67.2 |
| **Total** | **46.1** |

*Source*: Istat, Menghinello (2000)

More insights are offered in table A.4, which shows the share on national and world export of some of the best known Italian industrial districts. If we consider textiles, the district of Prato represents 28% of national exports and 3.4% of world exports. Similar figures are expressed by several other districts specialised in leather products. It is also worth noticing the relevant share on world export of ceramic tiles and flags detained by the district of Sassuolo.

Furthermore, as long as innovative behaviour is considered, innovative enterprises show a better performance, with persistently higher productivity (+15.5% in traditional sectors and +4.8% in the "other sectors"), labour cost (+7.4% and +4.2%), and hourly wages (+4.1% and +2%). Generally, the "impact" of innovation seems to be more effective in traditional sectors than in the "other" sectors: in fact, innovative firms in traditional sectors show higher levels in gross operating profit ratio, and this is particularly evident in small businesses.

Thus, the adoption of technological innovation is increasingly relevant for Italian traditional firms in order to improve their economic performance and competitiveness, and they are effectively using more technology than they did in the past. On the other hand, an econometric analysis performed by ISTAT has also shown that to be located in an "industrial district" positively affects the economic performance of Italian "traditional" enterprises (at least in terms of higher profitability). A mutually reinforcing effect is probably at work in diffusing the adoption of new technologies through the enterprise networks defining most industrial districts.

In any case, an evaluation of the ability of the Italian industrial sector in sustaining long-term growth based only on technological indicators could be misleading. A wider investigation, considering both technological and "non technological" factors (including leadership in technical and aesthetic design, the availability of highly skilled workforce in selected industries or the spill-over effects which can be observed within the industrial districts) is in fact needed, in order to highlight the factors that positively influence the productivity and competitiveness of Italian industry.

## Industrial policies and regulatory reforms

The history of Italian industrial policies is a very long and complex one. Here we underline only a few aspects concerning the recent evolution of state aid to enterprises' investments.[16] According to the Ministry of Industry (MAP, 2001), between 1997 and 2000 the total budgeted State incentives amounted to 0.5% of GNP, oscillating between 1.1% and 1.9% of total public expenditures.[17] In that period, State aid has had different facets: in the Central and Northern regions it has been addressed more frequently towards large enterprises, while in Southern regions State aid to smaller enterprises prevailed. In the Southern regions, State intervention is more relevant if expressed in terms of GNP (it averaged 0.8% in the four years considered), although there do not emerge large differences in absolute terms. Southern enterprises also received a larger average share of the investments financed, almost triple with respect to the Northern and Central regions' average (Table 12).

In effect, Italian industrial policies are based upon a relatively high number of different policy instruments. Incentives to investments have several objectives: state aid to underdeveloped areas; spurring activities that can generate important externalities, such as R&D and technological innovation; start-up help to weak categories (young entrepreneurs in Southern Italy, women, etc.). This notwithstanding, state intervention is also highly concentrated: more than 80% of total state aid derives from the four strongest policy instruments.

**Table 12 – State aid budgeted by kind of objective – Years 1997-2000** *(in billions of current liras)*

| OBJECTIVES | Year | | | |
|---|---|---|---|---|
| | 1997 | 1998 | 1999 | 2000 |
| Research and Development | 585 | 1.242 | 1.214 | 1.305 |
| Internationalisation | 487 | 281 | 244 | 387 |
| - *State aid to export* | 387 | 177 | 82 | 195 |
| - *State aid to FDI* | 100 | 104 | 162 | 192 |
| Economic development | 8.534 | 7.131 | 9.603 | 12.799 |
| - *Industrial sectors* | 8.073 | 6.707 | 7.841 | 11.090 |
| - *Tourism and trade* | 25 | 10 | 1.422 | 1.626 |
| - *Agriculture and fishing* | - | 25 | 37 | 83 |
| - *Enterprise creation* | 377 | 303 | 250 | - |
| - *Other measures* | 59 | 86 | 53 | - |
| Financial equilibrium | 170 | 80 | 853 | 1.017 |
| - *Increasing capitalisation* | - | - | 658 | 997 |
| - *Releasing debt constraints* | 170 | 80 | 195 | 20 |
| Rationalisation | 389 | 425 | 380 | 324 |
| Natural disasters | 90 | 100 | 163 | 210 |
| TOTAL | 10.255 | 9.259 | 12.457 | 16.042 |

*Source*: MAP (2001), p. 33

In the year 2000 about 30% of incentives have been dedicated to depressed areas, with a neat decrease of this share from 60% in 1998.[18] Industrial policies directed to R&D and technological innovation showed instead a remarkable increase, and in the year 2000 represented 18.5% of total state aid.[19] A decreasing share of state aid (still around 20%) is dedicated to traditional industrial policy objectives, referring to long-term interventions decided before 1990. An increasing share of total state aid (more than 20%) is instead dedicated to local programming activities and territorial pacts: these kinds of interventions show a systemic approach, not strictly oriented to helping single firms, but aimed at inducing a virtuous growth context in specific local productive systems. The year 2000 represents a sort of turning point for state aid to investments: firstly, a new step in the European Union Structural Funds programming has been made with reference to years 2000-2006; secondly, there is a growing tendency to the decentralisation of the interventions. This last phenomenon has been heavily spurred by EU policy guidelines, which assign about 70% of total resources to regional programmes.

## Concluding remarks

During the last decade, the Italian labour market and production system have had to face a profound structural change in competitive conditions, induced by trade globalisation, new technologies, and the strong acceleration in economic integration at the European level (especially through participation in creating the euro-zone). Such changes hit the Italian economic system deeply, due to its sectoral specialisation, as well as its technological and organisational features. In this respect, differences with the main partners seem to have remained wide – at least when measured by conventional indicators – whereas the macroeconomic performance has been similar (what has been described as the 'Italian puzzle'). Indeed, GDP growth has kept a pace just below the EU-4 average, notwithstanding the negative effect of the severe public debt reduction programme, while export growth in volume has been in line with the other EU-4 countries.

Competition has been eased (at least temporarily) by the lira depreciation, while part of the burden of keeping profitability levels has been addressed by a reduction of 5 percentage points of the labour share in value added. The Italian labour market, indeed, is still experiencing a phase of profound reorganisation: increasing female employment and flexible work arrangements are leading a process of convergence with the prevailing European dimensions and features, while labour market policies appear to have been a major factor in the inflation control needed to join the "euro club" from the beginning. An increase in competition and a reduction in costs have also been helped by some traits of industrial policy. To this purpose, it is worth mentioning that the reduction of state aid has been accompanied by the privatisation of state firms and the subsequent monopoly-breaking actions for some key utilities, as well as by measures for easing administrative burdens on firms, such as the adoption of one-stop shops.

In the face of these transformations, the production system seems to have followed the international pattern of change only (and still partially) in terms of sectoral composition and employment growth, while business size seems to have maintained its divergence. This difference appears as a major problem in the growth perspective. Until present, in fact, the interaction of some structural competitive factors has contributed to the acceptable, though weak, Italian performance. Such factors, very typical of the Italian case and at the very roots of the "Italian puzzle", are different but often related elements, such as: "systemic vertical integration"; "relational networks"; built-in capability of embodying technology in otherwise "traditional" products; persisting "niche economies" in a wide range of industrial activities. Today, the crucial question, then, appears to be whether such positive aspects and peculiarities could be maintained in the future – a question that crucially depends on the possibility that the diffusion of ICT opportunities on a mass scale into such a highly relational production system might help in overcoming its traditional, harsh structural imbalances.

## Notes

[1] Calculated as imp-ex flows average. In the case of Italy, in the year 2000 the export and import shares of the three other EU-4 countries were nearly 37 and 38% respectively.

[2] For instance, per capita income would be lower, were it measured in currency terms.

³ Indeed, Italy's stock of multipurpose and dedicated industrial robots is comparatively high, and steadily growing: according to the UNECE -IFR (2000) estimates, Italy's share in EU4 yearly installations has grown from 22.8% in 1997 to 27.9% in 2000, and is forecasted to reach 32.9% in 2003.

⁴ The following types of employee are eligible for regular benefits: production and clerical workers, middle-level management and technicians temporarily laid off or working reduced hours in industrial firms. Special regulations apply to the agricultural sector. Regular Cig compensation is fixed at 80% of the gross wage for the hours not worked, from zero up to the collectively agreed maximum (never more than 40 hours a week). The compensation is paid over a continuous period of up to three months; in exceptional cases it may be extended quarter by quarter, up to a maximum of 12 months during any given 2-year period. The benefits are paid by the employer at the end of each pay period, and then reimbursed by the Social Security Administration (*Istituto Nazionale della Previdenza Sociale* – Inps).

⁵ The purpose of the special short-time compensation programme (Cigs) is not only income maintenance, but also employment protection for the workers once productive activity in a company has resumed, following restructuring, reorganisation or conversion. Cigs can be conceded also in case of a work-sharing agreement. Eligibility is open to industrial firms (including construction and related firms) that in the six months prior to application employed, on average, more than 15 workers. The benefits are available to production workers as well as to clerical and white-collar staff (including travelling sales persons) and managerial staff. Workers made redundant lose their entitlement to earnings compensation if they refuse to attend a vocational training or retraining course, or engage in self-employment or salaried employment while drawing benefits. The special compensation benefit amounts to 80% of the pay the workers would otherwise have earned, up to a gross monthly ceiling that in 2000 was 744 euro (for workers earning up to about 1,500 euro gross). For those earning more, the benefit is raised to 899 euro. In the case of a crisis within the enterprise, the benefits last 12 months. This is extended to 24 months for firms undergoing restructuring, reorganisation or conversion. Exemptions from the 12-month limit may be granted by the Ministry of Labour for particularly complex programmes, in consideration of the technical characteristics of the manufacturing processes, the employment effects of the restructuring or reorganisation measures, etc. Firms that consider they will not be in a position to re-employ the redundant employees may proceed according to the regulations governing redundancies. The workers affected are placed on the *Mobility rolls* to facilitate their reintegration into the labour market.

⁶ The number of Italian firms is even larger than Japan's. According to the Establishment and enterprise census of Japan, in 1996 there were in Japan 1.7 million firms, half the Italian figure, employing more than 60 million persons (four times the Italian figure). Japanese small firms represent only 70% of the total, with lower share in trade sectors (24%) and manufacturing activities (54%). The sharpest differences between the Japanese and the Italian firm structure concern both size and industry. Japanese firms are in fact larger: in manufacturing the average size is more than 4 times the Italian average; in trade and transport and communication sectors more than 10 times; in financial services about 13 times; in construction more than 6 times. Japanese firms show also a larger number of local units per firm: the average manufacturing firm in Japan has 2.3 local units (in Italy 1.1); the average trade firm has 4.7 local units (1.1 in Italy). See: Statistics Bureau & Statistics Centre, Ministry of Public Management, Home Affairs,

Posts and Telecommunications, *Establishment and enterprise census of Japan. Volume 4. Summary results and analysis*. Tables 2.1, 2.1, 10 and 11.

[7] The pattern of their diffusion is very similar to that of zero-employee firms: in most services sectors (trade, business services, other services) more than two thirds of the firms are unincorporated. Both zero-employee and unincorporated firms have a relatively greater presence in central and southern regions.

[8] More specifically, if we consider 100 manufacturing sectors (corresponding to the three-digit level of Nace rev.1 classification), in 19% of the sectors the five largest firms account for less than 5% of total employment: 57% of total manufacturing firms operate in these sectors, involving 42% of total employment. Instead, 29% of firms in the manufacturing sectors are highly concentrated (showing a concentration ratio above 30%), but represent only 14% of total employment.

[9] In aggregate terms, industry and energy sectors accounted for 35.8% of total employment and 43.5% of total value added; service firms accounted for 54.4% of total employment and 49.6% of total value added, while the construction sector shares were, respectively, 9.7% and 6.9%. The share of small firms is higher in services sectors (where they account for 70.1% of employment and 55.9% of value added), and in the construction sector (80.7% of employment and 70.7% of value added). In manufacturing sectors, they represent 40.1% of employment and 26.2% of value added.

[10] Independent workers (i.e. working proprietors, partners working regularly in the unit and unpaid family workers, all of them not appearing in the payroll) represent 58.4% of total employment, insofar as small firms are concerned: in services sectors their represent 66.6% of employment, in construction 54.5%, and in manufacturing only 39.3%.

[11] In the case of productivity, the average record of Southern Italy's firms is about 69% of that of north-western firms, and 76-77% of that of firms in the Northeast and Central Italy. Labour costs, however, are 16.9% lower than those of north-western firms, 7.1% lower than those of north-eastern firms, and 10.8% lower than those of firms in the central regions.

[12] Within smaller firms, high export propensities can be found in leather and leather products' sectors (22.1%), while the highest value with respect to larger firms is generated by machinery and equipment sectors (52.8%).

[13] This may be a consequence of the lower average size of non-exporting small firms.

[14] In fact, the higher levels of labour costs among exporting firms are also associated with higher profit margins if compared with those of non-exporting firms. In smaller firms, the share of gross profits on value added is 36.1% among exporting firms, decreasing to 21.9% among non-exporting ones. The relative advantage of exporting firms can be observed in all size classes, with the exception of firms with more than 249 persons employed.

[15] Istat defines industrial districts on the basis of a multiple-step criteria, starting from the identification of 784 local labour market areas, obtained as an aggregation of the 8,102 Italian municipalities, on the basis of an algorithm related to the daily movements of the residential labour force. Istat then defines industrial districts as the subset of local labour market areas which satisfy both the following conditions: a) a concentration level of manufacturing activities, measured in terms of enterprise local unit employees, higher than the national average; b) a concentration level, within the local manufacturing areas, of small and medium-size enterprises above the national average. See Menghinello (2000).

[16] In particular, the complex set of measures and forms of State aid to enterprises aimed at increasing employment are not considered here. It is also necessary to remember that from 1990 onward, Italy has gradually undertaken regulatory reforms, taking important steps towards rules that are more transparent, market openness, and competition. This process has been primarily induced by EU obligations concerning the single market program, competition law and policy, the use of EU funds, the harmonisation of monetary and fiscal policy. EU liberalisation issues spurred also a strong commitment to privatisation. In 1990 an Antitrust Law has been adopted, carrying rules for cartels, market abuses and mergers: the Antitrust Authority focused especially on sectors occupied by traditional monopolies undergoing restructuring and private markets affected by anti-competitive practices. For a comprehensive survey of the Italian regulatory reform, see OCDE (2001).

[17] For a comprehensive evaluation of Italian State incentives to investment, see also MET (2001).

[18] See MET (2001).

[19] According to Istat estimates, more than 10% of Italian firm expenditure in *intramuros* R&D is publicly financed. In any case, according to Eurostat (2001), the Government budget appropriations or outlays for R&D (GBAORD) represents in Italy 1.12% of total Government expenditure, the third lowest share among EU countries. GBAORD include current and capital expenditure of Government-financed R&D performed in Government establishments, business enterprises, and private non-profit and higher-education sectors.

## References

Accornero A., et al. (1998), *Il protocollo del luglio 1993. Spunti per un dibattito*. Franco Angeli, Milan.

Eurostat (2001), How much do government budget for R&D activities. *Statistics in focus*, theme 9, 5.

Istat (1999), *Rapporto annuale. La situazione del paese nel 1998*. Roma.

Istat (2000), *Rapporto annuale. La situazione del paese nel 1999*. Roma.

Istat (2001), *Rapporto annuale. La situazione del paese nel 2000*. Roma.

MAP (Italian Ministry of Industry) (2001), *Relazione sugli interventi di sostegno alle attività economiche e produttive*. Roma.

Menghinello S. (2000), 'The demographic structure of the Italian exporting enterprises and the contribution of the industrial districts to *"made in Italy"* international trade', $2^{nd}$ *OECD Trade Statistics Meeting*, Paris, 20-22 November.

Met (2001), 'Una valutazione delle politiche "industriali" tra continuità e innovazione', *1° Rapporto Met*, Firenze, 12 Febbraio.

OECD (2001), 'Regulatory reform in Italy', *OECD Reviews of Regulatory Reform*.

Putnam, Robert D., Robert Leonardi, and Raffaella Y. Nanetti (1992), *Making Democracy Work. Civic Traditions in Modern Italy*. Princeton UP.

Tanda P. and Tronti L. (1998), 'Technical Progress, Life of Capital and Employment', *Labour, n.2, 1998*.

Treu T. (1993), *L'accordo del 3 luglio 1993: una nuova 'Costituzione del lavoro'* (mimeo). Milan.

Tronti L. (ed.) (1997), *Labour Market Studies. Italy*. Office for Official Publications of the European Communities, Luxembourg.

Tronti L. and Toma A. (1999), 'The relational side of employability: The Italian case', in Gazier, Bernard (ed.), *Employability: Concepts and Policies*. I.A.S., Berlin.

# APPENDIX

**Table A.1 – Number of firms and persons employed in Italy and in the EU by economic activity. Year 1996**

| SECTOR | ITALY | | | EUROPEAN UNION | | |
|---|---|---|---|---|---|---|
| | Average size (a) | Distribution by sector | | Average size (a) | Distribution by sector | |
| | | Firms | Number of persons employed | | Firms | Number of persons employed |
| Energy products | 74.3 | .. | 0.3 | 64.7 | .. | 0.5 |
| Mining and working of metals | 8.1 | 2.7 | 5.6 | 12.9 | 1.9 | 4.1 |
| Non-metallic mineral products | 9.1 | 0.9 | 2.1 | 14.8 | 0.7 | 1.6 |
| Agricultural and food industries | 6.5 | 2.0 | 3.4 | 13.4 | 1.8 | 3.8 |
| Textile industry | 10.2 | 1.0 | 2.6 | 13.2 | 0.6 | 1.3 |
| Clothing and leather | 8.1 | 2.1 | 4.3 | 9.2 | 1.2 | 1.9 |
| Wood and paper processing | 4.7 | 1.5 | 1.9 | 10.1 | 1.1 | 1.8 |
| Publishing print and reproduction | 6.8 | 0.8 | 1.3 | 9.5 | 1.1 | 1.7 |
| Chemicals, rubber and plastics industry | 21.4 | 0.6 | 3.1 | 35.5 | 0.6 | 3.2 |
| Machinery and equipment | 14.0 | 1.1 | 4.1 | 22.1 | 0.8 | 2.9 |
| Electrical and electronic equipment | 8.8 | 1.5 | 3.4 | 26.4 | 1.0 | 4.2 |
| Motor vehicles industry | 101.3 | 0.1 | 1.4 | 85.7 | 0.1 | 1.8 |
| Transport equipment (excluding motor vehicles) | 26.6 | 0.1 | 0.8 | 37.5 | 0.1 | 0.8 |
| Other manufacturing industries | 5.5 | 1.6 | 2.3 | 12.7 | 1.2 | 2.5 |
| Recycling | 4.5 | 0.1 | 0.1 | 7.2 | .. | 0.1 |
| Electricity, gas and water | 82.0 | 0.1 | 1.2 | 50.4 | 0.1 | 1.1 |
| **Total industry** | **9.1** | **16.0** | **37.7** | **16.3** | **12.4** | **33.0** |
| Construction | 3.1 | 12.6 | 10.0 | 4.2 | 14.6 | 10.0 |
| Sale and repair of motor vehicles | 2.8 | 4.6 | 3.3 | 4.3 | 4.1 | 2.9 |
| Wholesale trade and commission trade | 2.6 | 10.5 | 7.2 | 5.8 | 7.3 | 6.8 |
| Retail trade | 2.2 | 20.1 | 11.6 | 3.9 | 21.3 | 13.3 |
| Hotels and restaurant | 3.4 | 6.1 | 5.4 | 4.6 | 8.2 | 6.1 |
| Land transport | 4.2 | 3.8 | 4.1 | 5.4 | 4.4 | 3.8 |
| Air transport | 160.4 | .. | 0.2 | 110.4 | .. | 0.3 |
| Post and telecommunications | 188.5 | .. | 2.2 | 56.4 | 0.2 | 2.2 |
| Banking and insurance | 51.6 | 0.3 | 3.3 | 56.5 | 0.4 | 3.9 |
| Activities auxiliary to financial intermediation | 2.0 | 1.6 | 0.8 | 3.1 | 1.5 | 0.7 |
| Real estate and renting activities | 1.6 | 3.2 | 1.4 | 2.3 | 5.0 | 1.8 |
| Computer activities | 4.4 | 1.3 | 1.5 | 5.7 | 1.2 | 1.1 |
| Other business activities | 2.3 | 14.4 | 8.5 | 5.0 | 12.5 | 10.1 |
| Recreational, cultural and sporting activities | 2.8 | 1.0 | 0.7 | 4.1 | 2.8 | 1.9 |
| Personal services | 1.8 | 4.5 | 2.1 | 2.8 | 4.0 | 1.9 |
| **Services** | **2.8** | **71.4** | **52.3** | **4.8** | **73.0** | **57.0** |
| **Total** | **3.9** | **100.0** | **100.0** | **6.1** | **100.0** | **100.0** |

Source: Istat, Rapporto annuale 1998. Eurostat Enterprises in Europe, fifth edition
Notes: (a) number of persons employed divided by the number of firms.

## Table A.2 – Main economic indicators in industry and services sectors

| SECTOR CLASS OF NUMBER OF PERSON | Number of person employed | Number of employees | Turnover (euro bn) | Value added (euro bn) | Value added per person employed (euro bn) | Gross profit share of value added, by econ.activity and size class | Labour cost per employee (euro '000) | Wages and salaries per employee | Hours worked per employee | Hourly labour cost (euro) | Gr.investment per person employed (euro '000) |
|---|---|---|---|---|---|---|---|---|---|---|---|
| **Industry and energy** | | | | | | | | | | | |
| 1-19    | 1,973,365  | 1,199,294 | 161.1   | 51.4  | 26.1 | 27.0 | 19.4 | 13.9 | 1,779 | 10.9 | 4,6 |
| 20-99   | 1,271,000  | 1,214,364 | 186.8   | 53.5  | 42.1 | 40.2 | 25.2 | 17.8 | 1,724 | 14.6 | 7.5 |
| 100-249 | 529,713    | 524,961   | 103.5   | 27.0  | 50.9 | 37.8 | 31.7 | 21.9 | 1,712 | 18.5 | 9.8 |
| 250+    | 1,281,717  | 1,279,834 | 329.7   | 83.6  | 65.2 | 42.8 | 37.3 | 25.9 | 1,675 | 22.3 | 13.6 |
| Total   | 5,055,795  | 4,218,453 | 781.1   | 215.5 | 42.6 | 37.7 | 28.0 | 19.6 | 1,724 | 16.3 | 8.1 |
| **Construction** | | | | | | | | | | | |
| 1-19    | 1,098,497  | 499,981   | 77.1    | 24.2  | 22.0 | 12.5 | 19.7 | 13.5 | 1,754 | 11.2 | 4.0 |
| 20-99   | 178,137    | 169,521   | 18.8    | 6.4   | 35.9 | 29.1 | 25.5 | 17.1 | 1,742 | 14.6 | 3.2 |
| 100-249 | 35,921     | 35,613    | 5.7     | 1.7   | 46.6 | 27.2 | 33.9 | 22.7 | 1,733 | 19.6 | 4.1 |
| 250+    | 47,900     | 47,803    | 8.6     | 1.9   | 40.5 | 17.7 | 33.3 | 23.0 | 1,697 | 19.7 | 4.9 |
| Total   | 1,360,455  | 752,918   | 110.3   | 34.2  | 25.1 | 16.6 | 22.6 | 15.4 | 1,747 | 12.9 | 3.9 |
| **Services** | | | | | | | | | | | |
| 1-19    | 5,366,973  | 1,793,842 | 547.9   | 137.4 | 25.6 | 21.5 | 20.5 | 14.7 | 1,786 | 11.5 | 4.2 |
| 20-99   | 797,790    | 755,990   | 156.8   | 33.1  | 41.5 | 38.4 | 25.6 | 18.4 | 1,678 | 15.3 | 6.4 |
| 100-249 | 331,620    | 328,488   | 67.6    | 15.0  | 45.4 | 35.7 | 29.2 | 21.0 | 1,696 | 17.2 | 8.8 |
| 250+    | 1,162,799  | 1,160,876 | 18.7    | 60.2  | 51.8 | 37.0 | 32.6 | 23.7 | 1,671 | 19.5 | 12.9 |
| Total   | 7,659,181  | 4,039,196 | 956.0   | 245.7 | 32.1 | 28.4 | 25.7 | 18.5 | 1,726 | 14.9 | 5.9 |
| **Total** | | | | | | | | | | | |
| 1-19    | 8,438,835  | 3,493,117 | 786.2   | 212.9 | 25.2 | 21.8 | 20.0 | 14.2 | 1,779 | 11.3 | 4.3 |
| 20-99   | 2,246,927  | 2,139,975 | 362.4   | 93.0  | 41.4 | 38.8 | 25.4 | 17.9 | 1,709 | 14.9 | 6.7 |
| 100-249 | 897,254    | 889,062   | 176.7   | 43.7  | 48.7 | 36.7 | 30.8 | 21.6 | 1,707 | 18.1 | 9.2 |
| 250+    | 2,492,416  | 2,488,513 | 522.1   | 145.8 | 58.5 | 40.1 | 35.1 | 24.8 | 1,674 | 20.9 | 13.1 |
| Total   | 14,075,431 | 9,010,567 | 1,847.4 | 495.5 | 35.2 | 31.7 | 26.5 | 18.8 | 1,726 | 15.4 | 6.5 |

*Source*: Istat, Structural business statistics, 1998

**Table A.3 – Main economic indicators of exporting and non-exporting manufacturing firms, by size class – Year 1998**

| TYPE OF ENTERPRISE CLASS OF NUMBER OF PERSONS EMPLOYED | Average size (a) | Number of persons employed | Value added *(thousand million lire)* | Value added per persons employed *(million lire)* | Labour cost per employees *(million lire)* | Wages and salaries per employees *(million lire)* | Hours worked per employees | Hourly labour cost *(thousand lire)* | Gross investment per persons employed *(million lire)* | Profit margins (in %) of value added | Export / Turnover (in %) |
|---|---|---|---|---|---|---|---|---|---|---|---|
| **Exporting enterprise** | | | | | | | | | | | |
| 1-19 | 7.3 | 529.661 | 32.856 | 62.0 | 39.9 | 28.5 | 1.785 | 22.4 | 10.2 | 36.1 | 27.8 |
| 20-99 | 39.7 | 861.246 | 75.176 | 87.3 | 51.1 | 35.8 | 1.738 | 29.4 | 15.3 | 41.5 | 33.8 |
| 100-249 | 150.6 | 430.426 | 42.492 | 98.7 | 60.9 | 42.2 | 1.708 | 35.7 | 18.4 | 38.3 | 36.1 |
| 250+ | 823.8 | 1.033.019 | 110.027 | 106.5 | 70.6 | 49.1 | 1.681 | 42.0 | 21.3 | 33.8 | 35.8 |
| Total | 28.9 | 2.854.351 | 260.551 | 91.3 | 58.4 | 40.8 | 1.719 | 34.0 | 17.0 | 37.0 | 34.4 |
| **Non exporting enterprise** | | | | | | | | | | | |
| 1-19 | 3.1 | 1.418.598 | 64.484 | 45.5 | 36.1 | 25.9 | 1.776 | 20.3 | 7.9 | 21.9 | - |
| 20-99 | 32.1 | 391.432 | 26.046 | 66.5 | 43.1 | 30.8 | 1.692 | 25.5 | 11.3 | 35.2 | - |
| 100-249 | 147.1 | 88.832 | 8.076 | 90.9 | 61.8 | 42.3 | 1.740 | 35.5 | 16.6 | 32.0 | - |
| 250+ | 642.6 | 109.893 | 12.285 | 111.8 | 66.2 | 44.9 | 1.703 | 38.8 | 15.8 | 40.8 | - |
| Total | 4.3 | 2.008.755 | 110.892 | 55.2 | 42.2 | 29.9 | 1.745 | 24.2 | 9.4 | 27.9 | - |
| **Total** | | | | | | | | | | | |
| 1-19 | 3.7 | 1.948.258 | 97.340 | 50.0 | 37.4 | 26.8 | 1.779 | 21.0 | 8.5 | 26.7 | 11.8 |
| 20-99 | 36.9 | 1.252.678 | 101.222 | 80.8 | 48.6 | 34.3 | 1.724 | 28.2 | 14.1 | 39.9 | 26.0 |
| 100-249 | 149.9 | 519.258 | 50.569 | 97.4 | 61.1 | 42.2 | 1.713 | 35.7 | 18.1 | 37.3 | 31.1 |
| 250+ | 802.0 | 1.142.912 | 122.312 | 107.0 | 70.1 | 48.7 | 1.683 | 41.7 | 20.7 | 34.5 | 31.8 |
| Total | 8.6 | 4.863.106 | 371.443 | 76.4 | 53.0 | 37.2 | 1.727 | 30.7 | 13.8 | 34.3 | 25.9 |

(a) Number of persons employed divided by the number of firms

*Source*: Istat, Structural business statistics, 1998

**Table A.4 – Industrial districts' share on national and world export referred to some typical *made in Italy* products. Year 1996**

| INDUSTRIAL DISTRICT | REGION | PRODUCT | SHARE (a) on national export | SHARE (a) on world export |
|---|---|---|---|---|
| Sassuolo | Emilia Romagna | Ceramic tiles and flag | 50.4 | 26.7 |
| Sant'Ambrogio di Valpolicella | Veneto | Marbles and marble and stone products | 25.4 | 9.5 |
| Arzignano | Veneto | Leather and leather products | 28.5 | 6.2 |
| Santa Croce sull'Arno | Toscana | Leather and leather products | 20.8 | 4.5 |
| Montegranaro, Porto Sant'Elpidio and Monte San Giusto | Marche | Footwear | 8.5 | 3.9 |
| Pietrasanta | Toscana | Marbles and marble and stone products | 9.7 | 3.6 |
| Solfora | Campania | Leather and leather products | 16.5 | 3.6 |
| Prato | Toscana | Textile fabrics | 28 | 3.4 |
| Arezzo | Toscana | Jewellery and related artiche | 33 | 3.3 |
| San Bonifacio | Toscana | Tanks, reservoirs and containers of metal; central heating radiators and boilers | 13.8 | 2.1 |
| Treviglio | Lombardia | Agricultural and forestry machinery | 17.5 | 2 |
| Udine | Friuli-Venezia Giulia | Forniture | 11.6 | 1.8 |
| Vicenza | Veneto | Jewellery and related articles | 16.2 | 1.6 |
| Como | Lombardia | Textile fabrics | 13.4 | 1.6 |
| Bassano del Grappa | Veneto | Tanks, reservoirs and containers of metal; central heating radiators and boilers | 8.8 | 1.4 |
| Montebelluna | Veneto | Footwear | 8.6 | 1.3 |
| Modena | Emilia Romagna | Agricultural and forestry machinery | 11.1 | 1.3 |

(a) Excluded sales on national market

*Source*: Istat, Menghinello (2000)

# Comment

## Kenichi Sakai

First of all, I would like to express my great thanks to the Authors since I was able to learn a lot about the general features of the Italian economy and the changes in the Italian labour market and production system during the last decade. In particular, I was able to gain a better understanding of various aspects of the Italian labour market, especially the low rate of labour force participation, the high level of unemployment rates, the high degree of regional disparity, female and youth unemployment, the comparatively low percentage of highly educated workers and the low percentage of part-time and temporary employment within a European perspective, and various Italian labour market policies such as the intense use of the "short-time working compensation fund" (Cassa integrazione guadagni). I also learned of the importance of small and medium-sized firms in the production system, the remarkable openness toward foreign markets of the Italian manufacturing sector, the enterprise networks defining most of the industrial districts, and so on.

During the last decade the Japanese economy has also experienced a big change. The most important characteristic of the period between 1991 and 2001 is the very low – or even negative – growth rate. We have had a wave of large-sized bankruptcies. We suffer from an increase in fiscal deficit. And so, Japanese economists define the last decade as "The Lost Decade" or a period of depression after the bursting of the economic bubble of the 1980s. It seems to me that the recent depression is different from a simple cyclical recession. The Japanese economy has stagnated, and the country has not been able to revise its social and economic practices and its sense of values accumulated in the postwar period including the Reconstruction Period (1945-1955), the High Growth Period (1955-1973), the Stable Growth Period (1973-1986) and the Bubble Period (1986-1991). The most crucial issue facing the Japanese labour market is the increasing unemployment rate that reached an average of 5.0% in 2001, and as high as 5.6% (the worst record in the postwar period) in December of the same year. And we cannot disregard the 40 hour work-week, compared to the 35 hour work-week in Italy. The main reason for the increasing unemployment rate is that Japanese firms have suffered during the long depression, and that under severe competition from foreign companies they could no longer maintain industrial relation practices such as life-employment and seniority-oriented wages which were established during the High Growth Period and which supported the development of Japanese firms until 1991. As a result, Japanese workers, who once were guaranteed work and steadily increasing wages until retirement age, no longer have job security.

In conclusion, I would like to present the following four points. First, I feel that the comparison between unemployment rates across countries is to be taken with care as it heavily depends on how unemployment rates are calculated in each country. It is often said that the Japanese unemployment rate would be higher if we calculated it in the same way that Western countries do. In Japan, we don't count people who have given up looking for a job as unemployed. In addition, the rate includes only people who are looking for a job during the week when the survey is done at the end of every month. On the contrary, in the United States and Canada, all people who have looked for a job during the past four weeks are counted as unemployed.

Second, part-time workers and dispatched workers have become increasingly common in Japan. On the contrary these extraordinary types of labour are not so common in Italy. I think they will have a great effect on increasing labour force participation rates, especially for female workers. It would be interesting to understand the reasons preventing the adoption and diffusion of these types of workers in Italy.

Third, I understand that the unemployment situation of young people in the South (Mezzogiorno) is acute. I wonder if they get any support from pensions, from income of other family members, or from participation in an informal labor market to make their living. What are the concrete supports that compensate for the lack of income among the younger people in the South?

Finally, let me point out a few differences between small firms in Italy and Japan. In both countries there are a lot of small firms. But it seems to me that there is a difference in the way small firms are defined in the two countries. In Japan, small and medium enterprises are defined by the Small and Medium Enterprises Basic Law (revised in 1972) as those having no more than 300 employees and 100 million yen in paid-in capital.

I also think that there are structural differences between the two countries. For example, small firms are connected by flexible networks in Italian industrial districts. On the contrary, small firms are under the control of big business in Japan through a subcontracting system. In another words, small firms do not simply coordinate with big ones, they are dependent on them.

# PART II
# ASPECTS OF A DUAL ECONOMY

# Chapter 4

# Old and New Dualisms in the Italian Labour Market

Roberto Schiattarella
Paolo Piacentini

**Introduction**

The evolution of the Italian labour market in the last decade has been characterised by strong discontinuities. The financial crisis in 1992 has forced policy makers to adopt adjustment measures that have led, in the following three years, to the most significant employment shrinkage since the post-war period. By the end of the 1990s this heavy job loss had been almost completely reabsorbed, due to a matching increase in the number of employees (see diagram 1). Such a process of job-creation has in fact been exceptional, as the growth rate of GDP in the same period has been relatively small.

Looking at the absolute levels of employment, the differences between the beginning and the end of the last decade are not so striking. Nonetheless, there have been significant changes in the Italian labour market over the same period. Among these, one of the most striking has been the change in the composition of the work force in favour of female employees. Further, the so-called "atypical" jobs, i.e. contracts other than the traditional "permanent" and "full-time" positions, have more than doubled in the last decade.

Although the Italian labour market has changed significantly – in some cases for the better (e.g. the higher inclusion of female employment, mentioned above) – it seems that overall the typical problems of the Italian labour market have remained; indeed in some cases they have become even worse. In particular, one has to mention the high level of unemployment and the presence of strong inequalities, which represent the various types of the Italian "dualism".

Dualism is essentially an evocative rather than a rigorous term, encompassing the segmentation and differentiation of patterns of labour, which should be related more precisely to detailed taxonomies and definitions. In the Italian case, "dualism" is normally intended as territorial dualism, i.e. dualism at the most macroscopic level. A large portion of Italy's territory, in the South of the peninsula and the islands (the "*Mezzogiorno*"), has never been fully invested by the diffusion of self-sustained growth and modernisation, maintaining chronic conditions of low participation and high unemployment.

However, this is only one of the reasons why a simple survey of the characteristics and trends of the Italian labour market based on the "average" values at national level, would not be sufficiently informative of the Italian specificities.

The conditions of participation to the labour market differ widely in the country. At one end of the spectrum, we find workers who are relatively "protected" by the legislation and by contractual clauses, mainly employed in the public sector or in large firms; at the other end, we find the participants to the "irregular" (or "black") labour market, often not even detected by official statistics.

Our analysis will focus on "dualism" and, in particular, on a quantitative and qualitative assessment of the division of the labour market into a "regulated" segment, where legal and contractual guarantees are still in place, and a "deregulated" or flexible segment, where older and newer patterns of rather precarious work conditions prevail.

In the authors' opinion, this picture deserves particular attention and an in-depth analysis, as it is reasonable to believe that the patterns of the labour market will continue to change over the coming years.

The issue of "guarantees" is one aspect of the more general issue of labour flexibility. Nowadays, the necessity to increase market "flexibility", e.g. in the conditions of entry into and exit from job positions or in the relative wages across territorial segments, is pivotal to the economic and political debate on labour market reform.

In recent years mainstream economists, widely supported by international policy "think-tanks" such as OECD, IMF, Ecofin, etc., have stressed the important role of institutional factors – in particular the rigidities originating from legal and contractual protections that characterise the labour exchange – in the unsatisfactory performance of employment levels and growth, and in the persistence of territorial and other imbalances within the Italian context.

Unilateral interpretations centred upon the "rigidity/flexibility paradigm" would be, in the main, considered insufficient or biased from the point of view of a comprehensive diagnosis of the performance of the Italian labour market. However, the fact that legal and contractual clauses might have privileged "primary" segments of labour, contributing to a parallel expansion of a secondary market and of precarious work, might in principle be acknowledged. The demarcation lines between the segments of a "dual" market cannot be defined with precision, although it is apparent that protections have covered a section of the population predominantly consisting of "prime-age" male workers.

Lowering the level of guarantees might also affect the equilibrium within the family, in particular between guaranteed and non-guaranteed members of the family nucleus itself.

Our aim being mainly explorative, the analysis of the impact of the dualism between guaranteed and non-guaranteed employees on the family is beyond the scope of this work. Nevertheless, in the next paragraph we provide some empirical evidence and descriptive comments on the structural aspects of the Italian labour market, with the aim of identifying what is broadly defined as a territorially "dualistic" condition. In Section 3 and 4 we enter in greater depth into the issue of "guarantees", by analysing the current situation and the changes occurring within this domain. A brief discussion of the main points of the debate surrounding labour market regulation reforms will conclude the paper.

## Structural patterns of employment and unemployment in the Italian macro-areas in the 1990s

It is perhaps useful to start our survey by presenting an overall description of the medium-term evolution of that basic "institution" behind the supply of labour resources to the economy: the household.

Table 1 – Composition of Household per Type and Area (%)

| 1983 | CENTRE-NORTH | MEZZOGIORNO |
|---|---|---|
| Singles | 16.4 | 11.2 |
| Couples without children | 19.4 | 16.0 |
| Couples with children | 54.2 | 64.0 |
| Single parent, other | 7.3 | 6.6 |

| 1998 | CENTRE-NORTH | MEZZOGIORNO |
|---|---|---|
| Singles | 25.6 | 19.4 |
| Couples without children | 22.4 | 17.4 |
| Couples with children | 42.9 | 54.1 |
| Single parent, other | 8.0 | 9.0 |

*Source*: ISTAT & SVIMEZ

The structure of Italian society by type of component family is in fact a determining factor behind the behaviour and choices of participation. In this respect it is worth noting, as shown in Table 1, that within a time span of about fifteen years, the traditional family with children, on which most of the considerations of labour and welfare policies have been founded, has become marginal within the composition of statistical households in the Italian society. The percentage of "singles" has almost doubled from 1983 to 1998, and the territorial difference clearly reveals the gap between the more developed areas of the Centre-North and the "*Mezzogiorno*", where traditional family nuclei are still prevalent. It might be observed that the percentage of "single-parent" households, although increasing, is lower than that of Anglo-Saxon or Northern European countries. Low fertility and longer life expectancy for the larger cohorts of the "baby-boom" generations, combined with its demographic composition, are turning Italy into an exception in the world scenario. In January 2000, Italy had the lowest percentage of population below 14 years old within the European Union (14,6% compared to the 17.1% EU average) and the highest percentage of population over 65 years old (17.5% compared to 16%).

**Table 2 – Composition of Italian Employment in 1993 and 2000 (%)**

|  | 1993 | 2000 |
|---|---|---|
| Total | 100.0 | 100.0 |
| Male | 65.5 | 63.2 |
| Female | 34.5 | 36.8 |
| 15-24 years old | 11.4 | 8.4 |
| 25-54 | 77.1 | 81.1 |
| 55-64 | 9.9 | 8.9 |
| 65 and over | 1.7 | 1.6 |
| Independent | 28.7 | 28.2 |
| of which dependent: | 71.3 | 71.8 |
| Part time or short term contract | 8.1 | 15.7 |
| NORTH-WEST | 29.6 | 30.0 |
| NORTH-EAST | 21.1 | 21.9 |
| CENTRE | 20.1 | 20.2 |
| SOUTH & ISLANDS | 29.2 | 27.9 |

*Source*: ISTAT

The composition of the employed population, as reported in detail in Table 2, has been in part affected by this demographic transition; however, the changes in the structure of the working population during the 1990s do not appear so striking yet. The percentage of the younger cohort, up to 24 years old, has declined, as has the percentage of the over 55; thus employment in 2000 is more concentrated in the central age classes (81.1%). The share of dependent workers working part-time or with short-term contracts, has increased slightly, although the figures for Italy remain lower relative to other advanced countries. Finally, there has been, over the period considered, a worsening of the position of Southern Italy, which in 2000 accounted for only 27.9% of the national employment pool, compared to a percentage of the Southern population relative to the total Italian population of about 36%.

The data on the employment structure reveals an important characteristic of the Italian labour market, that is the low levels of employment for younger and older workers and the higher concentration in the central classes of age. This pattern might be interpreted as a consequence of a process of "social allocation" of the jobs available, which in situations of structural excess supply has favoured workers in their "prime-age", while younger workers find it difficult to enter the labour market, and older workers have limited chances of a longer active life.

**Table 3 – Employment Rates by Classes of Age in 2000 (%)**

|  | CENTRE-NORTH | | MEZZOGIORNO | | ITALY | | EU | |
|---|---|---|---|---|---|---|---|---|
|  | Males | Females | Males | Females | Males | Females | Males | Females |
| 15-24 years old | 37.9 | 31.6 | 19.0 | 9.9 | 29.6 | 22.1 | 44.8 | 36.7 |
| 25-29 | 77.8 | 63.7 | 52.1 | 23.3 | 68.4 | 48.7 |  |  |
| 30-34 | 92.5 | 69.0 | 74.4 | 29.7 | 86.3 | 55.1 | 87.5 | 65.7 |
| 35-54 | 91.4 | 58.4 | 83.6 | 35.4 | 88.8 | 50.4 |  |  |
| 55-64 | 37.3 | 15.8 | 48.8 | 14.2 | 40.9 | 15.3 | 48.9 | 28.4 |
| 65 and over | 6.2 | 1.5 | 4.9 | 1.3 | 5.8 | 1.5 | --- | --- |
| 15-64 | 71.9 | 48.0 | 50.6 | 24.6 | 67.5 | 39.6 | 72.3 | 53.8 |

*Source*: ISTAT & SVIMEZ

The shortage of job opportunities for the weakest segments of a potential workforce is further confirmed by the differentials in the employment rates (i.e. employment/population ratios for age classes). We report here only the more recent estimates available for the year 2000 from the Labour Force Sample Survey (Table 3). In this regard it is worth recalling that, during the Lisbon Summit in June 2000, the European Union has set out precise targets for the employment rates in the Union, which by 2010 should reach a level of 70% for males and 65% for females. The current rate for Italy falls far behind this objective. However, a look at the specific rates will show how the problem of low employment activation in the country actually coincides with that of low employment rates for women, as well as with the structural weakness of labour demand in the "*Mezzogiorno*" regions. At present, the male employment rate in the Centre-North is 71.9%, already above the Lisbon target and in line with the EU average (72%). On the other hand, there is a gap of about 10% for the aggregate female employment rate with respect to the EU average (53.5% against 63%). The figures in Table 3 show the dramatic territorial gap characterising the "*Mezzogiorno*" where, in particular, the female employment rate falls to levels comparable to those found in an underdeveloped country.

In Tables 4 and 5, a territorial and sectional breakdown of the data on Italian unemployment is summarily presented. The territorial dualism of the Italian economy emerges again dramatically, and there is clear evidence of a divergent trend, over the period, between the two broad areas of the country. Male unemployment rates in Northern Italy are among the lowest in the EU and may be representative of a situation of virtual full employment for this particular segment of the national labour market. The "*Mezzogiorno*", on the contrary, shows the highest unemployment rates in Western Europe along with some Spanish regions. The female and youth unemployment rates are the highest in absolute within the EU.

**Table 4 – Unemployment rates (%)**

|  | 1993 | 2000 |
|---|---|---|
| Total | 10.2 | 12.6 |
| Males | 7.6 | 8.1 |
| Females | 14.6 | 14.5 |
| 15-24 years | 30.4 | 31.1 |
| 25-34 | 11.6 | 13.6 |
| 35-54 | 4.3 | 5.6 |
| 55-64 | 2.8 | 4.5 |
| 65 and over | 2.5 | 2.9 |
| **Males** | | |
| NORTH-WEST | 4.5 | 3.4 |
| NORTH-EAST | 3.6 | 2.4 |
| CENTRE | 5.8 | 6.1 |
| SOUTH & ISLANDS | 13.4 | 16.3 |
| **Females** | | |
| NORTH-WEST | 9.8 | 8.0 |
| NORTH-EAST | 8.8 | 5.9 |
| CENTRE | 13.2 | 11.6 |
| SOUTH & ISLANDS | 25.5 | 30.4 |

*Source*: ISTAT

Table 5 – Number of Unemployed Persons in 2000 ('000)

|  | CENTRE-NORTH | MEZZOGIORNO |
|---|---|---|
| 15-24 years old | 272 | 528 |
| 25-29 | 204 | 343 |
| 30-34 | 139 | 246 |
| 35-54 | 262 | 405 |
| 55-64 | 31 | 57 |
| 65 -> | 5 | 3 |
| Total | 914 | 1,573 |

Source: ISTAT & SVIMEZ

No country in the world, we believe, can account for such a wide divergence in the outcome of labour exchange among sections of its own territory. The data in Table 4, with details on the composition of the unemployed people according to age class and territorial areas, confirms the concentration of an excess of labour supply within well identifiable segments for gender, age, and area of residence.

An insufficient labour force mobility at regional level has been considered, in the economic and political debate, the cause for a persistence of territorial divergence in the Italian labour market. Also, because of the existing minimum contractual standard established at national level, the relative wages would not sufficiently differentiate the earnings among areas with wide differences between labour demand and supply. We shall return to this point in the discussion of policy issues in the concluding paragraph; however, it might be useful to recall here some additional factors regarding these issues.

In recent years, after high emigration from the South of the 1950s and 1960s, the geographic mobility of labour has been discouraged by a series of factors influencing the behaviour and choices on the supply side of the labour market. Initial salaries, considered insufficient to cover the transfer and subsistence costs in the Northern cities, together with the expectations of jobs in the public sector and of subsidies, might also have discouraged the mobility of the work force in the South. To this one may even add the existence of work opportunities in the so-called "irregular" labour market, even if at low wages and in the most precarious of conditions.

However, the conventional vision of a regional mobility "blockaded" by disincentive factors on the labour supply side is not, in our opinion, wholly correct. In the second half of the 1990s, in fact, the number of younger workers, often with qualifications, moving from the South to, in particular, the North-East, has significantly increased. The net balance of an outbound migration from the "*Mezzogiorno*" has been, in 1995-1999, of about 60,000 units per year.[1] If, as it appears to be the case, the propensity to emigrate is higher among the most qualified youth, this trend may imply, in the medium term, a risk of depletion of the "human capital stock", further hindering the growth potential of the most backward areas.

As for the argument that a contractual rigidity balances wages across areas with different conditions of demand and supply, official surveys for the manufacturing industries do show some differentiation in the labour cost, Southern Italian gross wages standing at about 81% of those of the Centre-North in the year 2000. However, this differential does not in fact sufficiently compensate for the differences in labour productivity: the value added in manufacturing per unit of full-time labour in the *Mezzogiorno* was 79% of the level in the Centre-North. The real cost of labour per unit of value added was, therefore, higher in the South. This, together with other disadvantages, such as marginality with respect to main European markets, an unsatisfactory endowment of "infrastructure capital" and higher rates of criminality, would explain why the *Mezzogiorno* has failed to attract long-term domestic and foreign capital. If the environmental and infrastructural diseconomies persist, further marginal "discounts" on the cost of labour may be ineffective or insufficient incentives to "catch up" with structural delays.

To conclude, we believe that the extent of territorial dualism in the economic development and the labour market should be recognised as the most dramatic and relevant specificity of the Italian economy. The patterns of growth in recent years have not shown any trend towards convergence. Graph $1^2$ shows the total employment in full time equivalents from 1993 to 2000. As shown, the impact of the 1993/94 recession and of the budget adjustments needed to meet the "Maastricht conditions" for budget deficits, has been paid mainly in terms of further employment losses in the weakest area of the country. Even after the cyclical recovery of 1999-2000, total employment in the *Mezzogiorno* has not fully recovered its 1992 levels, while in the Centre-North a net positive balance of about 650,000 additional jobs has emerged in the same period. Signs of vitality in the productive system of Southern Italy, with growth of investments and exports, have been recently registered; however, these are far from being a significant compensation for a historically accumulated delay. The *Mezzogiorno* accounts for about one third of the country's territory and population, yet it contributes less than 10% of the total Italian exports.

Beyond the macroscopic evidence of a persisting territorial divide, the Italian society is characterised, in other respects, by the different conditions and "protections" confronting the participants to the labour exchange. The next section is devoted to further aspects of dualism, or segmentation, of the Italian labour market, beyond its territorial dimension.

**Differing conditions of stability and employment protection: The handicaps of the weaker segments of the labour market**

In terms of labour market regulation, a further "dualism" can undoubtedly be seen between, on the one hand, workers covered by social security and holding a permanent job, and, on the other hand, workers not covered by social security, with jobs without perspectives of continuity.

As mentioned above, the "dual" labour market has, on one side, workers covered by the social security system; these are, in particular, the employees of public institutions and large market enterprises. At the other extreme we find the "irregular" jobs, commonly labelled as "black labour market". The two halves of the labour market are, however, not mutually independent. Rather, they are strongly interrelated. The presence (and the extent) of precarious jobs is often conditioned by the presence (and the extent) of a section of society that benefits from the social security systems.

**Table 6 – Employment and social protection**

|  | 1993 | 2000 |
|---|---|---|
| Total employment ('000) | 20,484 | 21,080 |
| of which: dependent ('000) | 14,611 | 15,131 |
| of which "regular contracts" ('000) | 13,705 | 13,423 |
| of which working in firms |  |  |
| with more than 15 employees ('000) | 10,767 | 10,429 |
| regular contracts as a percentage |  |  |
| of total employment (%) | 67.0 | 63.7 |
| regular contracts working in |  |  |
| Firms with more than 15 employees (%) | 52.6 | 49.5 |

*Source*: our elaboration from ISTAT

Precarious jobs become acceptable when the worker indirectly benefits otherwise from social protection, either in terms of family support or through the welfare system. Therefore, tackling this matter in terms of flexibility vs. rigidity of the labour market is misleading: the rigidity in some parts of the labour market results in lower social costs due to the necessary flexibility in other parts of the labour market.

We shall try to give an empirical dimension to these two components of the labour market. As mentioned above, the employees of the public sector and of large enterprises represent the protected segments of the labour market. They do not have part-time or precarious jobs and they are not self-employed, they are all dependent workers with a permanent status.

Tables 6, 7, 8 and 9 quantify the actual degree of "protection" characterising the Italian labour market. Table 6 shows the number (and the percentage) of dependent workers with a full-time, long-life contract.[3] This segment of the labour market fully benefits from the social security system. These workers are covered by health insurance, by on-the-job accident insurance and by retirement plans. In the beginning of the 1990s, as reported in the table, this segment represented about 67 per cent of the labour market. From 1993 to 2000, however, such percentage decreased by about 4 per cent. It can be inferred that the widespread diffusion of "atypical" jobs, namely part-time and short-term contracts, is rapidly changing the system of work protection and has reduced the percentage of protected workers. In light of what has been considered so far, it is worth recalling that changing the systems of protections has an effect not only on the behaviour of "guaranteed" workers, but also on that of the "non-guaranteed" ones.

Table 7 – Employment and social protection

|  | 1993 | 2000 |
|---|---|---|
| Males | | |
| Total employment ('000) | 13,415 | 13,316 |
| Of which dependent ('000): | 9,257 | 9,072 |
| Of which "regular contracts" ('000): | 8,950 | 8,572 |
| "regular contracts" as a percentage of total employment (%) | 66.7 | 64.4 |
| Females | | |
| Total employment ('000) | 7,069 | 7,764 |
| of which dependent ('000): | 5,354 | 6,055 |
| of which "regular contracts" ('000): | 4,755 | 4,851 |
| "regular contracts" as a percentage of total employment (%) | 67.3 | 62.5 |

*Source*: our elaboration from ISTAT

More in detail, Table 7 shows that the percentage of long-term and full-time employees in year 2000 was slightly lower for the female component of the workforce, although the gender differentials were not as relevant as it might have been expected. Therefore, if we must refer to discrimination, this is mostly related to opportunities and rates of employment, rather than discrimination in the degree of protection for female workers. This evidence is partially counterbalanced by a comparison between the levels and composition of employment in the beginning and the end of the decade under analysis. The degree of protection has in fact decreased more for females. The fact that in recent years, when the number of "atypical" contracts spread out, female employment has increased more than male employment, may partially justify this trend. It appears, however, that the weaker components of the workforce are further sustaining the social costs linked to the diffusion of new instruments of flexibility introduced within the contractual relationships in the labour market.

**Table 8 – Average number of people which the "guaranteed" worker is in charge of**

|  | 1993 | 2000 |
|---|---|---|
| North West | 3.95 | 4.17 |
| North East | 4.27 | 4.42 |
| Centre | 4.24 | 4.69 |
| South and Islands | 5.62 | 6.62 |

*Source*: ISTAT

Despite the fact that workers declaring to have chosen a temporary or part-time job (mostly females) have been considered as "guaranteed", the five point decrease in the percentage of female workers must be highlighted. This evidence confirms that the cost linked to flexibility is increasingly being paid by the female workforce.

However, a more in-depth analysis of the picture emerging in recent years reveals signs of change, in particular in so far as unemployment in the "mature age" segment is concerned. Table 9 reports the percentage of unemployed heads of family (excluding those in search of a first job). As shown, we can easily infer that, between 1993 and 2000, absolute and percentage values have rapidly increased in the national average. The growth results are especially concentrated among long-term unemployed people. Therefore the system of guarantees starts being "disproved" beyond the families' marginal workforce and earnings.

**Table 9 – Head of family as percentage of the unemployed**

|  | 1993 | | 2000 | |
|---|---|---|---|---|
|  | absolute value | percentage | absolute value | percentage |
| Northern Italy | 75 | 24.4 | 70 | 28.2 |
| Central Italy | 38 | 26.7 | 48 | 32.2 |
| Southern Italy and Islands | 181 | 48.8 | 230 | 46.8 |
| Total | 294 | 35.9 | 348 | 39.2 |
| Of which Long term | 40 | 13.7 | 74 | 21.4 |

*Source*: ISTAT

So far we have considered "guaranteed" workers those covered against on-the-job accidents and benefiting from the health system and from the Social Pension Fund. However, from the worker's point of view, one of the most important guarantees relates to job stability. In Italy the legislation guaranteeing benefits to employees in case of redundancy ("Statuto dei Lavoratori") applies only to those employed in firms with more than 15 employees. Although it is not possible to value the effect of this legislation on the employment trend, some empirical evidence has shown that employment turnover is structurally higher in smaller firms. The very natality and mortality rates of small and very small firms constitute a determinant factor of employment turnover.

For this reason workers of firms with less than 15 employees have been considered the least "guaranteed" in terms of job stability. Reconsidering the percentages of "guaranteed" workers discussed above, when "least guaranteed" workers of smaller establishments are not taken into account, the figures change significantly. Namely, the "most protected" component of the workforce becomes now some 50% of the total population employed (Table 6). The trend experienced during the 1990s, therefore, moves towards a relevant, although not dramatic, decrease of the "guaranteed" component of the workforce.

The picture becomes more complex if we consider the distribution of "guaranteed" workers across the four Italian macro-regions. Overall the North West, traditionally the macro-region with the oldest industrialisation, seems to be the area with the highest level of protection of the workforce, followed by the Central macro-region, due to the high incidence of public employees working in the capital city of Rome. The North East, the region where industrial development has been more brilliant in more areas, follows with percentages that are about 4% lower. The South and the islands (44%) have the lowest percentage of "guaranteed" workers.

Considering that the South is already characterised by lower rates of employment relative to the rest of Italy, we can derive (Table 8) that in the North West one person out of four (on average, one per family nucleus) is covered by the social security system, whereas in the South only one out of six/seven people have a "guaranteed" job. As shown above, in the South family nuclei are larger than in the North; nevertheless, we can infer that the number of families without any worker covered by the social welfare system is higher than in the rest of Italy.

The empirical trends shown tend to confirm these conjectures at the aggregate level. The level of protection of the work force is decreasing fast everywhere, both in terms of percentage of "guaranteed" workers relative to the total workforce and relative to the total population. Nevertheless, we shall underline that the level of social protection is decreasing the most in the least developed areas, namely, in the "*Mezzogiorno*".

Interestingly, the South of Italy also presents the highest percentage of unemployed among heads of family, reaching almost 50%. This figure can be considered as a proxy for the social "disease" affecting the South, which has been increasing during the last few years, though at a lower rate than in the Middle and the North of Italy.

## Table 10 – Employment and social protection, by geographic area (%)

| North-West | 1993 | 2000 |
|---|---|---|
| "regular contract" as a percentage of total employment | 68.4 | 63.2 |
| "guaranteed" workers as a percentage of total employment | 53.9 | 50.6 |
| North-East | | |
| "regular contract" as a percentage of total employment | 62.6 | 28.9 |
| "guaranteed" workers as a percentage of total employment | 48.1 | 45.7 |
| Centre | | |
| "regular contract" as a percentage of total employment | 66.1 | 60.3 |
| "guaranteed" workers as a percentage | 53.5 | 48.8 |
| South and Islands | | |
| "regular contract" as a percentage of total employment | 57.1 | 51.8 |
| "guaranteed" workers as a percentage of total employment | 48.7 | 44.4 |

*Source*: our elaboration from ISTAT

## Old and new forms of precariousness in working conditions: from the "black markets" to "atypical" labour

The dramatic gap in terms of higher unemployment and lower employment rates of the *Mezzogiorno* regions has been described in the above sections. These figures are based on the "official" statistical data, as drawn from the quarterly Labour Force Survey, or as elaborated within the system of the National accounts. According to expert opinion, however, the use of current statistic indicators would, in a sense, overstate the extent of a "job shortage" and consequently underestimate the actual amount of labour utilisation and income. This is the result of the significant extension of the so-called "irregular" economy, or "black" labour markets, hidden to the official statistics and fiscal records.

Definitions and guesses of the extension of the "irregular" economy would call for a specialist's expertise and a dedicated essay. We are compelled, in this occasion, to be extremely concise. It might be useful to specify that the "irregular" economy should be distinguished from any notion of "illegal" activities, and meant essentially as work and income which, if not engaged in criminal activity as defined by the Penal Code, is nonetheless not covered by the official statistical sources. These activities go unreported in order to avoid fiscal and social insurance duties, as well as to avoid meeting contractual standards for wages and work conditions.

In the sense defined above, "irregular" work is not a phenomenon limited to Italy, and it poses serious detection problems in all Statistical Offices. These are now obliged by the international SEC95 Standard for the National Accounts to include the contribution from "irregular" work in the estimates of national income and total input of labour. Moreover, the various types of unreported work do not necessarily interest exclusively or mainly the least developed regions of a country. This means that overtime work, or "second jobs", unreported in order to avoid tax payments, might be more readily available in the most advanced industrial or urban environments.

However, in the context of the Italian economy, "black" labour should mainly be seen as a way of escaping legal and contractual norms for those productive units that are unwilling or unable to meet the minimum standards for a "legal" cost of labour. The areas of irregularity may be thus considered, at the lower end of a productive and distributive context, as the extreme case of exploitation of a "flexible" segment of the labour force.

Although the reliability of the estimates is often challenged, from the information made available from the offices of the National Account System it is possible to derive the incidence of the "irregular" components on the total input of labour. Table 11 reports these estimates in terms of number of full time equivalent employees and their incidence on total employment. What emerges is that, as it could be expected, "black" jobs are more diffused in the *Mezzogiorno* than in the other parts of the country, as well as in the service sector rather than in manufacturing. The correction made possible by the inclusion of "black" labour would certainly raise the reported employment rates (and presumably reduce those for unemployment) for Southern Italy. Part of such a territorial gap could then be attributed to the result of the territorial distribution of the second "dualism" that has been considered so far, i.e. that between legally and contractually protected labour and "precarious" labour, within which "irregular" workers may be included.

According to some, an excess of regulation and protection in the "legal" labour market, and in particular the setting of minimum wages by national contracts and the employment protection norms, might be in part responsible for the relevance of the "black" labour market. Deregulation and liberalisation of hiring/firing practices, and the possibility of discounting wages relative to the national standards, in the less developed areas, would therefore favour a "surfacing" of the irregular work positions.

**Table 11 – Irregular Labour Market: Estimated Incidence on Total Employment (Full-Time Equivalents)**

| 1996 | Number ('000) | | % of Total Employment in the Sector | |
|---|---|---|---|---|
| | CENTRE-NORTH | MEZZOGIORNO | CENTRE-NORTH | MEZZOGIORNO |
| Agriculture | 168 | 261 | 22.0 | 35.0 |
| Industry | 274 | 247 | 5.1 | 18.5 |
| Services | 1,403 | 935 | 13.8 | 22.3 |
| Total | 1,844 | 1,444 | 12.0 | 21.5 |

| 2000 | Number ('000) | | % of Total Employment in the Sector | |
|---|---|---|---|---|
| | CENTRE-NORTH | MEZZOGIORNO | CENTRE-NORTH | MEZZOGIORNO |
| Agriculture | 160 | 246 | 22.9 | 38.0 |
| Industry | 284 | 253 | 5.3 | 18.6 |
| Services | 1,547 | 1,039 | 13.8 | 27.0 |
| Total | 1,990 | 1,538 | 12.3 | 23.5 |

*Source*: SVIMEZ

As a matter of fact, since the mid-1990s, the main objective of the revision of the labour law in Italy, as well as in other European countries, has been to increase employers' flexibility of choice of contractual arrangements, while conforming to the recommendations coming from international organisations such as OECD and the European Commission. As already discussed, if it is possible to define the regulation of the Italian labour market as "rigid", this should also apply in the case of individual dismissals of regular workers in the larger establishments. For younger workers, a series of legislative innovations have in recent years allowed the extension of conditional hiring on a temporary basis, with relevant discounts relative to standard contractual wages. Among the main instruments in this direction, we can mention the extensive application of "apprenticeships" and other contracts with a training clause, which are exempted from the payment of most social insurance contributions and may be terminated arbitrarily by the employer at the end of their duration (one to three years). One should further mention that the use of "temporary", or interim, work, intermediated by private agencies of job placement, has been liberalised and gradually extended following its legalisation in 1996; this form of employment has been increasingly utilised since then.

At this point, it is disappointing to see, from the figures of Table 11, that, from 1996 to 2000, the years in which the "flexibility policies" should have become effective, the incidence of "irregular" labour has marginally increased. Further incentives favouring the "emersion" from the "black" market, for example waiving penalties for employers regularising their workforce, are under discussion.

Finally, the trend of labour policies encouraging the flexibility of contractual forms may be considered from the point of view of its implications for the dualistic patterns of the market. We shall discuss this point in the conclusions. Some quantitative evidence is anticipated below.

In the Italian use, the term "atypical" labour includes, besides "part-timers" and "temps" with characteristics similar to those of other countries, a typology which is perhaps a paradoxical example of the Italian ability to find a "legal escape from legal norms". We are referring here to the case of the so-called "collaborators", i.e. workers formally counted as independent professionals, and hired as "consultants", but who are "*de facto*" a continuously working force in the same establishment or office. "Collaborators" do not earn a "salary", since they are not in principle employees of the firm; they are remunerated for a project on an "invoice-basis".

This can be seen as another example of flexibility in the use of labour. The relevance of this type of "subordinate", who is not formally a dependent worker, would not even have come to light, if in 1996 the National Insurance Fund had not obliged these workers to join a special Pension Scheme, towards which the firm must pay a contribution of 13% of the invoice. The number of registered "collaborators" has increased, from 974.000 in 1996 to 1.745.865 by the end of 1999.

"Collaborations", apprenticeships and short-term contracts have in fact become an obliged passage for most young people in their entry into active life. With a country registering the highest youth unemployment rates in Europe, incentives to increase firms' hiring propensity through the availability of flexible and reversible contracts, has generally been considered as an obliged passage for labour policy.

Flexible work arrangements for the younger workers might have helped their entry into the labour market, but they have increased the burden of an already relevant "dualistic" differentiation. Moreover, firms may now be motivated to substitute older workers with a permanent contract, and this may increase the difficulty of supporting a longer active life and postponing retirement.

There is controversy, among commentators, about the longer-term prospects for young people entering the labour market under contingent contracts; for optimists, it is mainly a passage on the way to stable job positions; for pessimists, there is the risk of feeding a permanent pool of precarious work. The evidence, based on occasional samples, is mixed. In the meantime, the experience of recent years shows that almost the totality of gains in employment are accounted for by the growth of "atypical" labour.

## Fig. 1 – Employees from Quarter I 1993 to Quarter I 2001 (thousand units)

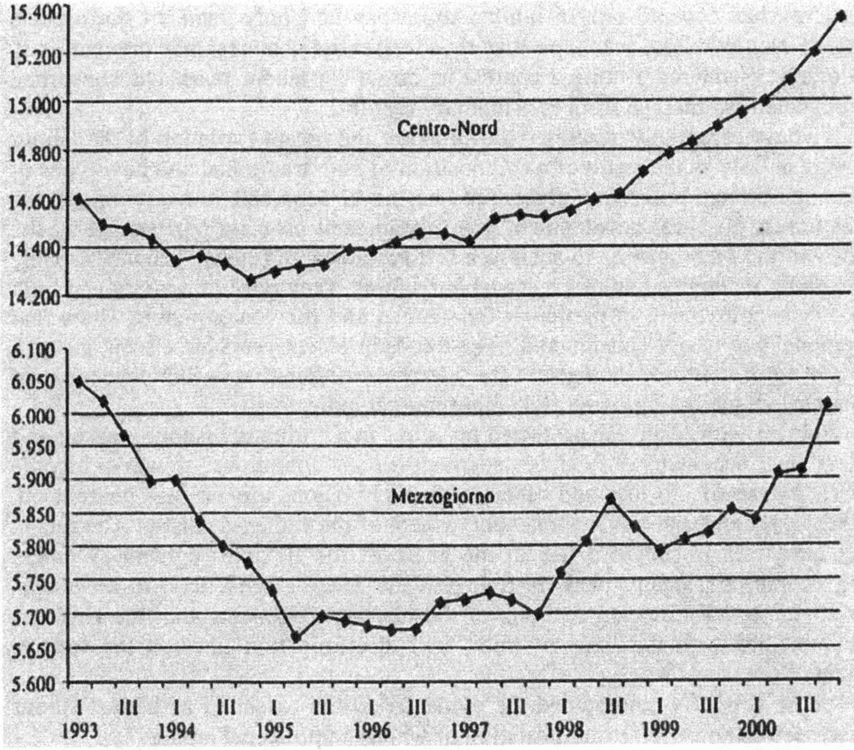

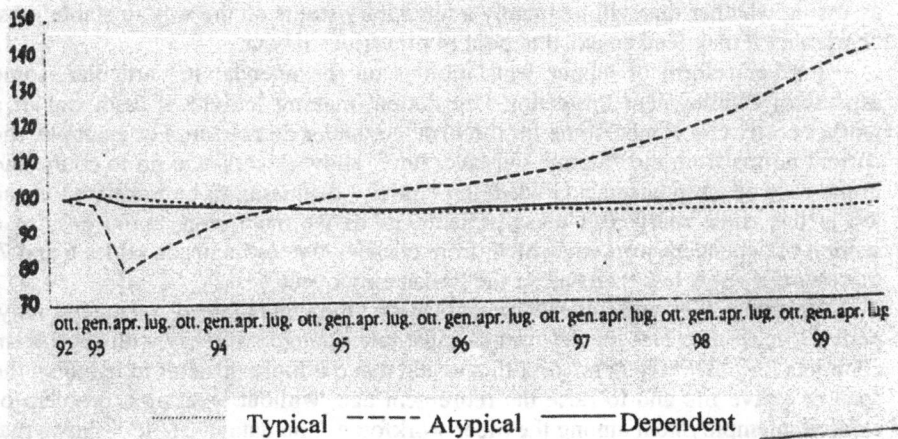

Fig. 2 – Growth of regular and atypical employment

## Summary and conclusions

The survey has covered only a limited time-span and only some of the aspects involved. Nevertheless, we hope that those essential features that prevent Italy from being considered a unified context as far as the labour market is concerned have sufficiently emerged from the summary report.

We have essentially described the situation and recent evolution of the labour exchange in Italy as the result of a composition of both traditional and new types of dualistic partitions. In the first place, Italy has never been able to overcome, in the decades of its post-war development, the fundamental problem represented by the inability of the *Mezzogiorno* to achieve a self-sustained and steady growth, capable of absorbing its large stock of excess labour supply. Low rates of activity and high rates of unemployment, in particular for women and for young people, show that the regional gap is still considerable. The trends in recent years have seen, instead, a worsening of the disadvantages of the *Mezzogiorno* relative to the other areas of the country, in terms of income and labour market indicators.

Workers with relatively protected positions in a "primary" labour market, and workers in a secondary, "flexible" segment where conditions of work, income support in case of job loss and other welfare provisions are far less guaranteed, represent a second, but not less relevant, aspect of the Italian dualism. The recent trends have clearly shown a rise in the share of the flexible segment. Women, young people, and again, workers living in the *Mezzogiorno*, tend to be under-represented in the protected sections of the market, evidencing that the partition often coincides with the lines of traditional discrimination towards the weaker segment of the workforce.

We have briefly commented the evidence on the extent of a "black" labour market, seen as an extreme manifestation of wholly unprotected labour.

"Deregulation" of the rules of entry, the diffusion of "atypical" contracts, temporary work, and so on, have certainly contributed to facilitating the entry into active life of many unemployed and inexperienced young people. The problem is assessing whether this will be merely a temporary status on the way to stable jobs, or whether it may feed an existing pool of precarious labour.

Further reform of labour legislation is on the agenda; in particular, some aspects of Employment Protection Legislation, making individual dismissal of a worker costly and cumbersome for the firm, are under discussion. For example, the current norms from the "Statuto dei lavoratori" allow a worker to go to court, and in the case of a sentence acknowledging "unfair" dismissal, to be reinstated in the job at the same salary. But these protections, as we have seen, apply only to a section of dependent workers, which, from our tentative estimates in tables 6 and 7, represents by now less than half of the Italian employees.

Relaxing this and other protections for the "guaranteed" segment may, perhaps, make it easier for the firm to substitute younger workers with short-term contracts for older "regulars". But this would make it more difficult to lengthen the span of active life and to raise the retirement age, without creating a problem of explicit unemployment among the older workforce. The data in Table 5 shows that the share of higher age classes in total unemployment is relatively limited in Italy.

This is also due to a generous provision for early retirement schemes (e.g. until 1996 all those having paid in 35 years of contributions could have access to a pension, independently of age; now a minimum age clause is set at 57 years). Deregulating exits from work and relaxing employment protection would likely increase the unemployment, or under-employment, of formally protected workers, in particular in the higher segment of age.

Such a trend may be considered as formally equitable, in the sense that it would correct a regulation *de facto* penalising women, young people, and so on. However, the primary segment is represented mainly by males with family charges, which may pose serious problems for the income and welfare enjoyed at the level of an "extended" family. We had estimated, in the case of the *Mezzogiorno,* a percentage of "regular" or "guaranteed" employees of only 15% out of the total population. The income of these workers and, moreover, the social insurance coverage extended to the members of their families, contribute to a social acceptance of the widespread conditions of low participation opportunities, "black" labour, long waiting time for young people to find a job, etc. If the income stability of the "fathers" is threatened, it is by no means certain that the opportunities and welfare of their sons and daughters will improve.

## Notes

[1] Cfr. Svimez, "Rapporto 2001 sull'economia del Mezzogiorno", Il Mulino, pp. 19-25.
[2] Cfr. ISTAT, 2000, see bibliography.
[3] The number of guaranteed workers has been derived from the difference between the total employment and the sum of: independent workers; dependent temporary/part time workers who had declared not to have chosen their type of contract (controlling for double counts); workers in small (less than 15 employees) firms who had not been already considered as independent or under-employed.

## References

A. Accornero, [et al.] (2000), *Solo una grande giostra? La diffusione del lavoro a tempo determinato,* Milano, Franco Angeli.
G. Antonelli. L. Paganetto (a cura di) (1999), *Disoccupazione e basso livello di attività,* Il Mulino, Bologna.
E. Baici, M. Samek-Ludovici (2001), *La disoccupazione. Modelli, diagnosi e strategie per il mercato del lavoro in Italia,* Carocci, Roma.
C.R. Bean (1994), 'European Unemployment: a Survey', *Journal of Economic Literature,* June.
P. Calza Bini (1972), *La disoccupazione. Interpretazioni e punti di vista,* Liguori, Napoli.
CEPR (1995), *Disoccupazione. Scelte per l'Europa,* Il Mulino, Bologna.
Fondazione G. Brodolini (1996), *Labour market studies: Italy, Employment and Social Affairs,* Series I, Commission of European Communities, Brussels.
ISTAT (2000), *Rapporto annuale. La situazione del paese nel 1999,* in particular, ch.5: *Trasformazioni del mercato del lavoro negli anni Novanta,* Roma.

Ministero del Lavoro e della Sicurezza Sociale, *Rapporto di monitoraggio delle politiche occupazionali e del lavoro*, Roma (Two reports years).
OECD (1999), *Employment Outlook*, Paris.
SVIMEZ, *Rapporto 2001 sull'economia del Mezzogiorno*, Il Mulino.

## Comment

### Sumi Iwamoto

The past two decades have seen significant changes in the working patterns in much of the advanced industrial countries. Hereafter most workers will experience atypical employment, such as part-time, temporary or contract-work, with a number of job, if not career, changes in their working lives.

The restructuring of working life, unemployment and labour market marginalization are among the most important contemporary social issues. It is a common observation that such changes in the world economy are taking place at a high speed, under the influence of the increasing globalization of markets and the implementation of new information technology. This process is furthered by the assumption that national economy has to secure competitiveness through a more flexible production and labour markets.

There has been, almost everywhere, a tendency towards significant deregulation of temporary contracts over the 1990s. Also in Italy, fixed-term jobs and contracts with temporary employment agencies are being used in a wider range of situations than before 1996, whereas such contracting was previously illegal in all circumstances. Its growing share in total employment has certainly contributed to the view that the standard or regular employment relationship belongs to the past. There is unanimous demand, from business circles and mainstream economists, for a more flexible labour market.

The Authors examine the trends in labour market disadvantage that frequently result in a territorial cleavage. We can find long-term unemployment of young people in the South and the new forms of atypical employment in the Centre-North. The problem of disparity between developed and developing regions is a kind of chronic Italian pathology. Therefore almost all the policies to fight unemployment are not able to prevent widening the gap in the unemployment rates between regions. Unemployment in Italy is a structural problem of increasing gravity that has required government intervention. The traditional actions of economic policy, aimed at increasing jobs especially in the South, have been replaced, since the 1990s, by legislative interventions on the work agreement that introduce more flexible ways in using workers. This has led to new forms of segmentation in the labour market and to new types of employment, although Italy is well below other EU countries in terms of diffusion of irregular work arrangements.

The imbalance is given by the marked dualism of protection which exists between the core sector of the labour-force and the more peripheral sector that reflect the social and economic diversity of the nation as a whole. On the other hand, workers located in the irregular or non-institutional labour market – the fairly extended "grey" or black economy – are almost wholly out of a welfare system insuring against standard risks. The decline in the average real wage and the rise in earnings inequality can be traced back to the late 1980s.

I discuss mainly two issues of the paper. The first concerns the long-term unemployment of young people seeking a first job. The second is the new forms of irregular employment. Also in Japan, recently, the average unemployment rate was over 5%; at the same time the uneployment rate for young people (from 15 to 19 years old) had risen to 13%. And then I must point out the tricks in the definition of the unemployed, namely, one who works only an hour per week under the survey is counted as being employed.

Young people for whom a neologism, "freeters", has been invented in Japan (youngsters apparently refusing to search for a regular job) count for more than 2 million. After leaving school, they spend a long time without looking for a regular job, by doing odd jobs, because their parents can afford to support them. We refer sometimes to them as "Parasite singles" or "Grown-up children". They are supported by close-knit family life. In Italy too, the young unemployed, not only in the Centre-North, but also in the South, shows a somewhat similar feature as the one mentioned above. This is in part due to a growing mismatch between supply and demand for different qualifications. In contrast to Japanese young people, a number of them would like to wait for a job opening that better corresponds to their level of ability.

The issue around atypical employment arrangements is concerned with social fairness, especially in terms of difference in wage and social contribution, etc. Having faced the mass unemployment problem, atypical employment arrangements were politically promoted in Europe, including Italy, with a view to create additional jobs. Also in Japan, between 1998 and 2001, regular workers decreased by 1,710,000, and irregular ones increased by 2,060,000. Actually, many of the new jobs being created are irregular ones. The part-time workers who were 10 percent of total employees (excluding agriculture) in the 1980s, rose to 23 percent in 2001.

Part-time work is mostly a permanent and regular form of work for women, while it is an exception for men. The majority of part-time workers, who are attending to family obligations, are over 35 and have expressed a preference for this work arrangement, indicating that this allows them to balance their work and non-labour market activities. On average, they work 5.6 hours per day, 4.7 days a week. However, approximately 30 percent of part-time workers work more than 7 hours a day, and over 20 percent of them work more than 6 days a week. There are no regulations as to the minimum length of hours and employment conditions. Among female part-time workers, 52 percent of them have over 3 years of employment duration, and 36 percent have over 5 years, according to the findings reported in a special Supplement to the Labour Force Survey (Japan Bureau of Statistics 2001).

Regarding temporary employment agency workers, in 1999, following the amendment to the Labour Dispatching Services Act, a change was made from a positive list principle (indicating jobs and cases for which use of temporary workers was admissible) to a "negative" one, that practically admits almost all jobs. In contrast to part-time workers, the share of involuntary "temps" ranges from 23.5 percent in 1988 to 30.3 percent in 1998 according to the survey for temps conducted by the Tokyo prefecture. A large majority of temps are young women between the age of 25 and 34 in clerical and machine operator positions (60%).

According to Barker & Christensen, there are three different models within an organization that govern the use of contingent workers:

1) Traditional Personnel Model: Firms have a set of secondary workers they use for substitution of personnel on leave or in order to smooth out peak or cyclical workloads. It is the use of traditional fill-in case type of contingent workers.

2) Crisis-Driven Model: The use of contingent workers shifts from fill-in/special case type to the substitution for regular workers.

3) Strategic Stuffing Model: The key to successful use of them lies in their strategic integration into an overall corporate plan (Barker/Christensen, 1998, 106-109).

Firms in Japan use temps as suggested by the crisis-driven model and part-time workers as suggested by the strategic stuffing model. The state-welfare programs serve as a indirect source of support for employers, who offer jobs that fail to provide a "living wage" and who assume that contingent workers are supported by other breadwinners.

The post-Fordist types of employment arrangement have also given rise to a new generation of home-workers with computers and of self-employed professionals who are however financially dependent from a contractor. Self-employment is increasing mainly in the services sector in firms which are able to outsource some of their functions. There are the two different groups among them. One is constituted by unskilled and casual workers, the other by autonomous and highly qualified workers. The use of the former is intended to exclude temporary or unskilled workers from social protection. The use of the latter is a typical form of post-Fordist labour, flexible in terms of time, place, type of service and cost.

The proportion of self-employed workers outside agriculture has increased in EU countries, but at a slower pace in respect to the late 1980s. On the contrary this proportion has continued to decrease since the 1960s in Japan, because these new types have not yet appeared, while Italy has the highest proportion in the EU countries and yet has increased from the late 1970s, particularly after 1983. According to the Authors, the highly qualified self-employed workers increased two-fold in the 1990s. Even when these workers are paid the same wage as regular workers, firms reduce their fringe benefit cost and avoid meeting labour standard requirements. Also they acquire a way to get part of the work done, without the workers showing up as heads on the balance sheet, giving the illusion of improving productivity.

They are often victims of layoffs and downsizing. For those who have lost a job it is relatively easy to become self-employed workers, but making a comfortable living out of this is far more difficult. The typical self-employed is part of a large labour reserve, that absorbs the decline in earnings during recessions, and then provides a flexible source of labour supply as the economy improves.

In the near future, the employment rates will increase at least for females, and in the same way, the proportion of atypical workers should further grow as the cases of Netherlands, Japan and USA already show. Although male and female work patterns are gradually becoming more alike, females remain substantially more likely to hold irregular jobs.

# References

Auer, P. and Cazes, S. (2000), "The resilience of the long-term employment relationship", *International Labour Review* (pp.379-408), n.139.

Barbieri, P. (1999), "Vecchi e nuovi lavoratori autonomi", *Stato e Mercato*, n.56.

Barker, K. and Christensen, K. (1998), *Contingent Work*, Cornell UP, Ithaca & London.

Bull, M. and Rhodes, M. (eds) (1997), *Crisis and Transition in Italian Politics*, Frank Cass, London.

Lewis, S. and Lewis, J. (1996), *Work-Family Challenge*, Sage, London.

Lind, J. and Moller, I.H. (1999), *Inclusion and Exclusion*, Ashgate, Hampshire.

Morin, M.L. and Vincens, C. (2001), "Redundancy, business flexibility and workers' security", *International Labour Review* (pp.45-67), n.140.

# Chapter 5

# Development Policies in the Italian Mezzogiorno: Lessons from the Past

Maurizio Franzini

## Introduction

If the future is to resemble the past the average inhabitant of the Italian region of Calabria will have to wait about 40 years before his income reaches today's level of the average citizen of Lombardia, another Italian region. Lombardia is a symbol of the rich North while Calabria is the poorest region in the poor Mezzogiorno.[1] It may be seriously misleading to base one's judgement on GDP only; however it is really difficult to argue that in the West there are other countries where development has been so uneven, in geographical terms, as in Italy.

This economic divide goes back many decades in the past. When Italy became a unified country in 1860 there were already significant social and economic differences between the Centre-North area and the South. Today these differences have become more marked, despite massive State intervention to support the Mezzogiorno, especially in the post-WWII period.

Therefore, it seems difficult to avoid the conclusion that the enduring backwardness of the Mezzogiorno is the most striking confirmation that government failures are inescapable. The main purpose of this paper is to understand whether the policies in favour of the Mezzogiorno are to be regarded without exception as a failure.

The experience of the last fifty years will be briefly reviewed and particular emphasis will be put on two features that are overlooked if one limits himself to comparing the GDP per head today with that of 40 or 50 years ago. The first refers to the fluctuating pace of several indicators with a positive trend initiated in the 1950s and interrupted in the 1970s when the oil crisis badly hit Italy and many other Western countries. The second feature goes beyond the idea that the Mezzogiorno is a homogeneous entity and points to the many differences existing within the Mezzogiorno itself, both at regional and subregional level. These two features demonstrate on the one hand that not all policy measures are doomed to failure and on the other that many areas in the Mezzogiorno have already moved away from a state of backwardness. The lessons of the past and the existence of many "Mezzogiorni" ought to be carefully considered in the shaping of future policies.

The paper is articulated as follows. In the first section a short description of the present day situation in the Mezzogiorno is provided. The second section reviews the different phases of policy-making since WWII. The third section discusses the present state of the debate – and in particular the need for bottom up policies – emphasizing the lessons that can be learnt from the past as well as the differentiated situations existing within the Mezzogiorno. Here the need for a policy aimed not at promoting a new start but at strengthening and consolidating previous development, as weak as it may be, will be stressed. Finally some conclusions will be drawn.

## The Italian Mezzogiorno today

### The growth rate

Between 1996 and 2001 the GDP has grown at a slightly faster rate in the Mezzogiorno than in the rest of the country: the yearly average rate was 2% against 1.8% (Svimez 2002).[2] The growth rates of the eight regions making up the Mezzogiorno were quite differentiated (see Tab. 1).

Tab. 1 – GDP, average yearly growth rate (1996-2001)

| | |
|---|---|
| Abruzzo | 1.5 |
| Molise | 2 |
| Campania | 1.8 |
| Puglia | 1.9 |
| Basilicata | 3.5 |
| Calabria | 2.2 |
| Sicilia | 2.2 |
| Sardegna | 2 |
| | |
| Mezzogiorno | 2 |
| Centre-North | 1.8 |
| Italy | 1.9 |

*Source*: Svimez 2002

The average yearly growth rate varies from 1.5% in Abruzzo to 3.5% in the tiny Basilicata. The variance declined over the last year of the period because in 2001 the better performers were the regions where the growth rate had been lower in the preceding years. In particular, Abruzzo one of the best performers in the long run, has shown sluggish growth in the last few years. There is, however, a noticeable tendency for growth to be higher in the smaller regions (like Basilicata, Molise, and Abruzzo itself).

## Income per head

The relatively good performance of the southern economy in the last years did little to reduce the gap existing in the GDP per inhabitant between the South and the rest of the country. In 2000 the GDP per inhabitant in the Mezzogiorno stood at 56,4 per cent of the Centre-North (see tab. 2),[3] hardly an exciting progress with respect to 1996 when the figure was 55.6 per cent. Part of the explanation is linked to demographic movements. In particular, in the last two years migration away from the Mezzogiorno – that had played a major role in the past – seemed to have resumed.

Differences between regions regarding income per head are again noteworthy. Abruzzo (see tab. 2) in 2000 had the best figure (83.8 per cent of the national average) and Calabria the worst (61.7). Only four regions (Abruzzo, Molise, Sardegna and Basilicata) were above 70 per cent and three of them are quite small. Reading these figures along with those on the growth rate we get a good picture of what is going on at regional level in the Mezzogiorno.

**Tab. 2 – GDP per head, 2000 (Index numbers, Italy=100)**

| ABRUZZO | 83.8 |
|---|---|
| MOLISE | 81.7 |
| CAMPANIA | 62.8 |
| Puglia | 65.7 |
| Basilicata | 71.7 |
| Calabria | 61.7 |
| Sicilia | 66.2 |
| Sardegna | 74.9 |
| Centre-North | 118.6 |
| Mezzogiorno | 66.9 |
| Italy | 100 |

*Source*: Svimez 2001, p. 100

As suggested by Piacentini-Sulis (2000), in order to gain a better understanding of this phenomenon it is useful to break up the income per head in its two components: productivity and employment rate. The employment rate carries the larger weight in the explanation of the gap although the rising trend in income per head of the last three years is due to the higher employment rate.

## Employment and unemployment

Both the rate of unemployment and employment in the south are very different from the national average: the former is much higher while the latter is much lower. These two features have characterized the last three decades, with minor changes in recent years.

In 2001 the employment rate was 43.1 per cent in the Mezzogiorno and 61 in the Centre-North (see tab. 3). In general Italy is far from the EU average[4] the only exception being represented by the male figure in the North. Over the last five years there has been a slight upwards trend in the South: also thanks to a more flexible labour market, employment in 2000-2001 went up by 2.7 per cent (i.e. 161 thousand units), more than in the Centre North where it increased by 1.8 per cent.[5] After the very hard years between 1993 and 1996 employment in the South is again at the level of the beginning of the 1990s.

**Tab. 3 – Employment Rate, 2001**

|  | Mezzogiorno | Centre-North | Italy | EU-15 |
|---|---|---|---|---|
|  | 2001 | | | |
| Male | 60.4 | 72.4 | 68.1 | 73 |
| Female | 26.1 | 49.6 | 41.1 | 54.9 |
| Total | 43.1 | 61 | 54.6 | 64 |

*Source*: Svimez 2002

**Tab. 4 – Unemployment rate, 2001**

|  | Males | Females | Total | 15-24 years |
|---|---|---|---|---|
| Abruzzo | 3.4 | 9.8 | 5.7 | 20.5 |
| Molise | 9.2 | 20.8 | 13.7 | 38.7 |
| Campania | 17.7 | 32.1 | 22.5 | 59.8 |
| Puglia | 11.1 | 22.1 | 14.7 | 39.5 |
| Basilicata | 11.4 | 25.8 | 16.5 | 45.5 |
| Calabria | 18.7 | 37.4 | 25.7 | 59.4 |
| Sicilia | 16.8 | 31.2 | 21.5 | 54.7 |
| Sardegna | 14.2 | 26.7 | 18.7 | 47.1 |
| Centre-North | 3.5 | 7.2 | 5 | 14.6 |
| Mezzogiorno | 14.8 | 28.1 | 19.3 | 50.8 |
| Italy | 7.3 | 13 | 9.5 | 28.2 |

*Source*: Svimez 2002

The unemployment rate was at 19,3 per cent in 2001. It was higher among women and reached stratospheric levels among the young: more than one out of two young people was unemployed, with relevant regional differences (see tab. 4).

In 2000-2001 the unemployment rate has been declining from the peak of 22 per cent reached in 1999. This is due to higher employment as well as migration outflows.

There were many differences at regional level (see table 4): Abruzzo stood at 5.7 (less than one northern region like Liguria and much less than Lazio, the region of Rome), Molise and Puglia below 15 per cent, Basilicata and Sardegna between 15 and 20 per cent, and the remaining three regions (Campania Calabria and Sicilia) well above 20 per cent; with Calabria touching 26 per cent. The differences are no less appalling in youth unemployment: in Calabria almost 60 per cent of young people are unemployed against 20,5 per cent in Abruzzo.

Campania is, however, the region that performs relatively better with respect to female unemployment, the rate of the latter is much less than twice the male rate. In Abruzzo that ratio is much higher.

Let us now look at some figures that help us to understand the main characteristics of the economic and social environment within which these results were forged.

*Labour costs and productivity*

Of special interest, also for their relevance to the policy debate, are the level and the dynamics of labour costs. The most recent data show that the labour costs per unit of output are lower in the Mezzogiorno than in other areas of the country. In particular, in 1999 they were 16.5 per cent lower than in the North-West and 6.8 per cent lower than in the North-East (Istat 2002, tab. 2.4, p. 69).

**Tab. 5 – Productivity, 1999 (Index numbers, Italy=100)**

| Abruzzo | 96.8 |
|---|---|
| Molise | 86.3 |
| Campania | 85.2 |
| Puglia | 87.8 |
| Basilicata | 83.3 |
| Calabria | 79.8 |
| Sicilia | 81.8 |
| Sardegna | 86.3 |
| *Centre-North* | *105.8* |
| *Mezzogiorno* | *85.3* |
| *Italy* | *100* |

*Source*: Ciriaci, 2001, p. 790

Given that productivity is much lower in the South,[6] wages and other non wage-costs are significantly lower in the Mezzogiorno. Indeed, the wage differential significantly increased in the 1990s. The largest gap seems to relate to unskilled workers, whose wage in the South has suffered most from the introduction of more flexible rules in the labour market and is quite low, leading to rising poverty among working people.

Tab.5 describes the situation in the eight regions in 1999. Again we see some marked differences, with Calabria and Abruzzo at the opposite ends of the list – the gap touching 18 per cent.[7]

## Credit markets

Another aspect which deserves attention is the financial structure and in particular the situation of the credit market, which is crucial for economic development. Several investigations show that passive interest rates are higher in the Mezzogiorno and rationing is much more common. The situation has changed for the worse in the last decade when many state-owned banks have been privatized, several local banks have disappeared – taken over by bigger banks based in the North – leaving the system without local banks with interregional activity which might play an important role in the financing of the development.

The share of uncollectable loans in 2000 was 15.7 per cent in the Mezzogiorno against 4 per cent in the Centre-North (Svimez 2001, p. 278). Moreover, interest rates on loans were on the average 8.69 per cent against 7.1 % in the Centre-North and rates on deposits were much lower in the South. As a consequence the interest rate differential was almost 2 points larger, namely close to 50 per cent in relative terms (Svimez 2001, p. 276). Bank intermediation is much more costly in the South. According to the prevailing interpretation this is due to higher risk of default.[8]

**Tab. 6 – Infrastructures, 1999 (index numbers, Italy =100)**

| GEOGRAPHICAL AREAS | Roads | Railways | Airports | Energy-Environment | Telecommuni-cations | Banks and Services | Cultural and Recreational | Education | Health | TOTAL |
|---|---|---|---|---|---|---|---|---|---|---|
| NORTH WEST | 107.7 | 97.2 | 143.4 | 137.2 | 143.2 | 130.2 | 100 | 104.5 | 123.8 | 119.3 |
| NORTH EAST | 104 | 105.6 | 72 | 126.2 | 96.3 | 117.7 | 110.6 | 102.9 | 96.2 | 102 |
| CENTRE | 102.1 | 126.1 | 150.6 | 96.4 | 117.5 | 118.6 | 175 | 105.8 | 112.2 | 122.2 |
| MEZZOGIORNO | 91.8 | 84.7 | 60.5 | 63.8 | 65 | 61 | 57 | 93 | 81.9 | 74.6 |
| ITALY | 100 | 100 | 100 | 100 | 100 | 100 | 100 | 100 | 100 | 100 |

*Source*: Istituto Tagliacarne-Unioncamere as in Istat, Rapporto Annuale. La Situazione del Paese nel 2001, p.107

*Infrastructures*

The Mezzogiorno is, at least in relative terms, very poor in infrastructures. As shown in tab. 6 the gap is larger in the so called cultural and recreational structures, in the airports and in the energy and environment networks as well as in telecommunications. All the figures are below the national average and only a few of them show a positive trend in the decade. This is particularly worrying given the disadvantaged geographical position of the Mezzogiorno.

*Criminal activity and social capital*

Several indicators reveal that in the South almost any type of criminal activity is more recurrent, partly as a consequence of organized crime (*mafia* in Sicilia, *'ndrangheta* in Calabria, *camorra* in Campania and *sacra corona unita*, largely an outgrowth of *camorra*, in Puglia). Tab. 7 reports the concentration of different types of crimes. The indexes are obtained by dividing the number of crimes by 100,000 inhabitants and then making a comparison with the national average. The columns refer to murders by organized crime (OM), SU is for the number of people charged with usury (SU), TE for number of extortions and AT for criminal attacks.

The Mezzogiorno has higher rates than the North and there is the usual scattering of regional data. The role of organized crime is well evident in four regions, despite police success in recent years. Some argue that the presence of crime has adversely affected the level of productivity (Centorrino-Ofria 2001).

**Tab. 7 – Crimes diffusion, 1999 (index numbers, Italy=100)**

|  | OM | SU | TE | AT |
|---|---|---|---|---|
| Abruzzo | 0 | 235 | 89 | 11 |
| Molise | 0 | 205 | 100 | 41 |
| Campania | 450 | 323 | 129 | 68 |
| Puglia | 205 | 89 | 149 | 188 |
| Basilicata | 0 | 60 | 113 | 0 |
| Calabria | 507 | 177 | 188 | 839 |
| Sicilia | 220 | 199 | 183 | 265 |
| Sardegna | 0 | 112 | 118 | 560 |
| Centre-North | 0 | 475 | 72 | 248 |
| Mezzogiorno | 268 | 149 | 148 | 16 |
| Italy | 100 | 100 | 100 | 100 |

*Source*: Centorrino-Ofria (2001) as in Svimez 2001, p.924

Many of these aspects interfere quite clearly with economic activity. In particular the poor state of the credit market, the lack of infrastructures, the strength of organized crime coupled with the long lasting inefficiency of the Public Administration including civil justice – not a peculiarity of the South, however – may easily discourage investments, especially from foreigners. Some of the basic pre-conditions for development seem to be missing in the Mezzogiorno – here is a very good argument for the critics of past policies.

Recently, many scholars have drawn attention to another deficient precondition for development, social capital. Following a much quoted study by Putnam (1993) many believe that social capital is scarce in the Mezzogiorno and point to this as the main weakness of the Mezzogiorno. It is difficult to measure in a satisfactory way such a vague concept as social capital and it is also not fully clear how it may affect economic development and, above all, how it could be 'artificially created'. However, in designing the best policy for the South one should not forget to address the issue of social capital.

*Poverty and the informal economy*

Finally let us consider some aspects of the social situation, beginning with the informal or underground economy. According to a very recent estimate by Svimez (see tab. 8), 23 per cent of the employed in the Mezzogiorno were irregular, most of them in the agriculture sector. The Mezzogiorno figure is much higher than the national average, the latter touching a worrying 15 per cent.[9] Indeed informal economy is very large in Italy, as made clear by the data recently published by the University of Linz (Roma 2001, p. 65). The regional variance in the South is as usual very large. According to Istat (Istat 2002, p. 171) the rate of irregular workers varied from 13.2 in Abruzzo to 27.8 in Calabria

**Tab. 8 – Irregular workers as a percentage of total workers, 2001**

|  | Mezzogiorno | Centre-North | Italy |
|---|---|---|---|
| Agriculture | 40 | 24 | 32 |
| Industry | 19.5 | 5.3 | 8.2 |
| Service | 21.5 | 14.9 | 16.5 |
| Total | 23 | 11.9 | 15 |

*Source*: Svimez 2002, p. 61

The large informal sector may have contributed in a perverse way to increasing the overall flexibility of the labour market; moreover it helps explain some peculiar aspects of the Mezzogiorno, like the relatively high level of consumption per head as compared to GDP.

The poverty rates, as a consequence of many of the features listed above, are much higher in the South. We refer here to an index of relative poverty whose threshold is defined as follows: two-member households where monthly consumption expenditure is less than the national per-capita consumption expenditure (in 2001 this threshold was a bit less than 815 euro) are to be considered poor.

In 2001 66 per cent of the Italian "poor" (1,766 poor families over 2,663) were to be found in the Mezzogiorno. The number of families living in the eight Mezzogiorno regions were 7,524 out of a national total of 22,192. It is worth stressing that poverty is concentrated among the unemployed. The working poor phenomenon has not emerged so far in the Mezzogiorno, hence creating jobs should be an effective weapon also for fighting poverty.

**Tab. 9 Relative poverty, percentage**

|            | 1997 | 1998 | 1999 | 2000 | 2001 |
|------------|------|------|------|------|------|
| NORTH      | 6    | 5.7  | 5    | 5.7  | 5    |
| CENTRE     | 6    | 7.5  | 8.8  | 9.7  | 8.4  |
| MEZZOGIORNO| 24.2 | 23.1 | 23.9 | 23.6 | 24.3 |
| ITALY      | 12   | 11.8 | 11.9 | 12.3 | 12   |

*Source*: Istat (Note rapide 17th July 2002)

In all the surveys on the quality of life – however disputable the indicators used may be – the southern regions and provinces almost invariably figure in the bottom positions. This is not surprising because public goods in the South are generally of lower quality and smaller quantity and this reinforces the gap in personal income. There are, however, signs of territorial disparity also in this case. For example, Isernia, a small province in Molise, is frequently considered ahead of several northern provinces.

Human capital, on the other hand, is considered adequate both in quantity and quality in most of the Mezzogiorno thanks also to the several Universities that in the post war period have been located in the South. Here the problem may be represented by the outward migration flows fed just by the best-educated workers of the Mezzogiorno. The issue, as we shall see in detail, is a present day problem.

### A longer view: persistence and change in the Mezzogiorno

If we go beyond the picture of the situation as it appears today we discover three features that have shaped the history of the Mezzogiorno in the last fifty years at least. The three features are: the tendency for the gap in income per head not to narrow in the long run; the fluctuating pace of many aggregate variables in the post-war period; the uneven development and regional and subregional area inside the Mezzogiorno itself.

Therefore only focusing on the income gap means losing sight of other interesting features. The last fifty years or so have not been motionless. The indexes of the gap have known fluctuations. Moreover making reference to the Mezzogiorno as a whole is inadequate because its internal areas are very different and have undergone very different dynamic processes. There is not any single and homogeneous Mezzogiorno and maybe there has never been one. Let us look briefly at these three features.

## The gap in income per head

The gap between the Mezzogiorno as a whole and the Central and Northern regions of Italy in terms of per capita income has not narrowed in the long run, even though in more recent data some feeble positive signs may be noted. There is almost general consent among the historians that the gap between the North and the South was already marked at the time of Italy's unification in 1860, so that the hypothesis according to which the problem was created by the unification itself is not confirmed by evidence. Eckaus tried to estimate the gap: according to him the income per capita was 15-25% lower in the South and he registered more or less the same difference in the agricultural sector, at that time the most important sector in the whole country (Eckaus 1961).

At the end of WWII income per capita was about 50 per cent lower than the Centre-North and several other social and economic indicators brought out very clearly that the Mezzogiorno was lagging far behind. As we have seen, today the gap is only marginally less than the post war level but significantly greater than when Italy was unified. It is very disappointing to notice that today's income per capita in the Mezzogiorno is more or less where it was in the Centre-North at the beginning of the 1960s, so one can say that forty years is a reliable measure of the Mezzogiorno "delay".

These data carry a negative sense of immobility. On their basis and remembering that many attempts have been made by public bodies to sustain development in the Mezzogiorno, two opposite positions have been taken. The first argues that the situation is hopeless and the reason lies in the culture of the southerners, viewed as lazy people trying to live on State transfer and to free-ride collective resources.

The second position stresses the need for more determined and generally more financially generous state aid in order to overcome what has been called the "Southern question" (*la questione meridionale*), a term which has been extensively used to mean that the development of the Mezzogiorno is a national problem, not a local one, and there will never be a really unified Italy unless the Mezzogiorno enjoys a comparable level of well-being as the North.

Indeed, a closer look at the facts demonstrates that both these positions have weaknesses – if we want to call in this way the self-evident ideological (or self-interested) bias of the so called "cultural" position. In fact the Mezzogiorno has moved on. If one looks at the aggregate data and is satisfied with comparing data at fixed periods she will not get sight of what has been going on. Since WWII many aggregate indicators have fluctuated and uneven development has taken place within the Mezzogiorno.

## Fluctuations in aggregate variables

In the two decades prior to 1973 the GDP per head showed a tendency to catch up. In 1973 it reached its peak: 60.2 per cent of the Centre-North. In the following years the tendency was reversed with the lowest figures reached in 1997-1998.

The good performance up to 1973 is the result of several causes, of different nature and social relevance. The policies adopted in the previous years certainly exerted a positive influence, as we shall see below. The GDP yearly growth rate was quite high (above 5 per cent of the average over the whole period) and the gap in income per head narrowed despite the fact that the GDP in the North grew at a sligthly higher rate:[10] migration provides the explanation.

Migration away from the south has been a distinguishing feature of many phases of the Mezzogiorno's history.[11] It is estimated that between 1952 and 1961 almost 2 million people left (almost equally divided between those going to the Centre-North and abroad) and a further 2.2 million in the following decade, most of them going to the so called industrial triangle in the North-West (Milan-Turin-Genua) attracted by the "economic boom" and also by the wage differential that in those years was quite high.

These are appalling figures compared to the total population of the Mezzogiorno: they are of such a magnitude that they almost completely compensate the natural component of the demographic changes that has been sharply positive in the South for a very long time. As a consequence, population in residence grew at the poor average rate of 0.25 per cent per year during the 1962-73 period, half of the value in the preceding decade and more than half the value it would have taken in the following years[12] (Svimez 2000, p. 20).

The gap in income per capita declined, therefore, not only for the positive reason that growth was very fast but also because of demographic differences between the North and the South. However the merits of the policy adopted in those years should not be underrated. To this issue I shall return below.

Migration today seems to be important again. Europe is characterized by a rather immobile population. This is seen as a disturbing feature for building a unified European market and several commentators have strongly recommended policy intervention to foster regional mobility. However, in the last few years migration flows from the South to the North seem to have resumed in Italy (Svimez 2002).[13]

In 2000 and 2001 the population slightly decreased in the South with almost 140,000 people leaving their home. The phenomenon is stronger in Sicilia, Campania and Puglia while Abruzzo and Molise have had, on the contrary, a positive balance between outgoing and incoming migration flows. Also from this extremely significant point of view the Mezzogiorno is highly differentiated. The primary destination of the migrants today is the North-East of the country, where the industrial districts of the Veneto are situated.[14]

This tendency manifests itself in a period of low growth rates, a situation quite different from the 1960s. Moreover, contrary to the past, migration flows are very likely fed by educated people endowed with a high level of human capital. This loss of human capital – whose cost may never be recovered – could weaken one of the few adequate pre-conditions for development existing in the Mezzogiorno and impair the future prospects for progress.

## Uneven development in the Mezzogiorno

A lot of the data presented above witnesses the differences existing today between the regions in the South. But this is not at all a new phenomenon. A well known scholar of the Mezzogiorno (Rossi Doria 1982), writing decades ago, distinguished between the "meat" and the "bone" referring respectively to, coasts and mountains in interior areas. Today there are distinguishable differences also between countryside and the cities that make it more and more difficult to refer to the Mezzogiorno as a uniform territory.

Several studies have shown that the northern regions are more similar amongst themselves than the southern ones. Actually the latter exhibit a wide dispersion in several variables (Ciriaci 2001, p. 793).

Over a longer period of time it is easier to see how different the paths followed by the Southern regions are. One striking example is provided by Sicilia, on the one hand, and Abruzzo, on the other: very similar after WWII, today they are separated by enormous economic and social differences (Helg-Peri-Viesti 2000).

An interesting and difficult question is to understand what lies at the root of these differences. Were they due to the workings of spontaneous forces, to different economic structures or to the effects of policy measures? There is no easy answer to such questions. For instance, organized crime is very strong in Sicilia and virtually absent in Abruzzo. This is a striking difference. But it is also widely acknowledged that in Abruzzo political patronage and crony capitalism is widespread. How can we explain that the same factor considered one of the major causes of economic distaster and government failure in many regions – and in particular in Sicilia – did not hamper progress in Abruzzo?[15]

At subregional level we find perhaps even sharper differences within the Mezzogiorno. Good examples are the several areas of industrial development scattered in a number of regions. It is usual nowadays to refer to them as industrial districts. There are industrial districts within Puglia, Abruzzo, near Naples, in Basilicata and Molise, in Sardegna and also in Sicilia – practically in every region. What is worth stressing is that in the same region often a few miles away from the districts there are cities and countryside devoid of any form of economic development. It is also to be underlined that there are instances of industrial districts developing without huge aid from the State.

Summarizing, there is no one single Mezzogiorno and there are also some "Mezzogiorni" of the Mezzogiorno. This is not to say that there are southern regions more similar to some northern regions rather than other southern regions. This is not confirmed by almost all the most important indicators. Still the lack of homogeneity should be borne in mind both in the evaluation of past policies and in choosing the best measures for the future. In particular it clarifies that "some" development has taken place in the Mezzogiorno, therefore we are not facing a typical start up problem. This has been too often overlooked by the policy makers when designing the development policies for the Italian Mezzogiorno.

**The history of development policies: not only top down failures**

The policies enacted in the Mezzogiorno in the fifty years or so after the WWII are today the object of bitter criticism. In the all negative evaluations of the past experiences it is easy to single out the scapegoat: it is the centralistic bias of the State intervention, its indulgence in the worst type of top down approach to development policy, aggravated by the recourse to "extraordinary intervention" and special agencies outside the ordinary structure of Public Administration.

Most of the criticism is well deserved but one should refrain from a too simplistic condemnation. The risk is an oversemplification that, on the one hand, does not do justice to the rich and differentiated experience of the policies for the Mezzogiorno and on the other leads to drawing wrong conclusions from the past with negative consequences for the choice of the best policies to adopt today. Above all, one should bear in mind the two features recalled in the previous section: the uneven pace of economic variables in the past decades and the uneven development of regions and subregional areas.

Let us briefly outline which policies have actually been adopted from the end of WWII. It is common to break up the whole 1950-1997 period in three phases. The first lasts from 1950 to the oil shock of 1973-1974, the second from 1974 to 1992 and the last from 1992 to 1996-7, when an entirely new approach was initiated.[16]

*The post-WWII period*

At the end of WWII the task of promoting the development of the Mezzogiorno was a very hard one and a radically new choice was made. In 1950 a law was issued that gave rise to the "Cassa per il Mezzogiorno" (Mezzogiorno Fund), a special agency external to the ordinary Public Administration which materialized out of the belief that the Mezzogiorno needed "extraordinary intervention".

The International Bank of Reconstruction and Development had a major role in its birth. Eugene Blank, the Bank president, declared that his institution was ready to issue long term credit provided that the receiver of the funds were a single institution similar to the Tennessee Valley Authority, considered one of the winning choices of Roosevelt's New Deal (Barone 1996, D'Antone 1996). In particular the independence from ordinary government was considered a necessary condition for avoiding corruption and other distorsive practices like political patronage.

It is somewhat ironical, in the light of the following events, to learn that the choice to set up a special agency in charge of the development of the Mezzogiorno was the result of external authoritative pressures motivated by the fear that political patronage and corruption would stem from ordinary government.[17] Today many hold exactly the opposite view: the Cassa was doomed to failure because "extraordinary intervention" led to corruption and bad habits. Perhaps there is no universal law in this, as in many other cases.

Indeed the Cassa was born with the full involvement of some of the best Italian technocrats, most of them being part of the brain trust of the State holding IRI that had had such an important part in the rescueing of several private banks and firms during the dark thirties.[18] A new management style was therefore introduced, that paid a lot of attention to strategic long term planning, a striking novelty compared to the conservative and inertial behaviour dominant in the Italian Public Administration. Some years later this technocratic approach – with its strong component of social responsibility – was substituted by more mundane techniques of decision. This was a great loss for the possibility of managing the economy – and the development policies in particular – on the basis of rigorous evaluation of social advantage.

As a special agency the Cassa managed huge amounts of money in excess of the ordinary budget and this helped to shape a policy which, notwithstanding its many detractors, in the first two decades had some merit.

The Cassa's initial task was to help the Mezzogiorno to overcome its long lasting deficiency of infrastructures. The idea was that infrastructures were an essential precondition for development, a kind of collective good which was lacking both in quantity and quality in the area as a whole. Many roads, railways and water canals were built by spending a considerable amount of money.[19]

The second phase of the Cassa strategy began in 1958 when the main objective became the industrialisation of the area. The whole design was clear: after having at least partially removed one of the preliminary obstacles, the task was to stimulate industrialisation with direct measures.

While the role of the State was rather obvious in the first phase this is no longer the case when industrialisation is the issue. How to foster it was not such an easy question and an interesting debate about how to combine state and market in this particular respect, not devoid of some originality, took place among some of the best economists and policy makers of the country. Most of them were members of the National Commission for Economic Planning, set up in 1962.[20]

Two visions emerged in the debate on the "programmazione economica" (economic planning). On one side were those who believed that public enterprises – at the time considered an essential weapon in development policies – were to follow a private-like behaviour and make calculations on the basis of the opportunities disclosed by the market. On the other side were those who believed that in a backward economy the market is not a good guide to welfare enhancing investment and therefore public enterprise also had to make choices that private firms would not have done. The point was quite compelling: if the markets were well functioning why was development so sluggish?

One can think here of external factors or other types of market failures, however the position of those who suggested that public enterprises adopted private-like calculations probably originated from a very practical preoccupation: if the market is not the guide, who is? Here is a crucial weakness in the Italian system – may be of the Italian government culture – that subsequent development, especially in the 1980s, would have clearly brought to the fore: the substitution of market calculations not with rigorous social evaluations but with almost any other decision criterion, including the most extravagant whims of political leaders.

This preoccupation was shared also by those participants in the debate who insisted on the necessity for planning to be democratic, meaning that collective will and people's participation was an essential condition for success (Bianchi 2002, p. 111). Here one can find an anticipation of today's strong emphasis on the strategic importance of having local resources involved in the development process.

A mixing of different measures was chosen in practice. A 1957 Act introduced fiscal incentives for private firms, credit was subsidised and also capital contributions (initially directed to small and medium size firms only) were allowed. This has been interpreted as a policy of the bottom up type (Jossa 2001). The idea was to create "growth poles", exploiting agglomeration economies – something not very common at that time – following Perroux's indication (Perroux 1955). As a complement to this bottom up approach another weapon, of a top down type, was deployed. It is the strategy that obliged the state-owned enterprises ("Partecipazioni Statali") to set up 60 per cent of their new plants and 40 per cent of their investment in the southern regions.

These big firms – mostly created during the 1930s when State intervention rescued many private firms and banks on the verge of collapsing – normally employed advanced technology and were capital intensive. They were seen as the vehicle for spreading development in the South.

In those same years labour costs per unit of output were significantly lower in the South. Unemployment and the absence of bargaining at the national level, made the wage differential 10 per cent larger than the productivity gap. National labour agreements between 1961 and 1969 explicitly allowed for "wage cages" (gabbie salariali), i.e. different wage levels between the north and the south up to a difference of 20 per cent.[21] Some authors believe that the repeal (1969) of the "wage cages" and the tendency for wages to equalize (even if they are far from being equal) bears most responsibility for the interruption of the catching up during the 1970s (see, among others, Sinn-Westermann, 2001).

The whole set of measures enacted between the end of the 1950s and the 1960s is not devoid of strength and rationality. After focussing on infrastructures a push was given to industrialisation with an intervention from above (through the state-owned enterprises) and a push from below (incentives to small and medium sized firms), while labour costs were kept lower than in the North.

As already recalled, the growth rate of the Mezzogiorno was particularly high in these years and the GDP gap narrowed even if migration has contributed to this result. Also other indicators were positive: 25 industrial area started to work in the first years of the 1960s, the share of investments at the beginning of the 1970s climbed from around 15% to more than 30%, with a major role of state-owned firms. Other important changes – not all positive especially in the long run – took place: the productive structure changed and the role of agriculture, that had been dominant so far, declined dramatically. As a consequence, the cities gained in importance.

Changes took place also as an unintended consequence of development policies themselves. For instance, the creation of infrastructures made the southern markets more appealing to the northern firms and this had negative consequences for many firms in the south especially those in traditional sectors like food and wood (Faini 1983). Only too often we forget that development policies create losers and, putting other considerations aside, this is an obstacle for furthering development.

## From the first oil shock to the shutting down of the "Cassa"

The second period of the polices for the Mezzogiorno conventionally goes from 1974 to 1992. The beginning of the period coincides with the crisis after the first oil shock which had serious consequences in a country like Italy which is heavily dependent upon imported oil. The period ends when the Cassa per il Mezzogiorno was liquidated and the Maastricht Treaty leading to the European Monetary Union forced a massive financial tightening in the Italian Budget.

The second half of the 1970s were years of deep crisis and high inflation in Italy. The crisis imposed a change in the priorities of the government, northern industry becoming the first receiver of financial and fiscal incentives. More in general, industrial policy was primarily geared to help those firms.

The vulnerability of the most advanced industries in the country points to a weakness in the carrying out of economic policy in the preceding years. The not too strong northern industry now needed heavy aid from the State and, to some extent, it crowded out the Mezzogiorno as beneficiary of public resources.

Investment suffered enormously while soaring energy prices badly hit capital intensive firms in the South. As the crisis unfolded, many private firms faced very dramatic conditions and the state-owned firms tried to rescue most of them (located mainly in textile, aluminium and chemical sectors), often without any evaluation of their capacity to remain in the market in the long run. But a different course of action was not easy to implement neither is it fair to state that all the rescue operations were to be blamed. In some cases the crisis interfered with an ongoing development process which, at least in principle, was worth this kind of benevolent help.

The already weak catching up process stopped and reversed, even though just in those same years some regions and provinces started a development process.[22]

The labour costs differential was vanishing at the beginning of the 1980s. Earlier, in 1968, to counter this tendency fiscal exemption of social security contributions (*fiscalizzazione degli oneri sociali*) had been introduced in the Mezzogiorno. Thought of as a temporary measure, it lasted for a very long time becoming one of the most important tools for channeling funds to the South. Well into the 1990s it was the object of much arguing with the European Union which saw it as a not too disguised form of forbidden state help.

Another much criticized devolpment refers to the huge increase in social spending with transfers made in favour of both households and firms. Indeed the social situation was rapidly worsening because unemployment was climbing –

reaching an unprecedented 20 per cent in the mid-1980s – and migration was discouraged by the many difficulties of the Northern industries.

The slackening of development in the South, combined with the difficulties of the North, disclosed a really dramatic situation. The expansion of public employment – another feature criticized in subsequent years also for its indirect effects on the wages in the private sector – is to be understoood in this context.[23] This is usually called the "periodo assistenziale" (social support policy) – meaning that a large part of the Mezzogiorno was becoming dependent on public funds and resources.

As public spending increased in the whole country, State deficit soared and interest rates went up, even if increasing inflation did a lot to keep down real interest rates. Political connections and patronage worsened in these years and it is not easy to assess what part the economic crisis itself had in it. Political parties became directly involved – perhaps too much – in the managament of the economy. The 1992 burst of corruption known as "Tangentopoli" (Bribesville) was not too far ahead.

It is difficult to say what could have been done in these crisis years instead of a public spending policy. Undoubtedly there have been excesses and mistakes, magnified by the traditional inability to make rigorous evaluations when public funds are involved. But this is not the same as saying that public spending invariably leads to bad policies. According to some scholars (Trigilia 1992) the burst of social spending and the choice of this "social support" policy had long lasting negative effects because it helped to create a "dependence" culture in the south rather than a pro-active attitude towards the market.[24] It is difficult to say whether this is true or not. However there are good reasons to believe that letting the crisis "do its job" (as a free-market approach would have it) is hardly wise advice in a recently developed area where many firms are weak simply because they are young. Selective protection and reversible protection would have been a better alternative but it is not easy to carry them out, especially when you cannot count on wise political elites and there is no backing up by a good tradition of rigorous social evaluation.

What went wrong was exactly the bad performance of the politicians. As one of the fathers of the Italian planning (*programmazione*) bitterly wrote in 1985: "the worst feature of the system was the rising collusion between administrative and political power on the one side and enterprises supplying goods and services to the State via public procurement on the other side. This rising collusion, not rarely mixed with corruption, brought not only a worsening political and civil life but also a waste of resources, being an obstacle to development...This was the main problem of public policy in the Mezzogiorno" (Sylos Labini 1985, p. 20).

In the period as a whole, the Cassa per il Mezzogiorno financed a reduced amount of infrastructure and issued less investment incentives. But the general economic situation and some new institutional development introduced important changes.

In particular, in the 1970s the Regions started to act as autonomous entities, more than twenty years after the Constitutional Law had envisaged them. With their birth, the push towards power decentralization and a bigger role for local governments become stronger and today is at its highest. Already in 1986 a law was issued that actually reduced the powers of the Cassa in favour of a large number of subjects. The extraordinary intervention model took its sunset avenue. The Cassa moved from a public agency of the TVA type to a kind of development bank (Bianchi 2002, p. 213). But it was not easy to change a consolidated nature and to take on this very difficult task.

It is worth stressing that in the words of the politicians of the time one can find clear attention for a problem which was relevant then and is more relevant now: how to combine coordinated intervention with differentiated local situations. The greater role assigned to the Regions was considered an important component of the best strategy (Bianchi 2002, p. 214).

## After the "Cassa"

The last phase of the development policies refers to the post-1992 events. This year is remarkable because on the one hand the Cassa per il Mezzogiorno was liquidated and on the other a very tight fiscal policy was adopted as Italy seriously started to put its budget in order to comply with the rules set by the Maastricht Treaty for entering the European Monetary Union. Moreover a huge devaluation of the lira took place in September 1992 in the attempt to put a stop to a climbing speculative attack.

All these developments were very unfavourable to the Mezzogiorno in the short run at least. Rather then catching up it plunged into a dangerous lagging behind. The 1993-1996 period is one of the worst in its performance, also in terms of investment and employment. Of course there were exeptions and the most relevant came from some industrial districts whose exports showed a tendency to increase also in the worst years.

Many banks went bankrupt and widespread privatization also in the credit sector took place. Despite the high level of wage bargaining centralisation at the national level, the very weak labour market made for increased wages and labour costs differentials, reversing the trend of the previous decade.

After the death of the Cassa, incentives for new investments in the Mezzogiorno were virtually non-operating in the 1992-1996 years. In their place a new scheme covering not only Mezzogiorno but all "depressed areas" of the country was introduced. To many observers this interpretation of the Mezzogiorno as an area in no way different from other depressed areas in other regions of the country, meant the end of the "*questione meridionale*" as a specific national problem. The electoral success of the Lega, a party strongly based in the North aiming at capturing the consensus of most Northerners unwilling to "finance" the South any longer, also contributed to this development.

The political climate was deeply changing also as a consequence of the corruption scandals (the so-called Tangentopoli) that involved many leading politicians. In 1993 a new electoral law promised to renew the political elites at local level and to give the Mezzogiorno a more responsibile and enthusiastic ruling class. Many hopes were raised by these innovations, but after almost ten years there are very weak signs of really long lasting changes in the behaviour of local political élites.

The increasing importance of the European Union set another new element. It concurs with the growing power of the regions to force a new role for the national state. A redefinition of responsibilities among the different levels of government is essential. The new turn in development policies started in 1997 is also to be understood in this institutional context.

In the 1992-1997 there were also some clear steps backwards. Important plants were shut down often without a convincing explanation, at least in economic terms. The most striking case, almost a symbol, is the steel plant of Bagnoli in Naples, which was shut down after a lot of money had been poured in it and when its cost effectiveness was satisfactory. Bagnoli is often considered as one of the many useless "cathedrals in the desert" built during the period of the "extraordinary intervention". There are doubts that this is a wholly fair description of what happened.

In conclusion, after 1974 the following decades did a lot to clear off the progress of the preceding years. These two decades saw some objective difficulties and an inadequate management of the economy. It would be wrong to pool these different experiences in a unique interpretation dominated by the idea that the period was uniformly characterized by top down policies doomed to failure by their very nature. There were not only top down policies nor were they necessarily a failure.

## The debate today and the lessons from the past

The scrutiny of past policies provide us with some important lessons and helps clarify which are the most challenging problems ahead.

The first lesson is that a well coordinated policy needs time, resources and a responsible ruling class. During the 1950s and the 1960s most of these conditions were met and a series of coherent steps were strategically planned. When one of these conditions is missing some troubles are inevitable. No new policy will work unless it copes with them. In particular, if policy making is guided not by socially rational calculations but by opportunistic behaviour ending up in collusion and corruption the chances of success are dramatically diminished.

The second lesson is that some development – intermittent and uneven as it may be – has taken place in the Mezzogiorno also thanks to the policies adopted. After the building of infrastructures and the support to industrialization a third phase of "consolidation" was needed. The 1974 crisis – also through its negative impact on the policies for the Mezzogiorno – seems to have interrupted a coherent process the next stage of which might have been the strenghtening and spreading of the development process that has been anything but automatic in the Mezzogiorno. The several linkages envisaged by Hirschman (1958, 1989) and other distinguished scholars seem to have been largely ineffective. In a very few cases the devolupment process spread as was expected.[25]

The third lesson is precisely that more attention should be lent to the conditions upon which the spreading of development and its consolidation depend. The weakness of the linkages is probably due to the bad working of some essential mechanisms. There are good reasons to believe that a large share of the burden falls on the very imperfect credit market of the Mezzogiorno. Easily accessible and cheap credit is an essential condition for the consolidation of existing firms and the birth of new ones "around" those which characterized the first stages of development.

In the ongoing debate there is almost general consent that the experience of the post war period is to be regarded as a general failure – the epitome of all the negative aspects of the top down policies. Forgetting the positive aspects of the past may be a mistake. For instance, one may be inclined to believe that the problem for the whole Mezzogiorno is how to start the development process whereas in several areas the actual issue is the consolidation of development.

To forget that some development has taken place is also to forget that there are individuals and firms which may be damaged by further intervention. This is relevant also from a political economy perspective: development may have opponents in the Mezzogiorno too. The policy design should take both these aspects into consideration.

In the present debate on the Mezzogiorno at least two different positions can be distinguished. The first relies on free markets and argues that all the obstacles to their working should be removed. The second advocates a much more active role for the state and argues in favour of a bottom up approach that gives more power to local governments.

In the free market approach, the most frequently mentioned obstacle to the proper working of the market, is the web of institutions which makes the labour market not so flexible as it could be. In particular, it is argued that the main problem is the lack of coherence between wages and productivity, with the former kept too high by national agreements and by the large size of public employment (Aquino 1999, Sinn-Westerman 2001). This position is held by the vast majority of public bodies and international agencies and by the Italian Board of Industry (Confindustria). Indeed the debate on this aspect has always been very lively.

Another distinguishing feature of this approach is that it advocates more territorial mobility. Many believe that migration away from the Mezzogiorno should be facilitated, well above the level that migration flows have already reached. A single measure – geographically differentiated wages, with lower wages in the South – might engender both migrations and local development.

Facilitating outward migration flows is not the same as promoting development. Indeed these measures seem apt for reducing national unemployment rather than for promoting autonomous development in the South. On the one hand, migration may deprive the South of human capital; on the other, pushing wages further down – whatever the effect on employment – may not lead to higher productivity, a necessary condition for setting up an autonomous development process. A policy aiming directly at increasing productivity is to be preferred on this ground (Cella 1999).

The second approach is also critical to the centralistic policies of the past but does not share the idea that free markets are the best medicine for the Mezzogiorno. Public intervention is deemed necessary even though it is to be different from the past and must conform itself to the dictates of the so-called bottom up approach. More specifically, a lot of room is given to the idea of local development and a lot of emphasis is put on the role that an often neglected input can play in the development process: social capital. It is argued that by giving more power to local governments it is posibile to avoid the policy mistakes due to lack of information and to partial knowledge of local resources. Therefore the crucial role of policy is to promote accumulation of social capital (indeed not an easy task) and to favour circulation of information and knowledge.[26]

This approach is well funded but, as with any other type of policy, cannot automatically solve every problem. In particular, there is no guarantee that by giving more power to local governments the evil of collusion will be defeated. There are neither theoretical nor historical reasons for being sure that this will happen. Moreover, the content of the adopted policy is no less important than the subjects empowered to choose them. The reference here is to the consolidation problem mentioned before: is local government able to take the best measures to this end?[27]

If priority is given to collusion the interpretation of bottom up policies may be very different. They could amount to the provision of automatic and anonymous incentives with no discretional power on the part of the policy makers wherever they are. Here the idea is that the state has to bridge the negative differential in profitability as evaluated by single entrepeneurs. Nothing else is required, neither social capital nor knowledge diffusion. Automatic incentives (introduced in Italy by a quite successful law after the shutting down of the Cassa per il Mezzogiorno) are viewed as the best solution to collusion and corruption.

As these sketchy considerations show it is not easy to find a solution that tackles every issue in the best manner. As in many other instances one size does not fit all and we are forced to choose among imperfect alternatives. In this respect a better knowledge of the "costs" of each policy in terms of other foregone objectives is of paramount importance. To this end a well balanced evaluation of the past experiences may be of great help as well as a deeper understanding of the situation as it has been shaped by the developments already occurred in the past.

## Conclusions

The policies adopted in Italy for the development of the Mezzogiorno from 1950 to the mid-1990s are nowadays the object of harsh criticism. They are seen as the epitome of the worst type of top down policies – useless for everybody except the unscrupulous policy makers and bureaucrats who designed and managed them.

There is much truth in this statement, but the most interesting part of the story lies where the statement is untrue. There have been periods in which the blamed policies have worked well. They were part of a coherent design which was produced and managed by some enlightened bureaucrats that were not members of the unscrupulous lot referred to above – very often depicted as the only one in the town.

The quality of the ruling class – both at central and local level – is a decisive variable for development to succeed. The past experience brings this out very clearly. When collusion and corruption made their appearance, there was no chance for enlightened social calculus to drive development in the South.

The development that has already taken place – also thanks to successful past policies – sets a new framework for today's policies. Consolidation, rather than starting up, is the problem in most areas and this is a too-often neglected feature of the Mezzogiorno. Had the process started in the 1950s and 1960s not been suddenly interrupted by the 1973-74 oil crisis, the ongoing development might have gained momentum becoming stronger and more widespread.

This type of assessment – the validity of which is as limited as that of any counterfactual assessment – focuses our attention on what has been missing so far in the Mezzogiorno: a strong enough set of linkages that help spread the development process. It is not easy to say how they could be strengthened and it is also likely that the attempts to overcome the obstacles to the consolidation process will engender political resistance by all those (outside the South but also within the South) who could be hurt from them. Here lies the less comfortable lesson from the past and the most difficult challenge for the policies to come.

## Notes

[1] The Mezzogiorno consists of 8 regions: Abruzzo, Molise, Campania, Basilicata, Puglia, Calabria, Sicilia and Sardegna. About 21 million people live there, that is more than 36 per cent of the whole population of Italy.

[2] This small difference is entirely due to the 2001 performance because, the average growth rates were exactly the same in the 1996-2000 period (Svimez 2001).

[3] According to more recent estimates, the figure for 2001 has risen to 57.3 per cent (Svimez 2002, tab. 3).

[4] The low level of the employment rate is particularly worrying in the light of the 70 per cent target to be reached by 2010 according to European Union intentions.

[5] Most of the jobs recently created in the Mezzogiorno, especially in the 1996-2000 period, are termporary. This is a general tendency in Italy, due to the introduction of more flexible contracts in the labour market. In relative terms this tendency has been weaker in the Mezzogiorno (Svimez 2001, p. 43). The greater flexibility in the labour market has also markedly increased the elasticity of employment with respect to GDP, making employment much more responsive to the economic cycle.

[6] It was 31.4% lower than in the North-West and around 19% lower than in the North-East and in the Centre (Istat 2002, p. 68). This negative differential is larger in firms with less than 20 employees.

[7] Abruzzo is ahead of two Central regions like Umbria and Marche.

[8] On this aspect see Imbriani's paper in this volume.

[9] The most recent data released by Istat refer to 1999 and are very close to Svimez. Istat set the country avearge 15.1 per cent. On the contrary, OECD estimates are higher (OECD 2000, p. 129).

[10] Those were mostly the years of the so-called "Italian economic miracle".

[11] For a more detailed view on migration away from Mezzogiorno see Bevilacqua (1997).
[12] Of course migration has also influenced employment and unemployment figures, which have fluctuated in the period too.
[13] Only in Germany are there stronger migration flows than in Italy.
[14] In general, several regions in the North have a very strong capacity to attract workers, stronger than Ireland, according to some estimates (Svimez 2002). Here is more proof of the extremely dualistic nature of the Italian economy.
[15] Some researchers have addressed the issue, often offering interesting analyses. Cfr. Mutti (1994), Piattoni (1999). A fully convincing explanation, however, is very hard to find.
[16] On the new course see the essay by F. Barca in this volume.
[17] Actually the experience of extraordinary intervention was not totally new in Italy. During the fascist years extensive recourse was made to them but also in earlier periods this practice had been used (Barone 1996, p. 227).
[18] Among them the most prominent figures were the then Governor of the Bank of Italy, Donato Menichella and Francesco Giordani a scientist who was alternate of the Italian executive director at the IBRD. A few years earlier, in 1946, on the initiative of those same managers and of the northern socialist Industry Secretary, Rodolfo Morandi, The Association for the Development of the Mezzogiorno (Svimez) was created. This too was a sign of the new attention paid to the Mezzogiorno by enlightened technocrats very often coming from the North.
[19] According to Podbielski the Cassa quite evenly spent more than 0.75 per cent of Italian GDP between 1951 and 1970 while in the 1971-1975 period the figure jumped well above 1 per cent (Podbielski 1978, Tab. 5).
[20] It is worth remembering that in Italy liberalism and state intervention had already been blended in a singular way. Albert Hirschman, then an economist at the Federal Reserve, in 1948 annotated his surprise in witnessing how the economic policy of such a staunch liberal as Einaudi (on outstanding economist who was Budget Secretary in 1947 and was elected president of the Italian Republic in 1948) had led to greater, not lesser control of the economy by the government (D'Antone 1996, p. 52).
[21] The debate on the "wage cages" was very harsh. Vera Lutz (1962) in the 1960s was strongly in favour of them, even if she seemed to have some doubts when she realized that migration was also a consequence of the cages and that very often the living conditions of the migrants in the North were really hard.
[22] However, according to accurate estimates, they represented no more than 25 per cent of the whole area (Bodo-Viesti, 1997).
[23] It is estimated that the share of employees in the public sector rose from 14.5 per cent in 1970 to 21.3 per cent in 1989. The corresponding figures for the Centre-North are 13.7% and 17 per cent, respectively (Bodo-Viesti 1997, p. 13).
[24] Some authors refuses to consider this period as characterized by state social support, see Jossa (2001).
[25] One of the most interesting cases is represented by Sardegna, carefully analyzed in Brusco-Paba (1992); for a more detailed discussion of the linkage approach and the disappointing experience of the Mezzogiorno see Franzini (1998).
[26] For a thorough presentation of this approach see Barca's essay in this volume.
[27] A deeper investigation of that problem might also lead to the conclusion that to foster consolidation measures are required that a local government cannot take – i.e. higher coordination may be required also to exploit the advantages of strategic complementarities.

# References

Aquino, A. (1999), 'I termini essenziali del problema Mezzogiorno', in A. Giannola (ed), *Mezzogiorno tra stato e mercato*, Il Mulino, Bologna.

Barone, G. (1996), 'La Cassa e la "ricostruzione" del territorio meridionale', in L. D'Antone (ed), *Radici storiche e esperienza dell'intervento straordinario nel Mezzogiorno*, Bibliopolis, Napoli.

Bevilacqua, P. (1997), *Breve storia dell'Italia meridionale dall'Ottocento a oggi*, Donzelli, Roma.

Bianchi, P. (2002), *La rincorsa frenata. L'industria italiana dall'unità nazionale all'unificazione europea*, Il Mulino, Bologna.

Bodo, G. and Viesti, G. (1997), *La grande svolta. Il Mezzogiorno nell'Italia degli anni novanta*, Donzelli, Roma.

Brusco, S. and Paba, S. (1992), 'Connessioni, competenze e capacità concorrenziale dell'industria in Sardegna', in M. D'Antonio (ed), *Il Mezzogiorno. Sviluppo o stagnazione?*, Il Mulino, Bologna.

Cella, G. (1999), 'Differenziare i salari: quante volte?' in A. Giannola (ed), *Mezzogiorno tra stato e mercato*, Il Mulino, Bologna.

Centorrino, M. and Ofria, F. (2001), *L'impatto criminale sulla produttività del settore privato dell'economia. Un'analisi regionale*, Giuffrè, Milano.

Ciriaci, D. (2001), 'Convergenza e dualismo: Nord e Sud tra il 1970 e il 1999', *Rivista Economica del Mezzogiorno*, XV, pp. 763-802.

D'Antone, L. (1996), 'L'interesse straordinario per il Mezzogiorno (1943-1960)', in L. D'Antone (ed), *Radici storiche e esperienza dell'intervento straordinario nel Mezzogiorno*, Bibliopolis, Napoli.

Eckaus, R.S. (1961), 'The North-South Differential in Italian Economic Development', *Journal of Economic History*, XXI, pp. 285-317.

Faini, R. (1983), 'Cumulative process of de-industrialisation in an open region. The case of Southern Italy, 1951-1973', *Journal of Development Economics*, n.3, pp.277-301

Franzini, M. (1998), 'Il consolidamento dello sviluppo come problema teorico. Argomenti per la 'nuova programmazione' nel Mezzogiorno', *Rivista Economica del Mezzogiorno*, n. 3, pp. 565-584.

Giannola, A. and A. Del Monte (1997), *Istituzioni economiche e Mezzogiorno. Analisi e politiche di sviluppo*, La Nuova Italia Scientifica.

Helg, R., Peri, G. and Viesti, G. (2000), 'Abruzzo and Sicily: Catching up and lagging behind', *EIB papers*, vol. 5, n. 1 pp. 61-88.

Hirschman, A.O. (1948), 'Inflation and Deflation in Italy', *American Economic Review* XXVIII, September pp. 598-606.

Hirschman, A.O. (1958), *The Strategy of Economic Development*, New Haven, Yale University Press.

Hirschman, A.O. (1989), 'Linkages', in J. Eatwell, M. Milgate and P. Newman (eds), *The New Palgrave. Economic Development*, Macmillan, London.

Istat (2002), *Rapporto annuale. La situazione del paese nel 2001*, Istat, Roma.

Jossa, B. (2001), 'Il Mezzogiorno e lo sviluppo dall'alto', *Rivista Economica del Mezzogiorno*, XV, pp. 399-420.

Lutz, V. (1962), *Italy. A Study in Economic Development*, Oxford University Press, Oxford.
Mutti, A. (1994), 'Il particolarismo come risorse. Politica ed economia nello sviluppo abruzzese', *Rassegna italiana di Sociologia*, XXXV, n.4 ottobre-dicembre.
OECD (2000), *Economic Surveys –Italy*, OECD, Paris.
Perroux, F. (1955), 'Note sur la notion de poles de croissance', *Economie Applique*, pp. 307-20.
Piacentini, P. and Sulis, G. (2000), 'Crescita virtuosa e crescita neodualistica nell'ambito regionale: tendenze recenti per le aree europee in ritardo di sviluppo', *Rivista Economica del Mezzogiorno*, n.1, pp. 57-98.
Piattoni, S. (1999), 'Politica locale e sviluppo economico nel Mezzogiorno', *Stato e Mercato*, n. 55, aprile.
Podbielski, G. (1978), *Venticinque anni di intervento straordinario nel Mezzogiorno*, Giuffrè, Milano.
Rossi Doria, M. (1982), *Scritti sul Mezzogiorno*, Einaudi, Torino.
Putnam, R.D. (1993), *Making Democracy Work: Civic Tradition in Modern Italy*, Princeton University Press, Princeton.
Roma, G. (2001), *L'economia sommersa*, Laterza, Bari-Roma.
Sinn, H.W. and Westermann, F. (2001), 'Two Mezzogiornos', *National Bureau Economic Research, Working Paper 8215*.
Svimez (2000), *I conti economici delle regioni italiane dal 1970 al 1998*, Il Mulino, Bologna.
Svimez (2001), *Rapporto 2001 sull'economia del Mezzogiorno*, Il Mulino, Bologna.
Svimez (2002), *Rapporto 2002 sull'economia del Mezzogiorno*, Sintesi per la stampa, www.svimez.it
Sylos-Labini, P. (1985), 'L'evoluzione economica del Mezzogiorno negli ultimi trent'anni', *Temi di discussione del Servizio Studi della Banca d'Italia*, n.46, aprile.
Trigilia, C. (1992), *Sviluppo senza autonomia. Effetti perversi delle politiche nel Mezzogiorno*, Il Mulino, Bologna.
Viesti, G. (2000), *Come nascono i distretti indutriali*, Laterza, Bari-Roma.

# Chapter 6

# Rethinking Development Policies in Italy[1]

Fabrizio Barca

**Introduction and Summary**

A shift is called for and is slowly taking place in Europe in development policies for rural and less developed areas. This shift has begun to move away from subsidies and sectoral interventions towards supply-side, area-specific actions – both public investments and institution building – aimed at improving framework conditions and increasing indirectly the productivity of private investments in these areas.[2] These actions can be pooled together under the name of Territorial Competitiveness Policies (TCPs) since their end-result is to increase permanently the competitiveness of less developed areas.[3]

The failure of previous regional policies to reduce development gaps among sub-national areas, the creation of the European Monetary Union, the elimination of the exchange rate among most European countries as a tool to compensate for lower productivity growth, the slow growth of Europe as a whole: all these factors make the move towards TCPs necessary and urgent.

Together with enhancing competition in labour and product markets, TCPs are directed towards improving communications and social infrastructures and at two innovative targets: increasing the externalities of existing entrepreneurial agglomerations; enhancing accessibility to natural and cultural resources. These targets call for both tangible and intangible area-specific projects. These include: improving communication infrastructures in order to increase site accessibility and enhance opportunities for exploiting the local heritage; maintaining natural and cultural sites and diversifying their use; providing public services; educating, training and capacity-building of local actors; building business networks and developing area-linked quality labels; enhancing endogenous innovative initiatives; etc.

All these projects are highly knowledge-intensive. Knowledge is required of: the idiosyncratic features of local heritage, the strengths and weaknesses of human resources, the technologies needed to produce and to adapt local products to consumer trends, the skills and the "animal spirits" of local entrepreneurs, the quality of relations among local actors, the existence of potential leaders, etc. This knowledge tends to be dispersed among several private, largely local, agents. This is the main reason why public action is needed: if the projects are to be designed and implemented, high costs of coordination among many private actors need to be sustained. Furthermore, the State can guarantee credibility in the use of the acquired knowledge for common purposes, while the returns on projects are often public in their nature.

Two problems must be solved before TCPs can be implemented. First, knowledge must be extracted from several local private agents and then combined with global knowledge in order to devise territorial, multi-sectoral integrated projects. The right incentives must then be put into place in order to encourage private agents to reveal knowledge under the expectation that their own well-being will be enhanced. Second, the right incentives must also exist for local governments to perform this policy role properly and so that efficient interaction can take place among different levels of government. To solve these two problems, a territorial governance promoting an adequate mix of Contractualization and Partnership among levels of government must be designed.[4]

This paper outlines some problems and some solutions to this governance issue by reporting on a Territorial competitiveness policy experiment, implementing a European policy for economic development, recently undertaken in the Italian Mezzogiorno.

First, the outlines of the Mezzogiorno policy experiment are presented, together with a brief sketch of the vital statistics of the area and of the European policy framework (section 2). The main novelties of TCPs implemented through the Mezzogiorno Plan are then outlined (section 3) and the governance model which was enacted is presented (section 4). Finally some preliminary conclusions are drawn (section 5).

## The Italian Mezzogiorno and the New Development Plan 2000-2006

Since 1992-93, profound changes have taken place in the Mezzogiorno's economy and society which have created new opportunities for its development. They have followed three concurring events: the end of a 40-year top-down economic policy; a strong tightening of law enforcement; the beginning of a radical devolution of political and administrative power.

After 1995, the turnover rate – birth rate net of death rate – of southern non-agricultural enterprises started rising and became higher than in the Centre-North (3.2 percent against 2.5 percent in the year 2000). An increase in the competitiveness of the Mezzogiorno's enterprises has also taken place, as shown by a strong and continuous rise since 1993 both in exports and in the inward flows of foreign tourists (about 10 percent growth a year in real terms). Since 1997, after a long period of stagnation, GDP growth occurred and has risen to an average of about 2-2.5 percent a year. Employment has risen again since the beginning of 1999.

In spite of these new signals, a much higher growth is both warranted by the high unexploited potential of the area and needed in order to avoid the risk of a vicious circle. Following Italy's entry into the European Monetary Union in 1998, a new policy was devised to address the issue. The opportunity to start innovating was offered by the implementation of a new cycle of EU structural policy.

About one third of the EU budget, amounting today to 0.46 per cent of EU GNP, is assigned to the task of increasing "economic and social cohesion". Both public investments and subsidies for new investments and/or jobs can be financed with structural funds, which are allocated among member States according to criteria agreed upon at the beginning of each cycle. 195 billion Euro have been assigned to structural funds, of which 135.9 billion go to regions whose development is "lagging behind" – rather schematically selected as those which had an average per capita income in the years 1994-96 below 75 percent of the EU average (so called Objective 1 regions). The Italian Mezzogiorno was assigned about 22 billion Euro – to be matched by the same amount in national funds; the funds must be spent by the end of year 2008, which explains the decision to refer to the 2000-2008 period. These funds amount to about thirty percent of all public investments and incentives to be spent in the area in this period.

According to EU structural funds regulation it is up to each State to draw up a Plan for the use of these funds. The plan allocates the resources among "targets", allocates the responsibility for managing the resources and selecting projects among the levels of government, establishes the selection criteria and the evaluation and monitoring methods which must be followed, introduces incentives and sanctions, sets administrative reforms and actions that must be enacted, etc. The plan must be approved by the Commission before the spending cycle can start.

The drawing up of the plan provided an opportunity to initiate a new regional policy for the Mezzogiorno. It offered a way to enact at once a completely new set of principles, many of which were indeed coherent with those of the 1999 structural funds reform.[5] Most of all, EU guidance and supervision provided Italy, as had already happened in the case of macroeconomic restructuring, with an external bonding to enact a much-needed internal change.

The task of writing the plan was assumed by the Department of Development and Cohesion Policies (DPS) of the Treasury. Drawing up the Plan took 18 months of technical and political negotiation between the central state, regions, municipalities and social partners. The negotiation itself was a way to experiment and refine a new interactive approach between local and central powers. It was also the way to devise, through a consensus-building process, the governance structure of the Plan, the allocation of responsibilities and the checks and balances on which its success depends. It was approved by the EU in July 2000.

The main decision and rules of the plan can be summarised with reference to five general principles:

*Setting targets and devolving and enhancing responsibilities:* 71.4 percent of funds was allocated to Regions, the rest being assigned to central administrations in charge of law enforcement, nation-wide communications, reduction of school drop-out rate, research and development, allocation of automatic capital incentives Local governments were entrusted with the role and means to devise and submit projects. The allocation of funds among six general targets was determined (see figure 1): 18.8 percent to natural and cultural resources (water infrastructures, natural parks, etc.), 6.0 to cultural resources, 16.7 to human resources (training, R&D, school drop-outs, etc.), 32.9 to local development, both for rural and urban areas (including ten percent for automatic incentives), 4.4 to cities, 19.5 for tangible and intangible communication (including law enforcement), 1.9 for technical assistance to the managing authorities. While resources assigned to central administrations were set for specific targets, those transferred to the Regions were not: Regions were asked to negotiate among themselves on how much to allocate to each target so as to comply with the pre-set general target allocation. Because of the radical changes introduced by the Plan and the need to make profound adjustments in public administration entrusted with their implementation, the financial spending scheme was very back-loaded, with only 13 percent of all funds to be spent in the first three (out of nine) years.

**Table 1 – The Mezzogiorno Development Plan: Allocation of financial resources** (total public funds=100)

| Priority axes | Public funds | | | Private funds |
|---|---|---|---|---|
| | Central responsibility | Regional responsibilities | Total | |
| *Natural resources (water, land,...)* | 0 | 18.8 | 18.8 | 5.6 |
| *Cultural resources* | 0 | 6.0 | 6.0 | 0.9 |
| *Human resources:* | | | | |
| - Training and active labour market policies | 0 | 10.7 | 10.7 | 0.9 |
| - Education | 1.8 | 0 | 1.8 | 0 |
| - R&D | 4.2 | 0 | 4.2 | 0.8 |
| *Local development systems* | 10.2[1] | 22.7 | 32.9 | 0 |
| *Cities* | 0 | 4.4 | 4.4 | 0.7 |
| *Communications and networks* | | | | |
| - Tangible and intangible networks | 8.3 | 8.4[2] | 16.7 | 4.7 |
| - Law enforcement | 2.8 | 0 | 2.8 | 0 |
| *Technical assistance* | 1.3 | 0.4 | 1.7 | 0 |
| *Total* | 28.6 | 71.4 | 100 | 13.6 |
| Total *(Euro million)* | 11,400 | 28,500 | 39,900 | 5,400 |
| Performance reserve (10%) | - | - | 4,6 | - |
| **Total funds** *(Euro million)* | 11,400 | 28,500 | 44.500[3] | 5,400 |

(1) Data include resources managed by the Ministry of Industry on behalf of Regions allocated through regional ranking.
(2) Includes some regional measures for law enforcement
(3) The figure is made up of EU resources (Euro 23,8 billion) and national resources (Euro 20,7 billion) according to the additionality principle.
Source: Ministry of the Treasury - Department for Development Policy (DPS)

*Evaluation and administrative modernisation:* the plan was devised – and is making the most of a pioneering experience at the Treasury – to create public investments evaluation and monitoring units in all regional and central administrations, highly integrated with administrative units, so as to offer support and at the same time create the premise for their renewal; a preferential channel was created for projects equipped with feasibility studies and a new generation of such studies was initiated which is presently being implemented; sanction and rewards were designed – to which the allocation of 10 percent of total resources at the end of 2002 is partly linked – in order to accelerate some administrative reforms (the so-called Bassanini laws, named for the Minister who enacted them[6]);

a project financing unit, as in the UK, was established at the Treasury for promoting all public administrations with technical assistance in order to devise investment projects attractive to private capital.

*Incentive and diagnostic monitoring:* quantitative target values were set for macro and micro variables to be used to measure projects' effectiveness; a monitoring system concerning financial and output effects was implemented; use was made of the 10 percent reward resources also to create an incentive for Regions to actually favour truly integrated projects; a diagnostic monitoring system was created so as to provide areas falling-behind with the assistance needed in order to compete with the other areas.

*Institutional and social techno-partnership:* a system of institutional partnership was established through which each Region can cooperate with its local governments and the central administrations, namely the DPS, can cooperate with the Regions; the network of regional and central evaluation units which is being created should provide a solid technical framework for such partnership; the establishing and the current activity of regional monitoring committees comprising representatives of central administrations, municipalities and social partners should strengthen the partnership and open it to social partners.

*Enhancing credibility*: the role of general supervisor for the implementation of all rules was entrusted to one national Authority only, the Treasury Development Department (DPS), directly committed to the European Union via international agreement.

It is too early to assess results. The strong visibility and accountability of EU funds, the chance to make their use conditional on the implementation of a new and binding set of rules and on strong decentralisation of responsibilities, the credibility that all targets derive from being written into the framework of a European international agreement, as was the case for macro-targets through the Maastricht Treaty: these are all reasons why the 2000-2008 plan lends itself to becoming a turning point in the economic policy for the Mezzogiorno. The task, though, is no easy one: to accomplish it, time and political stability are required, while any move in this direction is bound to be resisted by coalitions of all local interests that have traditionally benefited from barriers to competition, subsidies, and the inefficient and unmonitored allocation of public funds.[7]

While the work to implement the plan is proceeding at all levels of governments, the guidelines of the plan, the first steps in its implementation, as well as previous TCPs-like experiences that have took place in the Mezzogiorno during the 1990s, allow to draw some general lessons from the whole experiments, which I will now discuss.

**Territorial competitiveness policy: an outline**

The rationale for TCPs implemented in the Mezzogiorno Plan is that for a given heritage of natural, cultural and human resources and for a given physical agglomeration – or dispersion – of entrepreneurship, the competitiveness of an area, as measured by returns to be expected from local investments, can be strongly influenced by "framework conditions". Six specific factors come to the fore:

- market competition for labour, products and capital;
- tangible and intangible communication with other areas;
- training of human resources and opportunities for innovation;
- social infrastructures;
- internal relations and externalities of entrepreneurs' agglomeration;
- accessibility of natural and cultural resources.

For the quality of all those framework conditions the "institutional capacity" of the area – the efficiency and effectiveness of its public administration, of its judiciary system, etc. – is clearly very relevant.

The first four factors are by now quite well established. Market competition, while putting peripheral areas under stress, is an indispensable requisite for their growth, since it allows the full exploitation of comparative advantages and a proper matching of demand and supply for resources.[8] The same holds for both tangible and intangible communications, once the initial negative impact due to the opening up of alternative supply sources is taken into account. In particular, Internet linkages can now allow remote and small producers to market directly and worldwide to consumers the specific features and producing conditions of their products.[9] Training of human resources and support to innovative action in entrepreneurial activities are both requisites in order for comparative advantages to be fully exploited. As for social infrastructures, the quality of housing, hospitals and schools is very relevant for the choice of location of both managers and workers and for their job satisfaction.

The other two factors deserve closer attention, since they represent the core of the new perspective for regional policies.[10] A way to approach the issue is to start from Krugman's New Economic Geography (NEG). At the cost of some drastic simplifications,[11] NEG has given "macro respectability" and revised long standing ideas of development theory and several schools of thought on economic geography.[12] It links the development opportunities of an area to its ability to attract mobile resources with strong bargaining power (let's say scarce resources): entrepreneurs, capital, skilled labour.

Together with relative prices, NEG emphasizes those cumulative factors of an area that, once set into motion, and together with "given" natural and cultural resources, attract mobile resources and by doing so tend to perpetuate themselves as a reason for the superior profitability of that area. The externalities of agglomerations' are cumulative factors of this kind.

Externalities stem from the size of entrepreneurs' agglomerations. The first relevant factor, as it is well known, concerns the volume of *demand* for consumer goods and intermediate inputs set into motion by the scale of the agglomeration. S*upply* side effects (Marshallian factor) concern *labour pooling, input specialization, technological spill-over* and *knowledge pooling* (as I would call the information sharing that can take place among the agglomeration's entrepreneurs on what public or quasi-public goods would enhance the productivity of their investments).

The role of agglomerations' externalities is shown by the fact that firms operating inside agglomerations have a higher productivity and rate of return than those not operating inside an agglomeration. This result has been recently proved for the Italian industrial sector by a research project carried out at the Bank of Italy.[13]

As a result of the working of the externality effect, initial conditions of an area matter significantly. Whether, as a result of past history or accidental circumstances, an agglomeration comes into existence can indeed set an area on a virtuous path. The same is obviously true for economic policy, which can change those initial conditions.

This is by now well known. But it is also where problems start. What kind of policy is warranted by this line of reasoning?

*The incentive option*

One might be led to think that the safer way to go is for economic policy to devise incentives directed at peripheral areas that can compensate for whatever profit differential they have accumulated relative to areas with strong agglomerations. The idea is to use incentives in order to create *artificial agglomerations*, relying on the fact that, once they are set into motion, agglomerations can become self-sustainable thanks to the externalities they develop, so that incentives can later be removed.

This policy has indeed been and still is often implemented.[14] But that occurs at the cost of severe problems and dubious results. Reasons for these failures are clear-cut. Policies aimed at compensating accumulated disadvantages via incentives and creating artificial agglomerations, are bound to degenerate into rent shifting wars,[15] *with no effect on total welfare*. Furthermore, in this war, unless a financial compensatory mechanism exists, backward areas have a disadvantage since their smaller financial resources reduce the weapons they can use in attempting to shift rents.[16] On the other hand, if central compensation is at work, it is bound to fall under the growing criticism of advanced areas, i.e. its political sustainability will be rather low.

*A fresh perspective*

An alternative emerges when, by drawing from the many insights of pre-NEG theories – those contributions that David (1999) puts together under the label of Old Economic Geography – it becomes clear that neither cultural and natural resources, nor the externalities of agglomerations can be taken as given.

First, natural and cultural heritage, though given in physical terms, is not at all given at any moment as a source of development. The long-term contribution of a "given" natural and cultural heritage to economic development can be strongly increased by projects changing the accessibility of that heritage. The design and implementation of those projects cannot directly depend on the choice of private agents because of the high coordination costs that they would require. The State is precisely the institution to which private agents entrust the task to devise those projects.

Second, for a given agglomeration, externalities can widely vary, depending on institutional factors.

This is first the case of demand externalities. For a given agglomeration, its consumer demand externalities depend on how dispersed residential areas are for workers employed in the agglomeration; this in turn depends on urban planning, cultural factors and other factors linked to the local government's provision of public services.

It is also the case of supply-side externalities. For a given agglomeration, supply-side externalities depend on whether market and informal relations exist among entrepreneurs making up the agglomeration, whether they purchase inputs from each other, exchange or share clients, exchange information on practices and technology, pool labour in order to improve matching between demand and supply, share business services. For the success of the agglomeration, it is also very relevant whether entrepreneurs pool together their knowledge in order to ascertain the needs of the area for infrastructure and immaterial public investments (in training, research, networks) and in order to devise projects to submit to the local governments. The relational capital of an area is then a crucial factor for externalities to come about.

Physical proximity certainly enhances the "economic proximity" necessary for bringing about input specialization, labour pooling, technological spill-over and knowledge pooling; but it does not necessarily imply it. Formal and informal relations necessary for economic proximity to occur strongly depend on past history. A strong path dependency exists, since initiating up of formal and informal relations is costly. But at any point in time appropriate institutional arrangements implemented by local governments can foster the establishment of such relations.

The Italian Mezzogiorno provides good examples of how both natural and cultural resources and agglomerations' externalities can be under-exploited and how much room for development exists in their greater exploitation.[17]

Protected natural areas represent seven percent of the Mezzogiorno, the same share as in Central and Northern Italy. They include vast and uncontaminated territories, home to many rare plant and animal species as well as archaeological sites dating back to Greek colonization, and cultivated slopes on the fertile volcanic soil of Etna. In spite of this variety, the number of visitors per hectare of land is one third that of the Centre-North. Archaeological sites cover 1,400 hectares, compared to 1,000 in the Centre-North; but only 38 percent of these areas are open to the public, often only very partially. On a composite index of tourist attractions, the Mezzogiorno scores 36 against 32 for the whole of the Centre-North. But natural and cultural sites are often locked, inaccessible or understaffed; marketing is inadequate, failing to implement proper strategies; opportunities to develop manufacturing – traditional crafts as well as sophisticated software products offering virtual reconstruction of sites – and agro-industrial productions linked to those sites (as could be done for a wine or any other product whose production dates back to the original inhabitants of the site) are rarely exploited. There are 62 tourists per 100 inhabitants in the South against 163 in the Centre-North.

Firms and agglomerations in the Mezzogiorno are also not exploited to their full potential. Entrepreneurs fail in their propensity to build a strong network of formal and informal relations within the agglomerations. Firms in the Mezzogiorno's agglomerations buy less from each other than in the Centre-North, and prefer to deal with firms outside the agglomerations, while subcontractors have less diversification of clients;[18] firms also fail to co-operate in setting up common high-quality services, in creating risk-sharing institutions that allow for lower credit costs, in lobbying together for specific improvements in their business environment. The reason for this differing behaviour largely lies – as interviews show[19] – in the lack of trust relations inside the clusters.

## An alternative: providing welfare-enhancing public goods

A clear policy conclusion emerges which is of general interest. Competitiveness of a peripheral territory can be enhanced by providing public goods in the form of comprehensive public investment packages – a mix of infrastructures for communication, for social purposes and for the use of natural resources, local heritage preservation and enhancement, training, R&D, etc. – and institution building specifically designed to reap the opportunities of that territory.

In order to make natural and cultural resources fully accessible, public investments must be realised to protect natural areas, to restore archaeological and historical sites and monuments, but also to improve transport communication to these sites, to establish attractive museums, to set aside areas and provide light infrastructure so as to allow the development of appropriate hospitality services for all types of tourism, but also to promote or to revive sustainable and environment-friendly agricultural productions (or to introduce new ones) suited for the climate and the cultural and public image of the territory and to market them through virtual networks.

More in general, existing agglomerations – or would-be agglomerations, comprising entrepreneurs and agents with specific skills and knowledge who share similar technologies or products – must be empowered with the requisites to develop co-operation and to pool their knowledge together. Policies aimed at this target include:

(a) modernisation of local administrations, with the introduction of accountable procedures for the selection of local projects, so as to create an incentive for firms in the agglomerations to pool their knowledge together and to lobby transparently by means of local associations to enact public projects which enhance their profitability (as is the case in the Mezzogiorno Plan of setting

reward criteria for integrated projects complying with given requisites; or of creating regional evaluation units);
(b) institution building, whereby private and public local actors are encouraged to come together and to contribute to the design of projects (as is the case in the Mezzogiorno Plan of only partly successful territorial pacts);
(c) strategic integrated planning in urban and rural areas (as is being experimented in the Mezzogiorno);
(d) promotion of knowledge networks and innovation capacities, making full use of new information technologies, offering high-quality small firms operating in the agglomeration the opportunity to market the "diversity" of their products with distant consumers;
(e) enhancing business services affecting externalities.

The TCPs described, if successfully implemented, are welfare-increasing and can command a consensus much greater than traditional policies aimed at subsiding peripheral areas. Incentive policies are openly aimed at reallocating firms from one territory to another: insofar as they produce additional externalities via "artificially" increasing the scale of a given agglomeration, they are at the same time reducing the externalities of another agglomeration. By shifting externalities from one territory to another they tend not to produce any improvement in general welfare. Welfare can actually be reduced if some of the negative effects of incentive policies were to apply. A very different situation holds true for TCPs: state intervention is aimed at turning potential externalities in effective ones, with no "artificial" reallocation taking place. Capital and entrepreneurs will move only if truly superior opportunities arise; general welfare will thus be increased.

There is obviously no guarantee that TCPs will succeed. They are indeed complex and knowledge intensive. They require strong discretionality by the State both in order to assess which specific interventions are more suitable to any agglomeration and to implement them. The high discretionality and high knowledge content of TCPs suggest that much care should be put into their institutional design. I will now discuss this issue.

*Governance*

In order to draw up the institutional framework most suitable for devising and implementing TCPs, the following six features deriving from the targets of TCPs can be pinpointed. Three of them concern the type of knowledge that is needed to carry out the policy; three others refer to the requirements of public administrations devising and implementing it.

*A knowledge based policy*

TCPs are strongly *knowledge based*: knowledge is largely held by private agents; public agents must extract this knowledge, combine it and use it in order to devise and implement projects.

General knowledge is needed (new technologies, information on international opportunities, quantitative, well established methods for evaluation), but the distinctive feature of TCPs is the need for *local knowledge* (about agglomerations' boundaries, failures of its relational features, existence of unused resources, etc.). Local knowledge is particularly necessary for any local project to be properly devised and implemented: as pointed out by Cheshire and Magrini (1999), only local coalitions have the knowledge to devise agglomeration-enhancing projects, and the incentive to actually reveal information – each member of the coalition to the others – to be pooled together in the project.

Since knowledge is *scattered* among many local and central agents the necessity arises for *knowledge pooling* to take place, both horizontally, at local level, between different branches of the administration, and vertically, between local and central agents.

TCPs are nothing but essential functions of the State – mostly in its "minimal" version – that are to be aimed at specific territories: education, providing for public services, institution building, urban planning, market regulation, planning (non necessarily financing) of infrastructure: TCPs attempt to solve failures of the state.

Since TCPs projects are complex and of a highly integrated, multisectorial nature, high reliance is needed on *ex ante evaluation*, to be performed via feasibility studies: public administration is asked to act as project allocator, largely relying on the market to perform these studies, but endowed with the in-house capacity to allocate, to monitor and to make use of these studies.

Finally, public administration and the State must be *highly credible* in devising and enacting policy and in performing the functions sub d) and e).

In order to draw the consequences from these six features suggesting what form and governance be devised, let's start from the classical issue of whether TCPs should be run by local or central governments. These are two very strong arguments for the devolution.

## Local vs. central

First, only local governments have the knowledge to pool together local coalitions of private agents capable of devising projects, to monitor their work in progress, and to enact the institution building activities than can increase the economic vicinity of an agglomeration.[20] Projects supervised by the European Investment Bank show that the very lack of responsibility or competence by local authorities in pooling local knowledge and interests and in designing appropriate negotiating procedures among different private interests is often responsible for project failures.[21]

Second, better monitoring can be performed by local political markets on the project achievement record of local governments: the incentive of local governments to act properly can be increased by territorial competition among different administrations. Furthermore, adjustments of projects to unforeseen contingencies can be devised and implemented by local governments in a more timely fashion.

On the other hand, three classical arguments call into question the efficiency of a significant devolution of power in devising and enacting TCPs.

First, some externalities can fall, as suggested, beyond the limits of administrative boundaries, making a co-operation among local governments necessary.[22] Secondly, some interventions of TCPs can still degenerate into rent-shifting wars:[23] this could be the case of several territories all investing in the development of similar niche-products exceeding existing demand, or in the direct transport communication between local and global markets. Finally, renegotiation of allocation rules can more easily take place at a local level between local government and local private agents: the monitoring of the political market could be too slow to prevent it.

A solution to these trade offs between devolution and centralization may be found by choosing an appropriate allocation of responsibilities.

*Local* cum *central*

Central responsibility will then be retained only in those areas of TCPs where strong indivisibility or wide externalities exist (mainly, local to global communication). Otherwise, all TCPs aimed at devising territorial projects for increasing accessibility to natural and cultural resources and for increasing relational capital inside agglomerations should be devolved: local governments will then be responsible for promoting, selecting and managing projects and for co-operating with other local governments whenever they perceive that the appropriate area of intervention exceeds administrative boundaries. This is the rationale behind the choices made in the Mezzogiorno Plan.

As in the Plan, central administrations will focus their role on rule-setting, monitoring and providing technical assistance. General guidelines and rules will regulate the allocation of resources and guarantee a proper project cycle. Diagnostic monitoring will be aimed at assessing performance while policy is being enacted and at detecting those circumstances where local governments fail to cooperate in projects which exceed their administrative boundaries. Technical assistance will be provided for local governments so as to improve the quality of the project cycle, namely of evaluation and feasibility studies, and to ensure that project competition among local governments for the allocation of resources does not damage more backward areas where leadership and administrative capacity are weaker.

This general solution needs first to be adjusted to take into account the fact that there are general more than two levels of government involved in devising and enacting regional policies. A four level government – federal, state, regional, local – is a better representation of the present state of affairs in most areas of the industrialized world. It certainly fits the Italian case, where the traditional central State (57 million inhabitants) is currently shifting an increasing share of responsibilities to the European Commission in Brussels, while at the same time a process of devolution is taking place from the Italian State to 21 Regions – with an average of less than 3 million inhabitants (ranging from 118.000 to 9 million) – and from Regions to local governments – 103 countries with an average of the half million inhabitants and about 8000 municipalities.

The allocation of responsibilities among levels of government adopted in the 2000-2008 Plan implementing TCPs in the Mezzogiorno can then be taken as a useful point of reference. The "division of labour" is as follows:

- counties and municipalities – which can be identified as truly local authorities – have been assigned the task of pooling together local actors and devising and elaborating local projects: drawing from various experiences of local projects planned in the 1990s by coalitions of private and public agents (Territorial Pacts, Local Action Groups for rural projects and Urban and Territorial Projects[24]), counties and municipalities can perform this task by forming horizontal coalitions which pool together administrative areas with similar opportunities;
- regions have been assigned the responsibility of managing about three fourths of all Plans' resources by selecting projects submitted by local governments and promoting some top-down interventions: regions have primary responsibilities in monitoring on both financial and economic results;
- the central State, as well as being assigned the responsibilities of managing funds to improve law and order, national communication, research and development and to reduce school drop out rates, has been entrusted with the three above-mentioned central responsibilities: guidelines and rules; diagnostic monitoring; technical assistance. All these co-ordinating functions are performed by a single Department at the Ministry of the Treasury.

The European Commission, by performing autonomous diagnostic monitoring, plays the role of guaranteeing the full compliance of all rules set by the central State in accordance with EU Regulations: it then gives credibility to the whole process.

For such a clear yet complex division of administrative tasks to be operational and efficient, governance must include a well-defined contractualization of relations among different levels of government.

*Contractualization and ...*

If one was to take the traditional principal-agent paradigm to describe the relation among different level of governments, one would say that each level acts both as a "principal" delegating functions to a lower level, which thus behaves as "agent", and as an "agent" receiving delegations from an upper level, which thus acts as "principal". To create the right set of incentives, delegation of tasks must then be accompanied by targeting them, monitoring their outcome and linking to them sanctions and rewards. This system also allows the political market to focus on the tasks of their appointed governments and on those of public managers and to demand results from them.

The institutional framework that arises so far is reminiscent of New Public Management (NPM), a system of public management that has been increasingly experimented in several industrial countries.[25] A similar contractualization is called for in ruling horizontal relations across agencies at each level of government: devising multi-sectoral projects requires different sectoral branches to make clear-cut commitments to each other. NPM represent a significant step forward in the implementation of TCPs especially for countries where the accountability of regional policies has long been extremely inadequate. But this can hardly be the whole story.[26]

In the many countries (mostly Anglo-Saxon) where NPM has been more widely experimented, it has become clear that a full contractualization of relations between different levels of government or among branches of the same level cannot suffice. Conceptualization and execution of policies cannot be fully separated, making the very principal-agent paradigm inadequate; targets cannot be completely verified, while general targets can highly bias local governments' actions. Both horizontal and vertical cross-cutting are necessary. These concerns are particularly relevant in the case of TCPs, where local knowledge plays such an extensive role.

Each level of government has some of the knowledge needed for enacting general guidelines, but much of it is "tacit", in the sense that it cannot be transferred via formal procedures but only via informal interaction with other levels of government. Local governments, in order to design local objectives, to select projects and to perform diagnostic monitoring need general guidelines handed down from the higher levels and information about how other local actors have been, and are currently, acting. At the same time, the central government cannot ex ante establish fully defined and verifiable targets without the local knowledge specific to each territory that alone can turn those targets into proper incentives. Let's consider the second issue in more detail.

If the centre insists in specifying targets in detail, serious biases can be introduced and local authorities will be induced to satisfy those targets even at the cost of reducing the effectiveness of the actions. On the other hand, a very general specification of targets will run the risk of losing any binding power.

Take the example from the Mezzogiorno Plan of targeting by the state level the establishment by regional governments of Evaluation Units with the mission of carrying out the ex-ante evaluation of projects, to monitor the execution of such studies by outsourced private consultants and to become part of a federate evaluation network (this is indeed one of the targets of the Italian 2000-2008 Plan).[27] If a detailed description of the tasks of such Units, of their required skills and methods, of their organizational setting, were to be carried out by the central government, one would run the risk of overseeing the specific requirements of each regional government. In order to comply with the target, wrong choices would very likely be made. Very general targets, on the contrary, run the risk of not guaranteeing minimum quality requirements necessary for promoting a sound basis for project selection. Similar problems concern, at each level of government, the relations among specific sectoral agencies. Contractualization is necessary, but account must be taken of the fact that both horizontal and vertical "contracts" are bound to be largely incomplete, i.e. to contain provisos that cannot be specified in a way that can be fully verified by third parties.[28] While the governance of TCPs should aim to contractualize the delegation of responsibilities as far as is reasonably possible, it should also aim to manage contract incompleteness. A complementary governance tool is clearly called for.

*... partnership*

Contract incompleteness can be managed in two complementary ways: by setting targets in a way that takes incompleteness into account, i.e. by treating them as open-ended duties to be clarified along the way; and by setting up a flexible system of partnership, both horizontal and vertical, among government agencies that allows for the case-by-case clarification of the meaning of those duties through a continuous exchange of information and knowledge.

While contractualization of relations among different levels of government (via targeting, incentives and monitoring) is necessary, these relations must then be governed by a partnership network that allows these "incomplete contracts" to be completed via technical co-operation. Targeting can become more effective and biases can be avoided. Take the previous example of Evaluation units. One can now be content with a very general target of "establishing evaluation units of high quality, with the task of assessing feasibilily studies": the implementation of this target can now be promoted, monitored and assisted by a partnership technical unit, made up of representatives of both regional and central governments (this is again the solution adopted in the Italian 2000-2008 Plan).[29]

Institutional partnership must be both horizontal and vertical. Different sectorial branches of government, both at the central and local level, will then co-operate in devising ex-ante evaluations needed to assess the feasibility of integrated projects. Together with this horizontal partnership, vertical partnership will be established among different levels of governments: to establish and monitor targets (and, by doing so, give meaning to them), to develop standards and methods for evaluation of local projects, to monitor major feasibility studies, to implement projects and devise compensatory mechanisms for the differentiated impact on local interests.

A similar kind of partnership, based on knowledge pooling, is required in the relationship between public and private agents.

As has been made clear, a great deal of knowledge is unavailable to public agents; only private agents, whether local or external to the area, whether holding specific local interests – entrepreneurs, rent-holders, workers, citizens, unemployed, etc. – or acting as professional consultants, are often privy to it. Inside knowledge of this kind can only be "produced" and made available for devising territorial projects via interactions among many of these agents, all (or most of all) opportunistically motivated by their private interest. For such knowledge pooling to occur, local governments need to make a relevant and preliminary part of their TPCs the establishment of technical partnership with some or most of these agents, taken either individually or via their coalitions or associations.[30] As the Mezzogiorno experiment once again shows, this is a very delicate part of the whole strategy. Local private agents behave in an opportunistic way and they individually favour direct, exclusive relations with local governments, in the pursuit of the highest return; this attitude goes strictly against the implementation of knowledge-pooling, which is the main requirement of good projects. Furthermore, private agents tend to be particularly resilient in cooperating in backward areas where this behaviour has not yet been seen as a catalyst for growth. Nor can the problem be circumvented, as it is often believed, by relying on the knowledge of private consultants. First of all, they themselves can only design good projects if, together with some crucial general knowledge, they pool together the knowledge of several local actors. Secondly, they have an incentive to do so only if the local government has the skill to ask the consultants the right questions and to monitor their work closely.

Several TCPs-like experiences in the 1990s and the first steps of the 2000-2008 Plan offer some food for thoughts in this field.

## Local partnership: learning from experience

### Partner selection

A reduction in the (perceived) likelihood of including in the process knowledgeable agents increases the chance that all private agents will reveal their knowledge and that good projects will be designed. Local governance can help in these directions by setting up a competitive-enough process through which participants get "selected" to sit at the partnership table. Results from the Mezzogiorno experience of "territorial pacts"[31] show that a correlation exists between the success of public action and the openness of partnership (DPS, 2001).

Access must not be restricted to members of well-established associations of interests, always to be challenged by new-comers and representatives of less established interest groups. The latter might well have an incentive greater than average in using partnership in order to advance their weaker position.

As for the associations themselves – whether business or union or class action groups – their members will have a greater chance to improve their well being the more their representative at the table is concerned with members' interests rather than only the interests of his own group, as association bureaucrats. Competitive selection of association managers therefore becomes crucial. Failures of many experiences in the Italian Mezzogiorno depend on the complete lack of such a competitive selection.

### Timing and deadlines

A tendency might arise in partnership – once repeated interaction is allowed for, as is often the case – to dilute negotiation and to postpone decisions about whether to reveal knowledge or not, every partner waiting for the other partners to make the first step. Local governance can improve results by fixing deadlines and attaching costs to any time-delay, such as the reduction of financial resources made available by the regional or national government. The Mezzogiorno experience has shown that the success of territorial pacts was basically brought to a halt between 1996 and 1999 by the lack of central government credibility in setting deadlines. As soon as credibility was somehow restored (see section 5) most existing pacts became operational. Drawing from these lessons, a substantial reserve premium linked to targets and deadlines was introduced on a major scale for the implementation of EU regional policy (see again section 5).

*Accountability and uniqueness*

A strong incentive for local agents to take partnership seriously and to reveal knowledge comes from their firm conviction believing that no alternative ways will be provided by the State to design and select local projects.

Local governance of partnership can strongly enhance chances of success by increasing negotiation's visibility and accountability and making a strong commitment to the uniqueness of that negotiation. Drawing from the experience of the 1994-99 territorial pacts, the implementation of EU-financed local integrated projects in the new 2000-2006 programming cycle has increased accountability and the credibility of uniqueness.

*Project evaluation*

For local partnership to work, agents must truly believe that only good projects will be selected, i.e. that governments – regional governments in the Mezzogiorno case – which have the responsibility of selecting among projects submitted by several local governments, make use of well-established evaluation procedures. The very recent experience of an integrated territorial project being implemented in the Italian Mezzogiorno provides a set of clear-cut principles to follow. Local governance of partnership should be accompanied by an appropriate mix of contracts and partnership between the local and the regional government. Clear-cut criteria will have to be announced *ex-ante* by the regional government as far as concerns the selection of local projects. At the same time, the regional government will have to work in co-operation with local governments in order to continuously and transparently adjust and finalise those criteria.

*Cross-cutting among professional skills*

Finally, the Mezzogiorno experience shows that the success of local partnership depends on whether local governments command skills as diverse as those commanded by urban planners, scientists, economists, sociologists and lawyers (to mention only the main ones). A network of evaluation units composed of assorted skills is presently being set up in all Regions of the Italian Mezzogiorno (DPS, 2001). These criteria represent principles of good practice in partnership, which are both horizontal and vertical, as well as social and institutional. Whether this good practice is implemented or not will largely depend on local governments. The quality of public administration in emphasized once again in the implementation of TCPs.

**Preliminary conclusions**

The success of the criteria presented in section 5 very much depends, as the Mezzogiorno experience from which they are largely derived shows, on the existence and efficacy of a super-game capable to enhance the credibility of those criteria. In the Italian case, the super-game works as follows. The Italian Treasury-DPS has set the rules, monitors them and cooperates with the Regions in adjusting, interpreting and putting into practice those very rules. In doing so, a risk of undue renegotiation – rather than due interpretation – arises, which could threaten the whole scheme. In preventing this degeneration, and enhancing the credibility of the rules, the European Commission plays a very important role, but if it were to interpret this role too rigidly and were to try to enforce the "strictest interpretation of rules", it would also threaten the scheme. (A complex but indispensable interaction requiring trust between several layers of government is called for). The future of the Mezzogiorno experiment largely depends on this interaction.

For now, it is safe to note that a change is indeed taking place within most of the regional administrations entrusted with the enactment of the Plan, while central administrations appear to be much more resilient. Important changes are also taking place in the project cycle which lies behind the design of TCPs, with hundreds of studies proposed by local authorities (and financed by the Regions) being presently carried out to test the feasibility of territorial projects. While the participation in the process of local "leaders" has often been the driving force behind the proposal of territorial projects, and the mayors of small municipalities have often played a very relevant role, associations of either union, business or citizens interests have not yet proved adequate to the new phase.

It is therefore appropriate to refrain from drawing any final conclusions from the experiment. Some very general guidelines, though, can be inferred which could be of some use for other countries where some areas lag behind, and where unexploited natural and cultural resources, as well as physical agglomerations of entrepreneurial capacities lacking relational capital, exist. First, rather than attempting to create new agglomerations in selected areas and making use of incentives to influence firms' location – with a high risk of starting rent-shifting wars – a better course of action is very often that of pinpointing existing, although weak, agglomerations and enhancing their relational capital and framework conditions. Second, for this target to be pursued, substantial funds should be allocated to territorial policies, shifting them away from traditional sectoral interventions. Integrated, knowledge-intensive, area-specific projects should be the aim. Local, often largely unexploited, heritage of natural and cultural resources generally provides the best focal point for these projects. Third, local governments – municipalities, counties, self-organised coalitions of municipalities – are best suited to design these projects and carry out their feasibility checks. Regional governments should retain the power to select project proposals submitted by local governments and to allocate resources to them. A higher level of government is probably best suited to set the general guidelines, pinpoint the main targets (and possibly allocate funds among them) and conduct a diagnostic monitoring of the whole process. Fourth, the criteria for project selection should be known in advance so as to create a strong incentive for local governments to implement good partnership and to extract knowledge from local private actors. A governance system must be established that makes those criteria truly accountable and that allows no undue renegotiation to take place. At the same time there should be a continuous process of adjustment of criteria and rules on the basis of what all levels of government learn by implementing the policy. Fifth, for local partnership to be successful, several factors must be carefully dealt with: opening the selection of partners to less established associations of interests; setting credible deadlines that cannot be renegotiated; guaranteeing the uniqueness of the partnership table; implementing evaluation procedures; and combining different professional skills. Sixth and last, in order to put good partnership into place, to supervise the design of projects by private consultants, and to assess them, local, regional and super-regional governments need to have in-house evaluation capacity. The quality of the public administration is the indispensable tool of Territorial Competitiveness Policies.

## Notes

[1] The paper is drawn with minor adaptations from a paper called 'Rethinking Partnership in Development Policies: Lessons from a European Policy Experiment' presented at the conference 'Exploring Policy Options for a New Rural America' (Kansas City 30 April 1 May 2001) published by the Center for the Study of Rural America (2001), which I thank for kind permission.
[2] See OECD (1996), Pezzini (2001), Barca (2000) and the forthcoming OECD Territorial Review on Italy.
[3] For the expression see Cheshire, Magrini (1999).
[4] On the theoretical underpinning see Dorf, Sabel (1998).
[5] That was not the case for the move away from sectoral policies – which is part of TCPs. In spite of some announcements (see European Commission (1999)), a strong segmentation into sectoral policies and structural funds' sub-funds – Social Fund, Agricultural Guidance and Guarantee Fund, Regional Development Fund, Financial Instruments for Fisheries Guidance – have been retained by the EU reform.
[6] See Bassanini (2000).
[7] On this and on some countervailing factors, see again Barca (2001).
[8] See for a classical reference Krugman (1991).
[9] See for example Friedman (2001).
[10] For a full presentation of this view, see Barca (2000).
[11] See David (1999).
[12] See Krugman (1995) for a survey. See also Brusco (1975) and Becattini (1979) for the Italian contributions on the Marshallian concept of industrial districts.
[13] See Signorini (2000).

[14] See Puga (1998) and Cheshire, Magrini (1999).
[15] See Puga (1998) and Cheshire, Magrini (1999).
[16] See Puga (1998).
[17] For a presentation of these features and the policy that was drawn from them, see Barca (2001).
[18] See Mazzola, Asmundo (1999) and Omiccioli (2000).
[19] See again Mazzola, Asmundo (1999).
[20] See Trigilia (1999).
[21] See Rossert (2000).
[22] See Puga (1998).
[23] See David (1984, 1999), Markusen (1995) and Puga (1998).
[24] For a survey see Ministero Lavori Pubblici (2001).
[25] See O'Donnel, Sabel (2000).
[26] See O'Donnel, Sabel (2000) and Dente (1999).
[27] Together with 19 more targets to which the allocation to Regions of 10 percent of all resources of the plan has been linked. See European Commission (2000), Anselmo, Raimondo (2000).
[28] For a definition of "incomplete contracts" see Hart (1989) and Barca (1998).
[29] See again European Commission (2000) and Anselmo, Raimondo (2000).
[30] See on that Isham, Deepa, Lant (1995) and Stiglitz (1998).
[31] In territorial pacts public financing is provided both for incentives and for public investments to coalitions of both local governments and private actors which submit local integrated projects (including both private investments and infrastructure). For a critical assessment of this experience see the forthcoming special issue of the journal *Stato e Mercato*, winter 2001.

## References

Anselmo, I. and Raimondo, L. (2000), I criteri di premialità nel QCS 2000-2006, mimeo, (presented at the Fourth European Conference for the Evaluation of Structural Funds, Edinburgh, 18-19 September).

Barca, F. (1998), "Some Views on US Corporate Governance", in Columbia Business Law Review, n. 1.

Barca, F. and Pellegrini, G. (2000), "Politiche per la competitività territoriale in Europa: note sul Programma 2000-2006 per il Mezzogiorno d'Italia", presented at the First Annual Workshop of the Bologna University Centre at Buenos Aires, 26-27 April.

Barca, F. (2001), "New trends and policy shift in the Italian Mezzogiorno", in Daedalus, forthcoming.

Bassanini, F. (2001), "Italie, notre révolution silencieuse", in Fauroux R., Spitz B., Notre État, Paris, Robert Laffont.

Becattini, G. (1979), "Dal 'settore industriale' al 'distretto industriale'. Alcune considerazioni sull'unità di indagine dell'economia industriale", in Rivista di Economia e politica industriale.

Brusco, S. (1975), "Organizzazione del lavoro e decentramento produttivo nel settore metalmeccanico", in Flm di Bergamo (a cura di), Sindacato e piccola impresa, reprinted in Brusco, S. (1989).

Centre for the Study of Rural America (2000), Beyond Agriculture: New Polices for Rural America, Federal Reserve Bank of Kansas City, act.

Cheshire, P. and Magrini, S. (1999), "Evidence on the Impact of Territorial Competitive Policy and the Role of Transaction Costs in Conditioning Collective (In)action", Research Papers in Environmental and Spatial Analysis, n. 57, London School.

David, P. (1984), "The Economics of Locational Tournaments", Silicon Valley Research Project Discussion Paper, Stanford University.

David, P. (1999), "Krugman's Economic Geography of Development: NEGS, POGS and Naked Models in Space", International Regional Science Review, n. 22.

Dente, B. (1999), In un diverso Stato, Bologna, Il Mulino.

Dorf, M.C. and Sabel C.F. (1998), "A Constitution of Democratic Experimentalism", in Columbia Law Review, n. 2, March.

European Commission (1999), The Structural funds and their coordination with the Cohesion fund – Guidelines for programmes in the period 2000-2006, Communication of the Commission, July.

European Commission (2000), Community Support Framework for Objective 1 Italian Regions 2000-2006, August.

Friedman, T. (2001), "For the Villages, Global Good Sense", in International Herald Tribune, March 20.

Hart, O. (1993), "An Economist's Perspective on the Theory of the Firm", in Columbia Law Review, vol. 89, n. 7.

Krugman, P. (1991), Geography and Trade, London, MIT Press.

Krugman, P. (1995), Development, Geography and Economic Theory, London, MIT Press.

Isham, I., Deepa, N. and Lant, P. (1995), "Does Participation Improve Performance? Establishing Causality with Subjective Data", in World Bank Economic Review.

Markusen, A. (1995), "Interaction between Regional and Industrial Policies: Evidence from Four Countries", in Proceeding of the World Bank Annual Conference on Development Economics, World Bank.

Mazzola, F. and Asmundo, A. (1999), "Sistemi locali manifatturieri in Sicilia. Analisi dei potenziali distretti industriali", in Quaderni di ricerca, Banco di Sicilia.

Ministero dei Lavori Pubblici, Di.Co.Ter. (2001), Le domande di territorio – otto confronti per l'innovazione, presented at the Conferenza Nazionale del Territorio, Genova, February.

Ministero del Tesoro, del Bilancio e della P.E. – DPS (2000), Quadro Comunitario di Sostegno per le Regioni Italiane dell'Obiettivo 1 2000-2006, August.

O'Donnell, R. and Sabel, C.F. (2000), "Democratic Experimentalism: What to Do about Wicked Problems after Whitehall", mimeo, presented to the OECD Conference, Revolution and Globalization Implication for Local Decision-makers, Glasgow, February.

OECD (1996), Ireland: Local Partnership and Social Innovation, Territorial Development Report, Paris.

Omiccioli, M. (2000), L'organizzazione dell'attività produttiva nei distretti industriali, in Signorini LF. (2000).

Pezzini, M. (2001), "Rural Policy Lessons from OECD Countries", in International Regional Science Review, 24,1, January.

Puga, D. (1998) European Regional Policy in Light of Recent Location Theories, mimeo, November.

Rossert, B. (2000), "Contributing to Regional Development through Project Selection", in Cahiers Papers, v. 5, n. 1.

Signorini, L.F. (2000), Lo sviluppo locale, Roma, Donzelli.

Trigilia, C. (1999), "Capitale sociale e sviluppo locale", in Meridiana, n. 3.

UK Cabinet Office-PIU (2000), Improving Whitehall's Management of Cross-cutting Policies and Services, February.

# Chapter 7

# Evolution of Production Structure in the Italian Regions

Carlo Andrea Bollino
Marcello Signorelli

## Introduction

A new approach to planning in Italy centres on the idea of decentralizing of development policies. Local policies are conceived as coordinated actions aimed at enhancing the potential of specific factor endowment and, more in general, at raising the competition potential of local areas. This is called the "New Planning" or "*Nuova Programmazione*" (see *Ministero del Tesoro* 1999 and Barca F. – Pellegrini G. 2000).[1] Examples of this new approach were the "*patti territoriali*", "*contratti d'area*" and "*accordi di programma*" promoted between central and regional administrations, which called for increasing attention towards related aspects of the spatial dimension of the economy, including economic-productive issues, social environment problems, adequacy of capital endowment (public and private), environmental sustainability and others. The common strategy of the "New Planning" is to promote the attractiveness of local areas, to raise the potential value of (idle) local resources, to avoid migration of skilled labor, thus preventing resource-impoverishment growth.

The purported merit of this approach is threefold: from an institutional viewpoint, it satisfies a subsidiarity principle of closing the gap between public decision-making and democratic control; from an economic viewpoint, it opens the way to positive externalities, thus raising efficiency potentials of policy actions; from a social viewpoint, it allows for greater partnership (or "concertation") among local players, which is usually considered a positive benefit in its own right. The institutional partnership is considered a key element of this new approach and involves four levels (EU, national, regional and local). Regions are responsible for selection of (regional) priorities and projects; national administration has the power to define general objectives and to guarantee the observation of the rules; local authorities are involved in the presentation and management of projects; the EU approves the regional development plan and distribution of structural funds.

In an attempt to provide a quantitative methodological basis for the analysis of local policy, in this paper we focus on the issue of modeling the production side of the regional economy, using policy instruments to perform an ex-ante evaluation of the potential effects of policy actions.

We focus on two related aspects of policy. The first deals with evaluating the additivity of different elementary measures: we consider that only with an adequate model is it possible to evaluate the combined effect of different elementary measures, for mere inspection of partial elasticity may be misleading if measures have cross-combined effects, i.e. if there exists partial weakening or partial reinforcement of combined measures. Our simulations show that combinations of elementary measures are non linear, and that employment-increasing measures are typically sub-additive, when combined with other instruments.

The second issue is related to the existence of spill-over between areas: elementary measures in one local area may have an adverse or beneficial effect in a contiguous area and this is obviously even more crucial when assessing regional policies rather than diffuse and pervasive macro-policies. Our simulations show that spill-over effects exist between Italian regions.

Although aware of the limits of this approach, in the spirit of the "Lucas critique", we do not use this argument as a pretext for departing completely from historical and statistical evidence.

The paper has the following structure. In Section 2 the main regional gaps are highlighted, using different indicators and a comparative approach. Section 3 presents a theoretical model of a dynamic explanation of production decisions, entailing a production function, factor demand functions, investment; econometric results are given for four macro-regions: the northwest (NW), northeast (NE), centre (C) and south (S). We also present some new evidence on the existence of spatial spill-overs between Italian macro-regions. In Section 4, the institutions are considered as a particular and complex factor of production affecting (regional) production structures and employment performance. In particular, we analyse the main characteristics and changes in the Italian institutional system in the last 30 years, using a comparative approach. In Section 5, the results of Sections 3 and 4 are used to produce a quantitative assessment of the employment impact of different regional policies for the period 2000-2006, with simulations under simple and composite scenarios. Section 6 contains the main conclusions and policy suggestions.

## Some evidence of regional gaps

The main motivation for our analysis is obviously the persistence of regional gaps and especially the unsatisfactory employment performance of Italian macro-regions. The average growth rate of GDP in the period 1970-1995 was 2.7% for Italy and 2.2% for the NW,[2] 3.2% for the NE, 2.9% for C, and 2.7% for S. The gap in per capita GDP between south (S) and centre-north (CN) was steady over the entire period. In 1995, per capita GDP in S was 65.8% that of Italy. The equipment fixed investment average growth rate in the period 1970-1995 was 3.6% for Italy and 3.7% for NW, 3.9% for NE, 5.2% for C, and 2.0% for S. The final consumption average growth rate in the period 1970-1995 was 3.0% for Italy and

2.7% for NW, 3.1% for NE, 2.9% for C, and 3.2% for S. Recent new data for the period 1996-1998 issued by Istat and the preliminary estimate for 1999 released by SVIMEZ (2000) confirms that the south is lagging behind. On average, the growth rate in the nineties was higher in northern regions than the south. Centre and northern GDP grew by an average of 1.4% in the period 1992-1998 and by 0.4% in the south. As a consequence, the income gap increased further: the southern GDP was 58% of that of CN in 1992 and 54.6% in 1998. Regional gaps are striking in terms of the industrial manufacturing portion of GDP (in real terms): in 1995 it was 25.6% for Italy, 32.8% in the NW, 29.3% in the NE, 21.3% in C (26.6% in CN) and 16.1% in S. In 1970, the industrial sector was 60% in the CN, but only 10% in the S. Deindustrialization has only occurred in the N and concurrent industrialisation in the S has not been strong, despite the fact that the investment/value added ratio was higher in the S at the beginning of the period: in 1970 this ratio was 12% in CN and 15% in S. In 1995, the order was reversed being 16.5% in S and 18.2% in CN. As a consequence of the higher investment ratio, the capital/output ratio was higher in S. In 1995 it was 6.3 against 5.4 in NW, 4.5 in NE and 4.1 in C. Considering machinery only, the capital/output ratio was higher in CN than in S. This has two explanations: a lower share of manufacturing activities and a higher share of public infrastructure investment in S.

**Table 1 – Employment, unemployment and net job creation (1977-1996)**

|  | ER 1977 | UR 1977 | NJC 1977-83 | ER 1983 | UR 1983 | NJC 1983-93 | ER 1993 | UR 1993 | NJC 1993-96 | ER 1996 | UR 1996 | NJC 1977-96 |
|---|---|---|---|---|---|---|---|---|---|---|---|---|
| Northwest | 58.8 | 4.9 | -1.1 | 57.7 | 7.2 | -0.8 | 56.9 | 8.3 | -0.3 | 56.6 | 8.9 | -2.2 |
| Northeast | 59.1 | 4.6 | -1.0 | 58.1 | 7.6 | +1.2 | 59.3 | 6.9 | +0.3 | 59.6 | 6.9 | +0.5 |
| Centre | 53.8 | 7.5 | +0.2 | 54.0 | 9.0 | -0.4 | 53.6 | 12.0 | -0.9 | 52.7 | 13.7 | -1.1 |
| South | 49.1 | 9.8 | -0.9 | 48.2 | 13.6 | -5.3 | 42.9 | 23.4 | -2.9 | 40.0 | 28.6 | -9.1 |
| ITALY | 55.7 | 7.2 | -0.7 | 55.0 | 9.3 | -2.3 | 52.7 | 10.6 | -1.4 | 51.3 | 12.0 | -4.4 |
| OECD 18 | 66.3 | 4.4 | -0.2 | 66.1 | 8.0 | +0.8 | 66.9 | 9.3 | +1.0 | 67.9 | 8.5 | +1.6 |

*Legend:*
ER (Employment Rate) = Total Employment x 100 / working-age population (15-64 years).
UR (Unemployment Rate) = Total Unemployment x 100 / Labour Force.
NJC (Net Job Creation) = ER (year t) – ER (year m < t).
OECD 18 = Australia, Austria, Belgium, Canada, Denmark, Finland, France, Germany (West Germany before 1990), Japan, Netherlands, New Zealand, Norway, Portugal, Spain, Sweden, Switzerland, U.K. and U.S.A.

*Source:* OECD – Employment Outlook, 1997. The data for the Italian macro-regions are based on the database CNR-FGB-ISTAT 1, considering the age 15-64.

As well-known, the Italian economy was behind other developed countries in employment indicators, with remarkable regional differences (Table 1). In 1996 employment rate was 51.3% (against an average of 67.9% in the 18 OECD countries) and unemployment rate was 12.0% (against an average of 8.5%). Net job creation in the period 1977-1996 was –4.4 (against an average of +1.6 in the 18 OECD countries). Among "G7 countries", Italy and Japan are in last and first position for employment performance (Graph 1 and Tables A1-A2 in Appendix B).[3] With regard to Italian macro-regions, the south showed an extremely low employment rate (40.0% of the working-age population 15-64 years, in 1996), increasing unemployment rate (9.8% in 1977 to 28.6% in 1996) and remarkably negative net job creation (-9.1% in 1977-1996). In 2000 (April) the employment rate (calculated on overall population) was 43.4% in NE, 41.8% in NW, 38.4% in C and 28.5% in S. Unemployment rate was 4.2% in NE, 5.5% in NW, 8.8% in C and 21.0% in S. "Irregular" employment was around 18% in CN and 34% in the south.[4]

Comparing the performance of the Italian macro-regions with the average of the 18 OECD countries we see that (1) employment and net job creation are significantly lower than the OECD average in all regions and (2) unemployment is lower in the northeast, similar in the northwest, higher in the centre and much higher in the south.

Hence, the above economic and employment indicators show that the Italian economy is characterised by remarkable and persistent regional differences. In particular, the gap in employment performance between the south and the other regions is large and it is huge compared to the main developed countries.

## Regional differences in production functions

To highlight technology parameter differences across Italian regions, we used a four-factor (KLEM) production function, where output is identified as "extended value added", constructed as the sum of value added produced and total imports (of energy and raw materials, as well as other imports of semi-finished and finished products). The main characteristics of the model are quite simple: in the short period enterprises distinguish between variable factors of production and quasi-fixed factors of production (that are typically not minimising costs, due to the existence of adjustment costs). In this context, the functional characterisation of the technology in equilibrium in the short period is given by a restricted profit function or a restricted cost function (McFadden 1978); the existence of adjustment costs adds realism to the empirical analysis of relevant factor demand elasticities; investment is determined by partial adjustment to desired capital stock. The model is presented formally in the Appendix.

Operationally, the system is constituted by variable factor demand equations, optimal capital stock and investment equations, as described in appendix A. We applied it to industrial sector data of the Italian economy for the period 1970-1995, divided into the same four regions: northwest, northeast, centre and south. The data is therefore organised as time series of cross section data, for a total of 104 observations (4 regions x 26 years). Three variable factors were considered (employees and self-employed, imports of goods excluding energy, imported energy inputs) and a fixed factor of production (fixed capital). All data, estimation results and tests of specification and significance of the estimated system are presented and discussed in detail in Bollino-Signorelli (2001) and can be summarized as follows. Firstly, regional differences in the technological parameters are statistically significant at 99% confidence level. This is a new (econometric) result in the empirical literature, showing that the productive structure of Italy is different in the various areas. Secondly, tests show that there are not signs of wrong dynamic specification and of structural instability (up to three years, at beginning and end of the sample) at the 99% level. Finally, it is refused the hypothesis of full flexibility of all the productive factors, thus supporting the hypothesis that capital is a quasi-fixed factor, giving meaning to a measure of utilized capacity fluctuations due to the existence of a fixed factor. The $R^2$ and DW tests for the factor demand equations are as follows: labour 0.99 and 2.038; energy 0.94 and 1.727; materials 0.96 and 1.896, showing good performance and no autocorrelation.

**Table 2 – Estimated labour demand elasticities (selected years)**

NORTHWEST

| Year | labour price | Energy price | materials price | output | Capital stock |
|---|---|---|---|---|---|
| 1987 | -0.64 | -2.08 | 0.06 | 0.49 | 0.59 |
| 1990 | -0.68 | -1.59 | 0.87 | 0.49 | 0.62 |
| 1995 | -0.82 | -2.06 | 0.75 | 0.50 | 0.65 |

NORTHEAST

| Year | labour price | Energy price | materials price | output | capital stock |
|---|---|---|---|---|---|
| 1987 | -0.54 | -3.33 | 1.04 | 0.41 | 0.47 |
| 1990 | -0.56 | -3.07 | 1.04 | 0.39 | 0.62 |
| 1995 | -0.69 | -4.28 | 0.89 | 0.43 | 0.84 |

CENTRE

| Year | labour price | Energy price | materials price | output | capital stock |
|---|---|---|---|---|---|
| 1987 | -0.54 | -1.84 | 0.98 | 0.45 | 0.78 |
| 1990 | -0.58 | -1.0 | 1.02 | 0.46 | 0.84 |
| 1995 | -0.63 | -1.77 | 0.91 | 0.46 | 0.96 |

SOUTH

| Year | labour price | energy price | materials price | output | Capital stock |
|---|---|---|---|---|---|
| 1987 | -0.47 | -0.38 | 2.24 | 0.39 | 1.91 |
| 1990 | -0.47 | -0.35 | 2.43 | 0.40 | 1.05 |
| 1995 | -0.50 | -0.33 | 2.01 | 0.51 | 1.24 |

*Source*: Estimates by the Authors

Table 2 shows elasticities of labour demand for selected years. In general, own price elasticities are negative and lower for energy and higher for materials, as expected (Bollino-Signorelli, 2001). Also labour demand elasticities to labour cost are quite well determined, showing inelastic behaviour. Output elasticities generally increase over time, and are definitely less than one for labour and materials throughout the period, but tend to be greather than one for energy at the end of the period. As far as cross elasticities are concerned, there are signs of complementarity between labour and energy, and of substitutability between labour and imported materials, not surprisingly (Bollino-Signorelli, 2001). It is interesting that there are significant differences at regional level: labour own price elasticity has higher absolute value in NW, around 0.6-0.8, and is around 0.5-0.6 in the NE and centre and 0.4 in the south. Labour elasticities to output are higher in the NW and C (around 0.5) and around 0.4 in the NE and S. These elasticities are quite constant in the centre-north regions, but were increasing in the south in the 1990s. Indeed, in 1995 the output elasticity of labour in the south increased to 0.5, thus approaching the average of the other regions.

Changes in the capital stock induce positive increments in labour demand, as expected, and with relatively increasing intensity from north to south. The elasticity is near 0.5 in the northern regions, 0.8-0.9 in the centre and greather than one in the south. This pattern obviously reflects the degree of implicit rationing of capital stock in the short period.

Another interesting feature of the regional factor demand model is the possibility of investigating interactions between areas, i.e. spatial spill-overs. The presence of such interactions enriches the economic interpretation of the model. In the present case, these effects signal the possibility that output growth of an area may be apt to modify the development conditions of an adjoining area. The spatial connection between the regions is modelled through definition of a spatial weights matrix that ranks nearness. In this paper, we approximate the effects of spill-over between regions with the economic weight of a region, measured by output, and the physical proximity, measured by a distance index.

For each region we therefore added a new variable defined as a weighted average of other regions' output, the weights being obtained from distance indices between regions. Adding this variable to the factor demand model was statistically significant, confirming the importance of spill-over effects. The spill-over effects are differentiated on factor demand and across regions and are, as expected, of second order magnitude with respect to output elasticities (Table 3 reports the partial effects on labour demand computed for the year 1995). Recall that an output-augmenting spill-over effect on the production function entails an increase in efficiency and therefore, yields a negative effect on the dual cost function. Hence, a negative effect on factor demand can be interpreted as an increase in efficiency, given the regional level of production.

We find that output spill-over has a negative impact, *ceteris paribus*, on factor demand in the NW and S and a positive effect in the NE and C. In general, the effects on labour demand are greater in absolute size than those on the other two factors (Bollino-Signorelli, 2001). It is also interesting that there are asymmetries between contiguous regions: for instance, the effect of the NE on NW labour demand is about -0.6%, while the reverse effect of the NW on NE labour demand is about 0.13%. This means that an increase in economic activity in the NE has an indirect labour-saving effect on NW productive technology. The same is true between C and S: the spill-over on S labour demand from C is about –0.01%, and the reverse effect of S on C labour demand is 0.04%. Notice that growth in NW, NE and C, yields, *ceteris paribus*, an increase in labour productivity, i.e. a reduction in labour output ratio, in the south.

**Table 3 – Spill-over effects on labour demand – year 1995 (\*) (percentage elasticities)**

Northwest: Spill-over effect from region:

| S | NW | NE | C |
|---|---|---|---|
| -0.044 | 0.00 | -0.62 | -.052 |

Northeast: Spill-over effect from region:

| S | NW | NE | C |
|---|---|---|---|
| 0.005 | 0.13 | 0.00 | 0.006 |

Center: Spill-over effect from region:

| S | NW | NE | C |
|---|---|---|---|
| 0.044 | 0.11 | 0.015 | 0.00 |

South: Spill-over effect from region:

| S | NW | NE | C |
|---|---|---|---|
| 0.00 | -0.22 | -0.034 | -0.012 |

Note: (\*) partial elasticities computed from estimated parameters.
*Source*: Estimates by the Authors

**Institutions as a complex factor of production**

Institutions are considered a particular and complex factor of production affecting (regional) production structure and employment performance.[5] The institutional factors are distinguished in two groups. A first group of factors internal to the industrial relations system [co-operation and participation (+) vs. conflictuality (-); co-ordination of collective wage negotiations or decentralisation of wage negotiations with "price-taker" firms (+) vs. non-co-ordination or decentralisation with "price maker" firms (-); union and employer association membership plus "third actor"[6] role (+/-); effectiveness of the training system (+)]. A second group of factors partly internal and partly external to the industrial relations system [active labour policies (+); labour tax wedge (-); passive labour policies (-); rigidity of labour regulation (-). Starting from the negative institutional factors, we argue that Italy has long been characterised by an anomalous centralised system of normative and wage regulations. Rigid regulation of labour relations was introduced in 1970 (Law 300/70, so-called "workers' statute") and an automatic system of wage adjustments ("*Scala Mobile*") was reformed in 1975. In the 1980s there was remarkable use of certain "passive" labour policies (wage supplementation fund and early retirement). Some rigidities of the normative regulation were reduced in the 1980s (e.g. Law 863/84) and 1990s (e.g. Law 223/91), with a slow introduction of "active" labour policies. The rigid centralised system of definition of wage dynamics was only abolished in 1992. Largely due to union pressure, the "full-time and permanent contract" was the dominant type of contract until recently, with a consequent low diffusion of part-time, temporary contracts and more flexible structure of working-hours.[7] The conflictuality of Italian industrial relations was high from the end of the 1960s to the early 1980s, increasing systemic uncertainty[8] (Signorelli, 1997).

The "dualisms" of the Italian industrial relations system were particularly high in the past decades, with some partial changes. The normative favour (absence of firing risk; lower pensioning-age; long parental leave; etc.) and, in some periods, wage advantages for employees in the public sector were particularly high compared to other countries. The existence of differences between non-exposed sectors (the public sector and many private services) and exposed sectors (mainly the manufacturing sector), as regards the possibility of passing on the prices the higher wage increases, affected the wage bargaining process causing "wage runs". The complex wage negotiation system was substantially simplified in 1993 with the definition of two distinct levels: the sectoral level, co-ordinated at national level using planned inflation, and the firm level, linked to productivity dynamics. The "labour tax wedge" increased significantly in the 1970s and first half of the 1980s: in the 1990s the "total labour cost" for firms was around twice the "take-home pay" of workers. Obviously, this is a strong incentive for "irregular employment". From the demand side, firms can pay the same "net wage" as a regular contract with a saving of 50%.[9] From the supply side, the lack of regular job opportunities induces workers to accept irregular employment proposals.[10]

As for "positive" institutional factors, the degree of industrial relations co-operation at macro-level and participation at micro-level in Italy has been very low compared to most (western) European countries and Japan (the main "institutional" differences between Italy and Japan are presented in Appendix B, Tables A3-A7). Use of co-operative strategies by unions and employers associations increased remarkably in the 1990s with the so-called "concertation", while the degree of worker participation in firm decisions increased but is still very low. In recent years, decentralisation of placement offices and active labour policies have been major positive institutional innovations. Co-ordination and flexibility of wage negotiations were very low, especially in the period of rigid automatic wage adjustment (1975-1992) and many uncoordinated wage negotiation levels (until 1993). The low effectiveness of the vocational training system was partly due to its substantial absence in the bargaining process. Only in the 1990s did the topic of training (on-the-job training; permanent training; etc.) enter in collective negotiation and "concertation". Another important factor of industrial relations structure is related to membership and "third actor" role. The increasing weight of retired members (14.2% in 1981 to 40.7% in 1991) and the substantial absence of unemployed, strongly affected union strategies. On the other side, the major employers association ("*Confindustria*") was dominated by few large firms, especially in some periods, despite the fact that small and medium firms employed over 70% of the total employment. The union and employer associations membership and strategies interacted with a weak "third actor", mainly due to political instability.

In short, in Italy negative institutional factors outnumber positive ones in the last 30 years, with the (partial) exception of the 1990s. Some recent research (Signorelli, 1999 and 2000) highlighted the probable "asymmetrical" causal link between institutions and employment performance. In particular, a "good" institutional system seems to be a necessary but not a sufficient condition for high(er) employment performance, whereas a "bad" institutional system seems to be a sufficient (but not necessary) condition for low(er) employment performance. The "bad" institutional system with anomalous "centralisation" contributed to the persistence and worsening of regional (economic and employment) differences.

In the "New Planning" for southern Italy (*Ministero del Tesoro*, 1999) the institutional framework plays a major new role. Significant involvement of the regional (and local) level favours better selection of priorities ("*Piani Operativi Regionali*"), but the institutional partnership involves four levels (EU, national, regional and local). Regions are responsible for selection of (regional) priorities and projects. The national administration has to define general objectives and to guarantee observation of the rules. Local authorities are involved in the presentation and management of the projects and, finally, the EU approves regional development plans and distributes structural funds.

Moro (2001) argues that because the so-called "fiscal residue" is lower in southern regions than in other EU countries and the rest of Italy, it is useful to diferentiate fiscal incentives at regional level. Moro highlighted the importance of increasing the "fiscal residue" in southern Italy to create (international and internal) fiscal neutrality and to improve the economic and employment performance in the area. The author criticised the use of financial incentives (by the "New Planning") in favour of fiscal incentives. However, regional fiscal incentives are not yet (completely) permitted by European Union regulation.

The result of our analysis is that the (well-known) huge regional gaps in Italian economic and employment performance and (new) evidence of big regional differences in production functions make institutional "decentralisation" a necessary approach. For the implementation of effective institutional reform, based on the subsidiarity principle, there are two major related problems: (i) to identify the optimal size of the region for each (set of) institutional factor(s) and (ii) to consider and internalise (if possible) the (positive and/or negative) externalities due to the existence of regional interactions (spill-over effects).

**The impact of regional policy strategies**

Regional policy strategies were recently designated by the Italian Treasury ("*Programma di Sviluppo del Mezzogiorno 2000-2006*"), including measures to spur employment. Ex-ante evaluation of this policy design, in an attempt to provide a quantitative assessment of the foreseeable impact of the measures on relative factor prices and factor demand, especially labour demand, is interesting.

Before turning to policy assessment, we briefly assess the dynamic tracking performance of the model, simulated from 1972 to 1999, using available historical data.[11] The simulation results for the four regions were aggregated into national variables, in order to compare them with Italian historical data. Tracking performance was satisfactory.[12] Labour demand root mean square error (RMSE) translated into a percentage was about 2.5%, which is quite accurate. In general, the model tracked fluctuations in labour, energy and imports with fairly good precision.[13]

Let us now look at the future period, considering the horizon of the Structural Funds policy 2000-2006. We first simulated a baseline solution, which shares the main assumptions of the baseline adopted by the Treasury in the official planning documents transmitted to the EU for approval (*Ministero del Tesoro*, 1999), for output growth, interest rate and price developments. To study regional differences in response to policies, we simulated some alternative scenarios. A first group of five simple policy measures is given by: (i) a one point reduction in interest rate which enters the user cost of capital, capturing the essence of a monetary stance more favourable to investment growth; (ii) a one point reduction in wage rate, capturing a wage subsidy policy or a reduction in the "labour tax wedge"; (iii) an exogenous 2.5% increase in capital formation, capturing direct government intervention to spur investment via capital subsidy (like the subsidy funds of "*Legge 488*"); (iv) an exogenous 1% increase in output demand, which can be interpreted, given the budget constraint imposed by EMU, either as a balanced reduction in taxation and public expenditure (on non industrial goods) or as structural measure in favour of competitiveness of industrial goods; (v) a generalised 1% reduction in all factor prices, which can be interpreted as an improvement in institutional structure or as a reduction in production costs due to lower taxation on business[14] or as structural policy reforms aimed at enhancing factor flexibility and competitiveness. In order to study differences in regional responses, all shocks are equal across regions, e.g. a 1% reduction in wages is applied equally to all four regions, and so on.

Table 4 shows the effects on labour demand. The result are presented as geometric average period percentage differences in the last year of simulation between scenario and baseline, so they can be interpreted directly as growth rate differences between scenario and baseline. The crucial result is that there are differences in the responses of each variable to the same policy scenario across regions and there are differences in magnitude and direction of responses of each variable to alternative scenarios. Labour demand is more responsive to interest rate in the south than other regions (about 0.6%) but is less responsive to wage (about 0.5% versus 0.7%) as already highlighted in the elasticity analysis. The responses to investment increases are similar in north and south, while it is lowest in centre. As the cumulated exogenous increase in investment is 6%, a labour increase of 3% indicates that the technology improvement is labour-saving. Labour demand is the least responsive to output demand increase in S, and is considerably higher in NW and NE, confirming the ranking established by analysis of partial elasticities. Notice that when all factor prices decrease, mimicking a lower taxation policy, the labour demand response is highest in S (about 1.1%) and lowest in C. These results confirm the intuition that the old fashioned approach to stimulating demand is the least effective way to spur employment in the south. In fact, in this case the imported materials response in the south is almost double (about 0.35%) that in the rest of Italy: demand increase calls for an increase in imported inputs.

The results clearly show that a differential wage subsidy is not an effective policy in the south and that a direct investment policy subsidy does not exert a stronger effect than in the rest of Italy. Moreover, exogenous output demand growth results in a stronger increase in labour demand in regions where unemployment is lower, that is the NW and NE. The only particularly effective differential policy favourable to the south appears to be relaxation of constraints which hamper profitability, i.e. a reduction in all factor costs. Notice that the improvement in institutional structure can be considered as an implicit reduction of all factor costs.

Interest rate reduction has a relatively stronger effect in the S, mainly due to relaxation of bank credit rationing. In order to appreciate the relative effect of the different policies under the alternative scenario, let us consider the relative magnitude involved. The increase in labour demand is 1.08 under the scenario (v) and 0.18 under scenario (iv). Estimated production costs were about 88% of the value of output in 2000. This means that one Euro of public resources devoted to factor price reduction has to be compared with 1.13 Euro (the reciprocal of 0.88) devoted to obtain an output increase. If we assume an aggregate demand multiplier of two (which is obviously not captured in the present analysis of the supply side), this means that a policy of factor price reduction exhibits a relative effectiveness, in terms of employment growth in the south, almost 3.5 times that of a policy of direct public expenditure.[15] In addition, consider that investment is roughly 25% of the value output or 29% as a percentage of the estimated production cost in the year 2000. Thus, an increase in investment subsidy of 2.5% corresponds roughly to a policy of reduction of factor costs of 1%. The relative magnitudes of scenario (iii) and (v) responses are therefore directly comparable. It can be concluded that the relative effectiveness of investment subsidy is around one and a half times.

**Table 4 – Alternative scenario simulations (2000-2006)**

| (average percentage differences: scenario vs. baseline) | | | | | | |
|---|---|---|---|---|---|---|
| | | SO | NW | NE | CE | IT |
| | Scenario | *labour demand L* | | | | |
| (i) | interest rate reduction: -1% | 0.57 | 0.07 | 0.11 | 0.09 | 0.20 |
| (ii) | Wage rate: -1% | 0.53 | 0.82 | 0.67 | 0.60 | 0.68 |
| (iii) | Investment increase: +2.5% | 1.69 | 2.25 | 1.81 | 1.29 | 1.85 |
| (iv) | Output increase: +1% | 0.18 | 0.77 | 0.46 | 0.20 | 0.37 |
| (v) | Factor price reduction -1% | 1.08 | 1.02 | 0.90 | 0.79 | 0.96 |

*Source*: Estimates by the Authors

In order to investigate different set policy measures, we added an adverse interest rate increase of about 2 % to our scenarios, together with (vi) a 0.5% reduction in the wage rate throughout Italy, coupled with a 2.5% reduction in the south, thus implementing a favourable differential of 2% for the south; (vii) a 1% reduction in all factor prices throughout Italy and a further favourable differential of 2% in the south; (viii) a general factor price reduction as in (vii) with a 1% stronger wage reduction in the south (Table 5 shows the results for labour demand).

In the presence of a capital cost increase, investment and optimal capital stock are adversely affected and even substantial wage reduction (scenario vi) is not capable of spurring labour demand and has an adverse composition effect against the south.

This result, in our opinion, highlights the need for differential policies at regional level. The more courageous factor price reduction (scenario vii) brings about a 0.5-0.6% increase in labour demand in all regions. A further favourable wage differential in the south determines labour demand growth in this region considerably above the Italian average. It is important to highlight that combinations of elementary measures are non-linear and, in particular, employment-increasing measures are sub-additive.

**Table 5 – Alternative composite scenario simulations (2000-2006)**

| Composite Scenarios with interest rate increase (+2%) (average percentage differences: scenario vs. baseline) | | | | | |
|---|---|---|---|---|---|
| | S | NW | NE | C | IT |
| Scenario | | labour demand L | | | |
| (vi) wage rate reduction: -0.5% CN and -2.5% S | -0.68 | 0.28 | 0.12 | 0.12 | -0.01 |
| (vii) factor price reduction: -1% CN and -3% S | 0.66 | 0.83 | 0.58 | 0.53 | 0.68 |
| (viii) factor price reduction: -1% CN and -3% S and further wage reduction: -1% S | 1.69 | 0.83 | 0.58 | 0.53 | 0.93 |

Where CN=NW+NE+C

*Source*: Estimates by the Authors

These results show the difficulty of obtaining remarkable effects with simple (and composite) economic measures, suggesting the need for an integrated set of economic and institutional policies if economic competitiveness and employment performance are to increase significantly, especially in the south.

## Conclusions and policy suggestions

Huge regional (economic and employment) gaps and large regional differences in production functions interacted (perversely) with an inadequate and centralised institutional framework, contributing to the persistence and worsening of regional differences in economic competitiveness and employment performance.

In order to assess the main regional differences in production technology, we modeled a system of factor demand: labour, energy and imported materials (as variable factors), conditional to the existence of a quasi-fixed factor, capital stock, and investment, for four Italian regions (northwest, northeast, centre and south). The empirical results showed a meaningful difference in productive technologies at regional level, confirming the existence of quite different factor demand elasticities. In particular, labour price elasticity was higher in the northwest and lower in the south.

Analysis of spatial spill-overs highlighted interactions between the four areas. In particular, the growth in the north and centre yields an increase in labour productivity in the south (i.e. a reduction of labour output ratio), *ceteris paribus*.

Analysis of institutions showed that negative factors have outnumbered positive factors in the last 30 years, with the partial exception of the 1990s. For many years, the institutional framework has been characterised by (1) an anomalous centralised system of laws and wage regulations together with a low degree of co-ordination of wage negotiations, (2) high industrial relations conflictuality and, partly as a consequence, poor co-operation and participation, (3) the prevalence of passive labour policies over active ones, (4) inadequate training investment, (5) a high influence of social actors (union and employers associations) strategies, conditioned by the membership and favoured by a weak role of the "third actor", due to high political instability, (6) a high "labour tax wedge" on regular employment. The bad institutional system with anomalous "centralisation" interacted (perversely) with existing large regional differences, contributing to persistence and worsening of employment performance gaps. Some significant positive institutional changes have been introduced, especially since 1992, but the process of decentralisation and flexibilisation is still incomplete. For a better institutional framework, we suggest (1) improving decentralised negotiations and worker participation (e.g. favouring profit-sharing schemes and permanent training investment), (2) reducing certain rigid aspects of the regulations (e.g. increasing contractual flexibility) and completing the shift from passive to active labour policies, (3) favouring a stronger role of the "third actor", in line with the subsidiarity principle (e.g. reforms for greather political stability and completing the process of political, administrative and fiscal decentralisation), (4) decreasing incentives for irregular employment (e.g. reducing the "labour tax wedge"). However, the asymmetrical effectiveness of the institutional system on (regular) labour demand highlight that a "good" institutional framework is just a necessary (but not sufficient) condition for a high(er) employment performance.

In order to assess the effectiveness of the Italian Government development policy for the south presented to the EU for Structural Funds 2000-2006 and approved by the European Commission, we simulated alternative policy scenarios with the regional model, including a dynamic investment adjustment toward optimal capital stock, for the period 2000-2006. The results showed that alternative policies have different regional impacts: wage reduction, investment subsidy and output demand stimulus are most effective in the north and least effective in the south, whereas cost reduction policies have a higher impact in the south than the rest of Italy. In the south, the most effective policy, in terms of labour demand responses for a given level of public resources, is investment subsidy; lower business taxation is next, exhibiting a relative effectiveness of 2/3 of the former; direct demand stimulus is even less effective, about 1/5 of investment subsidy.

In order to spur employment in the south, it is therefore wise to give high priority to relaxation of capital constraints, especially in terms of public infrastructures. Notice, however, that capital subsidy is relatively less effective (in terms of employment growth) in the south than the north. Unless carefully differentiated by region, such a policy risks to widen rather than close the gap between north and south.

The results of the scenario of business cost reduction show that it is more effective for employment than direct public expenditure and benefits the south relatively more than the north. We consider this result an indication in favour of decentralisation: in fact, a policy aimed at cost reduction leaves more freedom of choice to the enterprise to optimally combine inputs and technology than a constrained subsidy to a specific production factor. Because improvements in the institutional framework can be mainly considered an implicit cost reduction, they would particularly benefit the south.

Notice that our simulations confirmed the existence of spill-over effects among regions and highlighted that combination of elementary measures for increasing employment are sub-additive.

The so-called "New Planning" for southern Italy contains some significant positive changes compared to the past extraordinary intervention. Two major positive novelties of the "*Programma di Sviluppo del Mezzogiorno*" (2000-2006) are that (i) involvement of regional (and local) levels is greather than in the past, and (ii) the main declared final goal is to increase regional productivity and competitiveness. However, the impact of the "New Planning" on employment in the south risks remaining quite low.

Some results of our research suggest increasing the effort to improve systemic flexibility and competitiveness by (i) completing institutional reforms and (ii) reducing taxation. We argue that only an integrated set of institutional and fiscal policies[16] can permit and favour a significant increase in economic and employment performance of the Italian economy together with a reduction in regional differences.

**Notes**

---

[1] For a critical analysis of the so-called "*Nuova Programmazione Economica*", see Moro (2001).
[2] We adopt the following symbols: NW for north-west, NE for north-east, C for centre, S for south, N for the first two regions combined and CN for the first three regions combined.
[3] Comparative analysis of Italian and Japanese labour market performance is given in Genda, Pazienza and Signorelli (2000).

⁴ See FGB (1997).
⁵ A large comparative literature exists on the link between institutions and economic performance (e.g. Tarantelli, 1986; Calmfors – Driffill, 1988; Soskice, 1990; Nickell - Layard, 1997; Signorelli, 2000).
⁶ The "third actor" is composed mainly by the central government, but also by the regional and local administrations.
⁷ See the proposal of Valli (1988) consisting in an integrated system of different types of contracts distinguished by working-hours in order to match the changing supply side need without ignoring the demand side conditions for widespread adoption of different contracts.
⁸ But the remarkable reduction in conflictuality in the 1990s was accompanied by a smaller reduction in its macroeconomic costs, due to the increasing direct effects of strikes on "third subjects" (e.g. strikes in some public services).
⁹ Irregular employment also guarantees the highest degree of "contractual, wage and numerical" flexibility for the firm.
¹⁰ Uncertainties about the future public pension scheme incentives young workers to accept irregular jobs, because the discounted value of the social contributions is quite low.
¹¹ Detailed official regional data is available for the period 1990-1996, some other regional data is available for 1997-98. Complete data is only available at national level for 1999. Some preliminary estimations for the south were released by Svimez (2000).
¹² Simulation statistics (correlation coefficient squared, root mean square error RMSE of historical vs. simulated values, regression coefficient of actual values on predicted ones and U Theil statistics), indicate that the tracking performance of the model is satisfactory. All correlation statistics were generally well above 90%, with particular accuracy shown by the labor demand equation, with correlations in the 98-99% range for all four regions and 99.4% for national aggregate.
¹³ For more information see Bollino (1999) and Bollino – Signorelli (2001).
¹⁴ It would be inappropriate to interpret this scenario as a measure of scale economies, for investment is endogenous and so the capital constraint is changing.
¹⁵ The computation is as follows: the relative response ratio is 1.08 / 0.18 which equals 6; this ratio times 1.13 and divided by 2 yields 3.39.
¹⁶ Notice that higher institutional efficiency and lower taxation both increase the so-called "fiscal residue". For an approach based on this concept, see Moro (2001).

## References

Atella, V. and Quintieri, B. (1995), "The Effect of technical Change in Input Demands in the Italian Manufacturing Industry", Quaderni CEIS, Wormig paper n. 49, Univ Tor Vergata, Roma, Aprile.

Barca, F. and Pellegrini, G. (2000), "Politiche per la Competitività Territoriale in Europa: Note sul Programma 2000-2006 per il Mezzogiorno d'Italia", *Working Paper*.

Bertola, G. and Ichino, A. (1995), "Crossing the River: A Comparative Perspective of Italian Employment Dynamics", in *Economic Policy*, n. 21.

Boarnet, Marlon-G. (1998), "Spillovers and the Locational Effects of Public Infrastructure", *Journal-of-Regional-Science*; 38 (3), August, pages 381-400.

Bollino, C.A. (1998), "Econometric Interpolation of Regional Time Series", *Journal of Applied Statistics*, n.1.

Bollino, C.A. (1999), "Technology and Factor Demand in the Regions of Italy", working-paper presentato al Convegno CNR su "Globalizzazione e Sviluppo Regionale", Perugia, 5-6 Novembre.

Bollino, C.A. and Signorelli, M. (2001), "Regional Differences in Technology, Institutions and the New Regional Policy Strategies in Italy", in *Economia, Società e Istituzioni*, 1.

Calmfors, L. and Driffill, J. (1988), "Bargaining Structure, Corporatism and Macroeconomic Performance", *Economic Policy*, n. 6, pp. 13-47.

Cellini, R. and Scorcu, A.E. (1998), "Aspetti Istituzionali e Crescita delle Regioni Italiane", in B. Quintieri (ed.) *Finanza, Istituzioni e Sviluppo Regionale*, Il Mulino, Bologna.

Ciciotti, E. and Spaziante, A. (eds.) (2000), *Economia, Territorio e Istituzioni. I Nuovi Fattori delle Politiche di Sviluppo Locale*, F. Angeli, Milano.

Diewert, W.E. (1971), "An Application of the Shephard Duality Theorem. A Generalized Leontief Production", *Journal of Political Economy* 79, 481-507.

FGB – Fondazione G. Brodolini (1997), *Labour Market Studies: Italy*, Brussels.

Genda, Y., Pazienza, M.G. and Signorelli, M. (2000), "Labour Market Performance and Job Creation", in A. Boltho, A. Vercelli, H. Yoshikawa (eds.) *Comparing Economic Systems: Italy and Japan*, Palgrave, London and New York.

Giannola, A. (ed.) (2000), *Le Politiche per il Rilancio dello Sviluppo del Mezzogiorno*, Il Mulino, Bologna.

Klein, L. (1960), "Some Theoretical Issues in the Measurement of Capacity", *Econometrica*, 28, 272-286.

Layard, R., Nickell, S. and Jackman, R. (1991), *Unemployment. Macroeconomic Performance and the Labour Market*, Oxford University Press, Oxford.

McFadden, D. (1978), "Cost, Revenue and Profit Functions", in M. Fuss, D. McFadden (eds.), *Production Economics: A Dual Approach to Theory and Applications*, Vol. I, Amsterdam, North Holland, 3-109.

Ministero del Tesoro, Programma di Sviluppo del Mezzogiorno, Roma, 1999, web site: http://www.tesoro.it/web/docu_indici/Area_Politiche_di_Sviluppo/Docu_Area_Politich e_di_Sviluppo.asp

Modigliani, F., Fitoussi, J.P., Moro, B., Snower, D., Solow, R., Steinherr, A. and Sylos, Labini P. (1998), "Manifesto Contro la Disoccupazione nell'Unione Europea", *Moneta e Credito*, September.

Moro, B. (ed.) (1998), *Sviluppo Economico ed Occupazione*, F. Angeli, Milano.

Moro, B. (2001), "Incentivi Fiscali e Politiche di Sviluppo Economico Regionale in Europa", *Moneta e Credito*, n. 3.

Morrison, C. (1985), "Primal and Dual Capacity Utilization: An Application to Productivity Measurement in the US Automobile Industry", *Journal of Business and Economic Statistics*, 3, 312-324.

Morrison, C. (1988), "Quasi-Fixed Inputs in US and Japanese Manufacturing: A Generalized Leontief Restricted Cost Function Approach", *Review of Economics and Statistics*, vol. 70, n. 2, 275-287.

Morrison, C. (1990), "Market Power, Economic Profitability and Productivity Growth Measurement, An Integrated Structural Approach", WP 3355, Cambridge: NBER.

Morrison, C.A. and Schwartz, A. (1996), "State, Infrastructure and Productive Performance", *American Economic Review*, vol 86, no. 5, december, pp. 1095-1111.

Nickell, S. (1999), "Product Markets and Labour Markets", *Labour Economics*, n. 6, pp. 1-20.

Nickell, S. and Layard, R. (1997), "Labour Market Institutions and Economic Performance", Institute of Economics and Statistics, *Working Paper N. 60*, University of Oxford.

OECD (1994), *The OECD Jobs Study: Facts, Analysis and Strategies*, Paris.

OECD (1995), *The OECD Job Study: Implementing the Strategy*, Paris.

OECD (1997), *Labour Force Statistics*, Paris.

OECD (1997), "Recent Labour Market Developments and Prospects", *Employment Outlook*, Paris.
OECD (1997), "Economic Performance and the Structure of Collective Bargaining", *Employment Outlook*, Paris.
Pellegrini, G. (2000), "I Fattori Strutturali dello Sviluppo Locale nelle Recenti Analisi Teoriche ed Empiriche della Crescita", in Ciciotti, E., Spaziante, A. (eds.) *Economia, Territorio e Istituzioni*, F. Angeli, Milano.
Quintieri, B. (ed.) (1998), *Finanza, Istituzioni e Sviluppo Regionale*, Il Mulino, Bologna.
Quintieri, B. and Rosati, F.C. (1991), *Mercato del Lavoro, Disoccupazione e Politiche di Intervento*, F. Angeli, Milano.
Reyneri, E. (1998), "Mercato e Politiche del Lavoro", in Cella and Treu (eds) *Le Nuove Relazioni Industriali*, Il Mulino, Bologna.
Scarpetta, S. (1996), "Assessing the Role of Labour Market Policies and Institutional Settings on Unemployment: A Cross-Country Study", OECD *Economic Studies*, n. 26.
Signorelli, M. (1997), "Uncertainty, Flexibility Gap and Labour Demand in the Italian Economy", *Labour*, 1.
Signorelli, M. (1997), "Industrial Relations Systems and National Employment Performances: Existence and Nature of a Causal Link", working paper presented at the AIEL annual conference, Milan, October.
Signorelli, M. (2000), "Relazioni Industriali e Occupazione in Italia in una Prospettiva Comparata", *Stato e Mercato*, 3.
Signorelli, M. and Vercelli, A. (1994), "Structural Changes in the Post-War Italian Economy", in *Economic Performance: a Look at Austria and Italy*, Boehm B., Punzo, L.F. (eds), Physica-Verlag, Heidelberg.
Solow, R. (1990), *Labour Market as a Social Institution*, Basil Blackwell, Oxford.
Somaini, E. (1998), "Politica Salariale e Politica Economica", in Cella, G. and Treu, T. (eds) *Le Nuove Relazioni Industriali*, Il Mulino, Bologna.
Soskice, D. (1990), "Reinterpreting Corporatism and Explaining Unemployment: Coordinated and Non-Coordinated Market Economies", in Brunetta, R. and Dell'Aringa, C. (eds) *Labour Relations and Economic Performance*, Macmillan, London.
SVIMEZ (2000), "I Conti Economici delle Regioni Italiane dal 1970 al 1998", Bologna, Il Mulino.
Tarantelli, E. (1986), *Economia Politica del Lavoro*, Utet, Torino.

## Appendix A: the Model

Formally, the variable cost function, $cv(w,y,t,k)$, defines the minimal cost to attain a given level of output y, given variable factors prices (w, of dimension n x 1), given the level of quasi-fixed factors (k, of dimensions m x 1) and for given technology (indicated from variable t). Shephard's lemma allows to derive the system of variable factors demand, that is

(1) $\quad x = \partial cv(w,y,t,k)/\partial w$

where x is the vector (of dimension n x 1) of the quantities of variable factors used. Given the conditional demands of variable productive factors, the maximisation of the profit is obtained equating marginal revenue to marginal cost, that is

$$(2) \quad p = -y \, (\partial d(y)/\partial y) + (\partial cv(w,y,t,k)/\partial y) = [1/(1 + e_{py})] \, cm(w,y,t,k)$$

where $d(y)$ is the inverse output demand function facing the firm, $e_{py}$ is elasticity of demand (inverse) and $cm(w,y,t,k)$ indicates the short run marginal cost. The description of the short term position of equilibrium of the enterprise does not preclude analysis of the long term position of the same firm, where long period means that total costs (variable costs, therefore, and costs imputed to quasi-fixed factors) are minimised. For a given level of quasi-fixed factors, the variable cost function is simply the difference between the short period total cost function ($ct(w,r,k,t,y)$) and the cost of the quasi-fixed factors, that is

$$(3) \quad ct(w,r,k,t,y) = cv(w,k,t,y) + r'k$$

where r is the vector (m x 1) of market prices (ex-ante) of the quasi-fixed factors. Evidently, the long run cost function $c(w,r,t,y)$ can be obtained minimising total cost (3) with respect to the quasi-fixed factors, given variable factors and output levels. The first order condition is

$$(4) \quad \partial ct(w,r,k,t,y)/\partial k = \partial cv(w,k,t,y)/\partial k + r = 0$$

or equality between market price r of the fixed factor and its shadow price q, defined as the potential reduction in variable costs consequent to a unit variation in the fixed factor level

$$(5) \quad q = - \partial cv(w,k,t,y)/\partial k > 0$$

If $k = k^*(w,r,t,y)$ is the solution of (4), that is the vector of "optimal" amounts of quasi fixed factors, substituting k in (3) yields the long run cost function

$$(6) \quad ct(w,r,k,t,y) = cv(w,k,t,y) + r'k$$
$$= cv[w,k^*(w,r,t,y),y] + r'k^*(w,r,t,y)$$
$$= c(w,r,t,y)$$

Notice that if constant returns prevail in the long period (and therefore ln $cv(w,k,t,y)$ / ln $y$ + $\iota'$ [ln $cv(w,k,t,y)$] / ln $k$)=1 for an appropriate unitary vector $\iota$) and output price equals marginal cost of production ($p = cv(w,k,t,y) / y$), it is possible to attribute the difference between the value of production and variable costs entirely to the remuneration of quasi-fixed factors

$$(7) \quad q'k = p \, y - cv(w,k,t,y)$$

In particular, if there is only one single quasi-fixed factor (capital stock), its ex-post shadow price q is simply the gross operating margin per unit of capital, i.e. the difference between value added and labour compensations.

Generalising the analysis to non constant returns and/or monopolistic competition cases (Morrison, 1990), we obtain the revenues/costs relationship as a function of the characteristic elasticities:

(8) $\quad py / ct (w,r,k,t,y) = e_{cy} (1 - e_{cK}) / (1 + e_{py})$

where $e_{cy} = \ln c(w,r,t,y) / \ln y$ (the elasticity of long run costs to output) is the reciprocal of scale returns, $e_{ck} = (r - q)' k / c(w,r,k,t,y)$ measures utilized capacity fluctuations derived from the presence of fixed factors, and finally $e_{py}$ (elasticity of inverse demand) measures the dependence of revenues on demand factors. If long run scale returns are constant, then $e_{cy} = 1$. If perfect competition prevails, i.e. $e_{py} = 0$, then (8) reduces to (7), with only one fixed factor.

The empirical application, with only one quasi-fixed factor, entails estimation of a Generalized-Leontief (GL) function due to Diewert (1971) and applied by Morrison (1988), in a regional context by Morrison-Schwartz (1996) and, in the Italian case, among others, by Atella and Quintieri (1995).

GL allows explicit solution for the restricted and unrestricted cost function, unlike the translog, which only allows numerical solution.

The GL with one fixed factor is

(9) $\quad cv(w,k,t,b,y) = y [\alpha_o + \Sigma_i\Sigma_j \alpha_{ij} w_i^{1/2} w_j^{1/2} + \Sigma_i \mu_{it} w_i t^{1/2} + \Sigma_i \mu_{iy} w_i y^{1/2} + \Sigma_i \mu_{ib} w_i b^{1/2}$
$\quad + \Sigma_i w_i (\phi_{tt} t + \phi_{yy} y + \phi_{bb} b + \phi_{ty} t^{1/2} y^{1/2} + \phi_{tb} t^{1/2} b^{1/2} + \phi_{by} b^{1/2} y^{1/2})]$
$\quad + y^{1/2} [\Sigma_i \mu_{ik} w_i k^{1/2} + \Sigma_i w_i (\phi_{tk} t^{1/2} k^{1/2} + \phi_{yk} y^{1/2} k^{1/2} + \phi_{bk} b^{1/2} k^{1/2}] + \Sigma_i w_i \phi_{kk} k$

where t is a time trend that approximates technological progress, b indicates the gross fixed investments that approximate the existence of adjustment costs, and $\alpha$, $\mu$, $\phi$ are technological parameters. Production coefficients of variable factors can immediately be derived from (9), that is

(10) $\quad x_i/y = (\partial cv(w,y,t,b,k)/ \partial w_i) (1/y)$
$\quad = \Sigma_j \alpha_{ij}(w_j/w_i)^{1/2} + \mu_{it} t^{1/2} + \mu_{iy} y^{1/2} + \mu_{ib} b^{1/2} + \phi_{tt} t + \phi_{yy} y + \phi_{bb} b + \phi_{ty} t^{1/2} y^{1/2} + \phi_{tb} t^{1/2} b^{1/2}$
$\quad + \phi_{by} b^{1/2} y^{1/2} + \mu_{ik}(k/y)^{1/2} + \phi_{tk} (tk/y)^{1/2} + \phi_{yk} k^{1/2} + \phi_{bk}(bk/y)^{1/2} + \phi_{kk}(k/y)$

and the envelope condition, that is the condition of equality of market price (ex-ante) of the fixed factor and its shadow price (ex-post)

(11) $\quad r = q \quad = -\partial cv(w,k,t,b,y)/ \partial k$
$\quad = -\{\Sigma_i w_i \phi_{kk} + \frac{1}{2} (y/k)^{1/2} [\Sigma_i \mu_{ik} w_i + \Sigma_i w_i(\phi_{tk} t^{1/2} + \phi_{yk} y^{1/2} + \phi_{bk} b^{1/2})]\}$

Obviously, (9) is homogenous of degree one in variable factors prices and therefore the demand system (10) turns out to be homogenous of degree zero. From (11) it is possible to derive the stationary state and the desired stock of the fixed factor.

Imposing the tangent condition between short and long run cost curves and therefore setting q= r and solving for k yields

(12)   $k = k^*(w,r,t,b,y)$
       $= \{-\frac{1}{2} y^{\frac{1}{2}} [\Sigma_i \mu_{ik} w_i + \Sigma_i w_i (\phi_{tk} t^{\frac{1}{2}} + \phi_{yk} y^{\frac{1}{2}} + \phi_{bk} b^{\frac{1}{2}})] / (r + \Sigma_i w_i \phi_{kk})\}^2$

Notice that (12) is homogenous of degree zero in prices, as required. Moreover, if $\phi_{kk} > 0$, the long run elasticity of capital with respect to $p_k$ is negative and therefore the curvature condition is satisfied. The convexity condition regarding k $((\partial^2 cv(w,k,y) / \partial k^2 > 0)$ is satisfied if the terms $\mu_{ik}$ are not all positive, which would imply a complementary of the fixed factor with respect to all other input.

The dynamics of investment is modelled with a partial adjustment mechanism:

(13)   $I = a + b [\log(K / K^*)]$

## Appendix B: Italy vs. Japan

### Graph A1 – Employment rates (1970-1996)

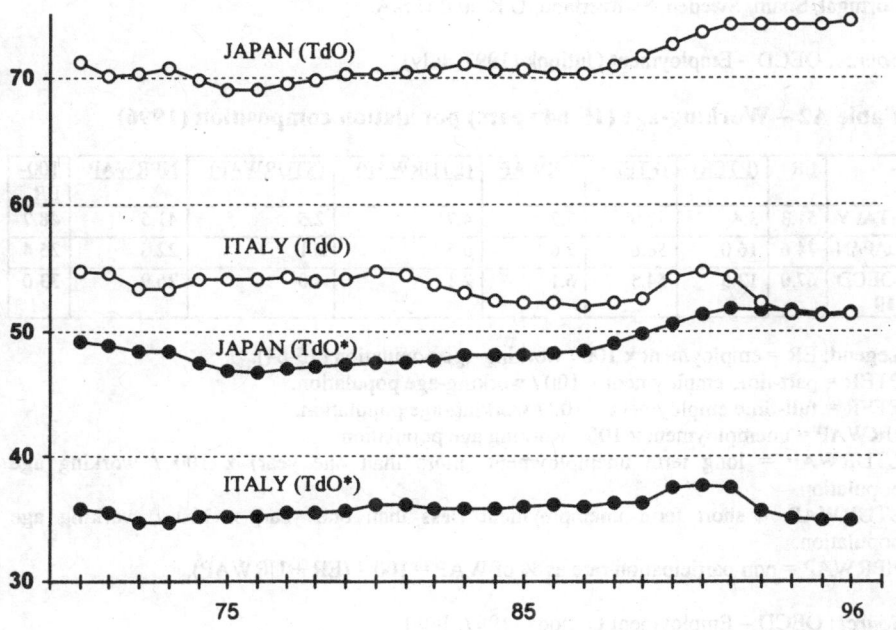

Note: TdO = employment x 100 / working age population (15-64 years)
      TdO* = employment x 100 / population
*Source*: OECD - Labour Force Statistics (1997)

## Table A1 – Dual structure of employment performances (1996)

| | Unemployment Rates (a) | | | | | | | | Employment Rates (b) | | | | | | | |
|---|---|---|---|---|---|---|---|---|---|---|---|---|---|---|---|---|
| | M | W | W-M | 15-24 | 25-54 | 55-64 | Y-A | O-A | M | W | M-W | 15-24 | 25-54 | 55-64 | A-Y | A-O |
| Ita | 9.6 | 16.5 | +6.9 | 34.1 | 9.3 | 4.3 | +24.8 | -5.0 | 66.4 | 36.5 | +29.9 | 25.4 | 65.5 | 27.3 | +40.1 | 38.2 |
| Jap | 3.4 | 3.4 | 0.0 | 6.6 | 2.7 | 4.2 | +3.9 | +1.5 | 88.5 | 60.7 | +27.8 | 45.1 | 79.6 | 63.6 | +34.5 | 16.0 |
| Oecd | 8.0 | 9.7 | +1.7 | 16.3 | 7.5 | 7.3 | +8.8 | -0.2 | 75.7 | 58.2 | +17.5 | 46.5 | 76.7 | 43.8 | +30.2 | 32.9 |

Legend: (a) = total unemployment x 100 / labour force. (b) = total employment x 100 / working-age population (15-64). W = Women. M = Men. Y = Young (15-24). A = Adult (25-54). O = Old (55-64).
19 OECD countries = Australia, Austria, Belgium, Canada, Denmark, Finland, France, Germany (West Germany before 1990), Italy, Japan, Netherlands, New Zealand, Norway, Portugal, Spain, Sweden, Switzerland, U.K. and U.S.A.

*Source*: OECD – Employment Outlook (1997, July)

## Table A2 – Working-age (15-64 years) population composition (1996)

| | ER | (PTER) | (FTER) | URWAP | (LTURWAP) | (STURWAP) | NPRWAP | 100-ER |
|---|---|---|---|---|---|---|---|---|
| ITALY | 51.3 | 3.4 | 47.9 | 7.2 | 4.7 | 2.5 | 41.5 | 48.7 |
| JAPAN | 74.6 | 16.0 | 58.6 | 2.6 | 0.5 | 2.1 | 22.8 | 25.4 |
| OECD 19 | 67.0 | 12.5 | 54.5 | 6.1 | 2.1 | 4.0 | 26.9 | 33.0 |

Legend: ER = employment x 100 / working-age population (15-64).
PTER = part-time employment x 100 / working-age population.
FTER = full-time employment x 100 / working-age population.
URWAP = unemployment x 100 / working age population.
LTURWAP = long term unemployment (more than one year) x 100 / working age population.
STURWAP = short term unemployment (less than one year) x 100 / working age population.
NPRWAP = non participation rate as % of WAP = 100 – (ER + URWAP).

*Source*: OECD – Employment Outlook (1997, July)

## Table A3 – Degree of regulation and active labour policies

|  | EMPLOYMENT PROTECTION (1990) (a) | LABOUR STANDARD (1985-1993) (b) | ACTIVE LABOUR MARKET POLICIES (1991) (c) |
|---|---|---|---|
| ITALY | 20 | 7 | 10.3 |
| JAPAN | 8 | 1 | 4.3 |

*Sources*: (a): OECD Jobs Study (1994), Part II, Table 6.7, Col. 5. Country ranking with 20 as the most strictly regulated.
(b): OECD Employment Outlook (1994), Table 4.8, Col. 6, extended by Nickell – Layard (1997). This is a synthetic index whose maximum value is 10 and refers to labour market standards enforced by legislation on, successively, working time, fixed term contracts, employment protection, minimum wages and employees representation rights. Each of these is scored from 0 (lax or no legislation) to 2 (strict legislation) and the scores are then added up.
(c): OECD Employment Outlook (1995). This variable is current active labour market spending as % of GDP divided by current unemployment. Expenditure on the disabled is excluded.

## Table A4 – Industrial relations conflicts (1986-1995)
(annual average number of working days not worked per 1,000 employees in all industries and services)

|  | 1986-1990 | 1991-1995 | 1986-1995 |
|---|---|---|---|
| ITALY | 315 | 183 | 249 |
| JAPAN | 5 | 3 | 4 |
| OECD 19 | 169 | 87 | 128 |

*Sources*: working days not worked: ILO; employees in employment: OECD

## Table A5 – "Labour tax wedge" structure (1996)

|  | ITALY Single worker | JAPAN single worker | ITALY married with two children | JAPAN married with two children |
|---|---|---|---|---|
| A) Take Home Pay / Total Labour Cost | 49.2 | 80.6 | 56.2 | 84.9 |
| B) Take Home Pay / Gross Earnings | 72.0 | 86.3 | 82.3 | 91.0 |
| C) Gross Earnings / Total Labour Cost | 68.3 | 93.4 | 68.3 | 93.4 |
| D) Average Total Tax Wedge (100 – A) | 50.8 | 19.4 | 43.8 | 15.1 |

*Source*: OECD, The Tax / Benefit Position of Production Workers, Paris (1997)

**Table A6 – Union density and bargaining coverage (%)**

|  | UNION DENSITY | | | BARGAINING COVERAGE | | |
|---|---|---|---|---|---|---|
|  | 1980 | 1990 | 1994 | 1980 | 1990 | 1994 |
| ITALY | 49 | 39 | 39 | 85 | 83 | 82 |
| JAPAN | 31 | 25 | 24 | 28 | 23 | 21 |
| OECD 19 | 46 | 40 | 40 | 71 | 70 | 68 |

*Source*: OECD – Employment Outlook (1997)

**Table A7 – Degree of co-ordination and centralisation of wage negotiations**

|  | DEGREE OF CENTRALISATION OF WAGE NEGOTIATIONS | | | DEGREE OF CO-ORDINATION OF WAGE NEGOTIATIONS | | |
|---|---|---|---|---|---|---|
|  | 1980 | 1990 | 1994 | 1980 | 1990 | 1994 |
| ITALY | 2- | 2- | 2 | 1.5 | 1.5 | 2.5 |
| JAPAN | 1 | 1 | 1 | 3 | 3 | 3 |

Note: A value between 1 (decentralised / uncoordinated) and 3 (centralised / co-ordinated) was assigned for degree of centralisation and co-ordination. The degree of co-ordination includes both union and employer co-ordination.

*Source*: OECD – Employment Outlook (1997)

# Comment

## Micaela Notarangelo and Giovanni Russo

The paper by Bollino and Signorelli is a very interesting one, as it addresses the fundamental issue of Italian macro-economic disparities among macro-regions and the consequences for economic policy, a subject that is often neglected by macroeconomic studies in spite of its capital importance in the Italian context.

The paper begins with a survey of the Italian development in the period between 1970-2000. It is found that between 1970 and 1995 regional inequality, although relevant both in terms of employment and production, remained more or less constant and did not display a visible enlargement of the gap between North and South. However, the gap increased substantially in the following period, i.e. between 1996 and 2000. This result is in line for example with Mauro (2001) who establishes the dualism of the Italian economy according to a variety of concepts (beta and sigma convergence) across different indexes (output per capita, productivity and wages) and using different methods (dynamic panel regression techniques and non-parametric multivariate kernel).

In this sense the new regional approach adopted by policy makers may indeed be good news. However, a regional approach to policy making implies that different policy instruments should be used when intervening in different regions and to this end it is very important to estimate regional production functions to highlight which policy instruments are more powerful in each given region.

The authors consider four production factors: capital, labour, energy, and intermediate goods (also imported) and find that technological parameters are statistically significant across regions (plausibly higher in the North). While the North's technological lead is thus emphasized (technological efficiency), the authors forgo the analysis of the Southern economy from the point of view of *economic efficiency*. Sarno (1999) defines a production process as *efficient in economic sense* (as opposed to technologically efficient) if the input costs associated to a certain level of production are minimum. Using this measure, he shows that the efficiency level in the South is almost equal to the level obtained in the North (although the production costs tend to be higher in the South). Following the same kind of analysis, Destefanis (2001) further finds that much of the differential in the economic growth between the South and the North is due to a lower exploitation of economies of scale in the South, explaining thus the divergence in production costs. Since Bollino and Signorelli reject the hypothesis of constant returns to scale it would be interesting to see whether their results agree with the rest of the literature.

Further in their analysis, the two authors find regional differences in the elasticity of labour demand to the four factors of production. In particular, labour demand in the South results as being quite elastic to variations in the interest rate and almost rigid to variations in the wage rate, while on the contrary, labour demand in the North results as being more responsive to changes in output, that is to say, technological progress turns out to be labour saving throughout. These are very interesting results in their own right. However, it is worth putting them into perspective. In fact, the rigidity of labour demand to the wage rate in the South of Italy may be due to the large share of employment that the public sector holds there. It is well known that public employment does not respond to the market logic and therefore it is not surprising if results obtained imply a lack of influence of the wage on the level of employment. This is in line with Autiero and Mazzotta (2001) who show that the reservation wage of workers in the South tends to be higher than the reservation wage of their colleagues in the North. These authors ascribe the differential to the higher wages paid to civil servants compared to the one received by employees in the private sector.

The paper by Bollino and Signorelli then carries on and touches on the institutional issue. The authors argue that the very centralized Italian wage bargaining setting has contributed to the development and increase of the regional gap. While it is true that Italy has performed worse than the rest of Europe as far as the employment rate and net job creation are concerned, the opposite is true as far as the unemployment rate (especially in the North) is concerned. This means that the same institutional setting that is responsible for the dismal performance of the South in terms of unemployment, is at the same time the agent of a brilliant performance in the North. Therefore it must be reckoned that to dismiss the Italian institutional setting as a 'bad system' altogether tends to overlook its complexity. The problem does not seem to be the level of centralisation of the wage bargaining (Sweden is an example), but rather it seems to be the lack of co-operation (or solidarity) between workers in the North and in the South of the country. The fact that the national wage has been bargained on the basis of the conditions existing in the northern labour market (disregarding the effects on the employment level in the South) may have been the culprit. Golinelli (1998) seems to imply this when he finds the existence of the Phillips relation in the North but not in the South (see also Mauro, 2001).

To conclude, the paper should be commended as it stresses the fact that macroeconomic policy may not have the desired effects when it is designed without considering the large regional differentials existing.

## References

Autiero, G. and Mazzotta, F. (2001), "Job Search Methods: the Choice between the Public and the Private Sector", CELPE Discussion Paper, 58.

Destefanis, S. (2001), "Differenziali territoriali di produttività ed efficienza negli anni '90: i livelli e l'andamento", University of Salerno, CELPE Discussion Paper, 59.

Golinelli, R. (1998), "Fatti stilizzati e metodi econometrici 'moderni': una rivisitazione della curva di Phillips per l'Italia (1951-1996)", *Politica Economica*, n. 3, dicembre.

Mauro, L. (2001), "The macroeconomics of Italy and convergence: an empirical survey", Trieste University, DISES Working Paper, 72.

Sarno, D. (1999), "I differenziali di efficenza economica dell'impresa meridionale", in Giannola, A., *Mezzogiorno tra stato e mercato*, Il Mulino, Bologna.

# PART III
# CORPORATE GOVERNANCE AND INDUSTRIAL ORGANIZATION

# Chapter 8

# Continuity and Change in Italian Corporate Governance: The Institutional Stability of One Variety of Capitalism

Ugo Pagano
Sandro Trento

## Introduction

The crucial economic role of the family has been one of the strongest elements of continuity in the extraordinary changes that have characterized Italian society in the last hundred years. This observation has been largely included in the stereotype of the representative Italian and has not escaped the attention of social scientists concerned with Italian society. For instance, Francis Fukujama (1995) views the central role of the family as a typical feature of "low thrust societies" that are unable to expand the size of their networks and organizations beyond the elementary thrust relations that characterize immediate family relations. In other words, according to Fukujama the limitations of alternative sources of thrust (rather than the relative strength of Italian family networks) explains the intensive adoption of family based organizations. Also Paul Ginsborg (1990) has observed that the relations between family and society are an important key to the understanding of post-war Italian history. However, according to Ginsborg, the intensity of Italian family relations is not to be seen solely as an alternative to more extended thrust relations. While the "familismo amorale" can lead to some disregard for wider social interests, it can also spur family members to undertake collective actions characterized by generous identification with the problems of other families. With reference to the topic of this paper, the importance of the role of the family is also very clear. Italy's form of "family capitalism" is, perhaps, a rather unique case among the industrialised countries where the largest firms are not usually run by family dynasties. It is true that small and medium firms, as well as recently founded large firms, are usually run by families also outside Italy. However, what is peculiar to the Italian system of corporate governance is that in large firms, control is passed more along family lines than through a mechanism of managerial meritocracy. Moreover, Italy is no exception in the sense that most capitalist countries have gone through a phase of family capitalism. However, the Italian experience is again rather different because this phase has never been overcome and no form of "managerial capitalism" has ever evolved. Thus, the question remains why in Italy large organizations have tended to stay under family control and why none of the alternative forms of capitalism has ever emerged. In this respect, the alleged Italian love for family may matter very little.

The structure of this paper is as follows. The first section we will analyze the relationship of Fiat and the Agnelli family. This is more than a case-study because Fiat and Agnelli account for such a disproportionate fraction of Italian capitalism. We will see that the cycle "Giovanni Agnelli (jr.)-Romiti-John Elkan" tends to repeat the earlier cycle "Giovanni Agnelli (sr.)-Valletta-John Elkan". In both cases a direct succession link between grandchildren and grandparents seems to solve some intergenerational tensions between father and children, while in the gap left by the intermediate generation non-family managers tend to acquire an important role. External intervention in the imposition of external managers characterized the second cycle although it was absent in the first. The vanishing power of Mediobanca may, in this respect, imply a return to the early "pure model" of family capitalism. In the second and third sections we will try to explain at a more theoretical level why different models of capitalism may co-exist and how the transition from one form of capitalism to the other tends to occur after major institutional shocks in countries where the preceding organizational forms were relatively weaker.

The last three sections consider three different phases of Italian capitalism. The fourth section consider the changes that characterized Italian corporate governance between the two world wars when a "bank-based system of corporate governance" was replaced by a sort of co-habitation between "family capitalism" and State-owned enterprises. The fifth section considers the missed opportunities of the post-war period when family capitalism was not replaced but rather regulated and reinforced (sometimes rescued) by institutions like Mediobanca, and when State-owned enterprises continued to play a very important role in Italy's economic development. Finally, the last section considers the nineties when privatization was intended to be linked to both the dismantling of State ownership and the birth of a new model of corporate governance. While a massive programme of privatisation took place, in the midst of such major change, the continuity of the model of family capitalism remained unbroken. Indeed, in many respects, with the end of the role of State-owned enterprises and the dramatic eclipse of the power of Mediobanca the system of family capitalism has been "purified" and has come to resemble a Weberian ideal-type. We conclude by observing that the purity of the model may contrast with its institutional stability that requires the contribution of specific complementary institutions.

## Italian family capitalism: the case of Fiat

On 16 December 1945, Giovanni Agnelli, the founder of Fiat and the grandfather of the present honorary president of Fiat, "Gianni" Agnelli, died at the age of 79. Ten years previously his son Edoardo Agnelli had died in a plane accident. At the time of his grandfather's death Gianni, the eldest of Edoardo's sons, was 24 years old. He was clearly unprepared to take over his grandfather's job. The top Fiat manager was at that time Professor Vittorio Valletta. One Fiat executive recalls that during the difficult years of the war, "Valletta always said we would be good Germans, we would be good Fascists, but we had to save Fiat. That was the policy" (Friedman, 1989 p. 36).

After Giovanni Agnelli's death Valletta told Gianni that there were two possibilities: either the young Agnelli or Valletta himself must become the president of the company. According to Alan Friedman's account, the young Agnelli, who did not consider himself ready for the job, replied "You do it Professor." What followed was a period that is known as "The season of Valletta" or, alternatively, as the "Regency." The relationship between young Agnelli and Professor Valletta was indeed very similar to that of an absent sovereign and his regent. "While Gianni spent his time on fast cars and loose women, Valletta was very much in control of the Fiat empire, overseeing its reconstruction in the post-war period. Agnelli might have ruled from a distance, but Valletta governed" (Friedman, 1989 p. 44).

Valletta's regency ended in 1966. During his season Fiat had enormously prospered. At the time of Giovanni Agnelli's death Fiat was producing 3260 automobiles a year. In 1966, Fiat was turning out that number of cars every working day. By the year 1974, the direct involvement of Gianni Agnelli and his young brother, Umberto, was one of the factors that had precipitated FIAT into a serious crisis. While Umberto had consistently shown very poor skills, Gianni had, with comparable consistency, proven to be a better ambassador for Fiat than a manager. With Fiat in a mess, young Umberto tried to pursue a political career. This created the opportunity to appoint Carlo De Benedetti, who was later to become the president of Olivetti, as managing director. After a short time, Umberto had to give up his hopes of a successful electoral career and expressed his desire to return to his FIAT job. "De Benedetti had finally to understand what everyone already knew, that for the Agnellis, Fiat was more than a company to be run on strictly business grounds. It was family property, where matters such as keeping a dilettante brother happy were more important than a company clean-up. De Benedetti realised then that there was nothing more he could offer in the group" (Friedman, 1989 p.78).

Leaving the company to find his own way as an independent entrepreneur, De Benedetti predicted that the day was not far off when Fiat could no longer be run so incompetently. That day came in 1980 when the survival itself of Fiat as an independent company was at stake. Umberto finally gave up and admitted that he was not the man to run the company. Cesare Romiti, a manager who, before working at Fiat, had shown his skills in the public sector was placed firmly in the driving seat by Mediobanca in exchange for his continuing financial support of the family. Mediobanca[1] president, Enrico Cuccia, emerged even more clearly as the "master of the masters" and as the supreme authority regulating the transmission of power from one generation to the other. He had also acquired the right to give control to external managers when children and brothers were judged to be unsuited for the jobs that had been performed by their older relatives. The solution was accepted but with some outrage for this external interference. The combination of the diplomatic skills of Gianni Agnelli and the managerial skills of the tough Romiti was invincible. Gianni Agnelli had finally found his new Valletta. Together they expanded the frontiers of the Agnelli power network. Soon, the Agnelli group controlled one quarter of the Milan stock exchange making free use of the clout that derived from its 569 subsidiaries and 190 associated companies. Gianni Agnelli became the single most powerful individual in Italy and, according to Alan Friedman the uncrowned king of the nation.

In the midst of so much success, many problems emerged. Umberto's son, Giovannino Agnelli, the designated new head of the family, died of cancer in 1997. Edoardo (Giovanni Agnelli's own son) had always preferred meditation and Indian asceticism to the demanding family job and, in any case, committed suicide a few years after Giovannino's death. The family's relationship with Romiti had never been an easy one and finally soured when he left Fiat. While the world was changing and Fiat was forced to tighten its relations with GM, the master of the masters, Enrico Cuccia, finally died in 2000 at the age of 92. With the the power of Mediobanca eclipsed and the tragedies that had swept away the intermediate generations, Giovanni Agnelli could only hope to do with his young grandson (John Elkan) what his own grandfather had done with him. The cycle could now be repeated. Power could again be passed from grandfather to grandchild, leaping one generation. This trasmission could occur, as in the old days, without the interference of institutions like Mediobanca. Nobody (outside the family) was there to judge the qualifications of the new master's performance.

## The diversity of business organizations: a theory of the relevance of institutional shocks

Iwai (1999) has observed how, even when legal differences are not relevant, the modern corporation is compatible with different organizational forms. The modern corporation is based on a double ownership relationship. On the one hand, the corporation is a legal person that owns other assets as things. On the other hand the corporation is owned by others as a thing. This Janus-like form of the corporation implies that two extreme cases are possible. At one extreme, the corporation may be controlled by one person and can be completely treated as thing with discretional autonomy independent from this particular physical person. At the other extreme, the corporation may become a self-referential being (in some ways a "proper person", characterised by self-ownership and not just a "legal person"!) that owns its own assets buying back some of its shares. In a paper that we have co-authored with Barca and Iwai[2] we show that while both extremes are theoretical abstractions, post-war Italian and Japanese firms have tended until recently to be relatively closer to each of these two extremes. Italian firms, with their pyramidal structure with families like the Agnellis at the apex, most closely illustrate the example of a corporation which is just a thing in the hands of the family. By contrast, Japanese firms, with their cross-shareholding occurring within their *keiretsu* groups, have often approximated a situation where the *keiretsu*, taken as whole, could easily own the majority of its own shares. Thus, although located at two opposite extremes, both Italian and Japanese corporations share the characteristic of being somehow "protected" from hostile take-overs – a feature that distinguishes them from the Anglo-American corporation.

In our paper with Barca and Iwai (1999) we explained these deviations of Japanese and Italian corporations from the standard Anglo-American model towards opposite extremes by pointing out that both Italy and Japan were subject to institutional shocks of different nature in the immediate post-war period.

There is little in standard economic theory that can help us to explain why institutional shocks such as the American occupation should have had such a lasting impact on the organizational arrangements of Italy and Japan. In the Neo-Classical framework, the entire issue of ownership and control rights[3] does not make sense.[4] In a world of perfect competition and zero market transaction costs, agents could write a complete contract that specifies the conditions under which they participate to coalition of agents producing a certain good. In this framework, the assignment of control rights does not matter: there are no ex-post residual decisions left by the ex-ante contract, where the power entailed by the control of the organizations could be exercised. In the New Institutional and in the New Property Rights framework, the assumption of costly and/or incomplete contracts implies that some relevant ex-post residual decisions may be left to the holders of ownership. In this framework, the assignment of control rights does matter and the choice of individual who will employ other individuals is relevant to the organization's efficiency. In a second best world, some agency costs are likely to be sustained by any individuals controlling the firm which must employ other individuals. Because of the specificity of other investments, each individual will have to share the fruits of its investment with other agents who can threaten to leave the coalition. Moreover, because of asymmetric information, each agent will have to sustain some (monitoring and/or bonding) costs. Thus, in comparison to the first best solution, no agent, can obtain the whole fruits of his/her investments and therefore tends to underinvest. The "second best" solution is to assign control rights to those agents who imply the highest agency costs when they are to be employed by other agents. In a market characterized by zero transaction costs this second best solution should always be attained. In this second best framework, the re-assignments of ownership and control rights that occurred under the American occupation should be irrelevant. If the new rights implied lower agency costs, they would have occurred independently of the American occupation whereas if they implied higher agency costs they would have been undone by the market after the end of the political constraints created by the occupation. In both cases, institutional shocks are irrelevant and the control of the organization would go to the high-agency-cost agents.

The relevance of institutional shocks becomes, instead, evident if we move beyond the New Institutional and the New Property Rights framework and acknowledge that in a transaction costs world where the control of firm does matter it is inconsistent to assume the existence of a costless perfect market for control itself. Three distinct problems arise in such a world whereby institutional changes come to have a decisive influence on the allocation of control rights.

i) <u>Information problems</u>. Due to asymmetric and imperfect information concerning who the highest-agency-costs individuals actually are, efficiency enhancing transfers of control might not take place and efficiency – reducing ones might well take place. As the result of this market failure, institutional shocks which, either directly or indirectly, bring about a forceful reallocation of control, can indeed make a difference by changing the default – no transfer-option.

ii) <u>Multiplicity of organizational equilibria</u>. Technology (i.e. the degree of specificity and the difficulty of monitoring of individuals) is not to be taken exogenously but is rather influenced by control allocation. Multiple combinations of technological and control allocation can then exist. Institutional shocks, by transferring control rights, can therefore permanently shift the economy from one equilibrium to another.

iii) <u>Separation between ownership and control</u>. The allocation of wealth among members of a society does not necessarily coincide with the allocation of "skills" (specificity and difficulty of monitoring). Therefore, control must separate itself from ownership and institutions are needed to sustain this separation. Alternative institutions arranged in "property-rights systems" or, as they are now called, "corporate governance systems", can achieve separation in different ways and with different effects on the allocation of rights [as well as the content of such rights]. Since a diversity of corporate governance systems can in principle arise, institutional shocks can have permanent effects on the ways in which economic systems are organized.

While point (i) is well known we need to consider the latter two issues in more detail.

<u>Multiplicity of organizational equilibria.</u> In some ways, different given systems of property rights have an effect similar to different systems of relative prices. A change in the property rights increases the agency costs of using the non-owning factors relatively to those of the owning factors. Thus, similarly to changes in relative prices, changes in property rights have a substitution effect: the high-agency-cost resources of the non-owning individuals tend to be substituted away; for this reason non-owning factors tend to become low-agency-cost resources. Or, in other words, they tend to become less firm-specific and more difficult-to-monitor than owning factors. Thus, the effects of property rights on the technological specification of the resources, which has been typically advanced by "Radical economists" can be explained by a substitution effect similar to the one determining input composition in standard microeconomic theory.

The relationships considered by many New Institutional and New Property Rights economists can be inverted along the lines suggested by the Radical economists.[5] According to the former, the ownership of the firms is to be given to the factors which involve the highest agency costs, that is, to the most difficult to monitor and specific factors. However, as Radical economists have suggested, it can also be argued that owning factors will tend to save on these agency costs and, because of a standard substitution mechanism, will tend to become relatively more specific and difficult to monitor. Thus, according to the radical mechanism, owning factors tend to choose that technology under which, according to New Institutional theory, their ownership is to be preferred. In this way, initial ownership conditions tend to sustain themselves via the technology that it is optimal to sustain under those conditions. This self-reinforcing mechanism is consistent with the idea that initial property rights shocks, such as those due to the American occupation, could in principle have had a lasting effect. Indeed, the two mechanisms considered above are not mutually exclusive and can be combined since causation may flow in both directions at once: while technology influences the allocation of property rights, ownership influences the choice of the technology. This two way causation can generate multiple "organizational equilibria"[6] and major institutional shocks, such as the American occupation, may shift the economy from one organizational equilibrium to the other.

An "organizational equilibrium" can be defined as any combination of property rights and technology which has the following characteristics. With the given property rights, the current technology is the most efficient available; conversely, with this technology, the current property rights are most efficient. In such an equilibrium, property rights and technology are self-reinforcing since changing one component at a time damages efficiency, and hence reduces the total income available for distribution among the various parties.

Can competition imply that, independently of initial conditions given by the history of the economy, the market selects the most efficient organizational equilibrium? While this is a possible outcome, we argue that the effects of market selection may turn out to be rather ambiguous. Indeed, there are some circumstances in which competition may enhance stabilization instead of upsetting an inefficient organizational equilibrium. The complementarity between property rights and technology, characterizing an organizational equilibrium, inhibits the possibility of a gradual evolution from one equilibrium to another. The inferiority of hybrids implies that the transition from one type of equilibrium to another is likely to be abrupt and that evolution will have a punctuated character.[7] The inferiority of hybrids also implies that competition may have a negative effect, wiping out the necessarily inferior hybrids before they may transform themselves into superior organizational equilibria. In some respects the role of market selection is analogous to that of natural selection. While it favours the selection of the best members of a given species of organizations, it may inhibit the speciation of new organizational arrangements. This analogy is reinforced by the observation that in natural history, the efficiency of each species depends on its frequency. Also "organizational species" share the same characteristic. Network externalities in property rights and in technologies may imply that few firms characterized by different organizational equilibria are not viable. These firms would be out competed by firms that, even if inferior when they exist with the same frequency, can better benefit from network externalities because of their current large number.

In other words, the successful speciation of new organizational equilibria does not only require that each firm deal successfully with the complementarities between its own rights and technology, but because of network externalities there are also important complementarities among the organizational models adopted by different firms. The existence of network externalities can cause a homogenisation of technology.[8] A single technological standard may be the only possible equilibrium outcome when common inputs, produced under a regime of economies to scale, are used by all the firms. The case of property rights has not received the same attention. However, network externalities can also cause the homogenization of ownership systems. For all the firms using the same system of property rights, some pieces of legislation and the skills necessary to its application and enforcement, are common inputs produced and used under a system of pronounced economies to scale. A piece of legislation can be used an infinite number of times without being destroyed. The same type of legal expertise by the same law firms can be used, enjoying the advantages of increasing returns by all the firms using the same property rights system. The enforcement of contracts by courts of law is very likely to be more predictable and precise for the firms using the most widespread property rights system. Finally, customary law requires that a custom be well established and this is more likely to happen within the framework of the property rights system used by the majority of firms. The complementarity between technology and property rights that is encompassed by the concept of organizational equilibria implies that network externalities can act indirectly on property rights via technology and also indirectly on technology via property rights. Network externalities among firms' technologies may also imply the homogenization of property rights. Vice versa, network externalities among the ownership systems may also imply the standardization of technologies. When these complementarities between technological and property rights standards exist, the speciation of few alternative organizational models may become very difficult in situations where the competition of the old species of organizational equilibria is very strong.

The two way causation flowing between technology and property rights implies that institutional shocks, such as occurred during the American occupation in Japan, may have lasting consequences on economic systems. Moreover the complementarity between rights and technology at both intra-firm and inter-firm levels imply that a strong competitive pressure may stabilize rather than upsetting inefficient "organizational species". Thus, at least in principle, we should not be surprised if the speciation of new successful species of organization could occur as a result of a political decision. protecting the environment from the pressure of competitive forces. The creative activity of competitive markets could, in some cases, lag behind this organizational innovation.

The separation between ownership and control. Control could be achieved through ownership alone, the "second best" solution invoked by the New institutional framework would be achieved only insofar as skills, as previously defined, and wealth happened to be allocated in the same way among individuals. While such coincidence might indeed occur, especially as the result of both skills and wealth being transferred from one generation to the next in closed family groups, it will certainly not be the rule. Arrangements have then developed in all developed societies whereby ownership of financial resources is partly or fully substituted as a means to exert control and entrepreneurs can collect debt capital or raise share and still retain control. It can indeed be argued that it is only thanks to such arrangements and to the separation between ownership and control that they have allowed that economic development has achieved the extraordinary results seen in this century.

To allow separation, a fundamental conflict of interest has to be somehow resolved between investors – banks or shareholders – and entrepreneurs holding control. Devices must exist which protect investors from their failure to finance the right entrepreneur and from abuses of power control. Abuses might include the entrepreneur's enhancing his own non-monetary benefits which cannot be appropriated by investors, his acting in the interest of other concerns that he directly owns, or his embezzling of funds. In a world of incomplete contracts these problems cannot be addressed by writing contracts where all wrongful doing is ruled out. In the same way, since investors must not prevent marginal deviation of entrepreneurs' behaviour from good practice but must prevent major diversion of funds, mechanisms making entrepreneurs' income in some way linked to the market value of the funds they manage can have only very limited effects.[9] Investors must then be granted the power to monitor control. But, whatever the monitoring devices are, in a world of asymmetric information, monitored entrepreneurs can be punished (and lose control) when no mistakes or abuses have been committed. Alternatively, because of asymmetric information, nothing may happen to them when interference would have been justified.

A trade-off thus arises between certainty of control and the protection of investors. On the one hand, the harder it is for investors to interfere with control, the more deterred they are from financing and the more difficult it is to ensure that an efficient allocation of control is made. On the other hand, the easier it is to interfere with control, the less effective control is as a means to enhance investments and innovation by entrepreneurs. In the latter case entrepreneurs will no longer be guaranteed long-term unconditional use of the company's assets and will reduce their irreversible specific investments in human capital. A further, "multiplicative negative effect" can be produced by this interference through behaviour of lower rank managers. The more likely it is that investors' monitoring implies hostile changes of control, the more uncertain managers will be about their prospects of climbing the firm's ladder through the working of the "internal market". In turn this will lead also lower rank managers to underinvest.

The many alternative institutions which have developed to address the trade off we have now illustrated can be grouped in the following six categories:
a) inside monitoring through membership of the board or other corporate organs (this may be exercised directly by the non-controlling owners, or delegated to outsiders or to financial institutions with holdings in the firms);
b) *ex post* outside monitoring by courts of law through shareholders' law suits in order to obtain redress for breach of trust by entrepreneurs (or by the board which should monitor them);
c) market, or the threat of exit, such as the chance for non-controlling shareholders to transfer ownership and control to third parties, even without the entrepreneur's consent, if the former feel that the latter has misused or abused his/her powers;
d) monitoring through the political market, by nationalising firms and entrusting supervisory power to parliamentary or governmental bodies;
e) relations of trust between entrepreneur and owners that ensure the former's cooperation with the latter.
f) contractual means such as pacts among shareholders, statutory provisos and pyramidal groups – whereby the voting rights of non-controlling shareholders are spread out over a large number of firms while those of the entrepreneur are concentrated in the company at the top of the pyramid – which, while not providing any monitoring tools to investors, offers some shareholders a way to enforce control.

Two rather distinct roles can be played by inter-firm share-holdings. In the case of pyramidal groups, ownership links, by dispersing non-controlling shareholders' voting rights, allow the controlling shareholder to expand the allocation of control well beyond his/her personal means. In Italy, where this system has been exploited most, for the average of existing pyramidal groups with at least one listed company and controlled by one shareholder or a set of family shareholders, entrepreneur's share capital is about 12-13 per cent of total group's capital (about 5 per cent for Fiat). Alternatively, inter-firm shareholding (when it does not amount to the control of one firm on another) does not only provide a link among firms for strategic interaction. It may also help to consolidate managers' control: very intense cross-shareholdings among firms, either directly, or through "intermediate firms", can in fact allow managers with no or little shares to disperse shares and to sustain each other. This is the case of Japan, but an example of this system is also provided in the U.S. system by private pension funds of two firms investing in each other shares.

The prevailing of any one of these several corporate governance devices will affect directly the allocation of control by making more or less binding the existing allocation of wealth. It also affects the ways in which transfers of control take place and the multiplicative effect on the incentive to invest of all managers. Let's consider the three cases when monitoring relies on exit or courts of law – b, c – is exercised "internally" by a financial institution – a – or is entrusted to family relations. In the first case, the market for managers is mostly an outsiders market: internal carrier is highly risky and long-term commitment is discouraged, but higher chances exist for newcomers to step in. In the second case, the reverse occurs: internal managers can rely on the firm's leading financial institution to preside over changes of control and make sure that the best managers get selected. More controversial is the third case: the internal market can be effective but conflicting interests of the family's heirs can easily endanger the prospects of managers.

The corporate governance systems prevailing at a given time in history in any country can be interpreted as a combination of the different existing devices. In understanding why a particular mix prevails in any country at a given time one should very much rely on the self-reinforcing mechanisms that explain multiplicity of organizational equilibria. Once a corporate governance system prevails, the successful speciation of a new device is prevented by the high risks and costs that any individual entrepreneur runs in presenting investors with a new institutional "package" and that any individual investor runs in accepting it. The existence of very strong network externalities makes it extremely expensive for any group of investors or entrepreneur to experiment with new, privately developed legal devices. The compulsory change of existing ownership structure or the reform of corporate law, stock market regulation or bank-industry relation, whether due to endogenously developed social changes or to exogenous military rule, can then bring about deep and possibly irreversible changes in the way control allocation is transferred.

## Organizational equilibria and species of capitalism

The self-reinforcing characteristics of organizational equilibria may explain some puzzling features of the dynamics of capitalism. Different "national" forms coexist in spite of common technological innovations. Moreover, "new organizational species", whose success is often related to these new technological opportunities, tend often to emerge in countries that are different from those that were successful in the preceding phase of capitalist development.[10] Chandler (1990) pointed out how the managerial revolution (that was also to lead to the development of Taylor's "scientific management") was paradoxically inhibited in England by its prominence in the first industrial revolution.

In the first industrial revolution, where textiles allowed successful small scale production, family controlled firms were adequate. In this framework, while family members had an incentive to make firm-specific investments and could also, without serious organizational costs, become difficult-to-monitor factors the same was not true for non-family-member managers. These managers were trapped in an "organizational equilibrium" that was a vicious circle for them: because of the family system, weak managerial rights implied an unfavourable distribution of asymmetric information and of specific skills, that, in turn, implied that, the case for managerial rights remained very weak. In England this "organizational equilibrium" resisted the pressure of the "second industrial revolution" where the changes connected to development of the railways pushed towards the development of sophisticated managerial hierarchies. Thus, the self-reinforcing aspects of "organizational equilibria" can explain why the "new species" of managerial capitalism, together with the full strength of the second industrial revolution, blossomed with much greater intensity in the U.S. and Germany than in Britain. Still, the new species of capitalism co-existed with the original species and no country was purely characterized by a single organizational form.

Under "managerial capitalism", often independently of their ownership entitlements, managers acquired considerable rights in the organization and accumulated great amounts of hidden information and specific skills. By contrast, the development of "scientific management" implied that the large majority of workers were "expropriated" of the hidden information and of all the specific skills that had survived the first industrial revolution. Workers' weak rights in the organization were connected to an unfavourable distribution of asymmetric information and specific skills causing the self-sustaining organizational equilibrium that characterized Taylorism.

Also in the case of the "Tayloristic organizational equilibrium", one of the major challenges to its vicious circle failed to occur at the centre of the system in the U. S. where the competition among the numerous members of the "Tayloristic" species was strongest. By contrast, it came about in defeated post-war Japan, contributing in an impressive way to the exceptional development of its economy which, for a while, almost challenged the supremacy of American capitalism.

Besides its peripheral location, the new species did not emerge "spontaneously" as the exclusive outcome of the workings of market forces. By contrast, the strong "institutional shocks", that characterized the years of the military defeat and the American occupation of Japan, had a fundamental, and very often unintended role, in the complex arising of the new organizational equilibrium. While a comparison with American capitalism can be easily used to emphasise the numerous elements of continuity within the history of Japanese capitalism, the discontinuity between the *zaibatsu* and the *keiretsu* system is, indeed, striking[11] and cannot convincingly be explained without referring to the institutional shocks that characterized that period.

The American expropriation of the zaibatsu families and the compulsory retirement of senior managers were coupled with an initial period of strong unions rights. These factors quickened the birth of a new organizational equilibrium whereby the workers acquired strong rights in their organization. These rights favoured the accumulation of job specific and difficult-to-monitor skills,[12] which, in turn, reinforced the rights of the workers. In other words, the institutional shocks created the conditions for a new self-sustaining organizational equilibrium (Pagano, 2001a) characterized by a distribution of asymmetric information and of specificity characteristics, which was in sharp contrast with the theory and practice of Taylorism.

Similar self-reinforcing mechanisms characterize other modes of production such as Italian districts, "German Corporatism" and the enormous varieties of organizational forms that are emerging in the ex-socialist countries.[13] As in the case of the second industrial revolution, the "third industrial revolution" (based on ICT) will have a great impact on the reassessment of the relative merits of these organizational forms and some may not turn out to be viable. However, also in this case the diversity of organizational forms is unlikely to be reduced. While we have seen that the influence of informational technology has yet to bring about unidirectional transformations, pre-existing property rights will somehow continue to shape (also) information technology.

One possible argument, which foresees a reduction in the "biodiversity" of capitalism, could be based on the observation that information technology favours the process of globalisation of the world economy and that, in a "globalised world", imitation and other factors may bring about an increase of organizational homogenization. However, in a globalised world, the existing forms of national capitalism's may more effectively exploit their "comparative institutional advantage" in different sectors of the economy and some new viable forms of capitalism may even emerge in this process. In this sense, globalisation allows the specialisation of the economies in those sectors where they already have or may develop a "comparative institutional advantage" related to their own particular organizational equilibrium and may even favour the diversity of the forms of capitalism. Thus, there is no reason to believe that the "biodiversity" of capitalism is bound to decrease.

By contrast, at least in this particular sense, we are far from reaching an "end of history".[14] It is within this context of persisting diversity of organizational forms that we may seek to understand why Chandler's managerial revolution never took place in the Italian model and why family capitalism has persisted as the main organizational form for large corporations.

## Changes of Italian corporate governance between the two world wars

Italy is a typical late comer, industrialising only at the end of the nineteenth century, but the process remained fragile for decades and was not put on truly solid foundations until after the World War II. The country was traditionally marked by a shortage of capital (absence of primitive accumulation), scarcity of raw materials and the lack of a large market (due to its historical division into small, independent states).[15] The model of development that emerged in the closing decades of the nineteenth century was centred on heavy industries, sustained by public procurement and protected by high tariff barriers.[16] Moreover, Italy lacked a "specific industrialization ideology"[17] – be it the French myth of the firm or the ideal of building a new society as in the Soviet Union, in order to forge a mass consensus for the drive toward industrialisation.

In the absence of these factors, during the first phase of industrialisation beginning in 1895, the substitutes were the "mixed banks", some founded with German capital (e.g. Banca Commerciale Italiana and Credito Italiano). These financial institutions operated through a *mix* of credit relations and equity subscription. In the framework proposed by Gerschenkron, in Italy the mixed bank acted at first as a *substitute agent* to overcome the scanty primitive accumulation of capital. Later, it provided the channel by which diffuse and fragmented savings, which the holders had no intention of putting into illiquid form, could be funnelled into equity that would, otherwise, have had a great deal of difficulty finding buyers in the stock exchange.[18]

It was during the 1920s that this "bank-based corporate governance" degenerated due to a progressive erasure of the separation of interests between banks and large industrial corporations, combined with the weakness of the "rear echelons", i.e. the lack of a credible reserve of small and medium-sized businesses. In addition to sustaining growth, then, the large banks also acted as coordinators, seeing to the placement of new share issues (often enough, with the usual small circle of customers).[19] Corporate crises were regularly dealt with and resolved by the banks themselves; if a crisis was too large to be handled by a single bank, a rescue consortium of very large dimensions would be formed.[20]

The natural corollary to the prevalence of debt capital was the failure of the stock market to take off.[21] After the turn of the century, it was the mixed banks themselves that sponsored the development of the stock market, with a view to making their equity shares more liquid and more easily disposable.

With an inadequate stock market and stable, non-competitive relations between banks and industry, between 1900 and 1913, the groundwork was laid for an intensive concentration of control and the formation of "corporate pyramidal groups, based on family control". However, it was only because of the enormous profits deriving from military production (in steel, shipbuilding, mechanical engineering and chemicals), during WWI, that the relationship between banks and enterprises degenerated irretrievably. The main Italian industrial firms acquired significant equity stakes in many banks. In this way, they moved from a "German-style" toward a "Japanese-style" of banking. Public procurement orders and massive profits restored corporate finances to health and powerfully spurred further concentration, especially by mergers and buyouts. In these years, the power relations between banks and industrial corporations were inverted, and industrial pyramidal groups now made take-over bids for the leading banks, although unsuccessfully.

The stock market crash of 1929 thus hit the Italian financial system in a moment of pronounced industrial and financial concentration. The intermingling of credit and industrial capital and the underdevelopment of the stock market, but above all the creation of corporate groups based on cross-shareholding, made the crisis particularly acute, hindering adjustment and creating a domino effect. The tight monetary policy and the decision to defend the external value of the Italian lira contributed to amplify the destructive nature of the shock in Italy. The crisis struck huge industrial-banking colossi, and the organization into pyramidal groups amplified the repercussions of the plunge in share prices. The leading banks found it simply impossible to liquidate their assets, which consisted primarily in equity holdings in the crisis-torn industrial groups. This paved the way for the most sweeping reallocation of ownership in the history of Italy, and above all "for the State to assume the central function within Italian capitalism" which it had refused at the turn of the century. State ownership became a new device to ensure full separation between ownership and control and to enable a group of talented managers to acquire control over industrial and service firms.

The government decided to refinance the troubled banks by buying out their industrial holdings and transferring them to a new agency created especially for this purpose in 1933: the Institute for Industrial Reconstruction (IRI, Istituto per la Ricostruzione Industriale). Constituted as a holding company and as a corporation under private law, IRI took over the entire equity capital of the mixed banks, hence more than 21 per cent of all the equity capital of limited companies existing in Italy at the time.[22] Meanwhile, industrial concentration had increased notably, and in 1936 fewer than 1 per cent of all Italian limited companies accounted for half the total share capital.[23]

The creation of IRI was accompanied by the fundamental Banking Law of 1936, which prohibited banks from holding equities in industrial companies and required maturity specialisation in their credit business, assigning short-term credit business to ordinary banks and medium and long-term credit to special credit institutions. Thus the German-style mixed bank vanished from the scene. But the Italian solution, unlike the American case,[24] was not intended to relaunch the stock market as a means of attaining a broader ownership base and more diffuse corporate control; the dominant logic continued to view the banks as the linchpin of industrial finance. IRI, on May 6, 1937, was transformed into a permanent institution. The decision not to reprivatise the companies was due in part to the fascist regime's desire to use public corporations as an instrument of industrial policy, but primarily it was due to the difficulty of finding private buyers for so many public firms.[25]

For the Italian economy, the crisis of the 1930s thus represents a truly structural divide, with an outright transformation of the model of corporate governance occurring between 1930 and 1936. With the direct, massive intervention of the State, Italy moved from an ownership pattern based on the corporate family group and mixed banks (similar in some ways to the German model) to one centred on the corporate group but subdivided into state owned and private groups controlled by families. A characteristic feature of the Anglo-American model of corporate control was introduced, namely separation of banking and industry. The bank as controller, mandated to oversee the rehabilitation and restructuring of firms in crisis, disappeared. The resulting vacuum was partly filled by the state holding company, which was repeatedly required to take over companies in financial distress. Due to the lack of other institutions that could have taken over the role played previously by the mixed banks, the state provided relevant resources and direct ownership over an important section of the Italian economy.

## Italian corporate governance in the post-war period

The Italian model of corporate governance after the restructuring of 1933-36 was based on two major actors: family-controlled pyramidal groups and State-owned pyramidal groups. The end of the war and the liberation of the nation from fascism by the Allied forces and by Italian partisan units, the end of the monarchy and the institution of a republic, the drafting of the democratic Constitution and the formation of a coalition government involving all the anti-fascist forces did little to alter the institutional structure of Italian capitalism. Most of the negative aspects of the Italian corporate governance were perceived by the Economic Committee of the Constitutional Assembly, but no reforms were implemented.[26]

From 1943 till December 1947 the Anglo-American armies were a powerful actor in the Italian political scene. The British Prime Minister, Churchill, had been preoccupied since 1943 with the defense and re-establishment of "traditional ownership relationships in Italy". Churchill had been an admirer of Mussolini in the 1920s and even during the last years of the war believed that the key issue in Italy was to avoid a communist take-over.[27] In 1944 a civil war broke out in Greece between the communists and the monarchists and the British troupes were sent to fight against the "reds"; this reinforced the conservative approach within the Allies. Churchill was not at all interested in purging Italy of the fascist presence in the State, the economic life and society at large, and considered the monarchy as the preferred institutional solution for the future Italian State. A military defeat of the fascist regime was enough in his view. For several months, the British government vetoed the first American recovery plans in support of the Italian industries.[28]

The American point of view was quite different. The Americans refused to recognise the King as the only legitimate representative of the new Italy and rapidly established relations with the Partisan forces organized in the National Liberation Committee (CLN); and unilaterally, from September 1944, decided to distribute food and financial aid. In general, however, the Allied occupation forces tried to speed up the process of reconstruction, with the explicit goal of preventing social disorder along with any possible left-wing insurrection. At the end of 1944, the CLN signed an agreement with the American general H.M. Wilson in Rome and received some assistance in the struggle against the Nazi-fascists in Northern Italy. However, they agreed to dismantle their military organization as soon as the war was over and to be considered not as a real government but just as a military group.[29] For almost two years Italy was divided into two separate States: a monarchy in the South, under the Allied protection, and a residual fascist regime in the North, under German control. The bureaucracy of the Southern government was a legacy of the previous fascist regime. Even after the re-unification of the country, the state apparatus was almost totally based on the fascist structure. The promised purges never happened and a general amnesty (June 1946), for fascist crimes was passed by the new government.[30]

The invasion by the Anglo-American forces certainly enhanced a liberal rule in Italy. On the other hand, following the armed defence of the factories against the German invaders in several firms in Northern Italy, workers had their first experience of participatory councils, which were fiercely opposed by the entrepreneurs. The necessity of accelerating the process of reconstruction and the emergence of a new conflict – the Cold War with the Soviet Union – induced, however, the Allies to support a quick return to the traditional system. Two other factors moved in the same direction: 1. the view of the leading party now emerging from the Resistance, the Communist Party, which held that existing institutions should at first be retained in order to allow rapid Reconstruction; 2. the positions – and the preferential links with the Americans – held by a small group of managers who had emerged in the State-owned companies and were now leading them.[31]

As a result of these several factors, State-owned companies were not dismantled, the family corporate groups were not reformed, and no major reform was devised. After a very short phase of coalition government which included the Communist Party, in 1947, in view of the promises of American financial help through the "Marshall Plan", the Christian Democratic leader Alcide De Gasperi formed the first government excluding the left-wing parties (socialists and communists). Italy clearly went under the American influence: it signed the Bretton Woods agreements (1947), received financial transfers under the European Recovery Program[32] (1948), and joined the NATO military alliance (1949). From May 1947 till February 1962, Italy was ruled by a series of governments firmly centred on the Christian Democrats and liberal parties. During this "liberal" phase, however, little was done in terms of traditionally liberal reforms: no antitrust laws; no reform of the commercial code; no steps toward a more developed financial market.

In the absence of financial institutions exercising, interim and *ex post* monitoring through equity or debt relations with the firms, all large firms, organized as hierarchical groups, were kept under family control or under the State control. The return to democracy was associated with the rise of a new governing class who had been formed largely in the opposition to fascism that opted for European integration and for free trade. This allowed the full development of the potential inherent in the model of corporate governance established between 1933 and 1936.

Furthermore, it can be argued that in the first 10 to 15 years after the end of the war some features of the governance framework, in the contingent economic and cultural context, were suited to very rapid development. State control gave a new generation of managers, mostly untainted by involvement with the previous fascist regime (and in some case, known opponents of it), the chance to acquire control of large, emerging enterprises. A sense of mission, linked to the post-war reconstruction climate, helped to make up for the monitoring failures of the model. Moreover, many of the relevant strategic choices were clear-cut (providing the country with an adequate and stable supply of energy, developing and modernising the steel industry to suit the needs of the engineering sector, building a highway system, etc.). At the same time, low wages due to an excess supply of labour allowed rapid growth in small and large family-controlled firms to be fuelled by abnormally high self-financing. Some groups (liberals and Communists, though for different reasons), maintained, after the war, that these public enterprises should be eliminated as a holdover from the fascist regime; according to others, the persistent backwardness of the economy made the privatisation of an enormous group like IRI simply impracticable. The representatives of the US government had also questioned the wisdom of retaining a public group created under fascism. In July 1944 Donato Menichella, one of the creators of IRI back in 1933, had addressed a report to Captain Andrew Kamark, the representative for IRI of the Finance Sub-Commission of the Allied Control Commission. Menichella had argued that the public ownership of banks and industries did not reflect the fascist regime's bent for planning but had stemmed from the rescue of the banks, whose purpose was primarily to protect savers and depositors and safeguard the stability of the banking system as a whole.[33] The impossibility of finding hands capable of running IRI's banks and industrial firms through private ownership, Menichella maintained, had compelled the government to transform IRI into a permanent structure.[34]

Over and above this historical judgement, the position that won the day (also for the Allied forces), in the late forties, was that public enterprises were a good tool for speeding up reconstruction.[35] State-owned enterprises were finally considered as a powerful tool to ensure a proper separation between ownership and control, probably one of the few tools available in a rapidly developing country without a real financial market. The structure of corporate governance in the state-owned industrial sector became one in which management exercises the power of control (i.e., of strategic design). The arrangement differed from the theory in that during this initial phase the supervision exercised by the political power structure was not stringent. State-ownership enabled, in Italy, a separation between ownership and control which was limited in the private sector. A new generation of public managers was empowered with the control of state enterprises. In the post-war period, this entrepreneurial fluidity in the state-owned sector contrasted with the immobility in the large private firms. In the state-owned pyramidal groups, the "residual right of control" seems to have been firmly in the hands of management. It was management, not the political tutors, that chose to focus the accumulation effort on rebuilding a modern industrial apparatus in steel, shipbuilding and engineering, and on major infrastructure (highways, the telephone network, etc.).[36] This institutional solution was all the more necessary because, in the absence of other models of corporate governance, the only alternative source of finance for such a project would have been bank credit and the leading banks (Banca Commerciale and Credito Italiano) were closely connected to the interests of just a few large Italian and foreign industrial groups.[37]

What explains the satisfactory performance of the state-owned groups in these early years of the new Italian democracy?

Three elements were present from 1945 till the end of the 1950s. Public managers were assigned to pursue relatively simple targets: reconstruct the economy and foster growth, build the basic transport and energy infrastructure and set the engineering sector on the solid ground of home steel production. Public management shared common experiences and a sense of mission often built through opposition to fascism. The ruling centre-right parties were strongly competing with left parties to prove that capitalism was capable of bringing about fast development.[38] All three conditions disappeared at the end of the 1950s. The market for political control failed: from 1945 to 1993 the government was uninterruptedly controlled by a series of alliances among an unchanging group of parties, the communist party was relegated to an often sterile opposition and failed to function as watchdog over the public enterprises. Indeed there was often collusion between majority and opposition in this regard (for instance, most of the measures on behalf of the public enterprises, including subsidies, were approved unanimously in Parliament).[39]

An attempt to introduce some monitoring devices in the management of the State-owned system was made in 1956 by creating of the Ministry for State Shareholding, designed to exercise political supervision of the IRI and the ENI groups. At the same time, multiple strategic goals were imposed on state-owned enterprises: to contest monopoly, to promote new industrial relations, to sustain employment and to foster the economic development of the South. By adding new goals to the original one it became very difficult for the Ministry for State Shareholding to perform monitoring activities. So-called "social objectives" could always be cited as an excuse for poor results obtained by public managers.

The development in the governance of large private corporations paralleled that of State-owned companies. The issue of reforming the corporate governance structure of Italian industry was indeed at the centre of the economic and political debate in the first two years after the war, in particular in the Constitutional Assembly, but no reform was enacted. Available data on major Italian private corporations shows that the pyramidal groups structure was indeed already widespread in 1947 but that it did not often allow for a great degree of separation between ownership and control (table 1). Together with the likely expansion of such leverage and the use of contractual tools (such as proxy votes entrusted to directors, multiple-votes share, etc.) the financing of the rapid post-war growth of large private corporations was then provided by extraordinarily high profits and self-financing. This in turn, occurred thanks to a rise of real wages which were much lower than productivity due to very uneven labour relations, weak Unions, high unemployment (in European-wide comparison).

**Table 1 – The control-ownership leverage in three major Italian Groups** [1]

| Years | Fiat | Pirelli | Falck |
|-------|------|---------|-------|
| 1947  | 1.9  | 8.9     | 2.5   |
| 1993  | 17.9 | 52.6    | 4.4   |

(1) Ratio between group's net share capital and share capital held by founding family.

*Source*: F. Barca, F. Bertucci, G. Capello, P. Casavola (1997), La trasformazione proprietaria di Fiat, Pirelli e Falck dal 1947, in F. Barca (ed), Storia del capitalismo italiano, dal dopoguerra a oggi, Roma, Donzelli.

This abnormal state of affairs slowly terminated at the end of the 1950s, in the same years when State-owned companies were undergoing major changes. Tensions in the labour market arose after 1958, wages rose very quickly and by 1962-63 the share of self-financing had drastically dropped. After a brief period of truce, tensions quickly resumed, keeping profits relatively low till the early 1980s. A growing need arose then for external capital and that, in turn, underlined the failures of the Italian corporate governance. It was not enough for relevant reforms to be enacted: some partial changes took place only in 1974 after long controversies. Pressure grew then for a much more intense use of pyramidal groups. New contractual means were introduced such as shareholders voting agreements; and a growing role came to be played by Enrico Cuccia's Mediobanca, founded in 1946.[40] Cuccia's merchant bank frequently allowed founding families to maintain their control over their companies by devising financial plans and holding strategic shares.

The intense recourse to pyramidal groups as a means to separate ownership and control is clearly illustrated in table 2 where data for three major corporations, Fiat, Pirelli and Falck, in year 1993 is reported. In 1993 the average degree of leverage in Italy was about 8 for private non-banking holders of control.[41] The very relevant increase in groups' leverage has been achieved by lengthening the group structure and by diluting the capital held by the family or by companies in the higher ranks of the group. This dilution led to a relevant weakening of the group structure: in other words, family control is no longer undisputed, especially in those companies of the group which, by being closer to the core business, are clearly preferred by external shareholders. Let's consider table 2 where a comparison is presented for Fiat, Falck and Pirelli of the major shareholders of the "key companies" of the groups in 1947 and 1993.

In 1947, only the Pirelli family no longer had the majority of votes in the key company Pirelli Spa: control was then exerted through the support of a set of well-established households, mostly from the same town (Milan) and sharing the same cultural roots. In 1993, the founding families still controlled an extraordinary high number of shares of all those key companies, partly thanks to group branches above those companies (as in Fiat); but this was certainly not enough to exert stable control, nor was financial support provided any longer by wealthy "rentier-households".

A new ownership structure has then arisen in these companies made of founding families, banks and insurance companies and industrial firms. The latter do indeed play a role in Pirelli and Falck through cross-shareholdings, which are similar to the Japanese case. In Fiat the supporting role is played only by banks and insurance companies, both through the holding of shares and through the threat of acting as "white knights" in case of takeovers. In such company a tripolar equilibrium has probably arisen through which control is exerted through some agreement or compromise between the founding family, the top manager and the leading financial institution (namely Mediobanca). A similar arrangement has arose in A.F.L. Falck in 1996. The instability of such arrangements might well explain the resilience of founding families in expanding their corporations, as the technological and competitive challenges required and the strong pressure to devise a reform of Italian corporate governance.

The same factors which had brought large corporations to a crises since the early 1960s had also unleashed small-scale, local entrepreneurial energies. In many areas of Central and Northern Italy and also in a few provinces in the South, so called "potential industrial district" had been in existence since the 1950s (see Brusco and Paba, 1997).

Technological knowledge and human capital had been accumulated and were ready to migrate from large firms to new more flexible small scale activities. Informal financing channels (family savings, etc.) and the provision of large State subsidies had been sustaining the survival and growth of small firms. Furthermore in Central and Northern Italy, locally based civic culture was thriving and ready to fuel micro-industry development. However, only at the beginning of the 1960s, when a "social shock" came from the crisis of the governance of large corporations, "potential districts" quickly developed into fully-fledged districts. Because of the "institutional shock", large companies tried to encourage skilled workers to set up their own firms which, because of their small size, could be isolated from the social conflicts impairing productivity in the large corporations.

**Table 2 – Main shareholders of "key companies" of three major Italian groups: 1947 and 1993** (As a percentage of total voting capital, ordinary and preferred. Number of shareholders – when known – in brackets.)

| Fiat Group Shareholders | Shares | Pirelli Group Shareholders | Shares | Falck Group Shareholders | Shares |
|---|---|---|---|---|---|
| **FIAT SPA (1947)** | | **PIRELLI SPA (1947)** | | **A.F.L. FALCK (1947)** | |
| *Agnelli family* | 70.2 | *Pirelli family* | 12.9 | *Falck family* | 73.1 |
| *Persons (37)* | 10.5 | *persons (75)* | 23.2 | *persons (40)* | 11.8 |
| *Vatican* | 0.4 | *banks (4)* | 2.6 | *Vatican* | 0.7 |
| *Banks (10)* | 2.8 | *non-banking firms (11)* | 2.9 | *non-banking firms(3):* | 14.4 |
| *Non-banking firms* | 2.5 | *"others"* | 58.4 | *"others"* | 0.0 |
| *"others" (2207)* | 13.6 | | | | |
| **FIAT SPA (1993)** | | **PIRELLI & C. (1993)** | | **A.F.L. FALCK (1993)** | |
| *Agnelli family* | 24.8 | *Pirelli family* (5) | 8.7 | *Falck family* (6) | 32.3 |
| Via IFI* (2) | 18.1 | banks | 16.4 | Banks | 4.8 |
| Via IFIL* (3) | 1.9 | Mediobanca* | 10.0 | IMI | 4.8 |
| Via Fimepar (4) | 4.8 | Banque Indosuez | 6.4 | Non-banking firms | 28.3 |
| *Banks* | 11.0 | *non-banking firms* | 32.9 | Italmobiliare * (Pesenti) | 11.8 |
| Istituto San Paolo | 3.4 | GIM* (Orlando) | 6.7 | Siderca Techint * (Rocca) | 5.9 |
| Mediobanca* | 3.2 | SMI* (Orlando) | 3.6 | Ilva* (IRI) | 4.9 |
| Deutsche Bank* | 2.4 | Gemina* | 5.3 | Finarvedi * (Arvedi) | 4.7 |
| Banco di Roma | 2.0 | SAI* (Ligresti) | 5.0 | Sofinda* (Danieli) | 2.9 |
| *non-banking firms* | 4.8 | CAMFIN* (Tronchetti Provera) | 5.0 | Pirelli & C.* | 2.0 |
| Assicurazioni Generali* | 2.4 | CIR* (De Benedetti) | 4.4 | Ras * | 1.0 |
| Alcatel * | 2.0 | SOPAF* (Vender) | 2.9 | *"others"* | 34.6 |
| *"others" 59.4* | | *"others" 42.0* | | | |
| * Belonging to shareholders' voting and block agreements | | * Belonging to shareholders' voting and block agreements | | * Belonging to shareholders' voting and block agreements | |

Source: F. Barca, F. Bertucci, G. Capello, P. Casavola (1997), *La trasformazione proprietaria di Fiat, Pirelli e Falck dal 1947 a oggi*, in F. Barca (a cura di), *Storia del capitalismo italiano, dal dopoguerra a oggi*, Roma, Donzelli.

This lucky development for the Italian economy occurred when the world was facing the consequences of the "shocks" related to the advent to information technology and programmable machines. These "technological" shocks made "small size" firms based on "flexible specialisation" very competitive in world markets. The fast growth of the Italian small firm sector created the conditions under which many individuals could enjoy the rights related to ownership of their firms. These individuals had the incentives to develop the specific skills that were necessary for their development and, having developed these skills, often became the most efficient possible owners.

The institutional shock of the 1960s had an important role in bringing about the virtuous circle characterizing this self-reinforcing organizational equilibrium. While new technological changes now made it possible for large sectors of the economy to be based on small size firms (linked however by various forms of untraditional cooperation), Italy was one of the few countries to exploit this opportunity to such a great extent. While (or, perhaps, because!) the organization of governance in the large firms was stuck in a form a family capitalism characterized by social immobility and class conflicts, the governance system characterizing small firms became a "model" to be studied and imitated in other parts of the world.

Italy, which had gone through major institutional shocks in the thirties and, unlike Japan, had missed the opportunities offered by the postwar institutional shocks, could, in some respects, paradoxically benefit from the social shock of the sixties. However such benefits could only postpone the need for a substantial reform of the corporate sector of Italian capitalism.

## The nineties: a decade of change...and continuity

The nineties can be considered a decade of deep change for Italy. The entire political system born after WWII came to an end. Labour and financial markets were also hit by reforms.

In the last decade, new laws have been passed concerning banking and financial sectors, a large program of privatisation has been implemented, an Antitrust Authority has been created and more attention to competition has been paid. Many sectors have been liberalised (electricity, telecommunication, natural gas; retail).

The crisis of Italy's state-owned companies dragged on for more than 20 years, though not without a few moments of recovery, when managerial skill combined with favourable developments in the political situation. On the whole, through the seventies and eighties, static and dynamic inefficiencies increasingly hampered both large private and state-owned companies. The former went through a "stop and go" process, in which long-delayed adjustments would be effected abruptly:[42] costs, both in long-term strategies and investment and in workers' conditions, were high. Many state-owned companies came to a virtual standstill.

Both presented their shareholders and the general public with dramatic examples of abuses of control and – with a few notable exceptions – largely failed to develop multinational strategies. The steady growth over two decades of the small enterprise sector partly made up for these swings and for dynamic inefficiencies by growing steadily throughout the two decades. But too many of its results have came at the unquantified cost of tax evasion, aided by the fact that personal and company interests are often inextricably linked, particularly in the model of family control; and too many opportunities for growth – to go "big" – have been missed due to failures of corporate governance.

By the beginning of the 1990s, increasing pressure stemming from these failures, together with stricter constraints on state funding from the European Community, the liberalization of capital mobility and an upheaval in the political market,[43] led authorities to take some steps. The decade of the nineties saw a thorough overhaul of the role of public intervention in the Italian economy, cutting back direct State management of economic activities and revising the rules governing the conduct of private enterprises.

In particular, privatization of the state-owned enterprises gradually gathered support in Parliament and among the public. Some privatization responded in part to the actions of the European Commission regarding state subsidies to corporations and the related need to adjust the finances of several major state corporate groups. In 1992, following the EC currency crisis and the devaluation of the lira, the government finally passed a strong privatization plan, calling for the sale of all the productive enterprises controlled by the State. The reasoning behind the strategy was twofold: on the one hand, the need to curb the rise of a huge and mounting public debt; on the other, the desire to improve the competitiveness of the Italian industrial apparatus, bringing more small savers into the financial market. An important role was played by the widespread feeling that the sphere of social life controlled by the political parties had to be drastically circumscribed.

The privatization process, which began its operational phase in 1993, can be considered as one of the largest ever realized in a European country. It generated total gross proceeds of more than 164 trillion lire (85.000 millions euros) between 1993 and 2001 (Tab. 3), nearly 8 per cent of the average GDP for those years. In the last three years proceeds averaged 1.8 per cent of GDP. By way of comparison, in the period of most intensive privatization in the UK, between 1985 and 1995, annual proceeds averaged 1.2 per cent of GDP. This process implied an increase in market capitalization of the Italian stock market which was 1,400 trillion lire in 2000 (714 billion euros) equal to 65 per cent of GDP. Also due to the public offerings of shares during the privatization process the concentration of ownership has declined in the second half of the nineties. In 1998 the successful leveraged takeover of Telecom Italia (former State-owned monopolist, privatized in 1997), one of the largest hostile takeover ever made in Europe, has implied a big change in the lethargic Italian market for corporate control.

The salient event of the decade in the area of regulatory reform of the markets was Law 287 of 10 October 1990, "Antitrust Law", which instituted a Competition

Authority. A new Banking Law was introduced in 1993 (Law n. 385 1 September 1993) eliminating the prohibition for banks to purchase shares in non-financial corporations and the regional and maturity specialization of banks. Banks can now play a much more active role. The option of a market relying on broad-based popular shareholding and on the market for corporate control requires modification of the civil code to safeguard the rights of minority shareholders and guarantee greater transparency in corporate management. It also requires more effective supervision of the stock market by the regulatory authorities. A new law was passed in February 1998 (Legislative Decree n.58, 24 February 1998) on financial markets, securities, corporate governance. In particular, new rules for corporate governance based on international standards have been adopted.

On takeover bids, the new rules are based on the obligation for a party to bid for all of a company's ordinary shares once it has purchased more than 30 per cent of the company's capital (mandatory bid rule). Other significant innovations are the admission of an auction system for competing bids and the possibility for shareholders' meeting to authorize defensive tactics against hostile bids. In the area of corporate disclosure, the scope of some reporting requirements has been broadened to cover unlisted companies that have issued widely held financial instruments. With the aim of making the ownership of listed companies transparent, the new law confirms the requirement to notify the Stock Market Authority of equity interests that exceed 2 per cent. The new law also enhanced the transparency of shareholder agreements, limiting their maximum duration to three years. If the parties have not fixed an expiry date for the agreement, they may withdraw at any time after giving notice.

Shareholders with at least a 1 per cent interest in a company may engage qualified intermediaries (banks, securities firms, asset management companies or specialized firms) to solicit proxies from the other shareholders for use in the general meeting. The votes for which proxies have been collected are cast by the delegated shareholder or, at the latter's behest, by the intermediary that was engaged to carry out the solicitation. The role of a listed company's board of auditors in exercising control on the running of the company has been strengthened by rationalizing the division of accounting-related tasks between the board and the external auditors. The rights of minority shareholders have therefore been more protected.

## Table 3 – Main privatization in the nineties (follows next page)

| Corporation (Group) | Method of sale | Percentage sold | Gross proceeds in billions of lire |
|---|---|---|---|
| **1993** – Italgel (IRI) | Private agreement | 62.12 | 431 |
| Cirio-Bertolli-DeRica (IRI) | Private agreement | 62.12 | 311 |
| Credito Italiano (IRI) | Public offering | 58.09 | 1,801 |
| SIV (EFIM) | Auction | 100.00 | 210 |
| *Total for year* | | | *2,753* |
| **1994** – IMI – *1st tranche* | Public offering | 32.89 | 2,150 |
| COMIT (IRI) | Public offering | 54.35 | 2,891 |
| Nuovo Pignone (ENI) | Auction | 69.33 | 699 |
| INA – *1st tranche* | Public offering | 47.25 | 4,530 |
| Acciai Speciali Terni (IRI) | Private agreement | 100.00 | 624 |
| SME – *1st tranche (IRI)* | Private agreement | 32.00 | 723 |
| Other companies *(ENI)* | | | 1,087 |
| *Total for year* | | | 12,704 |
| **1995** – Italtel (IRI) | Auction | 40.00 | 1,000 |
| Ilva Laminati Piani (IRI) | Private agreement | 100.00 | 1,929 |
| Enichem Augusta (ENI) | Auction | 70.00 | 300 |
| Other companies *(ENI)* | | | 336 |
| IMI – *2nd tranche* | Private agreement | 19.03 | 1,200 |
| SME – *2nd tranche (IRI)* | Accept takeover bid | 14.91 | 341 |
| INA – *2nd tranche* | Private agreement | 18.37 | 1,687 |
| ENI – *1st tranche* | Public offering | 15.00 | 6,299 |
| ISE (IRI) | Auction | 73.96 | 370 |
| *Total for year* | | | *13,462* |
| **1996** – Dal mine (IRI) | Auction | 84.08 | 302 |
| Italimpianti (IRI) | Auction | 100.00 | 42 |
| Nuova Tirrena | Auction | 91.14 | 548 |
| SME – *3rd tranche* (IRI) | Accept takeover bid | 15.21 | 121 |
| INA – *3rd tranche* | Conv. Bond issue | 31.08 | 3,260 |
| MAC (IRI) | Auction | 50.00 | 223 |
| IMI – *3rd tranche* | Public offering | 6.94 | 501 |
| Montefibre (ENI) | Public offering | 65.00 | 183 |
| ENI – *2nd tranche* | Public offering | 15.82 | 8,872 |
| *Total for year* | | | *14,051* |

## Table 3 – Main privatization in the nineties (follows from preceding page)

| Corporation (Group) | Method of sale | Percentage sold | Gross proceeds in billions of lire |
|---|---|---|---|
| 1997 – ENI – 3rd tranche | Public offering | 17.60 | 13,230 |
| Aeroporti di Roma (IRI) | Public offering | 45.00 | 541 |
| Telecom Italia | Core investors + public offering | 39.54 | 22,883 |
| SEAT editoria | Core investors + public offering | 61.27 | 1,653 |
| Banca di Roma (IRI) | Public offering + bond issue | 36.50 | 1,900 |
| Total for year | | | 40,207 |
| 1998 – SAIPEM (ENI) | Public offering | 18.75 | 1,140 |
| ENI – 4th tranche | Public offering | 14.83 | 12,995 |
| BNL | Public offering | 67.85 | 6,707 |
| Total for year | | | 20,842 |
| 1999 – ENEL | Public offering | 35.50 | 34,828 |
| Autostrade (IRI) | Auction + public offering | 57.00 | 8,105 |
| Total for year | | | 42,933 |
| 2000 – Autostrade (IRI) | Private agreement | 30.00 | 4,911 |
| Finmeccanica (IRI) | Public offering | 43.70 | 5,505 |
| Aeroporti di Roma (IRI) | Private agreement | 51.20 | 1,328 |
| Banco di Napoli | Public offering | 16.16 | 494 |
| Total for year | | | 12,238 |
| 2001 – ENI – 5th tranche | Accelerate Book Building | 5.00 | 5,268 |
| | | | |
| **Total proceeds** | | | (2,721) **164,458** (84,935) |

*Sources*: Company accounts (various years); Ministry of the Treasury, *Relazione sulle privatizzazioni* (various years); Financial Press.

The other essential condition for a new system of corporate governance to supplant the obsolete devices still in place is the emergence of control-oriented, activist financial institutions. The opportunity to develop universal banking has been reinforced, and banks are now allowed (although subject to restrictions) to acquire equity interests in non-financial companies. For the corporate culture of the banks to change, however, the legal framework is inadequate. Banks need to have a strong incentive to undertake a new role, and this absolutely requires their privatisation.

The previous equilibrium based on the interaction between large family-controlled firms and large State-owned enterprises along with the key role of Mediobanca does no longer exist. The privatisation process has basically eliminated the role of the State as shareholder. Mediobanca, since the death of its president, E. Cuccia, has been trying to keep its balancing role in family capitalism, but with little success. Family capitalism is still in power, in most of the country large groups are still family-controlled and small enterprises rarely increase in size.

The issue remains open whether the attempts to import "institutions" created during the last decade will enhance a new institutional equilibrium or rather this will have negative effects due to inconsistencies with in the structural features of the economy. The above mentioned new Financial Act (n.58/1998), for instance, entitled small shareholders to new rights in order to protect their interests, and this in turn implies a more frequent recourse to courts of law to enforce these rights. So far, empirical research has shown that courts are not equipped to handle these kinds of legal conflict, so the impact of the new law is quite small (Enriques, 2001).

A new law on takeovers designed to protect minority shareholders has not produced results expected in the recent case of the second transfer of the controlling stake of Telecom Italia from the previous raider Colaninno to the Pirelli group, while the Agnellis have expanded their control to the energy sector. Privatisations do not seem to upset the institutional stability of corporate family capitalism, but rather to widen its sphere of influence.

## Conclusion

At the beginning of the nineties, the Italian private corporate sector had still failed to undergo a managerial revolution. In the wishes of some reformers another failure – that of the public sector firms – might have spurred the advent of a new managerial model based on the "private" public company. Privatization would not only have meant the end of the state-owned companies, but also a new beginning for the private sector. The family control of large corporations should have been replaced or, at least, integrated by one of the forms of anonymous managerial capitalism (possibly in its "American version") and a different type of Italian capitalism should have emerged. (For a summary of all the different types of Italian capitalism see table 4).

While some changes, such as the growth of the stock exchange, would seen to be pointing in the direction desired by the reformers, in other respects, traditional family capitalism is expanding its control of the Italian economy. Indeed, one could claim that family capitalism has even "purified" its mechanisms of transmissions of economic power from any sort of spurious interference. No Cuccia is there present any longer to supervise the quality of the replacement of one generation by the next (or by the following generation). No manager like Romiti can be trained in the public sector and then imposed by a Cuccia on the private sector when the "family-self-appointed managers" fail. A pessimist may argue that, while the public sector corporations have been privatised, the Italian private corporate sector lacks both the complementary institutions necessary for the success of managerial capitalism and the complementary institutions necessary for the survival of family capitalism. We can only hope it is not really as bad as it sounds.

Table 4 – Types of Italian Capitalism

|  | Financial markets | Corporate governance |
|---|---|---|
| ITALIAN CAPITALISM "MARK I" | Universal banks (German type)<br><br>Till 1907 relatively developed stock mkt; | – process of ownership concentration<br>– creation of pyramidal group; high bank/corporate ownership; cross shareholding |
| ITALIAN CAPITALISM "MARK II" | – Separation of banks and non-financial<br>Firms (i.e. Glass-Steagal Act)<br>– Illiquid capital market;<br>– Weaker financial mkt pressures;<br>– 80% of the banks are state-owned | – creation of big state-owned groups;<br>– ownership concentrated and stable;<br>– high family and corporate shareholding;<br>– pyramidal groups<br>– high cross-shareholding |
| ITALIAN CAPITALISM "MARK III" (1970s-80s) | – liberalization of financial mkt<br>– liberalization of banking sector<br>– privatization of banks | – emergence of a very important small and medium firms sector;<br>– deverticalization of large firms;<br>– crisis of many state-owned groups;<br>- Mediobanca |
| ITALIAN SYSTEM | – new banking law:<br>banks are free to own shares; universal banking is allowed; process of banking | – reduction in ownership concentration;<br>– no institutional investors;<br>– cases of hostile takeovers; less collusive |
| IN THE 1990s | Financial markets mergers;<br>– privatisation enhances development of a More liquid stock market;<br>– new financial law: higher transparency;<br>More information;<br>mandatory bid over 30% of capital | Corporate governance climate;<br>– crisis of Mediobanca<br>– resurgence of family capitalism;<br>– emerging of some new groups |

*Source*: elaboration by the Authors

## Notes

1. More on Mediobanca on section 6.
2. See Barca, Iwai, Pagano Trento (1999).
3. Let us for now use the two as synonymous.
4. The neo-classical model is also characterised by a very restrictive vision of individual preferences. In this framework, preferences for work (Pagano, 1985) and preferences related to self-definition (Pagano, 1995) and identity are not considered satisfactorily. By contrast, they have played a very important role in determining the success of the organizations and, more generally, the outcome of the complex historical events that are the object of this paper.
5. See Pagano (1993).
6. The formal properties of organizational equilibria are examined in Pagano (1993) and in Pagano and Rowthorn (1994) and (1995).
7. See section 7 of Pagano and Rowthorn (1995).
8. See Arthur (1989).
9. See Hart (1995).
10. In other words the evolution of capitalism seems to be characterized by forms of "allopatric speciation" in the sense that new forms of capitalism tend often to emerge in countries different from those where the preceding forms had had a successful development. Pagano (2001a and 2001b) considers the problems related to the origin of new species in biology and some common laws of structure and change that characterize the formation of new organizational species. In particular, the emergence of American and German managerial forms of capitalism are considered in the framework of the theories of "allopatric speciation" developed in evolutionary biology.
11. The discontinuity between pre-war and post-war Japan capitalism and the relevance of post-war institutional shocks can be clearly understood by considering an alternative (an perhaps more appropriate) comparison with Italian capitalism. While the policies of the Allied Powers reinforced the Italian system of family capitalism, the American occupation terminated its Japanese version. The "institutional bifurcation" that was created had long lasting consequences and shaped the development of the two countries (Barca, Iwai, Pagano and Trento 1999).
12. In particular team work, which often replaced the assembly line in Japanese organizations, was necessarily characterised by the specificity of the skills (each skill becoming specific to those of the other team members) and by the difficulty to monitor the workers (it is difficult for an outsider to disentangle the contribution of a single worker from those of the other members of the team).
13. This multiplicity of feasible organizations is very important for economic policy and, in particular, for the problems related to the transformation of the former socialist countries (Aoki 1995, Pagano 2000). A comparative institutional analysis is required to consider the self-reinforcing mechanisms or the complementarities (Aoki 1996, 2001) that characterize each of the feasible alternatives.
14. Other reasons for which this is a very unlikely outcome are given in Hodgson (1999) who points out how the idea of the "end of history" is "deeply connected to an Enlightenment principle. This is the idea of a universal history: the notion of an

universal destination, underpinned by absolute rational principles" (Hodgson 1999, p. 153)

[15] In the words of a great Italian thinker of this century, Antonio Gramsci: "the Italian economy was very weak (and) there was no large and powerful economic bourgeoisie; instead there was a great number of intellectuals and petty bourgeois, etc. The problem was not so much to free already developed economic forces from antiquated legal and political fetters as to bring into being the general conditions for these economic forces to arise and develop along the same lines as in other countries", Gramsci (1975a), p. 57.

[16] As Gerschenkron noted, and as has been confirmed by more recent studies (Federico and Toniolo, 1991), protectionism was misdirected, favouring wheat production and basic industries with strong lobbying powers but poor long-term prospects.

[17] See Gerschenkron, (1962), p. 11.

[18] This thesis has not been dismantled even by subsequent studies emphasising the limits of the "German-type bank" experience. See Confalonieri (1974).

[19] On the eve of World War I, both Banca Commerciale Italiana and Credito Italiano had significant equity stakes in a number of major nascent enterprises.

[20] See Zamagni (1990).

[21] Until the reform of 1913 the primary source of law governing Italian stock exchanges was the French commercial code promulgated by Napoleon in 1807. The stock exchange, conceived of as the centre for directing savings into industrial and commercial activities, was a Napoleonic concept, introduced when Italy was in the French sphere of influence in the first decade of the nineteenth century. Bourses were founded in a number of Italian cities between 1802 and 1808, but this forcible innovation, not borne of any commercial necessity, was greeted with indifference if not outright hostility. The Italian exchanges were not structured as free associations of participants, on the English model, but were imposed from above, on the state-controlled pattern of the "Bourse du Roi". See Aleotti (1990), p. 29.

[22] 100 per cent of Italy's defense-related steel industry and coal mining, 90 per cent of its shipbuilding, 80 per cent of maritime shipping, 80 per cent of locomotive manufacture, 40 per cent of the non-military steel industry, 30 per cent of electricity generation, 20 per cent of the output of rayon and 13 per cent of the output of cotton. In addition, IRI owned a number of mechanical engineering firms, controlled the three largest commercial banks and the telephone service in central and northern Italy, and possessed very extensive real estate holdings. See Castronovo (1995).

[23] See Aleotti (1990).

[24] This was quite different from the path followed in the United States, where financial rehabilitation and the separation between banking and industry were founded upon the recovery of the stock market, with the formation of the SEC, the regulation of mutual funds and deposit protection legislation.

[25] See Cianci (1977).

[26] See Barca (1994), chapter VIII.

[27] See Ginsborg (1990).

[28] See Ellwood (1985).

[29] Sandro Pertini, future Italian President of the Republic, denounced this agreement as "the total surrender of the Italian Resistance movement to the English interests", see Ginsborg (1990).

[30] The judiciary system was not touched by the purge, so that the total majority of the purging trials held in the early months after the war issued not guilty sentences. As late as 1960, 62 of the 64 local government officers (Prefetti), all of the 135 Police chiefs (Questori) were appointed under the fascist regime Ginsborg (1990), p. 120.

[31] Barca and Trento (1997).

[32] Between 1948 and 1952 Italy received transfers of a total value of US$ 1,470 million, equivalent to 11% of the total ERP aid to Western Europe. See Romeo (1991), p.174.

[33] He offered a severe judgment of Italian financiers as a group: "Italy has never had a class of financiers who loved banking for banking's sake; that is, who were disposed to invest their money in bank shares and to operate banks with the sole aim of earning the largest possible dividends from those shares. Only industrial groups have manifested any interest, at various times, in acquiring stakes in the leading banks", Menichella (1944), pp. 127-128.

[34] This position belongs to a long-standing line of thought according to which Italian capitalism had always been fragile, bereft of legitimacy in the country and lacking a farsighted bourgeoisie. See Gramsci (1975b), p.56.

[35] See Bottiglieri (1984).

[36] In particular, at the turn of the decade, Oscar Sinigaglia, head of the steel division, drafted and implemented a plan for the construction of three full-cycle steel plants comparable in size and technology to the most up-to-date foreign facilities. Until then the Italian steel industry had been modest and antiquated, mainly reprocessing scrap metal. Sinigaglia argued that without a modern steel industry Italy would never have a true engineering or motor vehicle industry. See La Bella (1983), p. 53.

[37] See Colitti (1979), p. 117 ff.

[38] See Barca and Trento (1997).

[39] See Maraffi (1990).

[40] The 1936 reform had produced a banking system in which commercial banks were prohibited from medium and long-term lending. In 1944 and 1945 Raffaele Mattioli, chairman of Banca Commerciale Italiana, sponsored the formation of a new industrial credit institute mandated to offer five-year credit to firms. Originally, the plan called for close links between the new institute and Banca Commerciale, virtually replicating the "universal bank", with Banca Commerciale specializing in ordinary credit and the new institution financing longer-term industrial investment projects. In 1946, this project eventually led to the creation of a new medium-term credit institution, Mediobanca, whose equity capital was mostly subscribed by three IRI banks: Banca Commerciale, Credito Italiano and Banco di Roma. Originally intended in part to sustain the development of small firms, over the years Mediobanca was transformed into a true investment bank for Italy's leading private enterprises.

[41] See Barca (1995) and Barca, Bianchi, Brioschi et al. (1994).

[42] See Barca and Magnani (1989).

[43] A series of electoral reforms resulted in a British-style, first-past-the-post electoral system. At the same time judicial inquiries into political corruption overturned the political equilibrium that had prevailed for the entire postwar period, with the disintegration of the two leading government parties, the DC and the PSI. This transition is still under way, with intensive debate over the new constitutional rules that should be adopted.

# References

Aleotti, A. (1990), *Borsa e Industria. 1861-1989: cento anni di rapporti difficili*, Milano, Edizioni di Comunità.
Aoki, M. (1995), 'An Evolving Diversity of Organisational Mode and Its Implications for Transitional Economies', in *CEPR Discussion Paper Series*, n. 420, Stanford University.
(1996), 'Towards a Comparative Institutional Analysis: Motivations and Some Tentative Theorizing Presidential Address', in *Japanese Economic Review*, vol. 47, n. 1, pp. 1-19.
(2001), *Towards a Comparative Institutional Analysis*, MIT Press, Cambridge MA.
Arthur, B. (1989), 'Competing Technologies, Increasing Returns, and Lock-in by Historical Events', in *Economic Journal*, vol. 99, n. 394, pp. 116-131.
Barca, F. (1994), *Imprese in cerca di padrone. Proprietà e controllo nel capitalismo italiano*, Bari, Laterza.
(1995), *On Corporate Governance in Italy: Issues, Facts and Agenda*, paper presented at OECD Conference on: 'The influence of corporate governance and financing structure on economic performance', Paris, 23-24 February.
(1997), *Compromesso senza riforme nel capitalismo italiano*, in F. Barca (a cura di), *Storia del capitalismo italiano dal dopoguerra a oggi*, Roma, Donzelli.
M. Magnani (1989), *L'Industria fra capitale e lavoro*, Bologna, Il Mulino.
M. Bianchi, F. Brioschi, L. Buzzacchi, P. Casavola, L. Filippa, M. Pagnini (1994), *Assetti proprietari e mercato delle imprese. Gruppo, proprietà e controllo nelle imprese italiane medio-grandi*, vol. II, Bologna, Il Mulino.
S. Trento, (1997), 'State Ownership and the Evolution of Italian Corporate Governance', in *Industrial and Corporate Change*, vol. 6, n. 3.
F. Bertucci, G. Capello, P. Casavola (1997), *La trasformazione proprietaria di Fiat, Pirelli e Falck dal 1947 a oggi*, in F. Barca (a cura di), *Storia del capitalismo italiano, dal 1945 a oggi*, Roma, Donzelli.
K. Iwai, U. Pagano and S. Trento (1999), 'The divergence of the Italian and Japanese Corporate Governance Models: the Role of Institutional Shocks', in *Economic Systems*, vol. 23, issue 1, pp. 35-60.
Berle, A. and G. Means (1933), *The Modern Corporation and Private Property*, London, Macmillan.
Bottiglieri, B. (1984), 'Linee interpretative del dibattito sulle partecipazioni statali nel secondo dopoguerra', in *Economia Pubblica*, Aprile-Maggio, pp. 239-244.
Brusco, S. and S. Paba (1997), 'Per una storia dei distretti industriali italiani dal secondo dopoguerra agli anni novanta,' in F. Barca (a cura di), *Storia del capitalismo italiano, dal dopoguerra a oggi*, Roma, Donzelli.
Castronovo, V. (1995), *Storia Economica d'Italia. Dall'Ottocento ai giorni nostri*, Torino, Einaudi.
Chandler A.D. (1990), *Scale and Scope: the Dynamics of Industrial Capitalism*, Harvard University Press, Cambridge, MA.
Cianci, E. (1977), *La nascita dello Stato imprenditore*, Milano, Mursia.
Colitti, M. (1979), *Energia e sviluppo in Italia. La vicenda di Enrico Mattei*, Bari, De Donato.
Confalonieri, A. (1974), *Banca e industria in Italia, 1894-1906*, 3 volumes, Banca Commerciale Italiana, Milano.

De Cecco M. Ferri (1996), *Le Banche d'affari in Italia*, Bologna, Il Mulino.
Federico, G. and G. Toniolo (1991), 'Italy – Chapter 10', in R. Sylla, G. Toniolo (eds), *Patterns of European Industrialization*, London, Routledge
Ellwood, D.W. (1985), *Italy 1943-1945*, Leicester, Leicester University Press.
Enriques, L. (2001), 'Il nuovo diritto societario nelle mani dei giudici: una ricognizione empirica', in *Stato e Mercato*, 61, aprile, pp. 45-78.
Friedman, A. (1989) *Agnelli and the Italian Network of Power*. Mandarin Paperbacks, London.
Fukuyama F. (1995), *Thrust. The Social Virtues and the Creation of Prosperity*, London, Penguin Books.
Gerschenkron, A. (1962), *Economic Backwardness in Historical Perspective*, Cambridge (MA), Belknap Press.
Ginsborg, P. (1990), *A History of Contemporary Italy*, London, Penguin Books.
Gramsci, A. (1975a), *Il Risorgimento, Quaderni del Carcere*, Roma, Editori Riuniti.
(1975b), *Note sul Machiavelli, Quaderni del Carcere*, Roma, Editori Riuniti.
Hart, O. (1995), *Firms, Contracts and Financial Structure*, Clarendon Press, Oxford.
Hodgson, G.M. (1999), 'Economics and Utopia: Why the Learning Economy is not the End of History', Routledge, London.
Iwai, K. (1999), 'Persons, Things and Corporations: The Corporate Personality Controversy and Comparative Corporate Governance American Journal of Comparative Law, vol. 47, pp. 583- 632.
La Bella, G. (1983), *L'IRI nel dopoguerra*, Roma, Edizioni Studium.
Maraffi, M. (1990), *Politica ed economia in Italia. La vicenda dell'impresa pubblica dagli anni trenta agli anni cinquanta*, Bologna, Il Mulino.
Menichella, D. (1944), *Le origini dell'IRI e la sua azione nei confronti della situazione bancaria*, reprinted in Banca d'Italia, *Donato Menichella, Scritti e discorsi scelti, 1933-1966*, Roma, 1986
Pagano U. (1985), *Work and Welfare in Economic Theory*, Basil Blackwell, Oxford.
(1991a), 'Property Rights, Asset Specificity, and The Division of Labour under Alternative Capitalist Relations', in *Cambridge Journal of Economics*, vol. 15, n. 3, pp. 315-342. Reprinted in G. Hodgson G. M. (1993) *The Economics of Institutions* Edward Elgar, Cheltenham.
(1991b), 'Property Rights Equilibria and Institutional Stability', in *Economic Notes*, vol. 20, n. 2, pp. 189-228.
(1993) 'Organisational Equilibria and Institutional Stability', in Bowles S., Gintis H., Gustafson B. eds. *Markets and Democracy*. Cambridge University Press, Cambridge.
(1995) 'Can Economics Explain Nationalism?', in Breton A. et al. *Nationalism and Rationality*, pp. 173-204, Cambridge University Press, Cambridge.
(2000) 'Transition and the 'speciation' of the Japanese Model'. In Fabel O., Farina F. and Punzo L. in *European Economies in Transition. In Search of a New Growth Path*. Macmillan London and St. Martin Press New York pp.198-236.
(2001a) 'The Origin of Organizational Species', The Origin of Organizational Species. In A. Nicita, U. Pagano (2001) *The Evolution of Economic Diversity*. Routledge, London and New York, pp. 21-47
(2001b) *Information Technology and the 'Biodiversity' of Capitalism*. In G. Hodgson et al. *Capitalism in Evolution*, Edward Elgar, Adershot.
Rowthorn R. (1994) 'Ownership, Technology and Institutional Stability', in *Structural Change and Economic Dynamics*. vol. 5, n. 2 pp. 221-243.

Rowthorn R. (1995) 'The Competitive Selection of Democratic Firms in a World of Self-Sustaining Institutions', in Pagano U. and Rowthorn R. eds. *Democracy and Efficiency in the Economic Enterprise*, Routledge, London and New York.

Romeo, R. (1991), '*Breve storia della grande industria in Italia, 1861-1961*', Il Saggiatore, Milano.

Zamagni, V. (1990), *Dalla periferia al centro. La seconda rinascita economica dell'Italia, 1861-1981*, Bologna, Il Mulino.

Chapter 9

# Production Outsourcing in Italian Manufacturing Industry[1]

Alessandro Innocenti

**Introduction**

The debate on the role of dualism in the Italian manufacturing industry goes back to the 1970s. Since then it has been a key issue not only for industrial economics but also for economic policy. Only recently the Italian Parliament has recognised the autonomous role played by the local systems of small firms in economic development by introducing specific legislation to support industrial districts. At the same time, theoretical approaches interpreting the relationships between small and large firms solely as subordinate ones have been disputed on both empirical and theoretical grounds. Some arguments were suggested by the evolutionary theories of innovation. Innovation has been viewed as a localized process where progress can be obtained only gradually and within the path followed by each firm, independently of its size. Other insights were given by information economics. Firms have been described as information processors and repositories of explicit and tacit knowledge, that are made complementary to each other by the decentralised action of the network. By means of cooperative relationships with other small firms and of growing specialisation, small firms can remain small and become autonomous decision-makers. At the same time, vertical integration of large firm has been generally abandoned in favour of a refocusing on core activities joined with outsourcing through the subcontracting of the production of parts or of the provision of services to small and medium firms. Generally speaking, subcontracting can be defined as a pattern of co-ordination of production activities based on vertical relationships between separately owned and managed enterprises with distinct economic objectives.[2] The buyer decides not to internalise the development and production of a component, nor to directly procure it from a spot market. Instead, a sustained relationship is created, which includes the exchange of proprietary information and knowledge between the buyer and the supplier. The efficiency of this relationship depends on the fact that all the firms involved, whatever their size, share the knowledge necessary to solve problems of complementarities among different production phases but at the same time are protected from being expropriated of their own specific knowledge and their profits.

This paper analyses how these conditions for efficiency in networks of firms have been satisfied in the Italian manufacturing industry and proposes a theoretical interpretation to explain them. Section 2 surveys some evidence showing that since the 1970s production outsourcing was increasingly used in Italian manufacturing industry despite the high employment share of small firms. Section 3 argues that such a growth was characterised by the convergence between organizational patterns of vertical networks promoted by large firms and those characterising industrial districts. Both large and small firms increasingly externalised production phases by evolving from their past dependence on sourcing cheaper labour towards speciality subcontracting. Section 4 proposes a theoretical framework to interpret this process. It is argued that an explanation of the growth of outsourcing is given by the informational advantages of decentralised networks of firms over the vertically integrated firm. Section 5 sets out some concluding remarks.

## The extent of outsourcing

The high employment share of small firms is considered a distinctive characteristic of Italian industrial organisation since the 1970s.[3] All the same, economic activity in Italian manufacturing moved away from large firms to small firms in the 1980s and 1990s. As Table 1 shows, the rate of downsizing grew constantly during the 1971-1996 period. In particular, the employment share of firms with less than 50 employees increased from 38.8 per cent to 56.6 per cent. In the same period the share of firms with 500 or more employees dropped from 32.2 per cent to 17.2 per cent.

Table 1 – Manufacturing employment by firms size class (percentage shares)

|      | 1-9  | 10-19 | 20-49 | 50-99 | 100-199 | 200-499 | ≥500 | <50  | ≥50  |
|------|------|-------|-------|-------|---------|---------|------|------|------|
| 1971 | 19.1 | 7.9   | 11.8  | 9.5   | 9.2     | 10.3    | 32.2 | 38.8 | 61.2 |
| 1981 | 21.6 | 11.9  | 12.7  | 9.1   | 9.0     | 9.6     | 26.2 | 46.2 | 53.8 |
| 1991 | 24.4 | 14.7  | 15.3  | 8.9   | 8.1     | 8.8     | 19.8 | 54.5 | 45.5 |
| 1996 | 24.9 | 15.3  | 16.4  | 9.2   | 8.4     | 8.6     | 17.2 | 56.6 | 43.4 |

Source: Author's elaborations of Istat census database

This process has been attributed to a number of features of the Italian economy. First, small firms would have benefited from less rigidity in the labour market and more favourable fiscal treatment. A specific legislation approved in the 1970s affected primarily large-scale firms, by imposing them restrictive norms for dismissing workers. Moreover, it is well known that the practice of avoiding taxation was relatively more diffuse among small firms. Second, the prevalence of small size firms was fostered by the rapid growth of industrial districts. These local systems of production had gradually become the most innovative and profitable part of the Italian industrial system. In addition to these causes, firm downsizing showed in Table 1 cannot be explained without the spreading of outsourcing.

An indirect way to assess the extent of outsourcing is given by the degree of vertical integration. As Arrighetti (1999) shows, the index of vertical integration – namely, the ratio of value added over output – for the Italian manufacturing industry was stable on 0.35 – 0.39 from 1968 until the 1973. Then, it constantly decreased until 1997, when it was about 0.27. This trend is confirmed by disaggregated data. All the macro-sectors of manufacturing share the same tendency with the only exception of the food sector. Arrighetti also calculates the same index by firm size classes showing that the decrease was common to all the classes considered (20-199, 200-999, more than 999) but it was greater for large firms and more variable for medium and small firms. Not surprisingly, the comparison with a number of European countries confirms that although the rise in outsourcing was a very diffuse process, the Italian case was characterised by greater intensity and rapidity of change. Finally, it is interesting to note that according to some econometric tests performed by Arrighetti, the determinants of outsourcing were mainly connected to structural and organizational specificities of the countries under analysis rather than to uncertainty or variability of the demand in the final markets. Another indirect source of evidence for outsourcing is given by the sample measurements of the extent of subcontracting relationships. The main problem with this evidence is that it appears fragmented and piecemeal. In particular its evaluation is made difficult by the variety of definitions employed. However, available data confirm the widespread and growing use of outsourcing.

Sample data was collected by Mediocredito Centrale with the *Indagine sulle imprese manifatturiere*, that provides information both on the size and the evolution of subcontracting. So far the Observatory of Mediocredito Centrale has produced three surveys. The first was conducted in 1989-1991 and published in 1994; the second was conducted in 1992-1994 and published in 1997. In the second half of 1999 Mediocredito completed the third survey for the 1995-1997 period. All the surveys targeted manufacturing firms with more than 10 employees. The sample of 4.497 firms was stratified by census region and employment size.

**Table 2 – Firms by intensity of subcontracting (percentage shares)**

|  | 1994 | 1997 |
|---|---|---|
| Intensity of subcontracting | | |
| 0 | 66.8 | 62.5 |
| 0-10 | 15.6 | 3.9 |
| 10-25 | 8.0 | 2.8 |
| 25-50 | 6.1 | 4.0 |
| 50-100 | 3.5 | 26.8 |

*Source*: Author's elaborations of Mediocredito Centrale data

The dataset included information from balance sheets and subcontracting relationships. Only 1994 data are comparable with 1997 data because previous surveys considered different samples of firms. Table 2 gives data for the intensity of subcontracting, that is measured by the ratio between subcontracting activity and turnover.

In the 1994-1997 period, the share of subcontracting firms in the total of manufacturing firms rose by more than 4 percentage points (from 33,2 to 37,5 per cent). In just three years, the share of firms that subcontracted more than 50 per cent of their turnover grew from 3,5 to 26,8 per cent.

**Table 3 – Subcontracting intensity by firm size class and Pavitt sectors, 1997 (all firms)**

|  | Traditional | Scale | Specialized | High technology | Total |
|---|---|---|---|---|---|
| *Number of employees* |  |  |  |  |  |
| 11-20 | 27.9 | 27.3 | 30.1 | 18.3 | 27.9 |
| 21-50 | 28.7 | 34.4 | 30.0 | 23.5 | 30.3 |
| 51-100 | 28.1 | 28.0 | 26.0 | 35.2 | 27.8 |
| 101-250 | 25.8 | 27.6 | 20.2 | 23.9 | 24.7 |
| 251-500 | 22.4 | 23.3 | 33.1 | 25.9 | 26.1 |
| > 500 | 9.9 | 22.2 | 22.9 | 40.1 | 22.4 |
| Total | 27.4 | 29.3 | 28.3 | 26.2 | 28.1 |

**Table 4 – Subcontracting intensity by firms size class and Pavitt sectors, 1997 (only subcontracting firms)**

|  | Traditional | Scale | Specialized | High technology | Total |
|---|---|---|---|---|---|
| *Firms size* |  |  |  |  |  |
| 11-20 | 78.4 | 73.9 | 77.1 | 71.6 | 76.8 |
| 21-50 | 72.1 | 81.1 | 78.1 | 76 | 76.3 |
| 51-100 | 76.3 | 74.5 | 72.5 | 79.2 | 75 |
| 101-250 | 70.1 | 68.8 | 60.7 | 75.8 | 67.5 |
| 251-500 | 73.4 | 76.9 | 67.9 | 67.4 | 71.9 |
| > 500 | 40.6 | 68.1 | 74.6 | 77.5 | 67.3 |
| Total | 74 | 76 | 74.4 | 75.5 | 74.7 |

*Source (table3-table4)*: Author's elaborations of Mediocredito Centrale data

In 1997, subcontracting intensity (Tables 3 and 4) was on average about 28 per cent for the entire sample and 75 per cent for subcontracting firms and it was virtually constant across Pavitt sectors and firm size classes. In particular, no major difference emerges between scale and specialized sectors and across size classes with less than 500 employees. This suggests that similar patterns of relationships are shared to the same extent by different production techniques and various organisational structures.

The search for variables correlated with subcontracting is troublesome because there are a number of factors that are likely to increase the level of outsourcing. A possible correlate of subcontracting intensity may be export intensity. On the contrary Mediocredito data (Table 5) shows that non-export firms outsourced more than export firms. The source of this relation could suggest that relationships among small firms belonging to local systems account for a considerable part of subcontracting activity. However different evidence exists concerning the distribution of subcontracting activity according to geographical distribution (Table 6). The total share of sales in subcontracting to foreign firms (belonging or not to the same group) was 23.7 per cent in total, the total share of sales to national firms was 33.6 per cent and 33 per cent to firms located in the same area. Finally, the percentage of sales in subcontracting among firms belonging to the same group was about 40 per cent. This data could be evidence of the fact that, although the existence of widespread intra-group links was supported, subcontracting relationships among independent and distant firms were also significant.

**Table 5 – Subcontracting intensity by export activity, 1997 (all firms)**

|  | *Share of subcontracting activity in turnover* |
|---|---|
| Export Firms | 23.8 |
| Non-export Firms | 38.9 |
| Total | 28.1 |

*Source*: Author's elaborations of Mediocredito Centrale data

**Table 6 – Subcontracting activity by geographical distribution 1997**

|  | *Shares of sales in subcontracting* |
|---|---|
| Foreign firms belonging to the same group | 7.6 |
| Domestic firms belonging to the same group | 17.5 |
| Local firms belonging to the same group | 15.0 |
| Foreign firms | 16.1 |
| National firms | 46.2 |
| Local firms | 28.0 |

*Source*: Author's elaborations of Mediocredito Centrale data

Not surprisingly, the share of the main contractor (Table 7) shows a U-shape distribution that matches firm size distribution of Italian manufacturers. Largest and smallest firms established subcontracting relationships characterized by a higher share of the first contractor compared to the intermediate size firms. However, the share of the main contractor was, on average, 21 per cent, that is a value too low to substantiate the dominance of strictly hierarchical relationships between contractors and subcontractors.

**Table 7 – Shares of the main contractor by firm size class**

|  | Number of employees | | | | | | |
|---|---|---|---|---|---|---|---|
|  | 11-20 | 21-50 | 51-100 | 101-250 | 251-500 | > 500 | Total |
| First contractor | 21.5 | 20.7 | 20.3 | 19.7 | 21.2 | 22.1 | 20.9 |
| First three contractors | 36.6 | 36.0 | 34.3 | 33.8 | 34.1 | 37.2 | 35.6 |

*Source*: Author's elaborations of Mediocredito Centrale data

Mediocredito data also allow for a positive evaluation of the subcontractors' performance (Table 8). The values of Return on Equity (ROE) and of Return on Investment (ROI) and investment/turnover ratio for subcontracting firms were indeed higher than for non-subcontracting firms.

**Table 8 – Indicators of performance**

|  | $ROE^4$ | ROI | Investment/turnover |
|---|---|---|---|
| Subcontracting firms | - 8.2 | 30.1 | 6.3 |
| Non-subcontracting firms | -27.5 | 22.9 | 6.2 |
| Total | -20.4 | 25.5 | 6.2 |

*Source*: Author's elaborations of Mediocredito Centrale data

Finally, another piece of information is given by the Bank of Italy that has recently promoted a statistically significant sample survey of industrial districts (Omiccioli 2000). This survey gives an assessment of the average intensity of subcontracting of about 25 per cent of the turnover in industrial districts. This value, that matches exactly the results of Mediocredito surveys for the whole manufacturing industry, confirms the share of subcontracting in the local system of small firms and is similar to that of vertical networks co-ordinated by large firms. More interestingly, the analysis of the specific patterns of outsourcing shows that local systems increase the degree of specialization by outsourcing not only immaterial activities (design, marketing, advertising) but also productive phases. The prevalent pattern adopted by these subcontracting relationships among small firms is to create balanced contractual arrangements, where suppliers and users are protected from exploitation or replacement by the increase of their specialization.

To conclude, the spreading of outsourcing increasingly characterises the Italian manufacturing industry. Since the average size of Italian manufacturing firms has been steadily decreasing, the distance between the employment share of small Italian firms and that of other industrialized countries has been growing. These quantitative changes have been triggered off by qualitative transformations that are discussed in the following section, first the case of outsourcing of large vs. small firms is discussed followed by that of small vs. small firms within local systems of production.

## Changing patterns in production outsourcing

### The outsourcing of large firms

The downsizing or segmentation of large firms is conventionally viewed as the main cause of outsourcing. Such a process could depend on the maintenance of hierarchical arrangements between the supplier (usually small) and the user (usually large) and could ask for arm's length relationships safeguarding the retaliation power of the large firm.[5] Although the traditional patterns of exploitation of subcontractors through one-way communication channels and demands for cost reductions remains diffuse in traditional scale sectors and low-skilled activities, outsourcing between independent or partner firms has become the main source of downsizing even for large firms. Following the diffusion of the flexible production systems, which combine economies of scale and scope by pushing product differentiation to the last stages of the production process, large firms have progressively disintegrated vertically and established specific relationships with their suppliers. This expanding reliance on subcontractors, both for parts and for complete subassemblies, means that the way in which subcontracting relationships are organised becomes central to the efficiency of the whole production process and to the quality of products. The aim of large firms becomes the implementation of these relationship in cooperation with their small subcontractors by creating relational contracts, operating on a long-term basis and requiring active responses in terms of innovation and flexibility. To obtain this result, most large firms have outsourced by adjusting to subcontractor characteristics and by radically changing their internal organization. For instance, Camuffo and Volpato (2001) describe the case of the car industry, while Crestanello (1999) discusses the textile and clothing industry case. In these cases, outsourcing follows different channels, starting with spin-off within the same group and moving on to the start of new activities that is combined with large-scale specialisation strategies. The first level of the supply chain is progressively reduced and takes responsibility not only for the production of specific parts but also for technological innovation and components design. Finally, services have been fully outsourced, from those having lower added value and more labour-intensive (security, cleaning and catering) to more complex services such as logistics, computer maintenance, or transportation.

Generally, the process of outsourcing of large firms involves two main types of suppliers according to the degree of autonomy of the supplier. The first type is the dependent supplier, which just executes orders from the client firm. This kind of relationship is hierarchical, and information flows are typically one-way from the user to the supplier. The second type is more autonomous and is involved in the co-design of products. The subcontractor in this case faces more competitive pressure, from other potential suppliers, but has more bargaining power regarding the price of the product.

Insights into the characteristics of these relationships are given by the example of the carmaker Fiat. Recent work (Enrietti 2000, Volpato and Stocchetti 2000, Camuffo and Volpato 2001) shows that outsourcing is rapidly increasing, in both production and services. While in the 1970s and 1980s, Fiat outsourced mainly low value added production phases, since the late 1980s the same process involved important production phases such as the mounting of suspension units and crucial services like plant maintenance and logistics. An evident measure of the extent of this process is given by the reduction in employment level by 38 per cent from 133,431 units in 1990 to 82,450 units in 1999 despite the maintenance of the same production level.

The downsizing of Fiat has been accompanied by the restructuring of the suppliers relationships. Subcontractors are divided into three groups. The first-level subcontractors are those producing more complex components that are designed in close collaboration with Fiat and that are usually modules to be assembled internally by Fiat. The other two groups produce more standardized components and their activity is relatively more independent from Fiat.

The rationale for outsourcing appears to be the increase in the specialisation of activities. Subcontractors are chosen on the basis of their specialised technical knowledge and not in order to lower labour costs.[6] First-tier suppliers carry out specific tasks that correspond to a module. In order to make the different parts complementary, Fiat has organised car production by arranging the different phases in such a way that the information necessary to produce each of them can be processed autonomously. Generally, when a task is decomposed, the resulting units cannot only be arranged in different ways, they can also interact with each other in various ways. The amount and nature of interaction between the different modules can be described in terms of different kinds of modularity (Fodor 1983). The representational modularity, also known as information encapsulation, means that each module has its own exclusive representation of a kind of knowledge that is not accessible to any other module. Differently from functional modularity, where each module can interact with the other modules, in presence of encapsulated information a module is an exclusive source of knowledge and is independent on general architecture.[7] This implies that contrary to the past, when car components were designed and engineered by the car manufacturer leading the whole project and suppliers simply manufactured them, now the supply chain is fully decentralized among firms of equal importance:

"The fundamental aspect of coordination based upon ex ante planning is that any individual operator does not need information on the whole chain of operations. Any chain operator must know only start and end date for a given activity, and must be concerned about precisely meeting its specific deadline. This implies a hierarchical management of information. But forms of simultaneous coordination on the whole of operations, aimed at compressing chain slacks require on line access to the whole sequence of operations, in order to carry out adaptations any time in which downwards demand triggers a wave of change which involves the whole upward operation chain. In other words, this implies forms of network connections among operators. The decision-making processes related to product development involve both the car manufacturer and first tier suppliers. According to the continuous improvement both in product and process technology, nowadays the competencies that are necessary in order to manufacture a competitive car encompass a wide range of fields of expertise. As a result, critical decisions might often take place in an inter-firm process and thus an agreement among peers could be required" (Volpato and Stocchetti 2000, p. 9).

This arrangement requires that relationships between large firms and suppliers become contractually more balanced and long-term in such a way that their duration is determined by the product life cycles. Each time a new product is launched, the large firm makes a sort of call for the best offer from suppliers and suppliers are put into competition. After this initial phase, large firms continue subcontracting relationships with the same suppliers, so that product change is in fact an occasion to renegotiate the contract. The long duration of relationships allows deriving some of the benefit of vertical integration, while simultaneously avoiding its drawbacks, such as the lack of incentive for performance for the component maker.

Moreover, the flows of information in the suppliers network become more intense and complex. Technological and market information are shared depending on the necessity of co-ordinating the whole production process and a common language is established. On the other hand, the supplier specialises in an autonomous way and therefore can develop proper ideas and innovate. The advantages of this network can be characterized as the result of specialisation, namely to deal with a particular subset of the overall information set related to the development of the product, and of the sharing of generic knowledge, which brings both co-ordination and innovation, while the encapsulation of information safeguards incentives to introduce innovation because the residual claimant to the rents from innovation is protected from being expropriated.

One interesting point that is worth noting is that such partnership relationships are supported by technological progress (Mariotti ed. 1996). The co-ordination across firm boundaries is indeed helped by the use of information technology, and CAD (Computer Aided Design) systems in particular. Electronic data interchange was first used for structured tasks, such as scheduling, logistics and just in time. The increase of involvement of some suppliers in product development is associated with the use of information technology for complex and creative tasks, such as joint design and engineering. In addition, information technology helps to increase the efficiency of network relationships with suppliers since electronic data interchange and industry-wide platforms have been shown to help buyers to reduce the costs of finding an appropriate supplier, monitoring subcontractors and co-ordinating ordering, scheduling and payment systems (Bensaou, 1999). Such co-design requires close collaboration and intense communication between the engineers of the buyer firm and the supplier.

## The outsourcing of small firms

If the disintegration of large firms had a decisive influence on the further increase of the occupational share of small firms, the processes of outsourcing among small firms have reinforced the same trend. Carnazza, Innocenti and Vercelli (2000) study the processes of outsourcing among small firms of Italian industrial districts. Their discussion is based on the distinction between specialised and capacity-based subcontracting. Specialised subcontracting means a relationship between a contractor and a subcontractor where the former continuously relies on the latter for the supply of an input for which there is no in-house supply. In contrast, capacity-based subcontracting indicates a relationship where the contractor hands over supply to the subcontractor only in the case of temporarily high levels of demand. In many industrial districts, small firms have increasingly allocated part of the production process to other small firms, either by providing the financial resources needed to acquire machinery (since owners of the suppliers are often own previous workers), or by moving the isolated phases out of the district. Other contributions (Conti and Menghinello, 1998, Innocenti 1998, Corò and Grandinetti 1999, Gargiulo and Mariotti 1999) provide some evidence that local systems of small firms are characterised by processes of delocalisation, whereby production characterised by low knowledge specificity and intensive use of labour is shifted to low labour cost countries. The latter type of subcontracting is however considered valuable only if close co-operation between the contractor and the subcontractor is not crucial. On the other hand, subcontracting relationships characterised by high levels of knowledge specificity and product quality involve firms belonging to the same local system, among which vertical cooperation is arranged on the basis of long term duration, explicit ex-ante agreements and implicit renewal over time.

The difference between these two types of subcontracting can be shown better by describing what changes have concerned subcontracting relationships in industrial districts since the 1970s. These patterns of evolution are very similar to those characterising outsourcing of large vs. small firms. A significant part of these relationships among small firms turned from one-way to two-way communication channels. Two major factors explain this change. First, the increased technological level of production induces small firms to increase their specialisation. This implies the creation of more stable agreements, the multiplication of the tiers of subcontractors and more balanced contractual powers between suppliers and buyers. At the same time, capacity-based subcontracting, which was largely used in the past as excess capacity to be exploited during temporary phases of demand expansion, become less attractive. Secondly, the final markets in which Italian industrial districts are specialised become increasingly fragmented. The production of these local systems is largely concentrated on the high quality segments of three macro-sectors: the so-called "fashion system" (textiles, leather, clothes, shoes, glasses); goods for the house (wood, furniture, ceramics, accessories); the machinery produced for the previous two macro-sectors. These production systems have acquired the characteristics of niche markets, where customer needs are deeply diversified and the product life cycle has shortened. Rather than on price factors, firm market strategies are increasingly dependent on design innovation, product differentiation, customisation and after-sales services, and brand loyalty. These requirements can be satisfied only by intensifying the process of outsourcing and asking suppliers to co-develop products or parts.

To summarize, these examples point out how outsourcing of both large vs. small firms and among small firms is associated with the intensification of competition mainly based on non-price factors. Large firms have developed vertical networks with their suppliers, first tier suppliers being involved not only in cost reduction and time saving in production but also co-design and innovation. They have implemented a two phase outsourcing strategy. First, outsourcing aimed at cost reduction was limited to second tier suppliers involved in structured tasks such as scheduling and logistics. Second, first tier suppliers have been involved in product development, and thus have started to share strategic knowledge with their buyers. This process has shifted information flows from one-way flows, whereby the buyer gives orders to the supplier and the latter executes, to two-way communication. The extension of two-way communication to the processes of outsourcing has also concerned relationships among small firms giving them advantages relating to specialization and incentives. First, specialization provides small firms with the incentive to both actively participate in the production process and innovate. Although coordination costs may be higher in decentralised networks of small firms than in hierarchically managed organisations, horizontal competition contributes to increasing the efficiency of the system. Indeed small firms tend to base their competitiveness on the dominance of a narrow niche market, where the maintenance of monopolistic position is essential for making adequate profits. Therefore, small firms are particularly keen on keeping their strategic information and not leaking it out to potential competitors. The rise in both these two typologies of outsourcing can be interpreted on the basis of a unifying factor, the decentralisation of information in firm networks, this is the topic of the next section.

## The decentralisation of information in firm networks

A recent approach to the theory of the firm considers organisations as structures which aim at efficiently collecting and processing information (Radner, 1992, 1993; Bolton and Dewatripont, 1994; Marschak and Reichelstein, 1998). In this literature the key trade-off is between delay in decision-making (if there are more layers or more units within the firm, hence more intense communication is required) and the efficiency of decision-making (information processing is more efficient if the amount of information to be processed by each agent is smaller). For example, Radner focuses on the trade-off between reducing the delay in information aggregation by parallel processing and the rise in communication costs, while Bolton and Dewatripont emphasise the trade-off between specialisation and costs of communication and co-ordination. Hence the latter authors define the notion of specialisation: specialising on particular tasks allows the amount of information to process to be limited hence avoiding information overload and achieving more efficient processing.

A possible criticism to these contributions is that they do not distinguish between the various types of information to be processed and transmitted. In reality, information can be more or less complex, and some individuals in the firm cannot process any kind of information. Due to these differences in complexity, information is not always easily communicable. Different kinds of information therefore may carry different communication costs. Furthermore information has to be clearly differentiated from knowledge and knowledge can assume different meanings as well. More recent literature discusses the distinction between tacit and explicit knowledge (Grant 1996, Liebeskind 1996, Garicano 2000). Tacit knowledge is largely embodied in individuals and possessed without complete conscience of it. Hence tacit knowledge is typically acquired through experience and transmitted with difficulty, through metaphorical language or observation.

In this paper knowledge is considered, to some extent, always tacit, while information is the only part of knowledge that can be transferred. Knowledge can be considered as an infinite set – mainly because it is the outcome of a mental process – that includes information as a closed set.[8] While information can be communicated, knowledge cannot always be communicated perfectly. In other words, information is knowledge made explicit that can be communicated to others. The process of knowledge creation can be described as a sequence where the subject collects information, that is explicit knowledge communicated by others, and combines it with the knowledge stock, which is both explicit and tacit. The outcome is new knowledge that is only partially communicated to others.

To explain how the information is processed within the network it is useful to give a definition of hierarchy as well. Aoki (1986) defines the hierarchy as "the layering of specialised decision making in order to cope with emergent events for which detailed specification of appropriate actions cannot be formulated *ex ante*". According to this definition, the decision maker typically performs the activity of management by exception. Subordinates are assumed as not being able to cope with exceptional events. Any problem that is not solvable by ordinary skills of the subordinates is reported to the upper layer which is responsible for finding the solution. Consequently, the larger the range of activities assigned to each level of the hierarchy, the higher the number of unexpected problems to be reported to the upper levels will probably be.

Hierarchy can also be viewed as a system where "only a few individuals (or only one individual) can undertake projects, while others provide support in decision making", as opposed to a polyarchy, i.e. a system in which "there are several decision makers who can undertake projects (or ideas) independently of one another" (Sah and Stiglitz, 1986, p. 716). In this way the integrated firm, i.e. a self-contained hierarchical system, can be compared with the decentralised network, that is a polyarchy where several independent decision makers autonomously undertake productive projects. By the same token, if the integrated firm is the place where all residual rights of control accrue to the owner, then the decentralised network can be seen as a system in which multiple owners possess rights of control on separate competencies. The choice of an organisational pattern could thus be represented as the selection of a point on the line joining the extreme cases of the fully vertically integrated firm, which includes all the productive units, and of the "monadic" network that is a network where each producer is an autonomous decision-maker. In this way outsourcing, i.e. the decentralization of decision-making, would correspond to a movement along the direction going from the fully integrated firm to the totally decentralised network.

This representation points out how vertically integrated firms must solve informative problems similar to those of firm networks. Both kinds of organisation must indeed co-ordinate in the presence of specialisation. More specifically, the information necessary to make the specialist knowledge possessed by their components complementary has to be diffused and shared in order to improve the performance of both systems. But coordination has to be obtained while minimising knowledge transfers mainly, because "Communication, like decision making, is always imperfect. No individual ever fully communicates perfectly what he knows to another." (Sah and Stiglitz, 1986, p. 717). The informative efficiency of both organisations is the result of the equilibrium between these two opposed requirements and depends more on the patterns of information processing and knowledge creation rather than on the property assets of the firms. According to the first definition of hierarchy given above, the degree of decentralization is given by the assignment of the rights to decide on unexpected events. But this task cannot be accomplished if the subject in charge of the decision isn't able to manage the relevant information. Thus, it becomes important to analyse the information flows both in the firm and in the network, in order to compare their performance in terms of information processing capacity (static efficiency) and problem-solving capacity, hence also innovative capacity (dynamic efficiency).

What indeed makes a hierarchical firm or network different from a decentralised one beyond and for the very reason of the multiplicity of decision makers? A possible answer hinges on two issues. The first concerns the managing of information, that is, the process through which productive units collect, process and transmit information with the purpose of creating knowledge. The second involves making the different pieces of knowledge created through the managing of information complementary.

The managing of information can be viewed as being made up of three phases, each defined by problems, decisions to be taken and sources of costs (Figure 1). The first phase is information collection. The subject who collects information has to choose the senders to receive and the criteria for receiving information. Both decisions imply costs – selection and collection costs, respectively – that can be lowered through specialisation, mainly because this activity requires a prior investment in a receiving channel (Arrow, 1975; Demsetz, 1991). By contrast, the focus of information collection in too narrow a scope can prevent the organisation from taking advantage of the variety of information sources, in particular because absorptive capacity, and consequently the ability to create knowledge, can be weakened (Cohen and Levinthal, 1990).

**Figure 1 – The managing of information**

| Phases | Main problems | Decisions | Costs |
|---|---|---|---|
| 1. Collection of information | Information overload; ability to collect information information | Choice of Senders | Selection costs |
| | | Criteria for receiving information | Collection costs |
| 2. Processing of information | Matching problem with problem-solver; delay between the collection and the processing of information | Capacity of the processors | Matching costs |
| | | Communication among processors | Communication costs |
| 3. Transmission of information | Tacit knowledge and difficulty of communication; information appropriability | Modalities of transmission | Transmission costs |
| | | Capacity of the Receiver | Appropriability costs |

*Source:* elaboration by the author

The second phase is information processing. The information collected in the first phase is complemented with the knowledge previously possessed by the decision maker. Costs are given by matching the problem with the problem solver (matching costs) and by the elapsing time between the collection of information and its communication to the decision maker (communication costs). Both costs are influenced by specialisation. In particular, the efficiency of this phase depends on the net effect of the reduction of matching costs due to the narrowing of the range of specialisation of the subjects and of the increase in communication costs necessary for connecting the higher number of processors (Bolton and Dewatripont, 1994). De Canio and Watkins (1998) prove that an increase in the capabilities of processing allows a flattening of the organisations mainly by decreasing matching costs. The third phase is information transmission. In this phase modalities of transmission are chosen and channels for communicating with the receivers are created. (if knowledge is to some extent always tacit, only explicit knowledge is communicated and becomes information). Thus transmission costs depend on the ability of the sender to transform knowledge into information and by the absorptive capacity of the receiver to understand the collected information (Cohen and Levinthal, 1990). Information transmission may raise a problem of appropriability, whereby the receiver may exploit information to create knowledge that can be used to increase its own benefits at the expense of the sender.

By applying this classification, we define the decentralisation of information as an increase in the share of information processed by the same subject who collects it. In the firm the decentralisation of information increases when the task of coping with emergent events of a specified activity is transferred hierarchically downwards. This implies that the upper layers don't need to process information related to that specific activity and all the information collected by the lower layer is processed directly by the collector. Similarly, in the network the decentralisation of information is given by the increase of the share of the information processed by the same firm which collects it. We can define a network (or a firm) as fully hierarchical if it comprises a firm (or a subject) processing all the information, including that collected by other firms. By contrast, in a fully decentralised network, each piece of information is processed by the same firm who collects it. In any intermediate case, information will be partially transmitted by the collecting firm to another firm for processing. In as far as independent decision-making is the outcome of decentralised information processing, the difference to be emphasised is not the one between the firm and the network, but the one between the decentralised network (that is a polyarchy where autonomous suppliers undertake projects independently of one another) and hierarchical organisations, where decisions are taken on by a manager (in the case of the vertically integrated firm) or by the firm "overseeing" the production process (in the case of a network directed by a leading firm).

Thus, the relevant problem becomes fixing the optimal degree of decentralisation of information which corresponds to the optimal degree of decentralisation of the network that can be discussed by applying the division in phases defined above to the case of network.

*Phase 1. Collection of information.* The receiver chooses the senders and the criteria for receiving information. In a hierarchical network, these decision are usually taken by the same firm which collects the information and not by the firm which processes it. This splitting between collection and processing criteria can causes a loss of efficiency. The decentralisation of information reduces these inefficiencies by increasing the quantity of information processed by the firm which collects it. If the collector and the processor are the same subjects selection and observation costs are minimised. Moreover, selection costs decrease if relationships between supplier and user are long term. As senders are the same and the same criteria are used and improved over time, scale economies in the collection of information can be fully exploited.

*Phase 2. Processing of information.* The processing of information consists principally in making collected information complementary to previously possessed knowledge. This process takes place within a network in two sub-periods: the first is the source of matching costs, namely to match the information collected to the firm possessing the knowledge appropriate to solving the problem, the second is the source of communication costs, that are necessary for diffusing the different pieces of knowledge created within the network. The decentralisation of information has two effects. In the decentralised network the matching of the problem with the problem-solver becomes the outcome of competition. Firms belonging to the network co-operate vertically but compete horizontally in order to better perform this matching. The second effect is related to communication costs that are minimised by transmitting knowledge incorporated in the inputs produced by others.[9] Real communication is indeed limited to the vertical communication between supplier and user. The proximity of their productive phases enhances their ability to communicate in comparison with the case of a hierarchical network, where order rather than inputs are exchanged between supplier and user.[10] In this way, matching costs are decreased by reducing the number of problems delegated within the fully hierarchical network, and communication costs are decreased by restricting communication to adjacent productive phases, that are able to better extract tacit knowledge incorporated in the inputs.

*Phase 3. Transmission of information.* If the decentralisation of information allows for the substitution of direct communication with exchange of inputs, transmission can include elements of tacit knowledge because it concerns adjacent productive units which adopt similar codes of communication. Modalities of communication are consequently enhanced. At the same time appropriability costs are higher only if information is generic. The decentralisation of information increase the number of firms that process autonomously the collected information and take decisions that are incorporated in the product. The process of innovation is therefore based on inputs developed sequentially from the firms making up the productive chain. The selection of the productive paradigm is the result of a decentralised process in which local improvements are not distinguishable from the point of view of the whole productive process. Suppliers perform a specific task corresponding to a module based on exclusive knowledge which prevents other productive units from appropriating the specific knowledge of the specialized unit.

This specific pattern of information managing also regards the other issue to discuss, that is how the decentralised information and knowledge is made complementary in the network. Hierarchical and decentralised networks are differentiated by the way this activity is performed. The main problem to be solved in decentralised networks is indeed how to guarantee complementarities among the knowledge created by the various firms without hierarchy and at the same time to minimise imperfect communication of tacit knowledge. This task is accomplished by means of the shared body of knowledge.

The existence of the shared body of knowledge within the network is the consequence of the fact that improvement in tacit communication reduces the dependence on the hierarchy. The individuals who share common knowledge can directly communicate tacit knowledge because they rely on common cognitive frameworks determined by various factors, including the awareness of "reciprocal" or "group" interdependence, which necessitates co-ordination by mutual adjustment (Grant 1996). This outcome is obtained by limiting co-project to productive adjacent phases, that establish communication which becomes progressively free from error. By establishing stable relationships characterised by a continuous and frequent exchange of information not only is information but also tacit knowledge is shared allowing efficient complementarities between the two productive phases.

This exchange of information between supplier and user can be seen as a process involving three phases that differ according to the state of the prominent information:

a) The information is disseminated. The user decides to outsource the production of a new input and addresses a population of potential suppliers with a general idea of the new input. Some suppliers study the feasibility of the product specifying the range of possible investments.

b) The information is shared. The user accepts some proposals on the basis of an outline of the general characteristics of the product. The user and supplier co-project the prototype of the input and make the investments.

c) The information is encapsulated. The supplier produces the input and autonomously decides any change to the process that can derive from local shocks and unforeseen contingencies (errors, imperfections, adaptations to its own productive process). The user inserts the input in its product, autonomously introducing only the adaptations that come from unforeseen contingencies relative to its production process. Signals of problems can be derived from the market and are solved in the decentralised mode by means of the relevant information.

The shared body of knowledge is created and made common to supplier and user in the information sharing phase. The efficiency of subcontracting relationships depends indeed on the capacity of sharing not only information but also tacit knowledge necessary for solving the problem of complementarities between two adjacent stages. After solving this problem in the co-project phase, the process of information encapsulation allows the firms' contractual power to be balanced since it prevents weakening the incentives for introducing innovations. If the firm collects, processes and transmits information and is also the residual claimant to the rents from innovation because it is protected from being expropriated of its specific knowledge, it will have strong incentives for improving its performance by introducing innovations. It is specifically the increase in the amount of information processed by the collecting firm (i.e. the decentralisation of information) which creates better incentives for knowledge creation.

To summarize, the decentralisation of information, by delegating the processing of information to autonomous suppliers rather than keeping propriety or maintaining control over the whole productive chain of the network through the exercise of leadership, made the production process complementary not through hierarchical arrangements but through the shared body of knowledge. Furthermore suppliers are provided with higher incentives for developing specialised knowledge related to the particular stage of the production process they are dealing with because their contractual power is protected and enhanced by the encapsulation of information.

This theoretical framework can explain why in the Italian manufacturing industry the process of large firm downsizing has changed from the traditional pattern searching low labour costs to a different pattern characterized by the weakening of leadership in a way that makes the network created by large firms more and more similar to local systems of small firms. Both for large and small firms, the decentralization of information is the means whereby the capability of subcontractors to create knowledge is enhanced. But it is also the way through which incentives are enforced because users cannot easily replace suppliers and contractual power is more equally distributed. The balance of contractual powers between suppliers and users has a number of implications for local economic policies as well. In particular, the creation of medium and large firms in local systems may not be that advantageous in as far as they establish or maintain control over the network and take measures to monitor the activities of the suppliers, thereby reducing their innovative potential. Likewise the provision of business services or the public support to consortiums and associations of firms are bound to fail if they are perceived as harmful for such a contractual equilibrium. This problem is particularly relevant for industrial districts where public policies promoting cooperation have been often unsuccessful because they could have undermined the historically determined equilibrium and prompted the emergence of leaderships in a way that would have weakened incentives. Policies aimed at establishing new local systems of production should take this point into consideration.

## Conclusive remarks

This paper has examined production outsourcing in the Italian manufacturing industry from the perspective of information advantages, relying on some empirical evidence on vertical disintegration of both large and small firms. Aggregate data and case studies show that since the 1980s Italian manufacturers made widespread and increasing use of outsourcing. This process was triggered off by qualitative transformations. Supply chains were re-arranged in such a way that the number of first tier subcontractors decreased, functions previously considered as strategic were decentralised and the inter-firm relations were modularised. This evolution, that was common to the outsourcing of large vs. small firms and of small vs. small firms, prompted more intense information sharing and knowledge creation, coupled with higher incentives to innovate for the suppliers since they increased their specialisation.

In order to explain this process, decentralised networks have been contrasted with vertically integrated firms. A network has been defined more decentralised if the amount of information processed by the same subject who collects it is higher. The increase of the ratio between this quantity of information and all the information processed by the firm has been defined as the process of decentralisation of information, the consequences of which have been analysed for the managing of information. It has been argued that the informative advantages of a decentralised network are given by two factors: first, the existence of a shared body of knowledge that allows complementary information to be disseminated without hierarchy and, second, by vertical communication between suppliers and users that is based on the encapsulation of information. This status of information makes each module in which production is divided independent from general architecture and based on exclusive source of knowledge. In this way, specialisation gives better incentives for innovating because contractual powers of the firms are more balanced. If the same firm collects, processes and transmits information and is also the residual claimant to the rents from innovation because it is protected from being expropriated, it will have strong incentives to create knowledge and to introduce innovation. Furthermore, this interpretation implies that economic policies should consider the balance of contractual powers between suppliers and users as powerful means for creating and developing local systems of production.

## Notes

1. The author would like to thank Sandrine Labory for many valuable comments. This paper is a by-product of a joint research with her.
2. Outsourcing is used to describe many different activities, included the hiring of workers in non-traditional jobs such as temporary and part-time workers, but this paper focuses on the processes of outsourcing among firms that usually assume the form of subcontracting relationships. In this perspective, outsourcing involves turning over the functions that fall outside firm's core competencies to another firm whose core competencies are the functions being outsourced.
3. For comparative analyses, see Loveman and Sengenberger (1991), Acs and Audretsch (1993), Arrighetti (1999), Traù (1999).
4. ROE's values below zero are due to a restricted numbers of big firms with negative returns.
5. This interpretation may be defined orthodox in so far as it assumes that the only aim of entrepreneurs is to cut costs and increase managerial control over the labour process. Thus, it may be justified on the basis of the neoclassical production function.
6. This change of perspective has important consequences for collective bargaining. Trade unions are indeed successful in extending their bargaining power to the subcontractors. For example, an agreement signed in 1998, which externalises logistics from Fiat Mirafiori's establishment to a Dutch multinational, applies all the rights provided by the old agreement (the kind of employment contract, the benefits available in Fiat, the guarantee of job security and insurance for accident) to the new relationship.
7. This discussion of the role of information encapsulation in industrial organizations relies on Aoki (2001).
8. This distinction between *knowledge* and *information* is made by assuming that knowledge is open-ended because it is a process, while information is "closed" because it can be derived on the basis of specific data (see Loasby 1986 and Fransman 1998).
9. According to Demsetz (1991, pp. 28-29): "The boundary of firms is shaped by the relative costs and advantages of putting specialised knowledge to use by means of orders or by means of selling goods accompanied by instruction on uses. The latter is advantageous when the best use of an asset does not strongly depend on it being used at a particular time and place. Giving orders and producing goods embodying specialised knowledge is thus two different way of economising with the costs of transferring knowledge. This explanation indicates that a decision to make or buy must also depend on the trade-off between taking advantage of low costs experimentation within the boundaries of a firm and taking advantage of specialised knowledge located in other firms".
10. In a hierarchical network the leading firm has to give orders to all the firms located in the lower layers of the hierarchy. These orders have to be given in an intelligible way for the subordinated firms. Therefore, all the subordinates must know the vocabulary and the rules necessary to understand the orders. This implies that tacit knowledge must be excluded from the content of the orders

# References

Acs, Z.J., Audretsch, D.B. (1993), *Small Firms and Entrepreneurship: An East-West* Perspective, Cambridge University Press, Cambridge.
Aoki, M. (1986), 'Horizontal versus Vertical Information Structures of the Firm', *American Economic Review*, 76, 971-983.
Aoki, M. (2001), *Towards a Comparative Institutional Analysis*, MIT Press, Cambridge.
Arrighetti, A. (1999), 'Integrazione verticale in Italia e in Europa: tendenze e ipotesi interpretative', in F. Traù (ed.), *La questione dimensionale nell'industria italiana*, Il Mulino, Bologna, 113-147.
Arrow K. J. (1975), 'Vertical Integration and Communication', *The Bell Journal of Economics*, 6, 173-183.
Bensaou, M. (1999), *Collaboration Support Technologies in Interorganisational Relationships: An Empirical Exploration in Buyer-Supplier Joint Design Activities*, INSEAD Working Paper 99/78 TM/ABA.
Bolton, P. and Dewatripont, M. (1994), 'The Firm as a Communication Network', *Quarterly Journal of Economics*, 99, 809-39.
Camuffo, A. and Volpato, G. (2001), *From Lean to Modular Manufacturing? The Case of FIAT 178 World Car*, IMVP Working Papers, MIT's Center for Technology, Policy and Industrial Development.
Carnazza, P., Innocenti, A. and Vercelli, A. (2000), 'Small Firms and Manufacturing Employment', in A. Boltho, A. Vercelli and H. Yoshikawa (eds.), *Comparing Economic Systems. Italy and Japan*, Palgrave, Houndmills, 158-76.
Cohen, W. and Levinthal, D. (1990), 'Absorptive Capacity: A New Perspective on Learning and Innovation', *Administrative Science Quarterly*, 35, 103-134.
Conti, G. and Menghinello, S. (1998), 'Modelli di impresa e di industria nei contesti di competizione globale: l'internazionalizzazione produttiva nei sistemi locali del made in Italy', *L'industria*, 19, 315-347.
Corò, G. and Grandinetti, R. (1999), 'Strategie di delocalizzazione e processi evolutivi nei distretti industriali italiani', *L'industria*, 20, 897-924.
Crestanello, P. (1999), *L'industria veneta dell'abbigliamento. Internazionalizzazione produttiva e imprese di subfornitura*, Franco Angeli, Milano.
Demsetz, H. (1991), 'The Theory of the Firm Revisited', in O.E. Williamson, S.G. Winter (eds.), *The Nature of the Firm*, Oxford University Press, Oxford.
DeCanio, S. and Watkins, W. (1998), 'Information Processing and Organisational Structure', *Journal of Economic Behaviour and Organisation*, 36, 275-294.
Enrietti, A. (2000), 'Outsourcing', *Strumentires*, IRES Piemonte, Torino.
Fodor, J. (1983), *Modularity of Mind. Essay on Faculty Psychology*, MIT Press, Cambridge, Mass.
Fransman, M. (1998), 'Information, Knowledge, Vision, and The Theories of the Firm', in G. Dosi, D. Teece and J. Chytry (eds.), *Technology, Organisation and Competitiveness. Perspectives on Industrial and Corporate Change*, Oxford University Press, Oxford.

Garicano, L. (2000), 'Hierarchies and the Organisation of Knowledge in Production', *Journal of Political Economy*, 108, 874-904.
Grant, R.M. (1996), 'Toward a Knowledge-Based Theory of the Firm', *Strategic Management Journal*, 17, 109-122.
Innocenti, A. (1998), 'Gerarchia e contratti. Il ruolo dei rapporti di subfornitura tra piccole imprese nell'evoluzione dei distretti industriali', *L'industria*, 19, 391-415.
Liebeskind, J. (1996), 'Knowledge, Strategy, and the Theory of the Firm', *Strategic Management Journal*, 17, 93-107.
Loasby, B.J. (1986), 'Organisation, Competition, and the Growth of Knowledge', in R.N. Langlois (ed.), *Economic as a Process: Essays in the New Institutional Economics*, Cambridge University Press, Cambridge.
Loveman, G. and Sengenberger, W. (1991), 'The Re-Emergence of Small-Scale Production', *Small Business Economics*, 3, 1-37.
Mariotti, S., ed. (1996), Mercati verticali organizzati e tecnologie dell'informazione. L'evoluzione dei rapporti di fornitura, Fondazione Adriano Olivetti, Torino.
Marschak, T. and Reichelstein, S. (1998), 'Network Mechanisms, Informational Efficiency, and Hierarchies', *Journal of Economic Theory*, 79, 106-141.
Mediocredito Centrale (various years), Indagine sulle imprese manifatturiere, Mediocredito Centrale, Roma.
Omiccioli, M. (2000), 'L'organizzazione dell'attività produttiva nei distretti industriali', in L.F. Signorini (ed.), Lo sviluppo locale. Un'indagine della Banca d'Italia sui distretti industriali, Meridiana Libri, Cosenza, 289-298.
Radner, R. (1992), 'Hierarchy: The Economics of Managing', *Journal of Economic Literature*, 30, 1382-1415.
Radner, R. (1993), 'The Organisation of Decentralized Information Processing', *Econometrica*, 62, 1109-1146.
Sah, R.K. and Stiglitz, J. (1986), 'The Architecture of Economic Systems: Hierarchies and Polyarchies', *American Economic Review*, 76, 716-727.
Traù, F. (1999), 'Il riemergere della small scale production, nei paesi industriali: rassegna della letteratura empirica e primi confronti internazionali delle tendenze di lungo periodo', in F. Traù (ed.), La questione dimensionale nell'industria italiana, Il Mulino, Bologna, 63-112.
Volpato, G. and Stocchetti, A. (2000), Managing Information Flows in Suppleir-Customer relationships: Issues, Methods and Emerging Problems, IMVP Working Papers, MIT's Center for Technology, Policy and Industrial Development.

# Comment

## Katsuhito Iwai

The nature of the business corporation is undergoing a fundamental transformation all over the world. Huge conglomerates have downsized themselves by selling off many of their businesses and spinning off many of their divisions. Large manufacturers have flattened their vertically integrated organisations by delegating many of their production activities to independent suppliers. In recent years, business press, policy makers and academic economists are busy in documenting these changes, identifying their causes, and discussing their implications. Professor Innocenti's thought-provoking paper on production outsourcing in the Italian manufacturing industry is a welcome addition to the growing literature on this historical transformation in the nature of the business corporation.

In this paper Professor Innocenti focuses on the process of outsourcing that assumes the form of subcontracting relationships – firms turn over some of their former activities to other firms but at the same time keep long-term co-operative relationships with them. He first presents several empirical examples on outsourcing in the Italian manufacturing industry. Among them two facts are most intriguing. The first one is that not only large manufacturers but also small suppliers have shown a strong tendency for downsizing. The Italian economy is known to have a large share of small-scale firms, and this national characteristic has now become much more pronounced than ever. The second intriguing empirical fact is that the downsizing of Italian manufacturing firms began in the 1970s. This fact should be contrasted with the much reported trend of corporate down-sizing in the US economy. It was during the 1980s when the rise of hostile take-overs and pressures from institutional investors strengthened the power of shareholders that large US corporations began to outsource some of their production activities and loosen their hierarchical structure. That fact should also be contrasted with the history of the Japanese subcontract system. It is well-known that major Japanese manufacturers have kept their size relatively lean by having outsourced many of their production activities to subcontractors since around the 1950s. But there seems to be no discernable trend in Japan for further expansion of its subcontracting system from the 1970s to the 1990s. On the contrary, some of the Japanese manufacturers, a notable example being Nissan Motors, began to dismantle old subcontracting networks and replace them by the more market-orientated supply systems in recent years. The Italian experience appears to be quite different from that of the US and of Japan.

Professor Innocenti claims that the increase in outsourcing in *both* large manufacturers and small suppliers in the Italian economy since the 1970s can be explained by a unifying theoretical framework – the decentralisation of information in firm networks. In order to cope with the intensification of non-price competition in ever globalising markets, large manufactures have decomposed their products into independent modules and delegated the production of many of these modules to other firms with long-standing relationships. The resulting network of subcontracting relationships can be regarded as a hybrid of a fully integrated hierarchical firm with a centralised decision-making unit and a totally decentralised assemblage of autonomous firms at-arm's-length relationships with each other.

Professor Innocenti then argues that such organisational form can indeed enjoy the merits of the totally decentralised assemblage of firms and of the fully integrated firm simultaneously. The self-contained nature of the information concerning the module each subcontractor is specialised to allows it to work out improvement and innovation in its own shop or plant without worrying about the possibility of hold-up by its parent manufacturer. Of course, this would complicate the parent manufacturer's task of co-ordinating production activities because it is no longer able to use commands to gather the necessary information from suppliers of the modules that are now legally autonomous firms. But Professor Innocenti asserts that such a task has been made easier by the recent development of information-processing technology, such as CAD, which has rendered exchanges of complex information much more efficiently than before even between independent firms. More fundamentally, he insists that the problem of co-ordination can be solved by means of sharing the knowledge, especially tacit one, between the parent manufacturer and its subcontractors through long-term contractual relationships. The existence of the shared body of knowledge makes the information they possess complementary to each other and encourages their co-operation in exchanging the information that is vital for production and development.

Professor Innocenti then maintains that the same logic applies equally well to the explanation of the steady increase in outsourcing in the horizontal networks of small firms in those industrial districts that are specialised in "fashion" goods, housing goods and machinery specific to these goods. Indeed, success in markets for these highly differentiated goods is highly dependent on designs, customisation, after-sales services, and brand loyalty, which demand constant adaptation and innovation on the part of producers.

I believe that Professor Innocenti has made an important contribution to the field of industrial economics. He has not only given us an informative survey on the growth of product outsourcing in Italian manufacturing but also presented us a broad framework for its theoretical explanation. In particular, his emphasis on the informational advantage of the subcontracting system over the vertically integrated firm as well as over the totally decentralised network of firms would be a useful starting-point for the comprehensive policy-design for the Italian manufacturing sector, especially for its local industrial districts, in the 21$^{st}$ century.

My only concerns are that the information-theoretic framework presented in this paper is too general for differentiating the experiences of the Italian manufacturing industry from those of the US or of the Japanese manufacturing industry. In fact, in the case of the US manufacturing industry the process of outsourcing has not led to the expansion of the subcontracting system. It has gone to the far end of decentralisation by relying more and more on open markets for procuring necessary supplies. Also in the case of the Japanese manufacturing industry which is known to have a long-held tradition of relying on the intricate subcontracting system, some major manufacturers have abandoned that tradition and begun to adopt the more market-orientated supply system. Of course, the industrial structure is quite different between Italy, the US and Japan (though Italy and Japan have many similarities), and part of the variation in their experiences can undoubtedly be attributed to such a difference. I, however, doubt that that is all. In order to explain the uniqueness of the recent Italian experiences, it is necessary to investigate such factors as the difference in corporate government system, the extent of financial deregulation, the structure of labour markets, and even the geography of the country, along with the management of the information system. I am, however, also convinced that Professor Innocenti must have already thought about these factors. I hope that in the near future he will give us a more detailed picture of this dramatic structural change in the Italian manufacturing industry, which was one of the most exciting developments in advanced industrial societies in the $20^{th}$ century and will continue to be so in this new century.

# Chapter 10

# Italian Districts in the International Economy

Rodolfo Helg

## Introduction

The notion that Italy's comparative advantage is somewhat unconventional[1] receives support from the direct analysis of the Italian pattern of international specialisation. It can be synthetically characterised as being polarised and relatively persistent over the years. The first feature is described by the very strong specialisation in traditional sectors and in some specialised supplier industries, and the very weak position in scale economy based sectors and, especially, in high-tech industries (Iapadre, 1996).[2] This picture is robust to the taxonomy adopted. Figure 1 shows the evolution over time of the Balassa index of revealed comparative advantages (RCA) for the manufacturing sector and for three macro-sectors defined on the basis of factor intensity in production (Garnaut – Anderson, 1980).

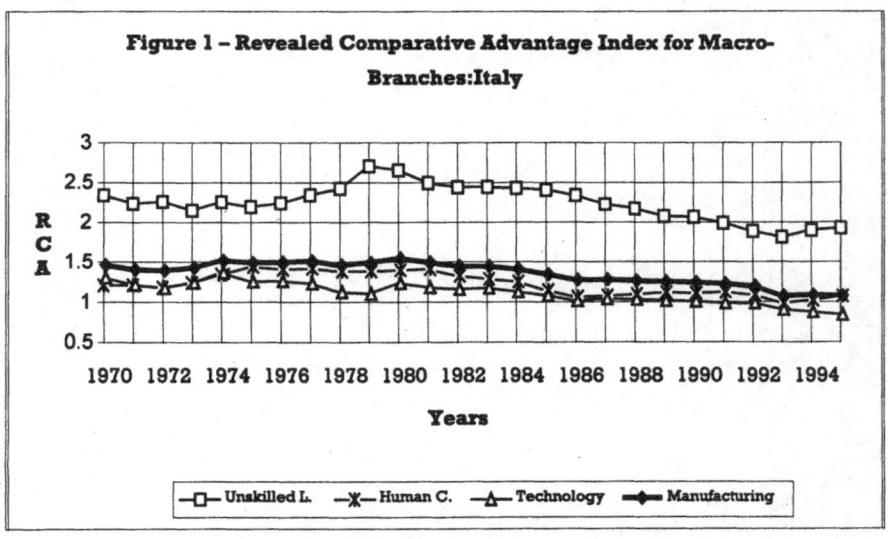

Source: WTDB - NBER and PC - TAS Database

In 1995 the RCA for the unskilled intensive sectors is around 2 (i.e. strong specialisation), while it is below one for the high-tech sectors.[3] The stability overtime of the Italian trade pattern is clearly shown in Figure 1. At a lower level of aggregation (two digits of the SITC rev.2 classification system), a similar message is obtained by analysing the similarity of the Italian trade specialisation in 1971 and 1992. Table 1 shows a high rank correlation coefficient (.87) between the RCA of the country over the two years.[4] In the same table results are also reported for the other G-6 countries and for the four NIEs[5] and the remaining 4 most developed ASEAN[6] countries. Italy has the highest trade pattern persistence among the G6. As expected the other Asian countries considered have a higher degree of mobility in their pattern.[7]

Table 1 – Stability in international specialisation patterns: Spearman's rank correlation coefficients between RCA in 1992 and in 1971 (* = significant at 5%)

| ita | hk | sin | tai | sko | phi | mal | tha | ind | jap | ger | fra | uk | usa |
|---|---|---|---|---|---|---|---|---|---|---|---|---|---|
| .87* | .75* | .46* | .58* | .62* | .58* | .52* | .40* | .26* | .76* | .78* | .69* | .77* | .81* |

*Note*: for country symbols see notes 5 and 6 and: ita = Italy; jap = Japan; ger = Germany; fra = France; uk = United Kingdom; usa = United States
*Source*: Helg (1999)

The peculiarity of the Italian trade pattern is reinforced by analysing how similar it is to that of other countries. Table 2 shows that Italy has more in common with the four NIEs (with the exception of Singapore) than with the remaining G6 countries (similarity is measured with the rank correlation coefficient between the RCA of two countries).[8]

Does such a pattern of specialisation make Italy particularly vulnerable to the competition of the new labour-abundant entrants? This concern is often raised, especially in the press. It may well be warranted, but some other elements concerning Italy's pattern of trade should also be considered.

In fact, as soon as we move to a lower aggregate level of analysis (both in terms of sectors and of production factor definition), the picture becomes more complex. It is a common finding indeed that within the traditional/labour intensive sectors, Italy is mainly specialised in the top end of the vertically differentiated spectrum of products. Many of these products are characterised by a relative high level of skill intensity and by a low price elasticity of demand.[9] By catering for the price rigid segments of the market for differentiated goods, Italian firms and workers may then be less exposed to competition from developing countries. New evidence in line with this interpretation can be found in de Nardis and Traù (1999). They show that "competitive pressures on Italian industries are rather low, when measured by quality-adjusted export similarity indices".

**Table 2 – Similarity in patterns of international specialisation: Spearman's rank correlation coefficients for RCA in 1992 (\* = significant at 5%)**

|     | ita  | hk   | sin  | tai    | sko   | phi  | mal  | tha  | ind   | Jap  | ger  | fra  | uk   | usa |
|-----|------|------|------|--------|-------|------|------|------|-------|------|------|------|------|-----|
| ita | 1    |      |      |        |       |      |      |      |       |      |      |      |      |     |
| hk  | .43* | 1    |      |        |       |      |      |      |       |      |      |      |      |     |
| sin | -.12 | .36* | 1    |        |       |      |      |      |       |      |      |      |      |     |
| tai | .54* | .60* | .22  | 1      |       |      |      |      |       |      |      |      |      |     |
| sko | .45* | .52* | .26* | .58*   | 1     |      |      |      |       |      |      |      |      |     |
| phi | -.01 | .16  | .26* | .14    | .17   | 1    |      |      |       |      |      |      |      |     |
| mal | -.09 | .04  | .54* | .12    | .22   | .44* | 1    |      |       |      |      |      |      |     |
| tha | .06  | .51* | .27* | .56*   | .50*  | .41* | .36* | 1    |       |      |      |      |      |     |
| ind | -.06 | .00  | .15  | -.01   | .10   | .61* | .47* | .24* | 1     |      |      |      |      |     |
| jap | .08  | .37* | .45* | .44*   | .53*  | -.15 | .08  | .18  | -28*  | 1    |      |      |      |     |
| ger | .30* | -.08 | .04  | .02    | -.08  | -.21 | -.08 | -.23 | -.27* | .49* | 1    |      |      |     |
| fra | -.02 | -.05 | -.13 | -.24 * | -.15  | -.20 | -.15 | -.02 | -.20  | -.08 | .22  | 1    |      |     |
| uk  | .03  | -.11 | .06  | -.19   | -.08  | -.22 | -.21 | -.14 | -.28* | .23  | .30* | .24* | 1    |     |
| usa | .30* | -.26 | -.08 | -.32 * | -.27* | -.05 | -.14 | -.15 | -.21  | .02  | -.14 | -.18 | .29* | 1   |

*Source*: Helg (1999)

Recently, it has been argued that to understand the Italian pattern of industrial (and as a consequence international) specialisation one should take into account the peculiar geographical location of industrial activities in Italy. Italian industrial structure is characterised by the small dimension of its firms (in 1991 average dimension of a manufacturing firm was 9.1 decreasing to 8.9 in 1996 (ISTAT; 1999)) and by the clustering of certain industrial activities in specific locations. The fact that Italian specialisation (at the production and at the export level) has something to do with the industrial districts, emerges clearly when one looks at the distribution of this districts across sectors. In 1991 34.7% of them specialised in textile and clothing activities; 13.6% in the leather and footwear macro-sector; 19.6% in the furniture and related product industries. This sums up to approximately 68% of total industrial districts. The remaining important group of industrial districts are the mechanical engineering macro sector (16.1%) and food (8.5%) (ISTAT, 1996).

## Italian districts and international trade

Studies on industrial districts have for a long time been characterised by their qualitative or case-study nature. Only in the last 10 years have we started having quantitative studies presenting a comprehensive picture of Italian industrial districts.[10] The reason for this delay in the arrival of quantitative studies is the very nature of an industrial district: a mixture of economic, cultural and territorial elements. One of the most important basic forces that contributes to creating an industrial district is the existence of external economies. Unlike its companion (internal economies of scale), the measurement of external economies poses formidable difficulties. As a consequence every attempt to measure the industrial district phenomenon imposes approximation costs that are on average higher than those incurred in measuring other economic variables. From this point of view a path breaking study was made by Sforzi (1997) within the framework of ISTAT activities. Starting with a set of criteria and using data at "comune" level, that research project has produced a systematic classification of Italian industrial districts.[11]

In 1996, the 199 Italian industrial districts accounted for 43.3% of total Italian manufacturing exports. (ISTAT, 1999). For the sake of comparison, their weight in terms of total Italian manufacturing employment was 45%. However, this number (upper-limit method) tends to over-estimates the "district effect", since it includes all industrial districts manufacturing exports. In fact, each industrial district has been defined empirically on the basis of its importance in a specific manufacturing sector that characterises its specialisation (the major-sector:[12] for example, Prato is an "industrial district" because of its specialisation in textile and clothing; Treviglio for its specialisation in agricultural machinery). Some of the productive activities located within the industrial district have very little to do with the specialisation of the area (non-related sectors). At the same time focusing only on data related to the major sector of specialisation (lower-limit method) of the district would under-estimate the "district effect". It is well known that one of the features of an industrial district is the existence of backward linkages from the producer of the final product (textile, say) to the producer of the machinery required to produce that product (auxiliary or supporting sector). Data are only related to the primary sector of specialisation of the district, hide backward and forward linkages, and should be considered as a lower-limit for the "district effect". The relevance of industrial districts exports, considering only their primary sector exports,[13] is 22% of total Italian exports (Viesti, 1997 and Becattini, Menghinello, 1998).[14] Hence, as a first approximation, the "district effect" on export can be positioned between 22% and 43% of total Italian manufacturing exports.

**Table 3 – Industrial district major-sector contribution to total Italian exports by macro-sectors (%)**

| Macro-sector | 1996 |
|---|---|
| Textile and Clothing | 42.6 |
| Leather, Leather goods and Footwear | 47.4 |
| Furniture and parts, Ceramic goods | 37.9 |
| Jewellery and Musical instruments | 39.6 |
| Mechanical industry | 18.1 |

Source: ISTAT (1999)

This average picture of the industrial district contribution to Italian exports, hides a very heterogeneous pattern of the different manufacturing sectors. Table 3 presents figures for some macro manufacturing sectors adopting the lower-limit method. For the group of so-called traditional sectors, industrial districts contribute more than 40% to Italian exports in textile and clothing, and leather etc; for more than 35% in furniture and ceramic goods, and jewellery and musical instruments. At a lower level of aggregation the contribution is even higher. For example, in the leather industry the industrial district contribution to Italian exports is 696 %. In the tiles industry it is 66.2%. This number is even more impressive since they are a lower limit to the true contribution of the "district effect". In the mechanical industry, the industrial district has a lower impact (181 %). However, within this macro-sector there is the agricultural machinery industry in which the industrial districts accounts for 429 % of Italian exports.

Table 4 – Industrial districts contribution to Italian exports %, 1996 (major-sector in brackets)

| Textile and Clothing | |
|---|---|
| Biella (textile fibres) | 10 |
| Como (textile fabrics) | 11.7 |
| (knitwear) | 10.8 |
| Treviso (knitwear products) | 10.7 |
| Empoli (leather garments) | 20.8 |
| Prato (textile fabrics) | 24.6 |
| (knitwear) | 22 |

Source: ISTAT (1999)

Moving to the contribution of the single district, Tables 4, 5, 6, 7 and 8 present the industrial districts that contribute more than 10% to total Italian exports in their major-sector.

Table 5 – Industrial districts contribution to Italian exports %, 1996 (major-sector in brackets)

| Furniture and related products | |
|---|---|
| Desio (plywood etc.) | 15.1 |
| Di Valpolicella (cutting stones) | 25.6 |
| Udine (furniture) | 10.7 |
| (plywood) | 13.3 |
| Sassuolo (tiles) | 51.3 |
| Civita Castellana (ceramic not for construction) | 11.4 |

Source: ISTAT (1999)

Without entering into details, within the textile and clothing macro-sector, two districts, Como and Prato, represent more than 35% of Italian textile fabrics exports and more than 32% in knitwear (Table 4). Sassuolo alone covers more than 50% of Italian tile exports (Table 5).

**Table 6 – Industrial districts contribution to Italian exports %, 1996 (major-sector in brackets)**

| Leather, leather goods and footwear | |
|---|---|
| Arzignano (leather) | 26.8 |
| Montebelluna (footwear) | 10 |
| Santa Croce sull'Arno (leather) | 21.5 |
| Solofra (leather) | 16.3 |

*Source*: ISTAT (1999)

In the leather sector 3 districts (Arzignano, Santa Croce sull'Arno and Solofra) account for more than 60% of Italian exports (Table 6). A similar situation arises for jewellery where two districts (Arezzo and Vicenza) represent more than 50% (Table 7).

**Table 7 – Industrial districts contribution to Italian exports %, 1996 (major-sector in brackets)**

| Jewellery and Musical instruments | |
|---|---|
| Vicenza (jewellery) | 17.1 |
| Arezzo (jewellery) | 34.3 |
| Recanati (musical instruments) | 16.8 |
| Osimo (musical instruments) | 10 |

*Source*: ISTAT (1999)

Within the mechanical macro-sector the role of districts is less impressive, but it still has an important role especially in agricultural machinery where two districts (Modena and Treviglio) account for more than 25% of Italian exports (Table 8).

**Table 8 – Industrial districts contribution to Italian exports %, 1996 (major-sector in brackets)**

| Mechanical industry | |
|---|---|
| Treviglio (agricultural machinery) | 15.7 |
| Padova (optical instruments) | 10.8 |
| Pieve di Cadore (optical instruments) | 12.2 |
| Modena (agricultural machinery) | 10.1 |

*Source*: ISTAT (1999)

But how important are the industrial districts in their major-sector on world markets?

Table 9 shows how some industrial districts play a major role also in world export markets.[15] The most impressive case is again that of Sassuolo with approximately 40% of the world tile export market.

Table 9 – World export market share of some industrial districts (major-sector in brackets)

| Sassuolo | (tiles and ceramics) | 39.2 |
|---|---|---|
| Como | (silk fabric) | 25.9 |
| Prato | (wool web) | 19.6 |
| Belluno | (glasses) | 17.6 |
| Carrara | (marble) | 13 |
| Arezzo | (jewellery) | 13 |
| Verona | (marble) | 10.1 |
| Arzignano | (leather) | 10 |

Source: adapted from Fortis (1999)

Also Como is important with one quarter of the world silk fabric export market. Additional evidence of the link between industrial districts and exports can be found in Bagella, Becchetti and Sacchi (1998). They show[16] that export intensity of district firms is higher than for other firms (25.6 % against 21.1 %).

Are firms in industrial districts more efficient? In the previous section we have reviewed how important industrial districts are for Italian exports even when the lower-limit method is adopted. A natural question arising at this stage is whether firms within a district are more efficient than firms outside it. An attempt to answer this question can be found in a series of studies originally prepared within the research department of the Bank of Italy.[17] The study by Fabiani, Pellegrini, Romagnano, Signorini (1999) and Fabiani, Pellegrini (1998) analyse, on the basis of company accounts, the profitability of firms within the districts. Over the period between 1982 and 1995, firms within the districts have a higher profitability[18] than firms outside it. Moreover, within the districts firms specialised in the core business of the district (the major-sector) are more profitable than firms not belonging to it. The latter group of firms is heterogeneous in the sense that it includes firms with a backward or forward link to the major-sector firms (those belonging to supporter sectors) and those completely extraneous to the activity of the districts, but still localised within it (those belonging to the non-related sectors). The expectations are that the first group is more profitable than the second. No evidence is available at the moment on this issue.

Then, the higher profitability of industrial district firms can be due to lower labour costs and/or to higher efficiency. On the first issue (lower labour costs) the evidence is not very clear. The above quoted authors find that per capita labour cost seems to be lower for firms located in industrial districts. The labour market within the districts seems to be characterised by an average age of the young employee that is lower than outside it, by a higher mobility both among firms and towards an autonomous activity, by a higher wage when certain specific skills have been acquired (Casavola, Pellegrini, Romagnano, 1999). As for the efficiency issue, the message emerging from the available literature is that in general, district firms belonging to the major-sector are more efficient than all other firms (i.e. firms located in the district, but not in its core business and firms located outside it) (Fabiani and Pellegrini, 1998).

## Conclusions

In the previous sections we have reviewed some evidence on the Italian pattern of international specialisation. On one hand, the usual picture of a trade pattern biased toward traditional sectors emerges and a part of the mechanical macro-sector defined as specialised suppliers. This pattern is more similar to that of some emerging economies than to that of other industrialised countries. However, if the analysis is conducted at lower aggregate level, the similarities with the emerging economies are reduced since within the various macro-sectors Italy is specialised mainly in the medium-high quality segment that do not enter into direct competition with the portfolio of products of these economies. Not only is the Italian trade pattern is biased towards traditional and specialised suppliers macro-sectors, but also the distribution of industrial districts is characterised by a strong presence within these two macro-sectors. Industrial districts generate an important portion of Italian exports especially within the traditional macro-sector. We also have new quantitative evidence that, on average, firms within industrial districts are more efficient than those outside. Overall, the picture presented here is not as pessimistic as usually claimed. However, one should not hide the fact that the process of globalisation, even assuming net benefits in the medium run, imposes adjustment costs in the short run. The mobility asymmetry between capital (highly mobile) and labour (low mobile), in a situation of increasing competitive pressure, requiring that the majority of the adjustment be made on the labour side (higher flexibility, unemployment). In addition, the increasing fragmentation of the production process puts a lot of pressure on the network link between the firm and its territory. In the past, this link has been one of the cornerstones of the industrial district. The delocation abroad of some production stages should not be thought of as a necessarily negative sum game. It could be the correct strategic move that might allow other stages of the same production process to remain internationally competitive and located within the district. The final results will depend crucially on which phases of production are to be relocated. If the knowledge intensive phases remain in place, then the industrial district will not change very much in nature. If the attitude toward the delocation process is benevolent, what one should really worry about is the low attractiveness of the Italian system in direct foreign investment.

## Notes

1. This term referrs to the average pattern of specialisation for industrialised countries.
2. The macro-sectors considered here are those corresponding to Pavitt's (1984) taxonomy.
3. The RCA is defined here as the Italian share of world exports in the i-th sector divided by the same share which refers to total Italian exports.
4. Spearman's rank correlation coefficients have been computed on the bases of the 2 digits aggregation level of SITC rev.2 sector classification.
5. Hong Kong (hk), Singapore (sin), South Korea (sko) Taiwan (tai).
6. Indonesia (ind), Malaysia (mal), Philippines (phi) and Thailand (tha).
7. For a more detailed analysis of the dynamics in the trade pattern for all these countries see Brasili-Epifani-Helg (2000).
8. De Nardis and Traù (1999) find similar results including the pattern of specialisation of some Eastern European countries. See also Chiarlone and Helg (2002).
9. Not all, however. For a distinction between the low price-elasticity textile sectors and high price-elasticity clothing sectors see Faini (1991).
10. One of the first studies analyzing Italian export performance from a local system of production perspective (a concept that is similar to the one regarding industrial districts) is Viesti (1994). See also Conti (1995), Conti and Menghinello (1996).
11. For a discussion of the limits of the criteria adopted in the empirical definition of industrial districts see Brusco e Paba (1997).
12. On the basis of the INPS data base, Fabiani and Pellegrini (1998) estimate that on average only 35 % of the employees in an industrial district work within the major-sector.
13. This data is not strictly comparable with the one of 43,3%, since both Viesti (1997) and Becattini and Menghinello (1998) use export for 1995 at the "province" level to obtain information on the local system of production (differently from the most recent data in ISTAT, 1999, that are at the "comune" level). Fortis (1998) also utilizes exports data at the province level, but adopts the upper-limit method, to obtain a share for industrial district exports of 35.4 %.
14. Even if the procedure in the two studies differ, the same result is obtained.
15. The data in this table are not directly comparable to those of the previous ones, because of the different methodology used in the less precise definition of industrial districts in Fortis (1999). In his work the lack of export data at firm/comune level, impose the use OF the "province" as the unit of analysis, with obvious costs as far as precision is concerned.
16. They use the Mediocredito database based on a representative sample of 5000 firms.
17. Most of the research results has been published in Signorini (2000).
18. Measured either with the return on investment or with return on equity.

## References

Bagella, M., L. Becchetti and S. Sacchi (1998), "The positive link between geographical agglomeration and export intensity: the engine of Italian endogenous growth", *Economic Notes*, vol. 27, no. 1.

Becattini, G. and S. Menghinello (1998), "Contributo e ruolo del made in Italy 'distrettuale' nelle esportazioni nazionali di manufatti", *Sviluppo Locale*, V, 9, pp. 5-41.

Brasili, A., P. Epifani and R. Helg (2000), "On the dynamics of trade patterns", De Economist, vol. 148, 2, June 2000.

Brusco, S. and C. Paba (1997), "Per una storia dei distretti industriali italiani dal dopoguerra agli anni novanta", in F. Barca (a cura di), *Storia del capitalismo italiano dal dopoguerra ad oggi*, Donzelli, Roma.

Casavola, P., G. Pellegrini and E. Romagnano (1999) "Imprese e mercato del lavoro nei distretti industriali italiani", *Sviluppo Locale*, VI, 10.

Chiarlone, S. and R. Helg (2002), "Il modello di specializzazione italiano e le economie emergenti dell'estremo oriente" (con S.Chiarlone), in *Progetto 2002: La competitività dell'Italia*, volume I, "Le imprese", G.P. Galli e L. Paganetto (eds.), Il Sole XXIV Ore Editore.

Conti, G., (1995), "I sistemi esportatori italiani: un'analisi per province su dati 1985-1993", in *Rapporto sul Commercio Estero 1994*, ICE, Roma.

Conti, G. and S. Menghinello (1996), "Territorio e competitività: l'importanza dei sistemi locali per le esportazioni italiane di manufatti: un'analisi per province (1985-1994)", in *Rapporto sul Commercio Estero 1995*, ICE, Roma.

de Nardis, S. and F. Traù, (1999), "Specializzazione settoriale e qualità dei prodotti: misure della pressione competitiva sull'industria italiana", *Rivista degli Economisti*, Fabiani S. and G. Pellegrini (1998), "Un'analisi quantitativa delle imprese nei distretti industriali italiani: redditività, produttività e costo del lavoro", *L'Industria*, XIX, n. 4, October-December.

Fabiani, S., G. Pellegrini, E. Romagnano and L.F. Signorini (1999), "Efficiency and localisation: the case of Italian districts", in S. Biffignandi (ed.), *Micro and macro data of firms*, Physica-Verlag.

Feenstra, R.C., R.E. Lipsey and H.P. Bowen (1997), *World trade flows, 1970-1992, with production and tariff data*, NBER WP No. 5910, January. (http://papers.nber.org/papers/W5910)

Fortis, M. (1998), *Il made in Italy*, Il Mulino, Bologna.

Fortis, M. (1999), "I distretti industriali e le esportazioni italiane", in ICE-Club dei Distretti Industriali, *I distretti industriali: la via italiana al lavoro e allo sviluppo*, CD-rom.

Garnaut, R.G. and K. Anderson (1980), "Asean export specialization and the evolution of comparative advantage in the Western Pacific region", in Garnaut (ed.), *Asean in a changing Pacific and world economy*, Australian National University Press.

Helg, R. (1999), "East and South-East Asian Economies and the EU: Pattern of Specialisation and Intra-Industry Trade", in Suthiphand Chirathivat and Corrado Molteni (eds.), *ASEAN-EU economic relations: the impact of the Asian crisis on the European Economy and the long-term potential*, AESS, Nomos Publ, Baden-Baden, 1999.

ISTAT (1996), *Rapporto Annuale. La situazione del paese nel 1995*, Roma, Istituto Poligrafico e Zecca dello Stato.

ISTAT (1999), *Rapporto Annuale. La situazione del paese nel 1998*, Roma, Istituto Poligrafico e Zecca dello Stato. (www.istat.it/Primpag/Rapannuale1998/index.html)

Krause, L.B. (1982), *U.S. Economic Policy toward the Association of Southeast Asian Nations: Meeting the Japanese Challenge*, Washington, DC, The Brookings Institutions.

NBER (1997), *World Trade Database (WTDB)*.

Park, Y.C. and W.A. Park, (1989), "Changing Japanese Trade Patterns and East Asian NICs", in Krugman (1991) (ed.), *Trade with Japan*, Chicago, University of Chicago Press, NBER.

Sforzi F. (ed.) (1997), *I sistemi locali di lavoro 1991*, Argomenti, no. 10, ISTAT.

Signorini L.F. (ed.) (2000), *Lo sviluppo locale. Un'indagine della Banca d'Italia sui distretti industriali*, Meridiana Libri, Donzelli, Corigliano Calabro.

UN (1997), *COMTRADE Database*.

Viesti, G. (1994), "La geografia delle esportazioni italiane", *Rivista di Politica Economica*, April.

Viesti, G. (1997), "Le esportazioni dei sistemi italiani di piccola e media impresa", *ICE*, Quaderni di Ricerca no. 3, October. (http://www.ice.it/studi/quaderni.htm).

# Comment

## Yoshiyuki Okamoto

This paper concerns the Italian industrial districts qualitatively analyzed from an international trade point of view. In the first half, the author confirms a popular image of the Italian economy, the Italian trade pattern, the strong specialization in the traditional sectors, and the similarity of the pattern with the NIEs. At the same time, from a less aggregate level of analysis, the author mentions another result, that in the traditional labor intensive sectors Italian firms specialize in the top end of the differentiated spectrum of products which are characterized by high skill and low price elasticity.

In the latter half of the paper, the author concentrates on "industrial districts", the geographical location in which the products are manufactured. He shows the high share of exports of the industrial districts in the various sectors and each industrial district in the world trade. In addition, the firms within a district, in particular their core businesses, have a higher profitability than the firms outside the district, because the labour cost within the district might not only be lower than outside, but also the firms within the district are more efficient.

This paper is based on several papers including some by the author himself and there are really no new fact-findings. It may contribute to a survey of some findings by the quantitative analyses on industrial districts.

It is not clear how the discussion in the former half of this paper is related with that in the latter. In the former the author insists that the Italian firms are specialized in the top end products, avoiding competition with the firms in low labour cost countries, but he does not give any data. This point should have a relationship with the finding on the profitability and efficiency in the latter half of the paper. In the Italian economy, particularly in industrial districts, high skill should play an important role in producing "Made in Italy" products.

Finally, it is necessary to define some key concepts clearly, for example an industrial district. The concept of the industrial district must be defined for quantitative analysis, in particular from a geographical point of view, which would surely affect the results of the analysis. Most of the research on Italian industrial districts have been done descriptively, but more quantitative studies are needed to clarify the structure and function of industrial districts.

# Chapter 11

# Banking System and the Dualistic Development of the Italian Economy

Cesare Imbriani

## Introduction

Taking into account the dualistic development of the Italian economy, the purpose of this paper is to analyse recent changes in the Italian banking system. In section two, the main changes which have occurred in the Italian banks are reviewed; in section three the restructuring process of the banking system in Southern Italy is examined as well as its effects on the local productive system; finally, section four briefly presents a framework which aims to explain the reasons for the dualistic behaviours of the Italian banking system. Some concluding remarks will be presented in section five.

## The Italian banking system

The 1990s were a particularly important decade for the Italian banking system. The abolition of the administrative controls and market competition brought about by financial liberalisation (boosted by the participation in the European Monetary Union) directed the banking system towards a more efficient organisation. The early 1990s were characterised by an erosion of the profit margins; in particular, the banking sector was strongly affected by the 1992-93 recession. The Italian banks experienced lower profitability than their European counterparts. Estimates made by the Italian Banking Association (ABI) show that the ROE (the ratio between gross returns and equity plus reserves) was 1.6% in Italy, 6.4% in Germany and 17.1% in UK over the period 1993-95.[1] The situation of the Italian banking system improved during the last decade. Falling interest rates in the aftermath of the convergence process towards Monetary Union reduced interest margins in 1997-98. Productive diversification and stronger competition were boosted up and a switch from financial intermediation to the provision of services followed. According to estimates of the Central Bank, the ROE increased from 4% in 1995 to 9.7% in 1998.[2]

The problem of bad loans is still relevant for Italian banks. The ratio of unpaid loans on total credit was still around 7.3% in 1999. Although this figure has been decreasing over the last five years, it is still higher than the European average.

These problems have accelerated the restructuring process of the banking system and revealed the too-small operative size of Italian banks compared to other OECD countries. According to estimates made by the Bank for International Settlements, in the last 17 years the number of credit institutions has decreased by more than 37% in the USA, 33% in both the UK and Germany, 45% in France, and by no more than 15% in Italy. At the end of 2000, 60.6% of the Italian banks accounted for only 5% of total lending operations. Mergers and acquisitions have only started in recent years; the restructuring process is particularly difficult and slow due to labour market rigidities.[3]

Diversification of activities can be the only answer. However, this does not mean total disintermediation of the banking system since banks still offer savings management services, either directly or via controlled companies. Portfolio reshuffling has been significant due both to the development of the stock market and the purchase of foreign bonds. Estimates made by the Central Bank show that the return on investment trust has ranged between 3.5 and 4 percentage points from 1997 to 1998. However, the reduction of the amount of treasury bills in the agents' portfolios is not as significant as it would appear since they are still 55.2% of investment trusts. The share of households who entrusted their financial savings in investment trusts or asset administrations increased from 5% to 11%; while the households' assets invested in life insurance products increased from 21.5% to 23.3% of the total, between 1995-98. It is worth noting that risky assets ownership is almost restricted to wealthy households and is highly variable across regions.[4]

Asset management almost tripled in Italy between 1996 and 2000. Investment funds account for 58% of the increase. At the end of 1999, ten groups (including two insurance companies) managed 71% of the total market. By the end of September 2000, 83% of operators were controlled by Italian groups. In 1999, revenues from saving management were 12,000 billion lire, i.e. 10% of the intermediation margin, increasing to 13% in 2000.[5]

## Banking system and the South of Italy

The restructuring process of the banking system has not been homogenous across regions. In particular, banks in the South of Italy (the so called *Mezzogiorno*) increased competition from outside banks entering their market. The percentage of Southern banks decreased from 29% to 24% between 1990 and 1999.

Small size banks suffered mostly from such competition: 74 of them (which account for 17.25%) had to leave the market. The reduction of the number of banks in other areas was less drastic: 4.6% in the Centre, 9.1% in the North-East, while in the North-West there has been an increase of 7%.[6]

Looking at the market shares reported in table 1, we can observe that in Southern Italy the market share of outside banks rose from 38% in 1990 to 47% in 1999. At the same time in this area the market share of Southern banks fell from 62% to 52% during the same period. Finally, in the rest of Italy the market share of Southern banks – which was only 3% in 1990 – decreased to 2% at the end of decade.

At the end of 1999, bonds and investment trusts accounted for only 4.5% of the financial wealth in the South, compared to 18.6% in the North and 10.9% in the Centre.

Stocks accounted for only 3.1% of total financial wealth in the South compared to shares of 11.6% and 6.2% in the North and Centre, respectively. The ratio of bank assets to GDP was 84.5% in Central and Northern Italy, while only 48.6% in the South.

**Table 1 – Territorial indicators of banking activities**

| Indicators (%) | 1990 | '91 | '92 | '93 | '94 | '95 | '96 | '97 | '98 | '99 |
|---|---|---|---|---|---|---|---|---|---|---|
| **Banks** | | | | | | | | | | |
| Mezzogiorno | 28.9 | 28.8 | 29.3 | 29 | 29.3 | 29.4 | 28.7 | 27.6 | 26.2 | 23.6 |
| Rest of Italy | 71.1 | 71.2 | 70.7 | 71 | 70.7 | 70.6 | 71.3 | 72.4 | 73.8 | 76.4 |
| **Branches** | | | | | | | | | | |
| Mezzogiorno | 23.6 | 23.5 | 23.9 | 23.9 | 23.7 | 23.3 | 22.9 | 22.6 | 23 | 22.7 |
| Rest of Italy | 76.4 | 76.5 | 76.1 | 76.1 | 76.3 | 76.7 | 77.1 | 77.4 | 77 | 77.3 |
| **Mezzogiorno market shares** | | | | | | | | | | |
| of Southern banks | 62 | 61.4 | 62.7 | 63.2 | 60.6 | 63.8 | 61.3 | 59.8 | 57.7 | 52.6 |
| of no Southern banks | 38 | 38.6 | 37.3 | 36.8 | 39.4 | 36.2 | 38.7 | 40.2 | 42.3 | 47.4 |
| **Rest of Italy market shares** | | | | | | | | | | |
| of Southern banks | 3 | 3.1 | 3.2 | 3 | 2.8 | 3.1 | 2.5 | 1.9 | 1.8 | 1.8 |
| of no Southern banks | 97 | 96.9 | 96.8 | 97 | 97.2 | 96.9 | 97.5 | 98.1 | 98.2 | 98.2 |

Market shares are calculated in terms of loans.

*Source*: Bank of Italy

Moreover, because of the poor socio-economic context of the area in which Southern banks operate, it was impossible for them to gain efficiency enlarging and improving the quality of the services supplied. In table 2 we reported the loans/deposits ratio.[7]

**Table 2 – Loans and Deposits in macro-regions from 1990 to 2000 (billions lire)**

| Year | 1990 | | | | 2000 | | | | | |
|---|---|---|---|---|---|---|---|---|---|---|
| Macro-region | Loans | % | Deposits | % | Loans | % | Deposits | % | % Change Deposits | % Change Loans |
| Rest of Italy | 671.635 | 81.4 | 582.412 | 79.0 | 1.410.517 | 85.0 | 780.616 | 78.9 | 34.0 | 110.0 |
| Mezzogiorno | 153.813 | 18.6 | 154.955 | 21.0 | 250.567 | 15.0 | 208.801 | 21.1 | 34.7 | 62.9 |
| Italy | 825.448 | 100.0 | 737.367 | 100.0 | 1.661.084 | 100.0 | 989.417 | 100.0 | 34.2 | 101.2 |

*Source*: Bank of Italy

Its dynamics show the difficulties for Southern banks to find suitable occasions for developing their intermediation activity. In fact, looking over the 1990-2000 period, Southern Italy experienced an annual growth rate for deposits similar to the national one while the amount of loans granted decreased by 18.6% percentage points over the 1990s.[8] In addition, even if at the end of the period the loans/deposits ratio rose from 99% to 120%, the gap between Southern and Northern areas increased substantially, jumping from 16% to 60%. Other indicators, which support these difficulties, are the loans and deposits ratios of resident customers to the regional GDP. At the end of 1999, the loans to regional GDP ratios were 84.5% in the North and 48.6% in the South; the deposits to regional GDP ratios were 55.1% in the North and 44.4% in the South.[9]

It must be recalled that the propensity to save does not appear to vary across regions. Hence, savings flow from the South to the Central and Northern areas that are perceived to be safer and more remunerative. Lack of financial resources in the Southern areas, thus, is not due to inadequate savings, but rather to the inability of banks to properly channel financial resources towards the productive sectors. Increasing acquisitions of local banks from outside banks makes the problem of local financing even more severe.[10] All these constraints affected the profitability of banks of Southern Italy in a significant way, as shown in the following table.

The macroeconomic scenario for the South dramatically changed since the beginning of the 1990s. Special incentives were suspended in 1992 and the fiscal retrenchment imposed by the public finance constrains due to fiscal imbalances made subsidy policies more difficult. The ratio of total transfers to net imports fell from a peak of 9% in 1975 to an average value of 2% in the 1980s.[11] The policy of helping out firms to pay social security contributions by means of tax relieves should also have been abandoned, following the repeated *reprimenda* of the

European Union. The ratio of social security contributions to net imports was about 10% in 1988.

Table 3 – Gross income to total assets ratio

| Banks Headquarter location | 1996 | 1997 | 1998 | 1999 |
|---|---|---|---|---|
| North-West | 0.58 | 0.55 | 1.05 | 1.3 |
| North-East | 1.09 | 1.09 | 1.33 | 1.42 |
| Centre | 0.44 | -0.39 | 0.58 | 0.54 |
| Mezzogiorno | -0.74 | 0.14 | 0.32 | 0.23 |

*Source*: Bank of Italy

Investment in infrastructure declined during the 1980s to 15% of the net imports. The effectiveness of such investments has always been doubtful. Their productivity has been quite low over the years. The role of such expenditure has thus been *de facto* equivalent to income transfers. According to SVIMEZ estimates[12] there was a reduction of 10% in public investment between 1990 and 1999. Real income per capita in the South was 56.8% of the average of the rest of the country in 1980. The ratio increased to 59.8% between 1983 and 1992. The Southern economy has performed rather badly since then, due both to the adverse economic cycle and the reduction of government transfers. The rate of growth of GDP in the Mezzogiorno was only 0.6% between 1992-1999, less than one third of the rate of growth in the rest of Italy. Gross investment decreased at a yearly rate of 2.4%, compared to an average annual increase of 1.6% elsewhere. Population growth, on the other hand, was considerably higher in the South, so that the per capita GDP fell further to reach 54.9% in 1999, just as it was in the 1950s.

**An interpretative framework of the banking system behaviour**

In this unfair context, where the structure of the Southern economic system lagged far behind, the ratio total transfers to net imports fell from 25.91% (in the period 1980-1988) to 19.44% during 1989-1992. The ratio fell further to 13.6% over the period 1993-1999. The policy of totally removing government intervention and let the free market do the job has thus proved to be unsuccessful.

The forces of the market can only work in the presence of sound institutions and, especially, of a well developed financial market. A recent study of the Heritage Foundation rates Italy as a partially free economy. Excessive regulation and slow justice being the main culprits; such problems are obviously much more relevant for the South. The presence of the State in the banking system has typically been important for Italian and, especially, Southern banks. There are signals that the process of privatisation will intensify in the near future, although there is no consensus on this point. However, the three leading banks now operating in the South (Banca Intesa, IMI San Paolo, Banca di Roma) do have considerable expertise in dealing with project financing, merchant banking and venture capital. The banking system will increasingly perform its natural role of financing investments on the basis of risk and return considerations, paying particular attention to recent developments in risk evaluation techniques. They have, however, the dragging anchor of bad loans inherited from previous managements. As shown in table 4, at the end of 1990 the bad loans to total assets ratio was 20.3% in the South, compared to 5.0% in the rest of Italy.

Table 4 – Bad loans/total loans ratio

| Year | Rest of Italy | Mezzogiorno | Italy |
|---|---|---|---|
| 1992 | 5.0 | 12.5 | 6.1 |
| 1993 | 6.9 | 15.9 | 8.2 |
| 1994 | 6.6 | 18.2 | 8.3 |
| 1995 | 7.2 | 22.7 | 9.3 |
| 1996 | 7.0 | 24.2 | 10.1 |
| 1997 | 6.6 | 21.8 | 9.4 |
| 1998 | 6.1 | 22.6 | 9.1 |
| 1999 | 5.0 | 20.3 | 7.3 |

Source: Bank of Italy

Table 5 – Average interest rates on loans

| Year | Rest of Italy | Mezzogiorno | Italy | Mezzogiorno – Rest of Italy |
|---|---|---|---|---|
| 1992 | 17.59 | 19.23 | 17.85 | 1.64 |
| 1993 | 12.28 | 14.31 | 12.62 | 3.03 |
| 1994 | 11.46 | 13.89 | 11.81 | 2.43 |
| 1995 | 12.95 | 15.00 | 13.25 | 2.05 |
| 1996 | 11.26 | 13.61 | 11.56 | 2.35 |
| 1997 | 9.35 | 11.39 | 9.56 | 2.04 |
| 1998 | 7.19 | 9.16 | 7.40 | 1.97 |
| 1999 | 5.72 | 7.37 | 5.90 | 1.65 |

Source: Bank of Italy

Asymmetric information has had a particular negative impact on Southern banks. The problems of adverse selection and moral hazard have been particularly important in the South of Italy due to lack of information and transparency. This has led good firms to pay too high prices for the loans due to the inability of the banking system to properly distinguish bad projects from good ones:[13] in table 5 average interest rates on loans charged by banks in two macro-regions are reported.

It might be argued that the banking sector is not the only responsible for the failure of credit markets in the South; in fact, the responsibility has to be shared with firms, which were unable to properly signal their quality.

## Concluding remarks

The empirical evidence so far provided indicates that during the 1990s the more dynamic Italian banks managed to expand and diversify their activity in Southern Italy, where the deterioration of the economic structure over the same period strongly affected the local banking system. The merger and acquisition processes of local Southern banks by outside banks certainly, on the one hand, increased their operative efficiency; but, on the other, it compromised the potential for an expansion of an autonomous local banking system. There are too many objectives in the policy agenda. One is to plan the debt restructuring as well as new industrial policies for troubled firms with a good potential to recover. The other is to promote new financial instruments[14] and techniques such as investment banking and markets for derivatives. Merchant banking for large firms and venture capital for smaller size firms seem to be the right instruments for helping the South to escape from the underdevelopment trap in which it has been for much too long.

## Notes

[1] For more details see ABI (1999).
[2] See Bank of Italy (2000a).
[3] See Fazio (2000).
[4] See Desario (2000).
[5] All data: Bank of Italy (2000a).
[6] See Lopes (2001).
[7] For the efficiency analysis of the banking sector see Berger and Mester (1997).
[8] The ratio of the number of bank branches per 1000 billion lire of deposits and loans is another important indicator of the scarce propensity of banks to invest in the South and confirms that banks consider Southern regions especially to collect funds. In fact, with regards to the collection of deposits there is a substantial homogeneity among the areas (28.2 branches per 1000 billion lire of collection in the South, 26.3% in the North). On the contrary, regarding loans, there are strong differences between the Mezzogiorno and the rest of the country (26.2 branches for 1000 billion lire of loans in the South and 16.7 in the North).
[9] See for more detailed Bank of Italy data (2000b).
[10] See Imbriani and Lopes (1999).

[11] We use this ratio in order to compare the percentage of net imports which is "financed" by transfers. For more details see Giannola, Imbriani and Lopes (1990).
[12] See, in particular, SVIMEZ (2001).
[13] This behaviour of the Italian banking system is rooted in the presence of asymmetric information between banks and firms. This generates some important bias: on the one hand, the interest rate applied by the banks that do not have complete information on the ability of the recipient to return the loan, will be on average higher than the ones emerging in a context of complete information; on the other hand, a problem of moral hazard might arise: the most efficient firms will look for alternatives sources of funding while the less efficient firms will show a higher preference towards risky activities.
[14] For the role of non-traditional activities on efficiency of banking system see Rogers (1998).

## References

Associazione Bancaria Italiana (1999), Rapporto sui mercati finanziari e creditizi, Bancaria, supplemento al n. 6.
Bank of Italy (2000a), Relazione Annuale del Governatore per il 1999, Roma.
Bank of Italy (2000b), Sintesi delle note sull'andamento dell'economia delle regioni italiane nel 1999, Roma.
Berger, A.N. and L.J. Mester (1997), Inside the Black-Box: What Explains Differences in the Efficiencies of Financial Institutions?, Journal of Banking and Finance, 21, pp. 895-947.
Coelli, T., D.S. Prasada Rao and G.E. Battese (1999), An Introduction to Efficiency and Productivity Analysis, Kluwer Academic Publishers, London.
Desario, V. (2000), Il risparmio finanziario in Italia: strumenti, intermediari, mercati, in Bancaria, n. 12.
Fazio, A. (2000), Concorrenza, sviluppo e sistema bancario, in, Bollettino Economico della Bank of Italy, n. 35, Ottobre.
Imbriani, C., A. Giannola and A. Lopes (1990), Le politiche di lungo termine per il superamento del dualismo Nord-Sud: problemi e prospettive. In Scazzieri, R., Quadrio-Curzio, A. (a cura di), Dinamica economica strutturale, Il Mulino, Bologna.
Imbriani, C. and A. Lopes (1999), Intermediazione finanziaria e sistema produttivo nel Mezzogiorno tra efficienza e redditività. In Giannola, A. (a cura di), Il Mezzogiorno tra stato e mercato, Il Mulino, Bologna.
Lopes, A. (2001), Mezzogiorno e politica economica nell'ultimo decennio. Alcune riflessioni critiche sulle opportunità e sui vincoli allo sviluppo. In Anania, G. (a cura di), Scelte pubbliche, strategie private e sviluppo economico in Calabria. Conoscere per decidere, Rubbettino, Soveria Mannelli.
Rogers, K.E. (1998), Non-traditional Activities and the Efficiency of US Commercial Banks, Journal of Banking and Finance, 22; pp. 467-482.
SVIMEZ (2001), Rapporto 2001 sull'economia del Mezzogiorno, Il Mulino, Bologna.

# Comment

## Osamu Ito

Professor Imbriani argues that the Southern area of Italy is in the situation of a so-called "underdevelopment trap". Textbooks concerning development economics say that the causes of the "underdevelopment trap" are, in ordinary cases, the rapid increase of population, stagnating income per capita, low rate or fluctuation of savings and therefore investment, as seen in South African and Latin American countries.

However, on the contrary, in Southern Italy, the savings rate is not low. So, what is the cause? The author's answer is that the financial intermediation system does not work well in Southern Italy. He points out that:

Savings outflow from Southern Italy to elsewhere in the country through the "outside" banks

Such "capital flight" takes place because of insufficient ability of the Southern Italian financial system, above all, the banking system.

Why is this? The author answers that the reasons are:
- Burden of bad loans
- Lower return and less safety of financial instruments, that is, inefficiency
- Inferior ability of financial high technologies
- Incapability to investigate and monitor borrowers

I think that the last one, poor ability to investigate and monitor, is the most important and fundamental factor rather than the high-tech factor in both Italy and Japan, because the other factors are its results. And, at the same time, financial difficulties arise in the regional small-sized firms in both countries. Is this recognition correct or not? This is my first question.

And then, why cannot banks change or restructure themselves, for example, cut off bad loans? The same problem seems to be appearing in Japan, Thailand, Indonesia, etc. as well as in Italy. In the case of the East Asian countries, I think the critical point is the problem of organizational structure, in other words, the problem of corporate governance of banks.

In Japan in particular, we may observe a phenomenon of lack of authority and responsibility at the top of organizations based on "context dependency". For example, in difficult times following the collapse of the bubble economy, the top management of Japanese enterprises, including financial institutions, has often been irresponsible and caused confusion.

The tendency for organizations in Japan is that job duties and therefore authority and responsibility are provided only in the context of the relationship to the surroundings. The foundation of top manager positions, and therefore their authority and responsibility, is due to the fact that they have been nominated by superiors. As the standards of personnel evaluation are not objective enough, such a system in which high-ranking persons nominate the people under them readily promotes the power of superiors and the dependence of their subordinates. Top managers are usually selected and nominated by their predecessors, who in many cases remain in the companies as "chairmen", "counselors" or "advisors." And the shareholders' monitoring of managers is weak in Japanese companies. So the top management is never checked by anyone except in such exceptional situations where others in power, including their predecessors, move against them. In other words, they have unlimited authority in "normal" circumstances. But in the special cases when their management responsibilities come into question, they become conscious that their position and authority are limited by the "context." They maintain that they were only doing their best in their given roles. As a result, those responsible do not take responsibility. This is the reason why the problems of Japanese organizations are dramatically evident in times of crises.

As stated above, because of the lack of check mechanism and responsibility discipline in top management, banks cannot change their way and restructure themselves. This is the reason why such problems as bad loans continue to exist for a long time. I wonder whether this picture fits the Italian situation.

# PART IV
# SOCIAL INSTITUTIONS AND NETWORKS

# Chapter 12

# The Fiscal Decentralization and the Autonomy of the Local Government

Carlo Filippini
Giampaolo Arachi

**Introduction and summary**

In the last decade Italy has experienced a gradual process of fiscal decentralisation. The reforms implemented in past years have substantially changed the structure of the Italian system of public finance.

Until the beginning of the 1990s, the local governments were responsible for important sectors of public expenditure (e.g. health) but they were financially dependent on grants from the central government.

This system suffered from serious inefficiency. The reforms implemented in the 1990s have increased the autonomy of local governments both concerning expenditure and revenue. The central government now devolves to local governments a large share of its tax revenue and new local taxes have been introduced. A new system of equalising grants has been designed to support regions with small tax bases.

We will provide an evaluation of the Italian experience by focusing on the following critical issues:

a) the consistency between the objective of enhancing efficiency through fiscal decentralisation and the objective of ensuring reasonable uniform standards for essential public services (e.g. health) in every local community;

b) the trade-off between interregional redistribution and the incentives of local governments to pursue active tax policies;

c) the effects of local governments' fiscal autonomy on the North-South dualism.

In this paper we will deal mainly with the regional level of government in relation to the central or national level. The case of municipal and provincial governments is touched on very briefly. The main reason is that presently in Italy, fiscal federalism – quite a relevant and hotly debated issue – means mainly decentralisation at the regional level while solutions for the lower levels are considered less relevant and have been less subject to debated.

## Central and local governments in Italy

The present situation is the outcome of a long process of both political and economic transformations that have marked Italy in the past twenty-five years. The roots of this process can be traced back to the pre-WWII regime.

It is therefore useful in order to understand why and how the different solutions and reforms have been adopted – in particular for an audience that has not directly experienced these events in Italy – to review the main points of this rather bumpy process.

According to Italian Basic Law or the Italian Constitution – in force since January 1, 1948 – Italy is a republic with strong elements of federalism. Five regions (out of 20) were given extensive powers from the very beginning thanks to a special statutes (some of which were passed even before the Constitution) and all the others had legislative powers over a number of problems – including local transport, urban planning, agriculture, health. The five regions account for just over 15% of the total population. This new level of government with considerable autonomy was a reaction to the previous rigid and centralist structure modelled on the French system. The other traditional levels are the Provinces (104 in all, two of which – Trento and Bolzano/Bozen – have been endowed with the powers granted to the Special Statute Regions) and the Municipalities (about 8,100). More recently large towns have been divided into wards or boroughs with some responsibilities. All these institutions differ in size, population, income per person and even electoral systems. While the Special Statute Regions were established immediately after WWII (with one exception) only at the beginning of the 1970s did the ordinary regional governments come into existence, finally implementing this provision of the Italian Constitution.

Around the end of the 1960s and the beginning of the 1970s, economic policies changed deeply because of the labour movement straggle and, more generally social unrest typical of those years, and also because of the national and international macroeconomic scenario. The Italian government proposed and the Italian parliament passed many laws increasing social benefits to large sections of the population. According to the Italian Basic Law any additional public expenditure must be covered by some source of public revenue, in the annual budget. Very often the provisions in the first year of the reforms were rather limited, but the effects in the long run were much greater. This was one the reasons for public deficits during the 1980s, which resulted in a rather large public debt: from about 60% of the GDP to over 100%.

The first relevant fiscal reform in the first half of the 1970s abolished almost all sources of local revenue, substituting them with a system of grants from the central government. This created a sort of fiscal irresponsibility in all local governments: they could spend without taxing; bank credit and eventually special grants often covered deficits when they became too big.

## Reasons for a reform

In the 1990s, the situation became untenable. The Maastricht Treaty signed in February 1992 set a goal – a single currency – and some convergence criteria to be met in order to participate in the new monetary system. For a while in Italy there was uncertainty about "whether to be counted in" – that is in the group of the founding members – because almost everybody thought that it was impossible to meet the criteria. Eventually the decision was taken to make all possible efforts in order to participate in the Economic and Monetary Union from the very beginning.

To many decision makers – both in the political and economic sectors – one very important argument behind this decision was the possibility of proposing and enacting unpopular reforms under the justification of the EMU: Europe was used as an external pressure in order to break political and social opposition to change.

Many were the causes of the public deficits and mounting public debt. Some of them were of a general, national nature and possible solutions did not involve any kind of decentralisation or federalism. Others, on the contrary, were linked to the characteristics of the Italian administrative and political set-up. We are specifically interested in these and will now present them briefly.

## Local government financial accountability

One of the factors causing public deficits was the quite peculiar situation of regional, and more generally local, governments: they were given many responsibilities by the mere activation of all the provisions listed in the Italian Constitution. In order to fulfil these duties Italian regions did not have any relevant taxation power and relied on transfers from the central government; at the same time budget constraints were very soft because their deficits were almost always covered by additional resources granted the central government in Rome.

In many cases there was a perverse incentive to spend more and more because transfers were determined on a historical basis: so the biggest spenders were also the biggest receivers. Almost no fiscal responsibility existed, regions could spend without any economic or political cost: they were not required to make their citizens pay for the services received. The result was even worse because the implementation of the regional government reform coincided with the fiscal reform – which abolished almost all local revenue sources.

By the beginning of the 1990s, this anomaly became so evident that a vast majority was in favour of abolishing it and making regions more accountable to their citizens. Of course there were groups or local authorities that were very lukewarm about any change: after all it was quite convenient to provide services and protest against taxation by the central government. In addition, poorer regions feared the inevitable reduction in resources. Moreover, the prospect of fiscal competition between regions was rather new and costs seemed greater than benefits. Eventually the Italian Parliament had to pass legislation setting specific constraints on local and regional governments' deficits (the so-called "internal stability pact").

### Efficiency in the local public sector

The Italian public sector expenditure is not (and was) out of line with most countries of the (now) European Union – contrary to a commonly held view. The real problems were public deficits, the inefficiency of the bureaucracy and the low quality of the services provided.

The first problem dates back many decades and is due to the rather low wages and salaries paid to civil servants (at least compared to payments in the private sector) and to the selection and training processes: the former was biased by political patronage and the latter almost non existent.

Moreover, a bureaucrat's main responsibility was supposed to be the interpretation of law and by-laws, very often quite complex and ambiguous, rather than implementation of given policies.

In time the influence of the trade unions grew and it became almost impossible to impose disciplinary measures even on bureaucrats guilty of rather serious crimes: this was widely accepted by people and institutions involved because it nullified the idea of personal responsibility.

The general public had very few chances of seeking redress for inefficient – or even unfair – behaviour of a civil servant. The quality of the services produced by the public sector was generally quite low. Here too there was little that could be done: competition by private producers was difficult or prohibited, even if human ingenuity and resourcefulness could sometimes make a difference.

The situation was quite similar for the central and the local governments: the behaviour of the two did not differ in a significant way because the kind of controls and political pressure by citizens had almost the same effect. Of course there were a few "islands" of efficiency concentrated mainly in northern areas of Italy because of the historical tradition of local autonomy and good government in these areas.

As some sort of compensation taxation in Italy was lighter than in other European countries and tariffs for public goods or services were even lighter. Evasion too was quite widespread, in particular for some specific groups or taxes: income taxes for self-employed people or VAT in some productive sectors or in small and medium firms. There was a balance, even if a perverse one: the services were bad but the price one paid was low. For example local (and rail) transports were slow and unreliable but fares were very low (trains in Italy were two thirds cheaper than in the UK or Germany and one half than in France).

### Interregional equalisation

Another problem that worsened from the 1980s to the beginning of the 1990s was the interregional redistribution of resources operated by the central government.

The most relevant and criticised feature was the huge transfer of resources from the North (and the Centre) to the South of Italy. When budget constraints were soft and growth rates not negligible, this did not raise much opposition, but with harder times (and a changing political situation – as we shall see in the next paragraph) dissatisfaction grew. Interregional redistribution was partially justified by the much lower income per head in most Southern areas but the lack of positive effects – as the gap did not narrow – was (rightly) interpreted as misuse of the funds due to inefficiency and corruption. The problem was made more acute by the fact that other kinds of inequitable, or at least unexplainable, transfers occurred: from the ordinary statute regions to the special statute ones, from large regions to small ones – even at similar income per head levels. The biases could not be explained by the aim of providing every person, with an equal amount of (public) goods and services.

Other redistributive factors were important: the intergenerational factor and also other social factors. The former operates mainly through state pension schemes and is now at the centre of political debate. There is a widespread opinion that state pensions are too generous with elderly workers and recently retired people (in particular women) because the prevailing system was a redistributive one and the benefits were fixed at the time when the ratio of retired to active workers was low. With the ageing of the population and longer life expectancy, younger generations will have to bear an excessive burden. Other social factors are also geared against the younger generations, or, more specifically, against people in search of work, because labour legislation protects employed persons to the disadvantage of the unemployed. These aspects are now being hotly debate but, prior to the beginning of the 1990s, they were not considered to be such sensitive issues.

## Changes in the political scene

At the same time, the collapse of the communist regimes in the Soviet Union and other Easter European countries deeply modified the Italian political scene. In the mid 1970s, many laws were enacted and policies adopted with a large "bipartisan" support: opposition parties voted for (or abstained over) most bills after an intense bargaining process that led to modifications of the original draft proposed by governments. The boundary between government political parties and opposition ones on the left became blurred; very often the result was compromise not reform, delay not action. At the same time a veto existed, barring the then so-called Communist Party from active participation in the Italian government. With the disappearance of the world bipolarisation between East and West the veto too lapsed. Politics in Italy became more flexible, meaning that for the first time since WWII, there was a real possibility for an alternative force in government.

A second important element appeared: the rapid growth of many regional parties in the North (economically the most important area) including the Lega Nord or Northern Alliance, based mainly in Lombardy, which drew the greatest support. The main reason for the success of these political parties was a growing dissatisfaction with the inefficiencies of the central government and, more specifically, with the low quality of the public services and goods provided coupled with the transfer of relevant amounts of resources from the northern regions to the southern ones. The latter reason in particular played an important role in winning votes for these parties. The 1990s saw a reversal of previous attitudes and preferences in European public opinions, from a marked concern for social issues and, especially, for a more equalitarian personal income distribution to rather individualistic if not selfish attitude. In many European countries – Germany, Switzerland, among others – richer social groups and regions objected to equalising transfers by central governments. In Italy this happened simultaneously with the decline of the two main political parties (the Christian Democratic and the Socialist parties) due to bribes and corruption charges, by means of a novel but effective clean up campaign carried out by the judicial branch in order to rid politics of corruption. The regional political parties became essential in forming local governments in the northern regions and fluctuated between federalism and separatism. They stressed the inefficiencies of the central government and the excessive (in their opinion) transfer of funds from the North to the South. Another hot issue was the centralisation of rules and bylaws: everything was decided in Rome, in the same way for every part of Italy. The examples of Germany and Switzerland – with large autonomies given to each *land* and canton – were taken as possible solutions for Italy too. The mere administrative and operational decentralisation was now no longer enough.

No political party could neglect this appeal to federalism and decentralisation. The Northern regions make up about 40% of the population – and votes – and much more of the GDP – and taxes. The result was a rather deep change in the Constitution giving regions (but not provinces and municipalities) much wider powers. The shift was essentially from a positive list to a negative list: while previously regions could legislate on a given number of problems they can now decide on everything that is not excluded and reserved to the central government.

## Decentralisation and devolution in the 1990s

The reform implemented in the 1990s has radically reshaped the finance of both Regions and Municipalities. Here we will focus on the Regions as they currently represent the central government's counterpart in the political debate on fiscal federalism.

### *The enlargement of the fiscal autonomy of Ordinary Statute Regions*

At the beginning of the nineties, Ordinary Statute Regions (*OSR*) had basically no fiscal autonomy. Up to 98% of total revenue consisted in transfers from the central government. Furthermore, nearly all of these grants were conditional to the financing of the National Health Service (*NHS*) (which represented nearly 80% of total regional expenditure) and of other minor expenditure programs.

Over the decade there were several attempts to increase the fiscal autonomy of *OSR*. We can single out two phases in the reform process. In the first phase, the central government introduced the essential instruments for fiscal autonomy through the devolution of relevant taxes to the *OSR*. In 1993, Regions received the yield of the health pay-roll tax, levied on salaries and on self-employed incomes. As a consequence transfers dropped to 54% of total revenue. In 1998, the health payroll tax and some minor regional taxes were abolished and replaced by a new tax, named Irap (Regional business tax), and by a regional surcharge (0.5%) on personal income tax. Irap is a value-added tax implemented through the subtraction method and levied on basically all business, both in the production of goods and services and in the financial sector. The base rate is 4.25%. The tax operates under the origin principle of taxation: the yield accrues to the Region where the value added is produced.[1] The actual Irap yield has been far lower than government's estimates (29 billion against the expected 34 billion euros). This explains why own revenue as a share of total regional revenue drop from 50% in 1997 to 44% in 1998. In practice, this first phase of reforms had a small, if any, effect on the Regions' fiscal autonomy. As to the health payroll tax, the Regions had no control over either the base or the collection procedures. They just received the tax yield from the central government Treasury as a part of a conditional grant, equal to each Region's health needs. Actually, the Regions do have the power to change the tax rate, in a given range around the base rate, but regional politicians have no incentive to propose unpopular tax increases given that health financing is secured by government transfers. This state of affairs has only been partially affected by the introduction of Irap. In theory, the Regions have wide powers concerning collection and auditing but, in fact, regional administrations lack the technical skills to manage any of the procedures involved and passively rely on the central government. As a consequence, all the information from the tax returns is in the hands of the Treasury, and is released quite parsimoniously in order to curb the demand for greater political autonomy coming from the Northern Regions. As to the tax rates, the 1998 reform confirms the right of the Regions to increase or reduce them[2] but does not remove the disincentives to fiscal effort. On one hand, the entire revenue from the personal tax surcharge and 90% of the Irap yield are still conditional to health financing. On the other hand, any gap between the Regions' own revenue and health expenditure is filled by grants from the central government.

The second phase of the reforms, completed in March 2000, aims at introducing the right incentives to encourage active tax policies. As previously remarked, it was widely acknowledged that regional politicians had no incentive to manage the taxes assigned to them for two reasons. Firstly, they faced a soft budget constraint, as any deficit in the health sector was ex-post financed through the State transfers. Secondly, almost all revenue was conditional to health financing. Furthermore, the Regions claimed that the uncertainty surrounding the amount of transfers (we must remember that the transfers were discretionarly determined by the central government, year by year, in the budget law) hindered any serious financial planning.

The 2000 reform tackles these issues by abolishing almost all existing grants and replacing them through the sharing of national VAT and the increase of the base rate of some other minor surcharges (personal income tax, excise on gasoline). The VAT sharing rate is fixed at 38.55% in order to leave unchanged the total amount of resources in regional budgets. The VAT is apportioned to Regions in proportion of the estimated consumption of their residents. Clearly, the distribution of the abolished grants is different from that of consumption. Therefore the substitution of the grants with the VAT sharing generates large fiscal imbalances in almost every Region. To correct these imbalances the reform has designed a new system of equalisation transfers. In the first year (2001) the transfers simply redistribute regional resources in order to guarantee each single Region the same resources it would have received under the old grants. After a long transitional period, which will end in 2013, the new system of transfers will equalise resources across Regions according to a formula which takes into account fiscal capacity and health needs. In theory, the equalising transfers are horizontal: "rich" Regions will give up some of their revenue to finance "poor" Regions.

Overall, the new system of regional finance should guarantee a hard budget constraint, as the central government will no longer finance the Regions through discretionary transfers. In addition, in order to strengthen the incentives to autonomous tax effort, the reform abolished all restrictions on the use of revenue: the additional yield generated by an autonomous tax increase can be spent freely to finance any regional expenditure program. Through the abolition of discretionary transfers, the new system of finance allows for a normal financial planning as each Region can estimate future revenues, which depend on the dynamics of their tax bases and on the equalising formula.

*Equalising transfers*

As previously emphasized the 2000 reform entails a long transitional period from the present system of equalising transfers (which basically redistributes the regional VAT in order to meet historical expenditure in each Region) to a new system in which the transfers are determined according to a formula which takes into account fiscal capacity, health needs and the economies of scale in the provision of public services. In particular, at the end of the transitional period, the transfer to Region $i$, $T_i$, will be determined as the difference between the amount of VAT assigned according to an equalising formula ($EVAT$) and the VAT assigned to the Region on the basis of the estimated consumption of that Region's residents ($CVAT$). Formally:

(1) $\quad T_i = EVAT_i - CVAT_i$

and

(2) $$EVAT_i = n_i \left[ \frac{RVAT}{\sum n_i} + \beta \sum_j \bar{\tau}_j (\bar{b}_j - b_{ij}) + (g_{h,i} - \bar{g}_h) + \gamma (p_i - \bar{p}) \right]$$

where $n_i$ is the Region's $i$ population, $RVAT$ is the regional share of national $VAT$, $\bar{\tau}_j$ is the base rate for regional tax $j$, $b_{ij}$ is the base of regional tax $j$ in Region $i$, $\bar{b}_j$ is the average base of tax $j$ over all $OSR$, $g_{hi}$ is the expenditure required to meet the health needs of the Region $i$, $\bar{g}$ is the average expenditure to meet the overall health needs of the $OSR$, $p_i$ is the estimated standard expenditure, excluding health needs of the Region $i$ and $\bar{p}$ is the average of the $p_i$ among the $OSR$. All variables contained in the square brackets are expressed in per-capita terms. The parameters $\beta$ and $\gamma$ are equal to 0,9 and 0,7 respectively. By substituting (2) into (1) we obtain:

(3) $T_i =$
$$n_i \left( \frac{RVAT}{\sum n_i} - \frac{CVAT_i}{n_i} \right) + \beta \sum_j \bar{\tau} i (\bar{b}_i - bij) + (g_{hi} - \bar{g}_h) + \gamma (p_i - \bar{p})$$

where the first two terms are the fiscal capacity, the third the health need, and the last the economies of scale. This formula highlights the three criteria that determine the size of the transfer received or paid by the Region $i$. The first two terms equalise fiscal capacity among the Regions, the second term redistributes resources according to health needs and the third one corrects the distribution of resources in order to compensate smaller Regions that cannot fully exploit the economies of scale in the providing services.

To evaluate the final impact of the equalisation formula on the distribution of revenue among Regions, we must consider each of the three corrections separately. Let us assume that Region $i$ keeps its tax rates at base levels. The Region's own revenues are equal to

$$R_i = n_i \sum_j \bar{\tau}_j b_{ij} + CVAT_i.$$

If the region receives (or pays) a transfer, $T'_i$, truncated to the first two terms in (3), total revenues are:

$$G_i^I = \qquad R_i + T'_i =$$

(4) $$n_i \left[ \frac{RVAT}{\sum_i n_i} + \beta \sum_j \bar{\tau}_j \bar{b}_j + (1-\beta) \sum_j \bar{\tau}_j b_{ij} \right]$$

If $\beta$ were equal to 1 each Region would have total per-capita regional revenue equal to the average per-capita yield of the VAT sharing and of regional taxes (e.g. Irap, regional surcharge on personal income tax) when levied at the base rates. In fact fiscal capacity is completely equalised only with respect to VAT, while the differences in all remaining regional revenue are equalised up to 90%, as $\beta=0,9$.

In order to describe the impact of the third component of (3) on total regional revenue, it is convenient to rewrite equation (4) taking into account that the VAT sharing rate has been chosen in order to leave unchanged the total amount of resources flowing in from regional budgets. Thus, for the year when the reform was first implemented (2001), the following equation is valid:

(5) $$\frac{RVAT}{\sum_i n_i} + \sum_j \bar{\tau}_j \bar{b}_j = \bar{g} + \bar{p}.$$

In fact, as we will clarify in section 5.1, the reform is based on the implicit assumption that almost these same conditions will be repeated in subsequent years. We may therefore substitute (5) into (4) to get:

(6) $$G_i^1 = n_i \left[ \bar{g} + \bar{p} + (1-\beta) \sum_j \bar{\tau}_j \left( b_{ij} - \bar{b}_j \right) \right].$$

When we add the transfers generated by the corrections for health need, total revenue becomes:

(7) $$G_i^2 = n_i \left[ g_i + \bar{p} + (1-\beta) \sum_j \bar{\tau}_j \left( b_{ij} - \bar{b}_j \right) \right].$$

If $\beta=1$ every Region would receive, at base rates, revenue equal to its health needs plus the average per-capita expenditure of all OSR in programs other than health services.

Finally, by adding the third component, we obtain:

$$G_i = n_i \left[ g_i + \gamma p_i + (1-\gamma) \bar{p} + (1-\beta) \sum_j \bar{\tau}_j \left( b_{ij} - \bar{b}_j \right) \right].$$

If $\beta=\gamma=1$, each Region would receive, at base rates, the money needed to finance its health needs and standard expenditure for other programs. In fact, being $\beta$ and $\gamma$ smaller than 1, Regions with larger than average tax bases and population would enjoy revenues exceeding the amount required to cover healt needs and standard expenditure, while those with smaller than average tax bases and population would be unable to finance healt needs and standard expenditure at base rates.

In order to illustrate the impact of the transfers on the distribution of regional revenues we simulated the implementation of the new transfer system based on formula (3) in the year 2001. The results are reported in tables 1 and 2. Table 1 shows the data concerning interregional transfers. The values in per-capita terms show that the sign and magnitude of the transfers are mainly determined by the fiscal capacity component due to the large divergence in tax bases across the Regions. All Northern Regions, with larger than average tax bases, must give up some of their revenue, while all Southern Regions receive a positive integration to their own resources. The situation of the Regions in Central Italy is somewhat mixed: roughly, large Regions (like Emilia R. and Lazio) are contributors while small ones (like the Marche and Umbria) are beneficiaries. The transfers activated by the correction for health needs are in general smaller and they flow in quite different directions. The Southern Regions are now mainly contributors as their health needs are lower than average due to a younger population. The main beneficiaries appear to be the Central Regions and Liguria, which is the Region with the highest percentage of elderly people in its population. The last term in the equalisation formula benefits the small Regions (Liguria, Marche, Umbria, Molise, Basilicata) irrespective of their geographic location.

In absolute terms, the total amount of money transferred from "rich" to "poor" Regions amounts to 6,326 million Euros (10% of *OSR* total revenue). The outflow and inflow are extremely polarised: the largest Northern Region, Lombardia, pays out more than half of total contributions and the two largest Regions of the South, Campania and Puglia, receive nearly 60% of all positive transfers.

**Table 1 – Simulated transfers among OSR according to the equalisation formula – year 2001**

| | Per-capita (Euro) | | | | | Absolute values (millions of Euro) | | | | |
|---|---|---|---|---|---|---|---|---|---|---|
| | Fiscal capacity | | Health need | Economies of scale | Total transfer | Fiscal capacity | | Health need | Economies of scale | Total transfer |
| | VAT | Other taxes | | | | VAT | Other taxes | | | |
| | 1 | 2 | 3 | 4 | 5= 1+2+3+4 | 6 | 7 | 8 | 9 | 10= 6+7+8+9 |
| Piemonte | -39 | -91 | 43 | -5 | -92 | -166 | -391 | 185 | -24 | -395 |
| Lombardia | -86 | -260 | -9 | -34 | -389 | -778 | -2337 | -83 | -303 | -3500 |
| Veneto | -53 | -96 | -9 | -8 | -166 | -236 | -428 | -40 | -37 | -741 |
| Liguria | -87 | 65 | 128 | 59 | 165 | -143 | 106 | 211 | 96 | 270 |
| Emilia R. | -101 | -165 | 69 | 0 | -197 | -400 | -650 | 271 | 0 | -779 |
| Toscana | -46 | -21 | 60 | 8 | 1 | -163 | -73 | 213 | 27 | 4 |
| Marche | -7 | 28 | 24 | 67 | 112 | -10 | 41 | 35 | 97 | 163 |
| Umbria | 19 | 66 | 57 | 104 | 247 | 16 | 55 | 48 | 87 | 205 |
| Lazio | -29 | -104 | -23 | -19 | -175 | -150 | -546 | -120 | -99 | -915 |
| Abruzzo | 70 | 152 | 11 | 75 | 309 | 90 | 194 | 14 | 96 | 394 |
| Molise | 122 | 243 | 27 | 166 | 558 | 40 | 80 | 9 | 55 | 184 |
| Campania | 164 | 312 | -62 | -26 | 388 | 950 | 1810 | -361 | -149 | 2250 |
| Basilicata | 176 | 294 | -32 | 125 | 563 | 107 | 180 | -19 | 76 | 344 |
| Puglia | 133 | 320 | -63 | -3 | 388 | 544 | 1312 | -258 | -11 | 1587 |
| Calabria | 143 | 311 | -51 | 43 | 446 | 297 | 644 | -107 | 89 | 924 |
| Sum of positive values | | | | | | 2045 | 4421 | 987 | 623 | 6326 |

Table 2 and figure 1, allow us to evaluate the effect of the implementation of the equalisation formula on the distribution of resources among the Regions. In particular columns 3 and 6 of table 2 report the percentage deviations from the mean of the Regions' total revenue in per-capita terms, respectively in the actual situation and in the simulated case where the equalisation formula is implemented in 2001. It is apparent that the equalisation formula mainly benefits the small Regions that experience an increase of their revenue in per-capita terms. Surprisingly, the largest Southern Regions are worse off, although they are the main recipient of transfers. This is the final result of the combined effect of the partial equalisation of fiscal capacity ($\beta<1$), and relatively low health needs (as their population is younger than the Italian average). Apart from the small Regions, the new transfer system brings about a strong equalisation of resources, as divergences from the mean are smaller than 10%.

## Table 2 – Distribution of total revenue – year 2001

|  | Actual revenue | | | Simulated revenue using equalisation formula | | |
|---|---|---|---|---|---|---|
|  | Total revenue (millions of Euro) | Total revenue per-capita (Euro) | Total revenue (deviation from mean) | Total revenue (millions of Euro) | Total revenue per-capita (Euro) | Total revenue (deviation from mean) |
| 1 | 2 | 3 | 4 | 5 | 6 | |
| Piemonte | 5709 | 1331 | 2.0 | 5804 | 1353 | 3.7 |
| Lombardia | 11688 | 1299 | -0.5 | 11621 | 1292 | -1.1 |
| Veneto | 5792 | 1296 | -0.7 | 5805 | 1299 | -0.5 |
| Liguria | 2386 | 1453 | 11.3 | 2439 | 1485 | 13.8 |
| Emilia R. | 5564 | 1409 | 7.9 | 5499 | 1393 | 6.7 |
|  | Actual revenue | | | Simulated revenue using equalisation formula | | |
|  | Total revenue (millions of Euro) | Total revenue per-capita (Euro) | Total revenue (deviation from mean) | Total revenue (millions of Euro) | Total revenue per-capita (Euro) | Total revenue (deviation from mean) |
| Toscana | 4844 | 1374 | 5.2 | 4851 | 1376 | 5.4 |
| Marche | 1896 | 1306 | 0.0 | 2024 | 1394 | 6.7 |
| Umbria | 1193 | 1433 | 9.7 | 1215 | 1460 | 11.8 |
| Lazio | 6752 | 1289 | -1.2 | 6679 | 1275 | -2.3 |
| Abruzzo | 1725 | 1352 | 3.5 | 1756 | 1376 | 5.4 |
| Molise | 471 | 1427 | 9.3 | 486 | 1471 | 12.7 |
| Campania | 6927 | 1195 | -8.5 | 6856 | 1183 | -9.4 |
| Basilicata | 813 | 1332 | 2.0 | 834 | 1366 | 4.6 |
| Puglia | 4947 | 1208 | -7.5 | 4932 | 1204 | -7.8 |
| Calabria | 2715 | 1310 | 0.3 | 2618 | 1263 | -3.3 |
| Total | 63418 | | | 63418 | | |

*Source*: estimations by the authors

## Open issues and perspectives

*The uniformity of health standards across the country*

As previously remarked, one of the main innovations of the 2000 reform was the abolition of any restriction on the use of regional revenues. Even if the transfer received or paid by each Region is calculated with reference to its health needs $g_i$, the Region may well spend less or more than $g_i$ in health. However, the reform has confirmed the principle of the uniformity of health services provision throughout the national territory. In fact, Regions are compelled to provide health services up to specified levels, both in terms of quality and quantity. If effective, control of performance may provide additional incentives to efficient management of health expenditure. The more efficient Regions, which are able to meet the required standards at a cost lower than $g_i$ may employ the money they have saved to finance other expenditure programs according to the needs and preferences of their constituencies. Nevertheless, the principle of uniformity in health services may be at odds with the new system of regional finance. As explained in sections *4.1*, the 2000 reform has formally abolished all vertical transfers from the central budget to the *OSR*. As a consequence, the Regions should now face a hard budget constraint as their total revenues, at base rates, depend only on the evolution of their tax bases. In the year when the reform was first implemented (2001), the VAT sharing rate was chosen according to (5) in order to guarantee sufficient resources to finance the sum of all Regions' standardised needs. When (5) is met the system of transfers redistributes regional resources in order to meet the health needs of every Region, as shown in section *4.2*.

The difficulties may arise in subsequent years if the regional tax bases grow less than health needs so that regional revenues are no longer sufficient to meet the health standards required by the central government. How likely is such a scenario? At first glance, the experience of the last two decades seems quite reassuring. In 1978, the year when the National Health Services was first created, public expenditure as a percentage of the GDP was equal to 5.3%. Twenty years later, in 1998, it was just marginally higher at 5.6% of the GDP. However, in the same period, total expenditure in health rose steadily from 5.9% to 8.4% of the GDP. In particular we may distinguish three sub-periods. From 1980 to 1986, both total and public health expenditure remained stable around respectively 7% and 5.5% of the GDP. Total health expenditure began to rise in 1987. Up to 1991, public health expenditure also rose, so that the share of public expenditure in total health expenditure stayed at about 76%. From 1992, public expenditure declined sharply and then stabilised at about 5.5% of the GDP. As a consequence, the share of public expenditure in total health expenditure dropped to about 66%. Overall, these figures may suggest that health needs are actually growing faster than tax bases, as shown by the dynamics of the ratio between total public expenditure and the GDP. The stability of public health expenditure over the GDP may reflect a reduction in the standards of the *NHS* due to the fiscal adjustment implemented since 1992 to meet the Maastricht criteria.

In order to evaluate the financial consequences of diverging growth rates of health needs and tax bases, we have estimated regional revenues and health needs in 2013. Ideally, in order to provide feasible projections of health needs one should forecast the quality and quantity of the services offered by the NHS and estimate their cost. Both projections are arduous and open to criticism. In particular, health care costs are affected by population ageing and by a variety of technological and economic factors such as incentives facing suppliers and patients, changes in price/costs of health care relative to other goods and services and increased underlying demand as incomes rise (Dang et al. 2001). There is no shared view on the relative importance of these factors in shaping the future dynamics of health costs. As to the impact of population ageing there are two opposing approaches (Dang et al. 2001, Roseveare et al. 1996). According to the former, health needs are strictly linked to age through a "J" shaped relationship: they are high in the first months of life, then decline during youth and adulthood and rise again in old age. As a consequence, health needs should rise as the percentage of elderly people increases in the population. In contrast, the second view emphasises that a large share of total lifetime health care costs occurs in the last year or two of life. Hence, population ageing may not lead to an increase in health needs if life expectancy rises too.

We do not cope with all these issues directly. Rather, we provide projections under two extreme scenarios that represent, respectively, the most favourable situation (where health needs grow in line with the GDP) and the most adverse one (where health needs grow faster than the GDP due to population ageing). In particular, in the adverse scenario we follow the approach that relates health expenditure to the age structure of the population. Hence *per capita* health care expenditures by age group have been projected using the national GDP growth rate and then multiplied by the number of people in each age group. The yield of the Regions' own resources has been estimated for each single Region on the basis of regional GDP growth rates. The results are reported in figure 1 and 2.

Figure 1 compares the simulated distribution of *per capita* revenue between the *OSR*'s in 2001 (table 2, column 6) with the distribution of projected per capita revenue in 2013 under the two alternative scenarios. The three distributions are quite similar. This confirms that the new system of interregional transfers can achieve a strong equalisation of resources under different dynamics of revenue and needs. The differences among Regions are wider in the adverse scenario. This may be explained as the Regions with a higher percentage of elderly people in their population (e.g. Liguria) experience a greater increase in their health needs and receive a higher share of resources through the equalisation formula. In contrast, Regions with a relatively young population (e.g. Campania) have lower health needs and receive smaller grants.

**Figure 1 – Per capita revenue in 2001 and in 2013 under alternative scenarios**
*(percentage deviations from mean)*

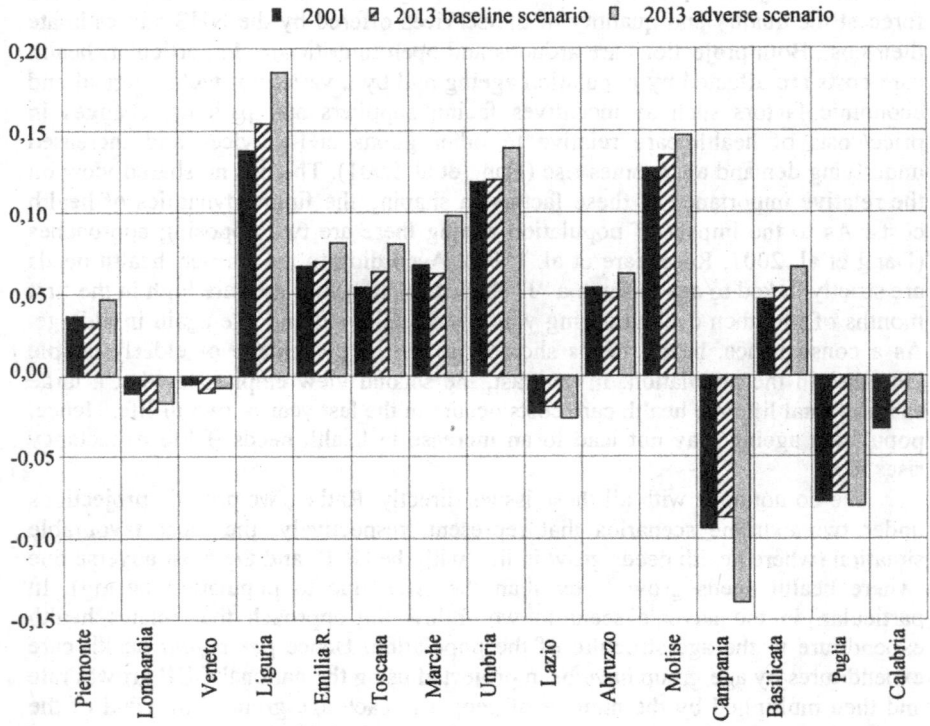

*Source*: estimations by the authors

However, as previously remarked, the problems may come not from the distribution of regional resources but from their absolute level. As shown in figure 2, in the adverse scenario total health needs are slightly higher than total resources at the Regions' disposal. As a consequence, many Regions cannot cover their health needs with the resources they receive at base rates. The worst situation is that of Campania with total resources equal to 94% of its health needs.

**Figure 2 – Total revenue/ health need – year 2013**

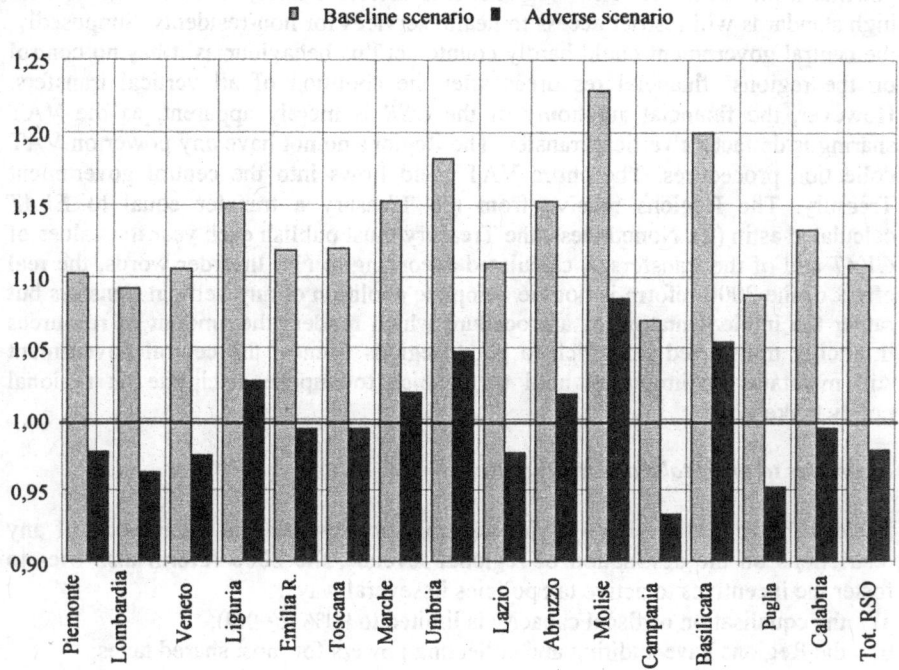

*Source*: estimations by the authors

In such a case how can a balance be drawn between resources and needs? The central government might follow two different strategies: it may either increase the resources at the Regions' disposal by raising the VAT sharing rate, or reduce the uniform standards of the *NHS*. Both strategies have serious shortcomings. The periodic revision of the VAT sharing rate may weaken budget constraints and foster opportunistic behaviour in regional politicians. As shown by the history of Italian intergovernmental relationship in the last twenty years, it may be quite hard to establish whether a future increase in health expenditure will have been caused by the inefficient behaviour of regional politicians and managers, or by an increase in health needs due to demographic, technological or economic factors. As a consequence, regional politicians will have the incentive to increase health expenditure and to claim that this is due to the grow of the health needs in order to receive more money through the increase of VAT sharing.

The alternative strategy at the government's disposal is a reduction of the health standards guaranteed across the national territory. The regions that value health care most and wants to keep high standards in public services will be forced to raise their tax rates to obtain additional revenues or to reduce expenditure in other programs. In this scenario, the slow disintegration of the *NHS* is at risk.

Large inter-regional differences in health standards will foster a high mobility of patients from "poor" to "rich" regions. It is therefore likely that the regions with high standards will restrict access to health services for non-residents. Supposedly, the central government could hardly counteract this behaviour as it has no control on the regions' financial resources after the abolition of all vertical transfers. However, the financial autonomy of the *OSR* is merely apparent, as the VAT sharing is de facto a vertical transfer. The Regions do not have any power on VAT collection procedures. The entire VAT yield flows into the central government Treasury. The Regions receive from the Treasury a transfer equal to *EVAT* calculated as in (2). Nonetheless, the Treasury must publish each year the values of *CVAT* and of the transfers $T_i$ calculated according to (1). In order words, the real effect of the 2000 reform is not the complete abolition of any vertical transfers but rather the implementation of a procedure which renders the amount of resources implicitly transferred from rich to poor Regions. Hence, the central government still maintains an important hold with which to impose discipline on regional policy makers.

*Incentives to undertake active tax policies*

Besides the formal abolition of all vertical transfers and the elimination of any restrictions on the destination of regional revenue, the 2000 reform also tries to foster the incentives to active tax policies in several ways:
a)  the equalisation of fiscal capacity is limited to 90% ($\beta=0.9$);
b)  the Regions have auditing and collecting powers for most shared taxes;
c)  there is no equalisation of the yield of autonomous tax effort above base rates.

The complete equalisation of fiscal capacity would have removed any incentive both to pursue policies aimed at enlarging the tax bases, by sustaining the growth of the regional economy, and to exert effort in auditing and collecting procedures. Nonetheless, the actual scope for regional policies that may broaden the tax bases is quite limited. It is evident that the ability to retain 10% of the yield produced by an increase in the tax bases is a rather weak motivation for regional policy makers. Furthermore, tax auditing and collection are quite difficult tasks for regional administrations. Firstly, as previously remarked, they lack, at present, the essential technical skills. Secondly, regional tax auditing is limited by the very nature of the main taxes involved.[3] As to Irap, the difficulties stem from the fact that the taxpayer may reside outside the Region where the value added is produced. In order to calculate the tax due by a non-resident the Region must first assess the total tax base of the taxpayer (i.e. the value added in all Regions where the taxpayer is doing business) and then apportion it according to labour costs. In the absence of interregional information sharing, it is quite hard for a single Region to gather the required information. Furthermore, tax auditing implies an externality: if a Region detects the tax evasion of a particular taxpayer, it benefits all Regions where the taxpayer is doing business. This reduces the incentives to actively create obstacles to tax evasion. Information gathering is also an obvious obstacle for the auditing of the personal income tax by regional administrations.

What about the incentives to vary the tax rates? The absence of any equalisation of the revenue stemming from an increase of tax rates above the base level leaves the motivation for tax effort completely unaffected. This may be a problem in the light of the huge differences in the Regions' tax bases. Table 3 reports the values of the additional revenue that each Region obtains by raising both the rate of Irap and the surcharge on personal income tax to their maximum levels. Total *OSR's* revenue raise of about 10% equal to 128 euro per-capita. The distribution of this additional yield is extremely uneven. On average, the Southern Regions collect less than half the revenue of the Northern Regions. The poorest Region, Calabria, sees its total resources increasing by less than 5%.

**Table 3 – Additional revenue from tax effort**

|  | Percentage of total revenues | Euro per-capita |
|---|---|---|
| Piemonte | 11.0 | 146 |
| Lombardia | 14.4 | 187 |
| Veneto | 11.2 | 145 |
| Liguria | 7.6 | 111 |
| Emilia Romagna | 11.3 | 160 |
| Toscana | 9.2 | 127 |
| Marche | 9.0 | 118 |
| Umbria | 7.3 | 105 |
| Lazio | 11.9 | 153 |
| Abruzzo | 6.8 | 92 |
| Molise | 5.1 | 73 |
| Campania | 5.5 | 65 |
| Basilicata | 5.0 | 66 |
| Puglia | 5.3 | 63 |
| Calabria | 4.8 | 63 |
| Total | 9.8 | 128 |

*Source*: estimations by the authors

These figures suggest that the Southern Regions will hardly exert any tax effort. This raises two concerns. Firstly, fiscal autonomy could reinforce the Italian dualism if the richest Regions use their fiscal autonomy to increase productive public expenditure in order to foster their economy. Secondly, if population ageing leads to a reduction of the standards offered by the NHS, it will be quite difficult for Southern Regions to cover their health needs through a tax increase. This will strengthen the drive towards dismantling the NHS described in the preceding section. There is however a different and positive view regarding this asymmetric distribution of the incentives to tax effort. The literature on tax competition suggests that the Southern Regions may benefit from low taxes: by keeping their rates below those of the Northern Regions they may be able to attract new investments that may promote their economic development. At the moment there is no evidence of this "positive" tax competition. In contrast, there are signs of some "harmful" tax competition among relatively "rich" Regions. Only three *OSR* (Liguria, Veneto and Toscana) have changed the rate of Irap. They have all *reduced* the tax rate for selected categories of taxpayers, such as newly established firms.

*Fundamental devolution*

While *OSR* financing was completely renovated through several reforms in the nineties, the devolution of expenditure responsibility is still at an early stage. In March, after years of heated but sterile debate and just before the general elections, the parliament introduced the subsidiarity principle in the Italian Constitution through an amendment supported by the center-left majority. Full legislative powers have been granted to the Regions except for limited number of matters of national interest (such as defence, foreign and monetary policy, social security, etc.). However regional powers will be limited within a framework of common rules set by national legislation.

The practical effects of this reform are still unclear. Under the pressure of the northern party "Lega Nord", which is part of the coalition that won the last general elections, the new government has declared its commitment to submit a new constitutional amendment for parliamentary approval. This proposal should be characterised by an even more radical devolution to Regions even if its exact contents are still unknown. Some suggestions may come from the proposals recently made by the Minister for Institutional Reforms and Devolution and leader of the "Lega Nord", Umberto Bossi. He suggested giving each single Region the choice between the status quo or complete autonomy in the field of health, education and local police. Furthermore, the new "autonomous" Regions should be left completely free to choose of their institutional arrangements (e.g. public vs. private provision, direct public production vs. public financing, direct public financing vs. quasi-markets).

In this complex and incomplete scenario it is hard to speculate on the future evolution of the regional finance. However, some useful insights may be gleaned by evaluating the effects of devolving a limited number of expenditure responsibilities in a simplified framework. In particular, we should consider the case of the complete and symmetrical devolution of education, health and local police (the functions indicated by Umberto Bossi) to all *OSR*. Table 4 reports the results of an estimate of the financial needs generated by this particular kind of devolution (Arachi and Zanardi 2001). The total amount of resources to be transferred to the OSR is equal to about 41 billions of euro, approximately the 65% of the actual total regional revenue. Obviously, expenditure in absolute terms is higher in the larger Regions (Lombardia, Lazio, Campania). In contrast, expenditure in per-capita terms is higher in the Regions located in the Center and South of the peninsula (e.g. in Calabria the expenditure is about one thousand euros per-capita) and in the small Regions (e.g. 829 euros per-capita in Liguria). The differences in per-capita expenditure are mainly due to two factors. Firstly, the small Regions face higher costs, as they cannot fully exploit the economies of scale. Secondly, expenditure for education is greater in the Regions with a higher share of the population in the 3-18 year age range.

Table 4 – Financial needs generated by devolution – year 2001

|  | Absolute values (millions of Euro) | | | | | Per-capita values (Euro) | | | | |
|---|---|---|---|---|---|---|---|---|---|---|
|  | Public order and safety | Education | University | Health | Total | Public order and safety | Education | University | Health | Total |
| Piemonte | 490 | 2090 | 416 | 24 | 3020 | 114 | 487 | 97 | 6 | 704 |
| Lombardia | 758 | 4228 | 874 | 82 | 5942 | 84 | 470 | 97 | 9 | 660 |
| Veneto | 353 | 2278 | 445 | 46 | 3122 | 79 | 510 | 100 | 10 | 699 |
| Liguria | 241 | 749 | 322 | 51 | 1362 | 147 | 456 | 196 | 31 | 830 |
| Emilia Rom. | 401 | 1818 | 658 | 104 | 2980 | 102 | 460 | 167 | 26 | 755 |
| Toscana | 478 | 1911 | 717 | 63 | 3170 | 136 | 542 | 203 | 18 | 899 |
| Marche | 160 | 865 | 168 | 29 | 1222 | 110 | 596 | 116 | 20 | 842 |
| Umbria | 107 | 526 | 183 | 11 | 827 | 129 | 631 | 220 | 13 | 993 |
| Lazio | 1405 | 3613 | 1003 | 250 | 6271 | 268 | 690 | 192 | 48 | 1198 |
| Abruzzo | 164 | 838 | 121 | 19 | 1143 | 129 | 656 | 95 | 15 | 895 |
| Molise | 63 | 234 | 19 | 4 | 320 | 192 | 709 | 57 | 12 | 970 |
| Campania | 774 | 4164 | 705 | 150 | 5793 | 134 | 719 | 122 | 26 | 1000 |
| Basilicata | 77 | 520 | 18 | 6 | 620 | 126 | 851 | 29 | 10 | 1016 |
| Puglia | 450 | 2577 | 289 | 52 | 3368 | 110 | 629 | 71 | 13 | 822 |
| Calabria | 343 | 1643 | 77 | 39 | 2101 | 165 | 792 | 37 | 19 | 1014 |
| Total | 6265 | 28053 | 6016 | 929 | 41263 | 129 | 578 | 124 | 19 | 850 |

Source: Arachi and Zanardi (2001)

How could the new regional needs be financed? We must verify whether the additional resources could be transferred to the Regions by increasing the existing VAT sharing or the surcharge on the personal income tax. Table 5 allows a comparison of these two alternatives by reporting the fiscal imbalances that would arise in both cases. In order to finance the devolution through personal income tax, the regional surcharge should be raised from 0,9% to 10,87%. Given the uneven distribution of income among Regions, this source of financing would generate large fiscal imbalances. The transfers needed to correct these imbalances are equal to about 8 billion euros (25% higher than the amount of transfers activated by the

2000 reform). As for the equalising transfers implemented by the 2000 reform, the flows are extremely polarised between two Regions: Lombardia and Campania. When VAT is used in place of personal income tax, the sharing rate should be set at nearly 100% (96.5%). If the yield is assigned to Regions according to the consumption of their residents, the total amount of the transfers needed to correct fiscal imbalances is much lower (about 6 billion euros). This reflects a more uniform geographical distribution of consumption with respect to income.

Table 5 – Alternative financing in case of fundamental devolution – year 2001

|  | Absolute values (millions of Euro) | | | | | Per-capita values (Euro) | | | | |
|---|---|---|---|---|---|---|---|---|---|---|
|  | | Personal income tax surcharge: rate 10,37% | | VAT sharing: rate 96,5% | | | Personal income tax surcharge: rate 10,37% | | VAT sharing: rate 96,5% | |
|  | Total needs | Revenue | Fiscal imbalances | Reven. | Fiscal imbalan. | Total needs | Reven. | Fiscal imbalan. | Reven. | Fiscal Imbalan. |
| Piemonte | 3020 | 4304 | -1284 | 3892 | -871 | 704 | 1004 | -299 | 908 | -203 |
| Lombardia | 5942 | 9867 | -3925 | 8812 | -2870 | 660 | 1097 | -436 | 979 | -319 |
| Veneto | 3122 | 4255 | -1133 | 4151 | -1029 | 699 | 952 | -254 | 929 | -230 |
| Liguria | 1362 | 1553 | -190 | 1610 | -248 | 830 | 945 | -116 | 980 | -151 |
| Emilia Romagna | 2980 | 4292 | -1311 | 3955 | -975 | 755 | 1087 | -332 | 1002 | -247 |
| Toscana | 3170 | 3277 | -107 | 3240 | -71 | 899 | 929 | -30 | 919 | -20 |
| Marche | 1222 | 1210 | 12 | 1249 | -27 | 842 | 834 | 8 | 860 | -18 |
| Umbria | 827 | 665 | 162 | 683 | 144 | 993 | 799 | 195 | 821 | 172 |
| Lazio | 6271 | 4659 | 1613 | 4675 | 1597 | 1198 | 890 | 308 | 893 | 305 |
| Abruzzo | 1143 | 831 | 311 | 949 | 194 | 895 | 651 | 244 | 744 | 152 |
| Molise | 320 | 183 | 137 | 220 | 101 | 970 | 555 | 415 | 665 | 305 |
| Campania | 5793 | 2837 | 2957 | 3494 | 2299 | 1000 | 489 | 510 | 603 | 397 |
| Basilicata | 620 | 306 | 315 | 357 | 263 | 1016 | 501 | 515 | 585 | 431 |
| Puglia | 3368 | 2091 | 1277 | 2660 | 708 | 822 | 511 | 312 | 650 | 173 |
| Calabria | 2101 | 917 | 1184 | 1314 | 787 | 1014 | 442 | 571 | 634 | 380 |
| Total | 41263 | 41247 | 0 | 41261 | 0 | 850 | 849 | 0 | 849 | 0 |
| Sum of positive values | 0 | 0 | 7967 | 0 | 6092 | 0 | 0 | 0 | 0 | 0 |

*Source*: estimations by the authors

This data shows that the actual system of OSR financing may accommodate a large devolution of expenditure responsibilities. VAT seems the best resource to rely on as it reduces the size of interregional redistribution even if, at the most, it could become a regional tax.

## The North-South dualism

Most of the drawbacks of the Italian system of intergovernmental relationships stem from the sharp economic dualism between the North and the South. The economic differences translate into asymmetric incentives for regional politicians to make efficient use of resources. We have shown that policy makers in the rich Regions of the North may have some incentive to actively manage the taxes within their power, while the poor Regions in the South have very limited tax autonomy and find it convenient to passively rely on grants.

**Table 6 – Projected transfers in 2013 according to equalisation formula**

|  | Baseline scenario for Regional GDP growth rates | | | | Higher growth in Southern regions | | | |
|---|---|---|---|---|---|---|---|---|
|  | Needs grow as GDP | | Needs grow faster than GDP due to population ageing | | Needs grow as GDP | | Needs grow faster than GDP due to population ageing | |
|  | Absolute Values | Per-capita | Absolute values | Per-capita | Absolute values | Per-capita | Absolute values | Per-capita |
| Piemonte | -408 | -96 | -270 | -63 | -210 | -49 | -72 | -17 |
| Lombardia | -4568 | -487 | -4446 | -474 | -3972 | -424 | -3851 | -411 |
| Veneto | -1055 | -225 | -1024 | -218 | -828 | -176 | -798 | -170 |
| Liguria | 243 | 160 | 348 | 228 | 305 | 200 | 409 | 269 |
| Emilia Romagna | -1437 | -350 | -1332 | -325 | -1179 | -287 | -1075 | -262 |
| Toscana | -314 | -88 | -182 | -51 | -147 | -41 | -15 | -4 |
| Marche | 344 | 227 | 461 | 304 | 383 | 253 | 501 | 330 |
| Umbria | 348 | 407 | 385 | 449 | 365 | 425 | 401 | 468 |
| Lazio | -1911 | -352 | -1997 | -368 | -1617 | -298 | -1703 | -314 |
| Abruzzo | 696 | 533 | 731 | 559 | 511 | 391 | 545 | 417 |
| Molise | 291 | 906 | 300 | 933 | 252 | 784 | 261 | 812 |
| Campania | 3384 | 577 | 2722 | 464 | 2612 | 446 | 1951 | 333 |
| Basilicata | 540 | 910 | 557 | 939 | 472 | 795 | 489 | 824 |
| Puglia | 2449 | 597 | 2383 | 581 | 1913 | 466 | 1848 | 450 |
| Calabria | 1375 | 682 | 1364 | 677 | 1120 | 556 | 1109 | 550 |
| Sum of positive values | 9671 |  | 9252 |  | 7933 |  | 7514 |  |

*Source*: estimations by the authors

The future evolution of Italian federalism depends crucially on whether the Southern Regions will catch up the rest of the Italian economy. Fostering the economy of the Southern Regions is one of the priorities of the new government. The Economic and Financial Planning Document has forecasted that in the coming years, the growth rate of Southern Regions will be one percentage point higher than the growth rate of the rest of the country. It is therefore expedient to analyse the effect of a differential growth of the South upon interregional financial flows. To this end, we have projected regional tax bases and needs to 2013 and calculated the ensuing equalising transfers in four different scenarios.

**Table 7 – Projected transfers in 2013 according to equalisation formula in case of fundamental devolution**

|  | Baseline scenario for regional GDP | | | | Higher growth in Southern regions | | | |
|---|---|---|---|---|---|---|---|---|
|  | Needs grow as GDP | | Needs grow faster than GDP due to population ageing | | Needs grow as GDP | | Needs grow faster than GDP due to population ageing | |
|  | Absolute values | Per-capita | Absolute values | Per-capita | Absolute values | Per-capita | Absolute values | Per-capita |
| Piemonte | -1057 | -248 | -872 | -205 | -689 | -162 | -511 | -120 |
| Lombardia | -6067 | -647 | -5809 | -620 | -5067 | -541 | -4830 | -515 |
| Veneto | -1600 | -341 | -1538 | -328 | -1176 | -250 | -1123 | -239 |
| Liguria | -519 | -341 | -392 | -257 | -372 | -244 | -248 | -163 |
| Emilia Romagna | -2940 | -716 | -2750 | -670 | -2469 | -601 | -2290 | -558 |
| Toscana | -1363 | -384 | -1191 | -336 | -1028 | -290 | -863 | -243 |
| Marche | 335 | 221 | 449 | 296 | 429 | 283 | 541 | 357 |
| Umbria | 341 | 398 | 375 | 438 | 387 | 452 | 420 | 490 |
| Lazio | -2286 | -421 | -2346 | -432 | -1756 | -323 | -1826 | -336 |
| Abruzzo | 994 | 760 | 1006 | 770 | 655 | 501 | 675 | 517 |
| Molise | 383 | 1192 | 385 | 1197 | 308 | 958 | 312 | 969 |
| Campania | 6611 | 1128 | 5783 | 986 | 5210 | 889 | 4411 | 752 |
| Basilicata | 850 | 1432 | 851 | 1434 | 720 | 1213 | 724 | 1219 |
| Puglia | 4082 | 995 | 3908 | 952 | 3090 | 753 | 2937 | 716 |
| Calabria | 2215 | 1100 | 2141 | 1063 | 1737 | 862 | 1672 | 830 |
| Sum of positive values | 15811 |  | 14898 |  | 12537 |  | 11691 |  |

*Source*: estimations by the authors

The first two scenarios have already been described in section *5.1* and figures 1 and 2. The first assumes that tax bases grow along with regional GDP whilst per-capita regional needs follow the average growth rate of GDPs among *OSR*. The second considers the additional effects of population ageing on regional needs. The third and fourth scenarios are analogous to the first two except for the assumption that the GDPs of Southern Regions grow one percentage point faster.

Table 6 reports the results of the four projections. A comparison between the data in the first part of the table and the data in the second shows that even a long term period of catching up will not radically reduce the scale of interregional redistribution. The total amount of transfers in favour of the "poor" Regions would be reduced by about one fifth.

Table 8 – Projected transfers among OSR according to the equalisation formula – year 2013, millions of euro

| | Without devolution | | | | | With devolution | | | | | |
|---|---|---|---|---|---|---|---|---|---|---|---|
| | Fiscal capacity | | Health need | Economies of scale | Total tran. | Fiscal capacity | | Health need | Education need | Economies of scale | Total transfer |
| | VAT | Other taxes | | | | VAT | Other taxes | | | | |
| | 1 | 2 | 3 | 4 | 1+2+3+4 | 6 | 7 | 8 | 9 | 10 | 6+7−8+9+10 |
| Piemonte | −145 | −501 | 313 | −74 | −408 | −364 | −501 | 313 | −431 | −74 | −1057 |
| Lombardia | −656 | −3102 | −146 | −663 | −4568 | − | −3102 | −146 | −514 | −663 | −6067 |
| | | | | | | 1641 | | | | | |
| Veneto | −280 | −603 | −71 | −101 | −1055 | −702 | −603 | −71 | −123 | −101 | −1600 |
| Liguria | −331 | 57 | 334 | 184 | 243 | −829 | 57 | 334 | −264 | 184 | −519 |
| Emilia R. | −733 | −1191 | 481 | 6 | −1437 | −1834 | −1191 | 481 | −402 | 6 | −2940 |
| Toscana | −442 | −324 | 366 | 87 | −314 | −1107 | −324 | 366 | −384 | 87 | −1363 |
| Marche | 20 | 108 | 63 | 153 | 344 | 49 | 108 | 63 | −38 | 153 | 335 |
| Umbria | 26 | 90 | 84 | 149 | 348 | 64 | 90 | 84 | −46 | 149 | 341 |
| Lazio | −406 | −1152 | −212 | −142 | −1911 | −1016 | −1152 | −212 | 235 | −142 | −2286 |
| Abruzzo | 171 | 345 | 25 | 155 | 696 | 429 | 345 | 25 | 39 | 155 | 994 |
| Molise | 60 | 124 | 15 | 93 | 291 | 150 | 124 | 15 | 2 | 93 | 383 |
| Campania | 1364 | 2821 | −622 | −179 | 3384 | 3415 | 2821 | −622 | 1176 | −179 | 6611 |
| Basilicata | 163 | 278 | −32 | 131 | 540 | 408 | 278 | −32 | 65 | 131 | 850 |
| Puglia | 788 | 2080 | −441 | 22 | 2449 | 1973 | 2080 | −441 | 448 | 22 | 4082 |
| Calabria | 402 | 969 | −177 | 180 | 1375 | 1006 | 969 | −177 | 236 | 180 | 2215 |
| | 2993 | 6873 | 1680 | 1159 | 12705 | 7494 | 6873 | 1680 | 2201 | 1159 | 15811 |

*Source*: estimations by the authors

It is interesting to note that population ageing does not increase the distance between "poor" and "rich" Regions. This is due to the fact that the main recipients, Campania and Puglia, have relatively young populations. Hence their health needs, and the ensuing transfers, do not greatly increase. The opposite is true for "old" Regions like Liguria and Toscana where health needs rise drastically bringing about a significant increase (reduction) of transfers received (paid) in per-capita terms. However, given that these Regions are relatively small, the total transfer they receive (pay) does not change significantly. Additional insights may be gleaned by projecting the equalising transfers under the assumption that education, health and local police will be devolved to the Regions. In order to forecast regional revenue one has to specify the source of financing and the formula for equalising the additional resources. We consider the case where the new regional functions are financed by increasing the VAT sharing to 96.5%. In the equalising formula we have introduced an additional term to equalise education needs. This term redistributes the resources towards Regions with higher than average education needs, in per-capita terms, higher than average (i.e. Regions with a higher share of their population in the 3-18 year age range).

Table 7 reports the results of four projections in the scenarios previously described. A comparison between the first columns of tables 6 and 7 shows that devolution enlarges the scale of interregional redistribution by about 50% as the total amount of equalising transfers grows from 10 to 16 billion euros. As shown in table 8 the increment is due entirely to the component that equalises fiscal capacity: the enlargement of the VAT sharing emphasises the effect of uneven distribution of consumption among Regions. Quite interestingly the introduction of a new correction for education needs in the equalisation formula reduces the interregional transfers.

As shown in table 8, the corrections for health and education needs are negatively correlated. This is easily explained because the older the population, the higher health needs and the lower education needs.

Overall, devolution strengthens the polarisation of financial flows between the Northern Regions, which have high consumption and low education needs, and the Southern Regions, where consumption is low but the education needs is high due to a relatively young population. As to the effects of higher economic growth in the South, devolution does not significantly change the results: the total amount of transfers is reduced by about one fifth.

## Concluding remarks

Throughout the seventies, local governments in Italy were financially dependent on grants from the central government. The lack of fiscal autonomy was the source of serious inefficiency and the main reason for large budget deficits at the local level. During the 1990s the fiscal autonomy of local governments was substantially increased: local governments now have the power to raise their own taxes and receive a large share of revenue from national taxes. A new system of equalising grants has been implemented to support regions with small tax bases. This fundamental reform has removed many deficiencies of the past system of local public finance. Yet, there are many issues that must be dealt with in the future. Firstly, the principle of uniformity in health standards across the country may be at odds with the decision to eliminate any kind of ex-post financing in order to foster the financial responsibility of local governments. Secondly, the incentives to implement autonomous tax policies at the local level might be hindered by the new mechanism of interregional redistribution. Finally, the viability of the entire system in the medium-long run is conditional on the evolution of the North-South dualism.

## Notes

[1] The total value added of a firm is apportioned to Regions where the production plants are located on the basis of labour cost.
[2] The Irap tax rate can be increased or reduced by one percentage point, the regional surcharge on the personal income tax by 0.5 percentage points.
[3] Recollect that VAT is equalised at 100%.

## References

Arachi, G. and A. Zanardi (2001), 'La devoluzione nel paese del dualismo' in L. Bernardi and A. Zanardi (eds.) *La finanza pubblica italiana – 2001*, Il Mulino, Bologna.
Dang, T.T., P. Antolin and H. Oxley (2001), 'Fiscal implications of ageing: projections of age-related spending', *OECD Economics Department working papers*, no. 305.
Giarda, P. (2000), *Intergovernmental fiscal relations in Italy*, mimeo.
Roseveare, D., W. Leibfritz, D. Fore and E. Wurzel (1996), 'Ageing populations, pension systems and government budgets: simulations for 20 OECD countries', *OECD Economics Department working papers*, no. 168.

# Comment

## Hiroko Kudo

### "The Italian Case" still existing

Among Italian political scientists, it had been said that there was no more "the Italian case", which used to be the diffused expression to describe exceptional situations and/or experiences of Italian society and politics. However, although this has been a strong temptation for all those who study Italy, it proved to be little likely. In fact, major political events during the last decade are quite unique to the country in question and just few cases show similar characteristics, at least in other European Union member countries.

For instance, the very case discussed in this paper of public finance restructuring in Italy is a very interesting experience. Public finance restructuring itself became one of the common targets for the European countries looking for political and economical integration, as a series of standards on their economical and social conditions was set for those countries by international agreements. At that time, Italy was on the borderline to enter the common currency as the first group and this situation determined its policy over the decade.

In fact, in 1996 Italian general election citizens were asked to choose between the EU economic integration with sacrifices and a liberal policy at the cost of not joining the common currency. Center-Left coalition won the election offering citizens the political reform and financial restructuring, thus the entrance to the common currency system as one of the countries of the first group. Since 1996, the government promoted public sector reform, political reform, and financial restructuring. They carried out an impressive drastic reform policy on bureaucracy. Concerning the financial restructuring, privatization and deregulation enabled the government to raise money and improve its public services, while market started to enjoy sound competition and thus improvement of services and conditions for the consumer-citizens.

Strategies and methods adopted for this public sector reform are in line with the reform strategies and methods practiced in many countries over the world. However, its articulation within the framework of reform for the EU integration is unique and, in fact, proved to be essential for the implementation. For example, privatization and deregulation can be seen also in Japanese public sector reform in the Eighties, but the extent and the speed with which Italy realized this strategy is impressive.

Public debt was the most serious and urgent problem to be resolved for the Center-Left coalition government led by Prof. Prodi, who now heads the European Union. Public debt problem was not less serious in Japan too and while Italy overcame the situation in a couple of years, Japanese public financial structure remained almost the same, despite the repeated announcements by the Prime Minister of forthcoming reforms.

"The Italian case" of overcoming public debt and restructuring public finances can be explained by various facts. One may argue that the requirements for the EU integration worked as an external pressure to the country, meanwhile Japan didn't and still doesn't have any urgent reason to do that, although it has been facing similar troubles because of its fragile financial structure. However, none of these was strong enough to force Japanese government to hurry its reform policy.

## Comparing public finance restructuring

Public finance restructuring itself is a rather common policy for developed countries when they face certain level of stagnation. Until the 1980s, many modern capitalist countries continued to promote growth and didn't care about their structural problems, as they still believed in a future of continuing growth.

In the 1980s, several developed countries, including Japan, realized that the situation has changed and started to implement reform policies. Compared to today's, reforms in that period were characterized by political difficulties and technical and/or methodological aspects. Today, governments are concentrating on fiscal restructuring, changes in the taxation system, and managerial reform of public services.

For instance to Japan, which has similar problems, the Italian experience of public finance restructuring is an interesting example of fiscal decentralization, allocation and/or equalization of financial resources, balancing between taxation and transfer, and linking taxation to public spending. Japan is in need of public finance restructuring, mainly to overcome its public debt problem under a persistent recession. In fact in Japan, public sector reform was given top priority since the middle 1990s, when the Prime Minister Hashimoto announced the need of so-called "Big Bang", which meant public finance as well as private business reforms. However, little has been implemented successfully to achieve this target by the following administrations because of lack of consensus. Some claimed that the stimulus package was badly needed to overcome a serious recession, some insisted that structural reforms were needed even if in the short term they might harm the economic situation of the country.

Other EU member countries, which were on the borderline together with Italy regarding the joining of common currency system, tried and implemented public finance reforms during the last decade, pushing other political and social issues aside. They were able to overcome the most urgent problems and hit the necessary target: however, other problems remained. Public finance restructuring sometimes causes further problems in the economy during the recession and thus obstacles recovery.

In fact, two Prime Ministers after the Hashimoto Administration in Japan preferred policies aimed at stimulating the economy instead of implementing public finance restructuring. Business Federations are not fully supporting the restructuring policy promoted by the PM Koizumi, however this is not the only reason for the delay in its implementation.

## Decentralization and tax reform

In Japan, decentralization policy has been promoted over the years, first, with respect to public administration, mainly to review and modify delegated functions, and second, with respect to taxation, mainly to increase sources of income for local governments and to create new taxes geared to certain purposes.

The newly enacted decentralization Law in Japan guaranteed power and autonomy to local governments. In fact, former delegated functions now need contracts between central administration and local governments, and local governments are given taxation autonomy, so that they can create and introduce new taxes and they can freely issue bonds without the authorization of the Minister. After its enactment, Japanese municipalities and prefectures have been competing each other to utilize this newly introduced possibility.

New taxes created and introduced recently can be classified into several categories and the most popular one is the "environmental" and/or "ecological" one. The targets vary from industrial waste to plastic shopping bags, reflecting their taxation systems and their economical and social structure. Very often, the income of these taxes is earmarked to specific spending, for example, the so called "environmental tax" has been designed for the environmental research and development, prevention of possible damage and protection of environment, environmental assessment, and any other use to create better environment.

Japanese reform of the taxation system has also been directed to widen the tax base. For instance, the Tokyo Metropolitan Government has been struggling to increase income from taxes and to balance it with the expenses. They created a "bank tax", which is similar to the business tax. Of course this has been strongly criticized by those hit and other concerned actors. Some also feared its impact on an already troubled economy. This new tax was criticized for being illegal by the group of banks and financial institutions and they actually won the case against prefecture government. This experience taught many lessons. The most important issue still remained unsolved is whether it is possible and/or legitimate for local governments to think about tax increases in order to deliver better public services. If we go back to the very principle of taxation, it seems to be legitimate; however, recent political decisions seem to deny this argument.

Meanwhile, the decentralized structure of public administration is and should be guaranteed through newly introduced actions such as citizen participation under "governance" model, citizen charter, merger and/or fusion among municipalities. Budget modernization, for instance, is focusing on; introduction of accrual accounting system, portfolio control, and performance based programme budgeting so that each local government can implement sound public management.

Japanese decentralization policy has been successful only to a limited extent, mainly because of political obstacles; Italian experience also proves the importance of political initiatives. The situation was unique to the Italian government and can be considered one of the reasons why they succeeded in this reform.

**Diversity and similarity (lessons learned)**

So what are the diversities and similarities between Italian reform and Japanese reform of the public sector characterized by public management reform, tax reform, decentralization, and so on?

Italy launched fiscal decentralization, namely "federalismo fiscale", distinguishing it from the political issues of devolution. Its decentralization policy was, in fact, a rather technical one, aimed mainly to reform public finance structure. Furthermore, public sector reform was aimed to realize "small government" and/or "smart government", which is to be complemented by taxation reform. The existence and impact of EU integration policy is unique to Italy and so is its articulation on social policy, including welfare policy.

In fact, the Bassanini Reform in Italy, which is called after the Public Function Minister who introduced the public sector reform since the first Prodi Administration, has several important aims: simplification, decentralization, managerial reform, rationalization, quality control, and performance management in public sector. These gave a solid framework to public institutions to implement further managerial policies and decentralization policies, including fiscal decentralization. The need of guaranteeing transparency and accountability of public institutions in order to be recognized as EU member country was realized through this reform. Through the balance of powers, decentralization guarantees control and transparency.

Furthermore, the Visco Reform focused on decentralization, rationalization, and unification, and reorganization of the taxation system. The rapid improvement of Italian fiscal structure cannot be explained without a fiscal decentralization policy.

In comparing Italian and Japanese policies, some questions can possibly arise. Was EU integration necessary for the success of Italian public sector reform? How much balance is needed between devolution of power inside one country and integration of different countries? The former question cannot be answered only by comparing the Italian case with that of Japan. It still has to be proved through history, whereas the latter question seems to have clear answer among European countries, as decentralization policy becoming more and more popular. However, the success of fiscal decentralization and thus public finance restructuring in Italy seems "the Italian case".

# Chapter 13

# The Italian Third Sector: An Overview at the Beginning of the Century

Marco Demarie
Stefano Cima

## Introduction

The dynamic of the third sector in Italy over the course of the last few years could be described with one image – which naturally, like all images, is only approximate. This is the image of a redefinition of the borders between the State and Society. On the one hand, the State is pulling back, narrowing the arena of its own direct activity; on the other, Society is moving forward, expressing a certain "business-like" desire in the areas of health, environment, culture and politics. Naturally, the process is not a perfectly harmonious one and this retreating and advancing do not completely correspond in all areas. There may be "no man's lands" as well as superimposition. But it is precisely in this two-fold movement that the opportunities and challenges of the Italian third sector lie.

Therefore, it is not just stylish to speak of the growing interest in non-profit organisations shown by the public, both Italian and international, as well as by legislators, politicians and administrators. Changes in the economic and social scenario, especially the problems with welfare systems and the models of citizens political participation, have given rise to development in the sector. The growth and expansion of organisations and the important increase, also in economic terms, of the non-profit sector that has occurred over the past decade has drawn the attention of scholars and institutions. Many of the reasons – both economic and socio-political – that explain the growth of the Third Sector in advanced economies are also valid here in Italy; at times even in a more accentuated form.[1]

The paper will firstly provide the reader with a synthetic presentation of the general economic, cultural and social reasons which explain the development of the third sector, with an emphasis on the Italian scene. An aggregate depiction of the economic size and composition of the sector will follow, and an attempt will be made to compare the Italian case with the different national types that have emerged from international research. The third section will consider the third sector actors, focusing on Italian idiosyncrasies. Conclusions will be drawn showing to what extent the future of the sector depends on several factors and their combination: the federalising process and its implications in terms of horizontal subsidiarity at all levels; the establishment of a friendlier legal framework; the sustainability of the supply of committed social entrepreneurs; and, last but not least, the political climate in which all the above will occur.

### Non-profit as response to market and state failures

Western economies suffer from an insufficient production of publicly useful goods and services. In other words, it seems that they have particular problems in creating mechanisms that encourage the private production of goods and services such as environmental quality, the protection of artistic and cultural heritage, health, assistance, education, scientific and technological research, the production of services for leisure time. These goods and services are considered crucial for the quality of civil co-habitation and the competitiveness of economic systems. Frequently, and the Italian case is typical, the public operator has had a sort of monopoly in guaranteeing the financing and production of these goods, with varying results (Ranci Ortigosa E., 1990). Caught between the need to produce welfare services that are becoming more and more costly – because of rapid demographic changes, among other reasons – and the difficulty of raising the funds necessary for financing them, governments have frequently ignored the production of other publicly useful goods and services. In Italy, these choices have produced widespread dissatisfaction: closed museums, a polluted environment, reduced scientific research, an insufficient average quality of health, education and social assistance systems (Borzaga C., Fiorentini G., Matacena A., 1996).

Even the public welfare system meets with many difficulties. Growing costs and the difficulty in finding the funds necessary to cope with them – because of the growing aversion of citizens in the West toward new taxes – make the economic system unsustainable over the long term, requiring drastic changes in direction. In addition the line of reasoning adopted by the public operator in supplying services is to make certain that these are frequently managed inefficiently and do not respond to the needs of the citizenry. Furthermore, public welfare systems have difficulty coping with the economic incentives that motivate citizens. For example, the free distribution of medicines tends to create a lack of control of pharmaceutical expenses and unemployment payments reduce the motivation to find a job, all this with destructive effects on the balance of the system.

Given the difficulties of an increasingly expensive welfare system considered to be inferior in quality, along with the inadequacy in the public production of other services of communal value, the idea has gained ground that non-profit organisations may provide an interesting solution. Considering those types of projects that the public operator does not perform well – such as the creation and management of public parks, the preservation and management of artistic and cultural heritage, the development of projects for cultural growth and opportunities for young people in the outlying areas of major cities, – all these could be effectively organised and managed by private organisations without affecting government spending any more than the poorly run public projects already do. Non-profit organisations can, in fact, easily utilise sources of public and private support, both monetary and non-monetary, that the public operator has difficulty in accessing. The most effective non-profit organisations bring together salaried and volunteer operators, just as they bring together public funds with individual and business donations, along with the interest from capital, in addition to an important amount of income of a "commercial" nature from the sale of goods and services to paying customers. There are even organisations that finance publicly valuable services and that support themselves with profits from the production and commercialisation of other goods and services. These also have, at least potentially, a more direct and equal feed-back with the users, both at the moment of defining the product/service as well as in verifying the capability of quantitatively and qualitatively satisfying the demand.

A model similar to the one just described could also be extended to traditional welfare services such as health, social assistance and education. This is a delicate and politically sensitive question and the working models, at least in Italy, must still be defined. The responsibility of supplying this service would continue to be public (in order to guarantee the universality of the treatment and strategic planning of priorities and projects), just as the most of the responsibility for financing these services would continue to fall on the public operator. Non-profit organisations would instead supply services able to integrate public and private support aimed at improving the quality of their products. Their financing could take on different forms, from agreements to credits for expenses.

## Non-profit as response to participation demand

A second group of reasons for which, beginning at the end of the 1980s, much attention was paid to non-profit and volunteer organisations can be found in the difficulties experienced by the system and models of political and social participation. The crisis in ideologies and growing disaffection with politics probably caused many citizens to shift their energies and desire for participation, to a world that still guaranteed space, the opportunity to make one's voice heard and decide for oneself, significant opportunities for interacting with other people and a response to the logical questions that many of us have. Social, cultural and environment volunteerism continues, to some extent, to guarantee all this. It is perhaps the discovery and re-evaluation of that "Tocquevillian" attitude of "coming together to solve problems" which presently has many supporters among scholars. It should be added that on the European scene, from the institutional point of view, the growth of the concept of assistance has created an environment favourable to the autonomy of social entities as producers of goods of both public and communal interest. First among these entities is the non-profit sector.

## The Italian non-profit sector: a general overview

An international comparison reveals a rather small Italian non-profit sector.[2] Data related to employment in the sector shows that it is lower than any other developed country, with an overall employment level (2.7%) only just a little higher than developing countries in Latin America and Central Europe (Table 1).

**Table 1 – Paid employment in the non-profit sector (standard work unit)**

| Country | PAID EMPLOYMENT Number | % of total employment* |
|---|---|---|
| Netherlands | 655.000 | 12.6 |
| Ireland | 119.000 | 11.5 |
| Belgium | 358.000 | 10.5 |
| United States | 8.555.000 | 7.8 |
| United Kingdom | 1.416.000 | 6.2 |
| Germany | 1.441.000 | 4.9 |
| France | 960.000 | 4.9 |
| Spain | 475.000 | 4.5 |
| Austria | 144.000 | 4.5 |
| Japan | 2.140.000 | 3.5 |
| Italy | 598.000 | 2.7 |
| Latin America | 1.932.000 | 2.2 |
| Central and Eastern Europe | 220.000 | 1.4 |

\* Agricoltural employment not included

*Source*: Estimates by the authors on Salamon L. M and Anheier H.K., 1998 and Istat, 2001

The percentage of employment compared to overall employment turns out to be lower vis-à-vis those European countries that are comparable to Italy such as Great Britain (6.2%), France (4.9%), Germany and Spain (4.5%). Finally, it should also be said that the Italian non-profit sector is smaller than that of Japan (3.5%).

There are three basic reasons traditionally identified in literature as an explanation of the small size of the Italian non-profit sector (see also Barbetta, 1997).

- There is a historical motivation that has to do with the pervasiveness of the State in Post-Unification Italy as well as in the underlying political cultures, in various ways suspicious of the autonomy of civil society. Consequently, in Italy collective needs – social, educational, and cultural – would be considered to be the appanage of the State. The production on the part of public institutions of all main services was probably much higher than in other countries, reducing the space for

private operators, both businesses as well as non-profit organisations. It is only now that the wind of subsidiarity has blown across Italian politics, and not without meeting some resistance.
- The second reason normally considered to explain this Italian anomaly is the importance of the informal economy that, in the present case, substitutes structured organisations, businesses or organised non-profit institutions that produce welfare services. In particular, the family, whose socio-economic role is still very important and maintains several traditional characteristics (the employment level of women in Italy is the lowest of all industrialised countries), takes on this role. Furthermore, in personal services, particularly assistance, the importance of unregistered workers is not insignificant (more and more frequently foreigners).
- Finally, this could have to do with an institutional bias. Some non-profit activities, though existing, seem to be invisible because Italian law has not traditionally offered adequate legal formats for their development with the possible effect of discouraging these projects. Whether these remain confined to the informal area or incorporated into "inadequate" legal forms – such as commercial companies – they end up being statistically invisible. On this subject, consider for example all those sectors of co-operation (but not the so-called social, see below), most of which are blocked by the problem of distributing profits, that remain excluded from the definition adopted on an international level. Even ethical banks, a sector in rapid growth over the past few years, that work for the development of non-profit organisations without following any profit making ends, are outside the sector since it is considered a commercial business.

But what is the present economic size of those organisations that make up the sector? What role do they play and what are their possibilities for the future? Even though the Italian non-profit sector is smaller than those of other major industrialised countries, the number of non-profits is high when compared both with profit-making businesses as well as public institutions.

There are 221,412 organisations overall active in Italy[3] (as of 31 December 1999). This is a large number considering that there are around 450 thousand profit-making businesses in the same sectors of specialisation (education, health and other public services). Let us examine some gross measures:
- The number of active organisations is equal to slightly less than half the profit-making businesses operating in the same specialised areas.
- More than 4 million people are employed overall in various positions in organisations in the sector, i.e. 17% of the active population and 10% of those of working age.
- In terms of salaried employment, Italian non-profit organisations show a level analogous to that of the banking and insurance industries, corresponding to 2.7% of non-agricultural employment.
- The overall expenditure of the sector is estimated to have been 69 thousand billion lire (more than 35 billion Euro) in 1999 (last estimate available), corresponding to 3.2% of the Gross Domestic Product.

If the above are some broad terms of reference concerning the sector as a whole, one has to add that the Italian non-profit sector is far from being homogeneous. In fact, it tends to be a very diverse landscape, like most of its counterparts all around the world.

Many small, almost invisible institutions coexist alongside a few institutions of important economic size with complex organisational structure. Organisations with a solid base of salaried workers exist side by side with organisations prevalently based on volunteer workers; there are organisations capable of paying their workers at the highest market levels and others that can only afford modest levels of expenditure. Legally, many different forms exist, some of tricky definition. Industry-wise, Italian non-profits are basically active in the areas of culture, sports and recreation, education and research, health and social assistance. These areas account for about three fourths of the sector according to any variable taken as a reference (employment, salaried or not, or expenditure). Though in a less clean-cut way, Italian non-profits conform to the most common model in European countries, in other words that of a social service oriented model (Barbetta G.P, 2000). From the ISTAT survey we also learn that private resources seem significantly to exceed beyond half the overall financing. As a matter of fact, more than 85% of organizations claim that public money accounts for less than 50% of their revenues of all kinds. This is interesting but rather controversial and should perhaps be investigated by future research. It would seem to reveal an orientation to "market" or "quasi-market" activities, given that the role of private donations is very limited.[4] Overall, Italian non-profits earn more than half their resources from sales on the market place (both public and private).

Public financing, which mainly entails payments through either contracts or agreements intended for specific activity, is particularly important in those sectors characterised by the supply of services to the needy or the disadvantaged. Advocacy organisations and those supplying other types of services (culture, leisure etc.) appear to be more autonomous.

The overwhelming majority of these organisations are made up of associations, unincorporated and incorporated. Fewer in number, but very powerful in economic terms, are the "other" legal types of groups (basically religious groups and mutual aid societies), social co-operatives and foundations (Table 2). The last two types are specifically dealt with later in this paper.

As mentioned, an overall total of almost 4 million people work in various positions in the sector (Istat, 2001). For the most part, these are volunteer workers, though the number of salaried workers is also significant. Non-salaried workers amount to about 3.2 million volunteers, 96 thousand religious staff and 28 thousand conscientious objectors. There are about half a million salaried workers (including 63,500 part time employees), 80 thousand collaborators (with regular contracts) and four thousand other workers generally seconded by businesses and/or institutions.

## Table 2 – Italian non-profit organizations by legal form and main activity sector – year 1999

| MAIN ACTIVITY SECTOR | LEGAL FORM | | | | | | |
|---|---|---|---|---|---|---|---|
| | Incorporated association | Foundation | Non incorporated ass. | Committee | Social coop. | Other form | Total |
| Culture and recreation | 37.102 | 827 | 97.444 | 2.327 | 476 | 1.557 | 139.733 |
| Education and research | 2.620 | 707 | 5.667 | 202 | 135 | 2.206 | 11.537 |
| Health | 5.338 | 167 | 3.483 | 64 | 362 | 262 | 9.676 |
| Social services | 6.557 | 768 | 8.056 | 321 | 2.396 | 1.136 | 19.234 |
| Environment | 1.274 | 15 | 1.738 | 155 | 66 | 29 | 3.277 |
| Economic develop. and social cohesion | 963 | 82 | 2.281 | 204 | 692 | 116 | 4.338 |
| Law, advocacy and politics | 1.582 | 21 | 4.948 | 171 | - | 120 | 6.842 |
| Philantropic intermediaries | 380 | 147 | 635 | 59 | - | 25 | 1.246 |
| International solidarity and cooperation | 420 | 36 | 847 | 90 | 10 | 30 | 1.433 |
| Religious educational activities | 1.250 | 207 | 3.090 | 117 | - | 2.138 | 6.803 |
| Professional associations, trade unions, etc. | 3.605 | - | 11.850 | 75 | - | 104 | 15.634 |
| Other activities | 222 | 31 | 707 | 48 | 514 | 138 | 1.660 |
| Total | 61.313 | 3.008 | 140.746 | 3.833 | 4.651 | 7.861 | 221.412 |

Source: Istat, 2001

In terms of standard work units, the salaried workforce amounts to around 598 thousand work units, a number comparable to employment in the automobile and non-electric machinery industries (539 thousand work units) or the sector of banking and insurance (640 thousand). The size of the non-salaried component is analogous, with 413 thousand standard work units. Overall, the workforce dedicated to the sector may be estimated to be slightly more than one million standard work units.

The distribution of these institutions by employment structure is noteworthy. It is confirmed that the Italian non-profit sector comprises, on the one hand, a swarm of small organisations that are almost exclusively based on volunteer work (84.8% of the total) and, on the other, a few, very big institutions (Table 3).

**Table 3 – Italian non-profit organizations by employment bracket and main activity sector – year 1999**

| MAIN ACTIVITY SECTOR | With no hired workforce | EMPLOYMENT BRACKET | | | | | Total |
|---|---|---|---|---|---|---|---|
| | | 1- 9 | 10 - 49 | 50 – 249 | 250 e più | Total | |
| Culture and recreation | 131.617 | 6.747 | 1.146 | 198 | 25 | 8.116 | 139.733 |
| Education and research | 6.046 | 3.553 | 1.447 | 408 | 83 | 5.491 | 11.537 |
| Health | 8.025 | 857 | 480 | 208 | 106 | 1.651 | 9.676 |
| Social services | 13.691 | 2.918 | 1.925 | 593 | 107 | 5.543 | 19.234 |
| Environment | 3.013 | 190 | - | 9 | - | 264 | 3.277 |
| Economic development and social cohesion | 2.762 | 853 | 587 | 119 | 17 | 1.576 | 4.338 |
| Law, advocacy and politics | 5.554 | 1.087 | 161 | 35 | 5 | 1.288 | 6.842 |
| Philantropic intermediaries | 1.106 | 134 | - | - | - | 140 | 1.246 |
| International solidarity and cooperation | 1.231 | 146 | 52 | 4 | - | 202 | 1.433 |
| Religious educational activities | 5.239 | 1.299 | 214 | 46 | 4 | 1.563 | 6.802 |
| Professional associations, trade unions, etc. | 8.632 | 5.082 | 1.600 | 296 | 24 | 7.002 | 15.634 |
| Other activities | 895 | 445 | 267 | - | - | 765 | 1.660 |
| Total | 187.811 | 23.311 | 7.945 | 1.972 | 373 | 33.601 | 221.412 |
| % | 84.8 | 10.5 | 3.6 | 0.9 | 0.2 | 15.2 | 100 |

*Source*: Istat, 2001

The high concentration in the sector is epitomized by the fact that the 373 largest organisations (1.1% of the total) employ 41.5% of the total, i.e. more than 220,000. Geographically, there is no homogeneous diffusion of Italian non-profit organisations. They are more present in the North (51.1% of the total) as compared to the Centre (21.2%) and the South (27.7%). Overall, there are 38.4 non-profit institutions for every 10 thousand inhabitants. This relationship tends to be higher in the northern and central regions. The positive relationship would then seem to be defined by the level of modernisation and development of an area and the presence of formal third sector as indicated in the literature. In terms of the age of the organisations, the majority are recently formed institutions: around 78.5% were formed after 1980 and 55.2% after 1990. Organisations found in Southern Italy tend to be younger. In fact, in this area, the percentage of organisations formed after 1990 (61.4%) is higher than that found in other geographical areas. This gives hope for a progressive reduction in the disparity between the areas.

**Table 4 – Total and average revenue by main activity sector – year 1999 (million of lira)**

| MAIN ACTIVITY SECTOR | REVENUE | | |
|---|---|---|---|
| | Million | % | average |
| Culture and recreation | 12.527.228 | 17.2 | 90 |
| Education and research | 9.423.108 | 12.9 | 817 |
| Health | 13.752.334 | 18.9 | 1.421 |
| Social services | 14.266.837 | 19.6 | 742 |
| Environment | 342.221 | 0.5 | 104 |
| Economic development and social cohesion | 2.846.097 | 3.9 | 656 |
| Law, advocacy and politics | 1.952.531 | 2.7 | 285 |
| Philantropic intermediaries | 1.504.441 | 2.1 | 1.207 |
| International solidarity and cooperation | 839.881 | 1.2 | 586 |
| Religious educational activities | 2.402.074 | 3.3 | 353 |
| Professional associations, trade unions, etc. | 8.107.683 | 11.1 | 519 |
| Other activities | 4.926.603 | 6.8 | 2.968 |
| Total | 72.891.038 | 100 | 329 |

Source: Istat, 2001

### A joint view: Italian non-profits and international models

Where is the Italian third sector located vis-à-vis to other international cases? By using prevalent sector(s) and utilising salaried employment as the key indicator, several patterns of specialisation can be identified, testifying to the peculiarity of the welfare systems in each country (Table 5).

A first model is the "health" one that includes Japan, the United States and Holland. In these countries, employment in this sector amounts respectively to 47.1%, 46.3% and 41.7% of the total. The high percentage of people employed by hospitals explains this fact. It is interesting to note that in all of these three countries the second area of activity, in order of importance, is education. The second model is the "educational" one, typical of several countries where non-profits have a greater importance in terms of employment. These include Ireland (where 53.7% of non-profit employment is in education), Great Britain (41.5%) and Belgium (38.8%). If in Ireland and Belgium the weight of primary and secondary religious schools is responsible for this result, in Great Britain that is mainly due (as in the United States) to secular institutions active in university education.

The most common model in European countries is finally that of "social service", also in Italy, though to a lesser extent. Austria is first in the social services sector, with a level equal to 64% of overall employment; thus it is the country with the most marked specialisation in the sector; followed by France (39.7%), Germany (38.8%), Spain (31.8%) and Italy (25.9%).

This phenomenon in Austria and Germany is the effect of the implementation of the subsidiarity principle, which leads the public administration to greatly rely on non-profit organisations for the supply of services to individuals. In Latin countries, non-profit organisations tend, instead, to perform a role complementary to that of public organisations – and sometimes a niche one.

**Table 5 – Paid employment in the non-profit sector, by main activity sector (%)**

| COUNTRY | Health | social services | Others |
|---|---|---|---|
| Austria | 11.6 | 64.0 | 24.3 |
| Belgium | 30.4 | 13.8 | 55.8 |
| France | 15.5 | 39.7 | 44.8 |
| Germany | 30.6 | 38.8 | 30.5 |
| Ireland | 27.6 | 4.5 | 67.9 |
| Netherlands | 41.7 | 19.0 | 39.3 |
| Spain | 12.2 | 31.8 | 56.0 |
| United Kingdom | 4.3 | 13.1 | 82.7 |
| Italy | 20.8 | 25.9 | 53.3 |
| Japan | 47.1 | 16.6 | 36.2 |
| United States | 46.3 | 13.5 | 40.2 |

*Source*: estimates by the authors on Salamon L. M and Anheier H.K., 1998 and Istat, 2001

**Table 6 – Italian non-profit organizations by source of revenue and main activity sector (%) – year 1999**

| MAIN ACTIVITY SECTOR | revenue predominantly from public sector * | Revenue predominantly from private sector | Total |
|---|---|---|---|
| Culture and recreation | 9.7% | 90.3% | 100 |
| Education and research | 20.1% | 79.9% | 100 |
| Health | 40.8% | 59.2% | 100 |
| Social services | 26.8% | 73.2% | 100 |
| Environment | 26.1% | 73.9% | 100 |
| Economic development and social cohesion | 26.4% | 73.6% | 100 |
| Law, advocacy and politics | 6.4% | 93.6% | 100 |
| Philantropic intermediaries | 9.0% | 91.0% | 100 |
| International solidarity and cooperation | 12.5% | 87.5% | 100 |
| Religious educational activities | 3.6% | 96.4% | 100 |
| Professional associations, trade unions, etc. | 2.9% | 97.1% | 100 |
| Other activities | 14.3% | 85.7% | 100 |
| Total | 12.9% | 87.1% | 100 |

(*) Includes: grants and contributions from institutions and/or national and international bodies; incomes from contracts and/or agreements with national or international public institutions.
*Source*: Istat, 2001

## Trends and actors in the Italian non-profit sector

*Volunteerism*

The Italian third sector is frequently confused, in its widespread representation, with volunteerism. From the 1970s, on, volunteer work developed a growing awareness of itself while its social impact grew very greatly both in relation to its activity as well as to the number of people involved. Contrasting research data exists concerning this point, estimating the number of people involved to be six million or even more. It is perhaps prudent to say that around 6-8% of the Italian population (of all ages) is either systematically or occasionally involved in volunteer work in all types of formal or informal organisations. Instead if we consider only those volunteer organisations which are registered, in accordance with a specific act of 1991, in special regional registers (11,710 at the end of 1997), volunteer workers definable in general terms as ones "with a high, stable level of commitment" amounted to between five and six hundred thousand units (ISTAT, 2000). Another typical assumption concerning Italian volunteerism is that it is believed to be a phenomenon of primarily religious inspiration. In reality, research data seems to confirm that though the weight of explicitly religious organisations is great, it does not exceed 40% of the total; even though it is possible that, in certain areas, the density of organisations of this type is higher.

The Italian volunteering sector continues to show great vitality and above all the ability to move into those problematic social spaces where other responses could hardly be applied (social exclusion, extreme poverty, delinquency, etc.), even with innovative organisational solutions and practices. More complex models are frequently found alongside organisations still naive and simple (Dipartimento Affari Sociali – Presidenza del Consiglio dei Ministri, 2001). Volunteer organisations seem to have a certain ability to generate, or to evolve into, organisational forms that are almost businesses such as social co-operatives (see below). There is a growing systematic collaboration with public bodies on the local level following recent legislation in the sector. There is, however, no lack of opinions contrasting the growth of efficiency with the risk of a certain hardening in motivations that could make the sustainable future of volunteer work itself uncertain.

## The emergence of the non-profit business: the social co-operatives

Social co-operatives are typically Italian institutions regulated by a specific national act of 1991. They have a purpose of social solidarity that is expressed either in supplying social assistance or educational services for the general population (type A) or in encouraging employment for disadvantaged people (type B). In this case, at least 30% of their members or employees must be made up of people with employment problems. First level co-operatives generally sell their services to the public administration, frequently on the local level, via systems of contracts, competitions or agreements. The second level co-operatives act on the market in competition with profit making businesses.

The 1991 law gave an organisation and a legal format to the experiences of non-profits that had emerged largely from the area of volunteer work and the "association revolution" of the 1980s, which strove to overcome the precarious nature of organisations with a completely volunteer basis. The model of the social co-operative is therefore interesting since it represents a profile of a business, or quasi-business, that is actually non-profit and not exclusively mutual-aid oriented. Social cooperatives are based on the theory that a synergetic and creative combination is possible between business rationale and philanthropic rationale. The growth of these subjects has been great, attesting to the usefulness and profitability of the model (Centro studi CGM, 1997 – Barbetta G.P., Cima S., 1999 – Ronchi A. 1999). In 1999 there were almost 4,700 cooperatives (Istat, 2001). Finally, it would be useful to underline the propensity of co-operatives to organise themselves into higher level networks, both sectorial and territorial. This model is useful in guaranteeing even the smallest subjects certain economies of scale and a more effective representation.

## Foundations: innovations and new roles

It is worthwhile to mention the sector of foundations because of the recent transformation it is undergoing and the conspicuous growth of its importance and visibility. Italy is one of the cradles of European foundations but the sector did not undergo that process of modernisation which witnessed, between the 19th and 20th centuries, the birth of a new philanthropy in English speaking countries, and especially in the United States. Many very complex reasons, common to many Latin countries are at the roots of this lack of development (Schluechter A., Then V. and Walkenhorst P., 2001). Among these, the diffidence in the prevailing political cultures toward intermediate social bodies, centralisation and the pervasiveness of the nation state, an economic and industrial structure which was either fragmented or controlled by the state, the powerful presence of the Catholic church as an important social actor. This does not mean that foundations did not exist in the twentieth century. Indeed they did, particularly in the cultural or welfare areas. However, aside from a few exceptions, these were institutions with limited social impact and niche roles. New dynamism was produced in the sector beginning in the 1980s, both in the growth of the number of foundations as well as in the emergence of new types of foundations. Overall, the ISTAT survey (2001) counted 3,008 foundations existing in 1999. In fact, the very broad and diverse range of foundation types can be summarised in two basic types: on the one hand, those created by the autonomous initiative of citizens, family businesses, other public or private bodies, according to general proceedings defined by the Civil Code. On the other, those created following special legislation designed to transform already existing institutions into foundations and to privatise public bodies and their management.

Generally, Italian foundations of the first type are noted for two aspects: their "operating" character and limited endowment (Demarie M., 1997). Most produce goods and services (prevalently cultural and educational or welfare-related). Their activity is only partially supported by the income from their endowment and is sustained by contributions (both public and/or private) and/or income from commercial activity. Those foundations that carry out activities actually definable as grant-making are instead a small minority. The amount and size of grants they make should be considered overall as very low. The appearance should, however, be noted, though still in its infancy, of an innovative type of grant-making such as that performed by some "community foundations", following the international pattern.[5] Other patterns of innovative behaviour – such as foundations contemporarily fund-raising and grant-making – are also emerging. On the average, these foundations are a rather young group, as confirmed by data from the ISTAT survey: 53.3% of the total of those foundations active have in fact only been created over the past decade. The progressive simplification – from 1977 till now – of bureaucratic practices for creating foundations and attaining legal status partially explains this wave of creation. It could be added that this legal structure has proved to be a manageable and flexible organisational solution for the formalisation and rationalisation of volunteer and philanthropic activities. The presence of this type of foundation has become more and more visible, with some outstanding individual examples, even though the fragility of their economic base constitutes an obvious problem. Due to its flexibility, the foundation model is increasingly used by the public sector in the process of privatisation or reform of public bodies – often historically originating as private organisations and later nationalised or de facto controlled by the state. Over the last decade, special laws have created types of foundations entrusted with functions previously performed directly by branches of the state in order to enhance their managerial effectiveness and attract private capital and expertise (D'Autilia M.L., 2001). This is true in the cultural fields, as in the case of the Opera Theatre Foundations (for example, the Teatro La Scala in Milan is now a foundation) and other individual cases (museums or institutes). This is also true in the welfare field where hundreds of a specific group of publicly controlled, local level welfare institutions (IPABs) are reacquiring their original status as private foundations (nationalised at the end of the 19th Century) (Ranci C., Costa G., 1999). On the other hand, local authorities or different branches of the public administration commonly establish new foundations often in partnership with private actors in order to run new non-profit joint ventures, ranging from heritage management to educational, social or welfare-related purposes. The cultural field seems to be the most promising.

However, we are still at the very beginning of a process, which is very much in its experimental stage.

Perhaps the most relevant single development in the area of Italian foundations in the 1990s was the emergence of a number of wealthy grant-making foundations as the outcome of a rather tortuous process of privatisation regarding the formerly state-controlled banking system. New legislation split each semi-public bank into two separate entities: a commercial, joint stock bank and a foundation as owner of the bank. Later, these special foundations were designed as non-profit, public benefit oriented bodies whose endowment consisted of the bank from which they originated (Ranci P. and Barbetta G.P., 1996 – Borzaga C., Cafaggi F., 1999). This measure had a degree of historical plausibility given that social concerns were among the very reasons why the original institutions had been established as private bodies pursuing collective aims. This transitional phase is now coming to an end and the new foundations have become private, charter-based foundations whose mission is to promote a wide range of social and cultural purposes as well as economic development in accordance with the law and individual statutes. The law also states the basic principles of their operational and managerial framework specified in the independently designed charters. There are about ninety so-called foundations of banking origin and they are wealthy (ACRI, 2000). A cumulative unofficial estimate for their overall assets is now (in 2001) around 50 billion Euro, with sizeable revenues growing over time. Individual size varies significantly, with a handful of real giants (with assets greater than 3 billion Euro). They are located almost exclusively in Northern and Central Italy. The foundations of banking origin have been and still are controversial. Considering their economic importance, their management and investment policies are sensitive political issues. Their growth into genuine and independent foundations, a process currently taking place rather quickly but not without attrition, will provide Italian civil society with those real, modern grant-making institutions it has always lacked to its serious detriment.[6]

## ONLUS

Scholars in the field of comparative research on non-profit sectors may have heard the term ONLUS. The introduction of the ONLUS legislation ("Organizzazioni Non Lucrative di Utilità Sociale" [Socially Useful Non-Profit Organisations], 1997) was the main intervention, at the system level, aimed at regulating but also encouraging the development of non-profit organisations. This fiscal act stated that non-profit organisations with certain formal and substantial characteristics could benefit from financial aid, at times considerable, in terms of their income. Donations to ONLUS organisations also are tax deductible. Among the needed requirements for becoming an ONLUS organisation, there is a clause strictly blocking the distribution of profits; furthermore, the activity of the organisation must have social aims and be carried out in set sectors to the advantage of determined groups – i.e. disadvantaged sections of the population. Under these conditions, there may be ONLUS foundations, ONLUS associations and so forth The request for recognition as an ONLUS is, however, optional while certain types of non-profit organisations are strictly excluded, such as labour unions and political parties. Special provisions and limitations are made for IPABs and foundations with a banking origin, the access to which is conditioned by the complete acquisition of a private character and the autonomy of its management. Aside from the complicated administrative procedure, rather burdensome for the subjects, and a certain strictness with respect to the actual definition of "social usefulness", the ONLUS legislation has met with the interest of numerous non-profit organisations, especially those with a certain level of commercial activity. Data from the Ministry of Economy, in fact, reveals the existence of more than ten eleven thousand ONLUS organisations as of 1999.

## Prospects

How can we evaluate the prospects of the Italian non-profit sector? It is only possible here to touch upon certain aspects that seem relevant. More than just one reason, however, would lead us to think that general conditions are favourable toward a sustained development of the Italian third sector. Just consider that, following a heated political debate, the Italian Constitution was recently amended to include a paragraph especially encouraging horizontal subsidiarity with the introduction of the formula: "State, Regions, Metropolitan areas, Provinces and Cities favour the autonomous projects of citizens, both individual and in associations, to carry out activities of general interest, based on the principle of subsidiarity". The constitutional legislature has in fact stated that horizontal subsidiarity is the necessary complement to vertical subsidiarity – the basic principle inspiring the movement in Italy known as "federalist reform". On the other hand, the new centre-right political majority (the winner the 2001 general political election) and the government have not failed to underline the crucial nature of civil society of and its organizations seen as a long term Italian resource and to stress their intention to create adequate legislation to promote this. An orientation favourable toward privatisation and "de-bureaucratisation" – at present widespread in Italian political culture – suggests that recourse to privatisation type solutions via the creation of non-profit organisations could become more frequent. These political intentions of a domestic origin are also part of a larger European framework of principles in favour of horizontal subsidiarity as incorporated in various official acts.

In this circumstance, politics seems to meet the needs dictated by reality. The dynamics connected to "glocalisation" make the containment of public expenditures unavoidable and will require a shift in policies, especially in policies related to issues of welfare, health, culture and environment, responding to the demand expressed by citizens at the local level and continually more attentive to the quality, both technical and human, of the supply of services. In this sense, the important processes occurring today of the devolution of powers from the central governmental level to local governments could find interesting partners in local, active and enterprising non-profit organisations. In particular, current political policies plan for the transfer to the regional level of full legislative powers in the areas of education and health. If the regions – many of which are already experimenting – express preference for organisational solutions that leave greater space to the non-profit sector and creatively involve them in defining policies, the latter could see very important opportunities open up and resume positions precisely in those sectors where, for historical reasons, a minor presence has been found.

Nevertheless, issues do exist that cannot be ignored. These are issues of a political nature, of the potential supply of social enterprise, of the regulatory framework. They will be mentioned in the following section. One of the dangers the non-profit sector must beware of is the danger of remaining stuck in a heated political, ideological conflict. It would be deadly for non-profits to find themselves hostage of a political struggle pitting the supporters of more traditional welfare guarantees against those who are calling for a reduction in the state's role in social policy. This could have negative consequences for the non-profits, both in terms of their public image, as well as their internal cohesion: different cultural components could find themselves locked in diametrically opposing political positions. A balanced relationship among all social components is necessary. The different legitimate political allegiances in the sector must keep the channels of communication open among themselves. In order to take place, the transition from a welfare state to a welfare society should be managed with the highest level of pluralism, without falling into useless confrontation. Another important issue will be the outcome of the policy of privatisation/reorganisation of public or quasi-public bodies via non-profit organisations, especially foundations. If non-profit organizations are substantially recognized as belonging to the private sphere, even though they are inscribed within the dialectic between the public sector and new entities, we may consider the process to have been successful. Otherwise we will have witnessed an interesting operation in terms of bringing efficiency but one that is basically just opportunistic. On the other hand, it should be asked whether or not a potential supply exists in Italy of widespread social enterprise able in the long term to take advantage of the opportunities for development in the sector. The interest of young people, as well as older people, is high but the level of strength and sustainability of enterprise and human capital in the third sector is not clear, especially in the presence of declining youth unemployment – which will create more competition with the business sector. This is a point that involves expectations, abilities and, in a broad way, ethical motivations. Formal education can do much here but not everything. Much will depend on the strengthening of the sector and thus its ability to give its personnel compensation and interesting professional prospects, but also what type of human, social and political values Italy will be able to express in the future.

Finally, legal frameworks. The Italian system should be renovated: the treatment of non-profit organisations is still rather imprecise and heterogeneous, a result of the stratification of special provisions, which are at times contradictory. Measures of encouragement and support (for example the ONLUS case) co-exist with legislation that still expresses at times even suspicion toward the non-profit sector. If the Italian third sector is to grow, and therefore take on the challenge of competition, it should be regulated by an adequate regulatory framework, able therefore to combine the needs for transparency and accountability that have been imposed by the objective of market efficiency and the present characteristics of many non-profit organisations, too fragile to support heavy bureaucratic burdens (Barbetta G.P. e Schena C., 2000). We need common principles for a very diverse set of institutions: and this is not going to be an easy problem. Another important aspect, as far as taxation is concerned, is the introduction of mechanisms encouraging donations on the part of families and businesses to non-profit organisations. The low level of this is one of the factors penalising the Italian third sector. Of course, much will depend on the current difficult plight of Italian financial accounts.

Political context, entrepreneurial potential, and legislation in the sector, these three aspects are interlinked and interdependent. Each of these must be open to innovation if the redefining of the borders between the state and the non-profit sector are to move happily toward a more flexible, responsible society, a society able to respond quickly and satisfactorily to the needs of its citizens and to make room for their desire to act for the common good.

## Notes

[1] The following paragraphs on economic and socio-political reasons for the development of non-profit sector follow the main findings of G.P. Barbetta (Barbetta, 1997 and 2001).

[2] As to statistical definition and classification of non-profit sector see: United Nations (1993), Eurostat (1995), Anheier H.K., Rudney G., Salamon L.M. (1994), Salamon L.M. and Anheier H.K. (1997), Cima S., Mancini A., Moreschi B., Zamaro N. (1999), D'Autilia M.L, Cima S. (2000).

[3] Data regarding Italian non-profit organization come from the first census of private institutions and non-profit businesses carried out by ISTAT with the collaboration of the "Centro di Ricerche sulla Cooperazione" [Center for Research into Cooperation] of the Università Cattolica and the Istituto per la Ricerca Sociale (Social Research Institute) in Milan. The first results were published by ISTAT in 2001 (Istat, 2001). The census was part of the second phase of the joint international research project on non-profit organizations of the Institute for Policy Studies of Johns Hopkins University in Baltimore (USA) that involved 23 countries between 1996 – 2000 period; Argentina, Australia, Austria, Belgium, Brazil, Colombia, Finland, France, Germany, Japan, Great Britain,

Ireland, Israel, Italy, Mexico, Holland, Peru, The Czech Republic, Romania, Slovakia, Spain, the United States and Hungary (Salamon L.M. and Anheier H.K., 1998). Estimates and elaborations by the Authors.

[4] In the 22 countries covered in an international survey (Salomon and Anheier, 1997), donations make up 12.5% of the overall income, other funds from private sources 48.2% and from public sources 39.3%. There are great differences between individual countries. The first noticeable difference is related to the level of private financing. In only three countries (Italy, Spain and the United States) this significantly does go beyond half the overall financing, respectively 63.9%, 67.9% and 69.5%. For most European countries, the situation is instead reversed. It is particularly interesting to note how among those countries with the highest private financing, Italy is the one with the smallest donation: 3.3% compared with 18.8% in Spain and 12.9% in the US.

[5] Community foundations have been introduced in Italy (Lombardy) by the Cariplo foundation, the largest among the foundations of banking origin.

[6] It is to be noted that the budget act (Law 448, 28/12/2001) passed by the new centre-right political majority introduces some substantial innovations in the governance and in the assets management patterns of the foundations of banking origin. These innovations have been received as extremely controversial and seen by the foundations as a measure jeopardising their recently acquired private legal status and therefore their autonomy from the public sector. The new act is now in the process of being implemented through governmental regulation and some kind of compromise is being looked for.

## References

ACRI, Associazione fra le Casse di Risparmio Italiane [2000], *Quinto rapporto sulle fondazioni bancarie [Fifth Report on the Foundations of banking origin]*, Roma.

Anheier, H.K., Rudney, G., Salamon, L.M. [1994], "Nonprofit Institutions in the United System of National Accounts: country applications of SNA Guidelines" in *Voluntas*, 4.

Barbetta, G.P., ed. [1997], *The nonprofit sector in Italy*, Manchester, Manchester University Press.

Barbetta, G.P., a cura di [2000], *Il settore nonprofit italiano [Italian Nonprofit Sector]*, Bologna, Il Mulino.

Barbetta, G.P., e Schena, C., a cura di [2000], *Regole e controlli sulle organizzazioni nonprofit [Regulations and checks concerning the Nonprofit Sector]*, Bologna, Il Mulino.

Barbetta, G.P., Cima, S. [1999], "Italy's Third Sector: Recent Trends and Perspectives", paper prepared for *Civitas*, Madrid.

Borzaga, C., Cafaggi, F., a cura di [1999], *Le fondazioni bancarie [The Foundations of banking origin]*, Roma, Donzelli.

Borzaga, C., Fiorentini, G., Matacena, A. [1996], *Nonprofit e sistemi di welfare [Nonprofit and Welfare Systems]*, Roma, Nis.

Centro Studi CGM, a cura di [1997], *Imprenditori sociali [Social Enterpreneurs]*, Torino, Edizioni della Fondazione Giovanni Agnelli.

Cima, S., Mancini, A., Moreschi, B., Zamaro, N. [1999], *Definizioni, classificazioni e variabili guida per le statistiche sulle istituzioni nonprofit, [Definitions, Classifications and Key Variables. Handbook for the First Census on Nonprofit*

*Institutions]*, Roma, Istat, Irs, Centro di Ricerche sulla Cooperazione dell'Università Cattolica, Mimeo.

D'Autilia, M.L. [2001], *L'impatto dei provvedimenti di riforma sulla identificazione delle unità istituzionali della pubblica amministrazione: profilo normativo [Reform of The State and Changes in the Institutional Profile of Ex-Governmental Institutions]*, Roma, Istat.

D'Autilia, M.L., Cima, S. [2000], *Le istituzioni nonprofit tra pubblico e privato [Nonprofit Institution between public and private governance]*, Roma, Istat, Irs, Centro di Ricerche sulla Cooperazione dell'Università Cattolica, Mimeo.

Demarie, M. [1997], "Le fondazioni in Italia. Un profilo empirico" [Foundations in Italy. An Empirical Profile] in Aa. Vv., *Per conoscere le fondazioni [Knowing Foundations]*, Torino, Edizioni della Fondazione Giovanni Agnelli.

Dipartimento per gli Affari Sociali, Presidenza del Consiglio dei Ministri [1999], *Volontariato. Rapporto biennale sul volontariato in Italia [Volunteerism. Report on Volunteerism in Italy]*, Roma.

Dipartimento per gli Affari Sociali, Presidenza del Consiglio dei Ministri [2001], *Volontariato. Rapporto biennale sul volontariato in Italia 2000 [Volunteerism. Report on Volunteerism in Italy]*, Roma.

Eurostat [1995], *European System of Accounts ESA*, Bruxelles.

Istat [2000], *Le organizzazioni di volontariato in Italia, Anno 1997 [Voluntary Institutions in Italy, Year 1997]*, Roma.

Istat [2001], *Istituzioni nonprofit in Italia. I risultati della prima rilevazione censuaria, Anno 1999 [Nonprofit Institutions In Italy. Findings of the First Nonprofit Census, Year 1999]*, Roma.

Nazioni Unite [1993], *A System of National Accounts*, New York.

Ranci, C., Costa, G. [1999], *Dimensione economica e caratteristiche delle Ipab. Un quadro nazionale [Economic Size and Profile of Ipab. A National Framework]*, Roma, Dipartimento Affari Sociali, Presidenza del Consiglio dei Ministri.

Ranci, P., Barbetta, G.P. [1996], a cura di, *Le fondazioni bancarie verso l'attività grant-making [ Foundations of Banking Origin Towards the Grant Making Activities]*, Torino, Contributi di Ricerca della Fondazione Giovanni Agnelli.

Ranci Ortigosa, E. [1990], "La politica assistenziale" [Welfare Policy], in Dente, B., a cura di, *Le politiche pubbliche in Italia [Public Policies in Italy]*, Bologna, Il Mulino.

Ronchi, A. [1999], *Le cooperative sociali in Lombardia [Social Cooperatives in Lombardia]*, Milano, Regione Lombardia.

Salamon, L.M., e Anheier, H.K., eds [1997], *Defining The Nonprofit Sector. A Cross National Analysis*, Manchester, Manchester University Press.

Salamon, L.M., e Anheier, H.K., eds [1998], *The Emerging Sector Revisited. A Summary*, Baltimore, Centre for Civil Study Studies, Johns Hopkins University.

Schluechter A., Then, V., e Walkenhorst, P. [2001], *Foundations in Europe*, London, Society, Management and Law, Bertelsmann Foundation, Directory of Social Change, CAF.

# Comment

## Yousuke Mamiya

First of all I would like to say that I am not a specialist in the field of the third, or non-profit, sector: of course I do not have any knowledge about this sector in Italy.

In spite of this, or rather because of it, I read the paper with great interest. Of course it was useful for me to know that Italy and Japan are coping with similar problems and groping for similar directions. However, far more interesting for me is the context or background against which the Authors set the problem. That is, the context of public-private relationship, or using the Authors' own words, State-society relationship.

What is society? What is the private sector? Usually by these words we mean the market economy composed of private firms and households. In this meaning the privatization, for example, amounts to transferring the control of the enterprise from State to profit-making bodies. In fact in Japan politicians use the word privatization in this meaning and promote privatization of public enterprises with this meaning in mind.

Now society is not the same as market economy in the Authors' meaning. I think this is an important point. For them society is not contained in market economy, but rather market economy is contained in society. That is, society has a residue which does not belong to the market sector, and which they call the third sector.

The first, the public sector, the second the private sector, and the third is, so to speak, the overlapping sector of the two. Overlapping means that this sector has characteristics of the first as well as of the second. In other words the third sector as a non-profit sector pursues public ends or, in the Authors' words, "the common good", and in spite of its public character it has an autonomy independent of State control, whether it be central or local.

As far as I understand, "civil society", a key word of the paper, is a society in which this overlapping sector plays a leading role. Therefore for the Authors, nourishing the third sector is nourishing civil society to which I give a blanket consent. This proposition also holds good in Japan as well as in Italy.

Lastly let me add one point. Usually when we study the third sector, stress is put on the private and autonomous character of it rather than the public character, as I have said regarding the privatization movement in Japan.

However even in the private sector a public character could be found. For example the private sector typically shown in the market system seems to have a public character. The Italian business system in which small or medium size firms play a vital role is often mentioned as an alternative model to large corporation system. The reason why scholars pick up this Italian model is probably due to its public-oriented character. I would like to know the Authors' view on this point.

# Chapter 14

# The Family and Social Networks in the Socio-Economic Development of Italy

Andrea Toma

**Introduction**

In Italy, we currently find ourselves facing a new phase, which has not yet been fully interpreted. The growing complexity of Italian society is generating a demand for discipline which can no longer be provided by the old rules previously in force. The labour market, for example, is still regulated by frameworks – of a mental, legislative and contractual kind – inspired by the prevalence of subordinate labour, whilst nowadays individual labour (entrepreneurial, self-employed, free-lance, atypical etc.) is more common. This type of employment now involves 13 million Italian citizens, but in this connection government culture has insufficient experience and government logic is completely impotent. In the welfare sector, too, many factors are undermining the old systems, while new solutions are forced to consider the strong need felt by individuals and families for self-protection and personalised intervention in both the field of health and of social security. This need is illustrated by the rise in private spending on health, by the increasing proportion of investments devoted to life insurance policies and pension funds, by the various forms of self-determination by patients and by user participation in decision-making processes. Furthermore, in this phase, another phenomenon is helping to define the changing picture of Italian society and its ability to react and take decisions when faced with new situations: the growing demand for collective security, which is spreading steadily throughout the country in response to the new realities of immigration and micro-crime (although these have perhaps been over-emphasised, with excessive collective emotion being fuelled by the media).

Within this general reference framework, the present project therefore attempts to review the last thirty years of Italian history, in an attempt to look at the combination of choices and adjustments made by the family in the light of the changing context outside the family and its needs. We shall therefore try to consider economic development from the family point of view, in its effort to achieve income, security, stability and well-being. Today, looking back, we can see that we followed the right approach: an approach that also enables us to reflect further on the present situation. It is now becoming extremely interesting to guess what new methods of adjustment will be chosen by families, faced as they are by a state of uncertainty – brought about by the unforeseen results of the globalisation process, the instability of the international political situation, increasing competition between regions and nations, the trend towards individualised labour, the phenomenon of migration – which is undoubtedly new to us and therefore difficult to interpret. This survey must also constitute the starting point for a proper study concerning other kinds of social safety-net that have accompanied the development process in Italy, such as the network of associations, industrial co-operation and the voluntary sector. These structures are now finding that they must adopt a new approach, from both an economic and a social point of view. In section 2, an analysis will be made of the structural profile of the Italian family and the important ways in which it is being affected by the choices of individuals with regard to procreation and childbirth. In section 3, we shall look at the large-scale transformation processes that have affected Italian society – urbanisation, immigration, industrialisation – together with the methods used by families to adjust to these processes. In section 4, the role of the family as the central unit in development will be defined. This will be done by observing how it behaves in seeking affluence, creating jobs, saving money and consuming goods and services. In section 5 we will make a detailed analysis of the natural tendency of the Italian family not only to act as an autonomous and self-sufficient unit but also, and more especially, to develop a vocation for extending the boundaries of the family group. The consequent inversion of roles with the outside world becomes, in its more advanced and more "virtuous" form, a means of developing social and relational capital. (And this lies at the root of those all-Italian models of success, ranging from the traditional presence of local industrial districts to the function of associations and voluntary organisations, which still represent alternative solutions and take collective responsibility for some of the main problems that have yet to be solved in Italy, particularly that of personal assistance.) In this connection, we shall mention innovative experiments in the formation of social capital that have acted as important mediators between institutions and individuals, giving positive added value – difficult to quantify but undoubtedly significant – in the creation of affluence in Italian society.

**Profile of the Italian family**

One of the most contradictory issues is that of recent trends in population statistics. This currently characterises and to some extent influences our ability to foresee other phenomena relating to the growth and development of affluence in Italian society. In the space of only a few decades, Italy has seen a rapid transition from a high birth rate to a negative trend in the natural population balance, and this has been only partially offset by the entry into Italy of individuals from countries outside the EU. Between the beginning and the end of the last century, the population of Italy almost doubled, increasing from 33 million in 1901 to almost 58 million estimated for this year. The birth rate is now 9.3 births per 1000 inhabitants, as compared with a rate of 16.8 in 1970 and 10.0 in 1990 (Table 1).

The number of families has risen from 7,350,000 at the beginning of the century to 21,850,000 at present. Only ten years ago, there were almost one million fewer families. In addition to the absolute figures for the total population, it is in the composition of the family that we see the most striking changes. There is a wider spectrum of different types of family: there are more one-person families (including both young and old individuals, who generally behave in different ways), with a reduction in the average number of members and an increase in the average age at which the family nucleus is formed. The average number of people in the family is now 2.6, whereas twenty years ago it was 3 and in the middle of the last century 4. Furthermore, while one-person families represented 19.3% in 1988, the figure had risen to 21.7% ten years later. The number of two-person families also rose in the ten years considered, increasing from 23.6% to 26.1%, while in the same period the percentage of families consisting of four members fell by two percentage points. Again in this period, the number of couples without offspring increased from 3,913,000 to 4,608,000.

**Table 1 – Population and households (1901-2001)**

| Year | Resident population (within present frontiers) (in thousands of units) | Density (population per sq. km.) | Number of households (in thousands of units) | Average number of components |
|---|---|---|---|---|
| 1901 | 32.963 | 112 | 7.350 | 4.6 |
| 1911 | 35.842 | 123 | 8.200 | 4.5 |
| 1921 | 39.397 | 126 | 8.600 | 4.4 |
| 1931 | 41.043 | 136 | 9.750 | 4.2 |
| 1936 | 42.399 | 141 | 9.850 | 4.3 |
| 1951 | 47.516 | 158 | 11.814 | 4.0 |
| 1961 | 50.624 | 168 | 13.747 | 3.6 |
| 1971 | 54.137 | 180 | 15.981 | 3.3 |
| 1981 | 56.557 | 188 | 18.632 | 3.0 |
| 1991 | 56.778 | 188 | 19.909 | 2.8 |
| 2001 (estimate) | 57.750 | 191 | 21.850 | 2.6 |

*Source*: Censis elaboration of figures from Istat and Svimez

One of the most significant features of the change in the Italian family, however, is that the decision to marry and have children is being delayed. The number of marriages per 1000 inhabitants has fallen from 7.9 in 1961 to the present 4.8, while the average age of women at the time of marriage is now just under 28, about three years more than in 1961 (Table 2). The average age of women at the birth of their first child is consequently greater: in this case, too, there has been an increase of about three years over a period of forty years (from 25.7 to 28.5 years of age). The phenomenon of people continuing to live in the family after adulthood is also of considerable interest, particularly in terms of its effects on the social level. In 1993-94, 18.5% of those in the 30-34 age group still lived at home, but by 1998 this figure had risen to 22.8%, with significantly more males than females.[1]

**Table 2 – Demographic characteristics (1901-2001)**

| Year | Live births per 1,000 inhabitants | Marriages per 1,000 inhabitants | Age of brides at marriage | Average age of women at birth of first child | Inhabitants aged 0-14 as proportion of total population (%) | Inhabitants aged 60 and over as proportion of total population (%) |
|---|---|---|---|---|---|---|
| 1901 | 33.0 | 7.2 | - | - | 34.4 | 9.6 |
| 1911 | 32.2 | 7.5 | 23.6 | - | 33.8 | 10.2 |
| 1921 | 30.5 | 11.5 | 24.2 | - | 31.1 | 10.4 |
| 1931 | 24.9 | 6.7 | 24.0 | 25.9 | 29.7 | 10.8 |
| 1951 | 18.1 | 6.9 | 25.0 | 25.9 | 26.3 | 12.2 |
| 1961 | 18.4 | 7.9 | 25.1 | 25.7 | 24.6 | 13.9 |
| 1971 | 16.8 | 7.5 | 24.5 | 25.1 | 24.4 | 16.6 |
| 1981 | 11.0 | 5.6 | 24.4 | 25.2 | 21.5 | 17.4 |
| 1991 | 9.9 | 5.5 | 26.6 | 27.1 | 15.9 | 21.1 |
| 2001 (estimate) | 9.0 | 4.8 | 27.8 | 28.5 | 14.3 | 24.5 |

*Source*: Censis elaboration of figures from Istat and Svimez

The figure that most clearly illustrates the current change in population trends, however, relates to the inversion in the quantitative ratio between the generations. If we start from the beginning of the 19th century, this is even clearer: In 1901 the under-14 age group accounted for 34.4% of the total population and the over-60 age group represented 9.6%, while one hundred years later we find a society where these figures have been inverted, with all that this implies on the economic and social plane. By 2001, the over-sixties represented 24.5% of the total population, while the under-fourteens accounted for only 14.3%. A comparison of these figures reveals an unknown quantity of some significance: overall population trends, together with the behaviour of individuals, are producing a radical transformation within the Italian family which could weaken the resources that have so far allowed the family to play a central role in the growth of the country.

The considerations expressed in the remainder of the present review will give an idea of the primary importance of this issue, particularly in the light of one fundamental aspect. Until now, the family has been extremely successful in dealing with the challenges presented by the transition from what was essentially a poor society to a wealthy society able to redistribute the fruits of development (although this redistribution has not always been entirely efficient and indeed has very often failed to observe market mechanisms and the rules governing proper participation by the various components of society). In addition, it must be emphasised that this effort, although frequently made without any external support from the institutions, has nevertheless succeeded in alleviating the negative economic consequences of development. In Italy, these have taken the form of great difficulty in creating jobs and extremely selective access to the labour market, to the disadvantage of the younger generation. A study of the resources brought into play by the family in the "straits" of the last twenty years allows us to start thinking about the projects necessary for dealing with the new framework of uncertainty which, as we have seen, is simultaneously the cause and the effect of population trends and of behaviour patterns chosen by single individuals.

## Effects of social and economic changes on the Italian family

If we look at the "great transformation" that took place in Italy in the latter half of the last century, it is immediately clear that the growth cycle was concentrated in the period 1957-1963 (the period generally known as the "economic boom"). It is also clear, however, that the spread of affluence continued – strongly, though often in an underground fashion – during the 1970s, too, despite the economic uncertainty generated by the oil crisis and by the overbearing rise of inflation and unemployment. This movement was due partly to force of inertia, as the result of the intense accumulation processes of the preceding decade, and partly to the progressive diffusion of professional skills and exposure to entrepreneurial risk, sometimes in spheres far removed from those in which productive activities had traditionally been concentrated. As had already happened in other countries, where industrialisation had previously taken place, economic development was accompanied by intense processes of urbanisation and by internal mobility involving large A strata of the population, owing to the wider productive base and the creation of new, more complex structures. At the same time, suitable conditions were created for a wider range of services for the community and for a variety of services which were later to meet the demand of enterprises and families. Between 1951 and 1996, the number of enterprises in Italy rose from 1,504,000 to 3,521,000 (Table 3). The greatest increase in absolute terms, amounting to over 600,000 units, took place between 1971 and 1981. In the same period, the percentage of entrepreneurs and free-lance professionals rose from 2.2% to 8.5% of the total employed population (Table 4). The distinguishing feature of the growth of the entrepreneurial system in Italy was that the organisations were of limited size: the percentage of one-person enterprises rose from 46.35% in 1951 to 55.6% in 1996. As the entrepreneurial system developed, the urbanisation process took on a decided trend in the period 1951-1971. At the beginning of this period, the total population of the six largest cities in Italy (Rome, Milan, Turin, Naples, Genoa and Palermo) was 5,834,000, but by the end of the period it had risen to 8,398,000 (Table 5).

## Table 3 – Growth of entrepreneurial system (1951-1996)

| Year | Enterprises recorded in census (*) | | Number employed | | Percentage of enterprises employing only one person |
|---|---|---|---|---|---|
| | a.v. | index (1951=100) | a.v. | index (1951=100) | |
| 1951 | 1.504.027 | 100 | 6.781.092 | 100 | 46.3 |
| 1961 | 1.938.724 | 129 | 9.463.457 | 140 | 44.3 |
| 1971 | 2.236.044 | 149 | 11.077.533 | 163 | 47.4 |
| 1981 | 2.847.313 | 189 | 13.001.187 | 192 | 48.1 |
| 1991 | 3.301.551 | 220 | 14.601.812 | 215 | 48.0 |
| 1996 | 3.521.416 | - | 13.792.962 | - | 55.6 |

(*) Including collaborators and partners in co-operatives
a.v.= absolute values

*Source*: Censis elaboration and estimates

## Table 4 – Population engaged in professional activity by position occupied (1901-2000) (% value)

| Year | Self-employed | | Employed | | Total |
|---|---|---|---|---|---|
| | entrepreneurs and free-lance professionals | other self-employed workers | managers, administrative staff and office-workers | other employees | |
| 1951 | 2.2 | 38.8 | 9.5 | 49.5 | 100 |
| 1961 | 1.4 | 30.2 | 12.7 | 55.7 | 100 |
| 1971 | 1.9 | 24.4 | 20.6 | 53.1 | 100 |
| 1981 | 3.4 | 19.7 | 27.4 | 49.6 | 100 |
| 1991 | 6.9 | 20.5 | 29.6 | 43.0 | 100 |
| 2001 (estimate) | 8.5 | 20.5 | 30.5 | 40.5 | 100 |

(*) including collaborators and partners in co-operatives

*Source*: Censis elaboration and estimates

**Table 5 – Growth of major Italian cities (resident population in thousands) (1901-2000)**

| City | 1901 | 1931 | 1951 | 1971 | 1998 |
|---|---|---|---|---|---|
| Turin | 330 | 591 | 719 | 1.178 | 910 |
| Milan | 490 | 962 | 1.274 | 1.724 | 1.308 |
| Genoa | 219 | 591 | 688 | 812 | 641 |
| Rome | 425 | 937 | 1.652 | 2.800 | 2.646 |
| Naples | 547 | 832 | 1.010 | 1.233 | 1.020 |
| Palermo | 306 | 380 | 491 | 651 | 686 |
| Total | 2.317 | 4.292 | 5.834 | 8.398 | 7.211 |

*Source*: Censis elaboration and estimates

But the peculiarity of the urbanisation process was the growth of medium-sized towns. At the beginning of the fifties, the total resident population of towns with over 50,000 inhabitants amounted to 14,025,000 and at the beginning of the 1970s it had risen to over 20 million, accounting for 37% of the total population of Italy. Although the urbanisation process – which is now almost over, in any case – was not entirely balanced, it made it possible for many medium-sized towns to acquire an important role in the economic system and in the distribution of the wealth produced, partly in relation to the innovative processes resulting from the use of new technologies in productive activities, both in manufacturing and in the service sector. So industrialisation was accompanied by an increase in employment in the tertiary sector, which in Italy has a very important peculiarity: growth of the tertiary sector coincides with an increase in the number of women employed in the labour market. As compared with 1951, when working women accounted for 25.1% of the active population, the proportion represented by women today has risen to 38%. The most decided contribution to this indicator can easily be found astride the 1970s, during which period the figure rose from 27% to 32.9% (Table 6). All these aspects are therefore worth analysing in detail because of the effects, in real terms, that they have on the family. After so many years, however, we can safely say that the Italian family does not seem to have been overwhelmed by the extent of the transformation brought about by economic development. The adjustment techniques adopted by families have represented an important factor in compensating for the risk of crisis and imbalance that necessarily accompanies rapid growth. This ability to adapt has undoubtedly been helped by the higher standard of living and the potential offered by markets that are increasingly accessible and extensive, making it much easier to obtain new goods and services and to take advantage of solutions which help to save time and greatly facilitate traditional tasks within the family. But at the root of all this we can glimpse a greater willingness, on the part of the population in general and families in particular, to supplement the income of the head of the family with revenue from other sources: chiefly from jobs, which are frequently undeclared and illegal, but sometimes from a sort of "sale" of all available resources. These may derive from real estate (which, not infrequently, has also been created illegally) or from a sort of "tacit agreement" with the state for the purchase of government debt bonds (a phenomenon that was particularly in vogue during the 1970s and 1980s). Essentially, it is in this phase that we see the full development of a particular "combinatory" ability in Italian families, most of which are far removed from the need to ensure their survival and are now orientated towards finding ways of hoarding and acquiring wealth in its various forms.

Table 6 – Female population engaged in professional activity (1901-2001) (% value)

| Year | Women engaged in professional activity as % of total population |
|---|---|
| 1901 | 32.5 |
| 1911 | 31.3 |
| 1921 | 28.6 |
| 1931 | 22.9 |
| 1936 | 28.7 |
| 1951 | 25.1 |
| 1961 | 24.8 |
| 1971 | 27.0 |
| 1981 | 32.9 |
| 1991 | 35.3 |
| 2001 (estimate) | 38.0 |

*Source*: Censis elaboration of figures from Istat and Svimez

**The role of the family as a protagonist of development**

Within the processes described above, the family implements very effective methods of adaptation. It increases its ability to act as a buffer against critical factors and its ability to exploit the new openings and opportunities deriving from the extra room to manoeuvre found in the processes of creating and accumulating capital. The word "capital" is used in a wide sense: it may be capital in terms of moveable or immovable property, or human and professional capital, or again social capital produced by "putting up for sale" the networks of personal relations typical of the wider family. In the first case, the proliferation of micro-enterprises and enterprises of a family nature in many areas of northern Italy represents the family's response to the massive processes of restructuring and outsourcing carried out by the large enterprises to counter increasing competition from internal and external markets; in the second case, we see a high capacity for acquiring new sources of income and affluence by combining as effectively as possible all the family's sources of revenue (such as social security or real estate) or by launching undeclared or illegal economic activities involving other members of the family, whose participation is varied and flexible. One figure above all others seems to be significant, confirming the tendency towards integration and the creation of a wider base of available income: the number of people in the family having an income. In 1968, about 55% of Italian families lived solely on the income of the head of the family, but by 1973 this percentage had fallen to 51%; at the same time, there were already 36 families out of 100 that benefited from two sources of income, as compared with 30% five years previously.[2] Today the average number of people in the family with an income has risen to 1.74, with peaks of 1.79 among families resident in the northern regions and 1.85 among families of self-employed workers. Overall, 44% of Italian families have only one person with an income, while 42% of families have two incomes and the remaining 14% can count on incomes from three or even four people (Table 7). The sources that allow families to have an income are of widely varying kinds. As far back as the 1970s, Censis noted the growth and persistence of illegal forms of labour, which on the one hand offered Italian families greater opportunities but on the other corresponded to taxes not collected by the state and, above all, widespread precariousness with no apparent prospects for an enormous number of individuals, who were very often exploited and paid minimal wages. Detailed studies carried out in that period estimated that there were about 5 million jobs in addition to those officially declared. In the light of this figure, it was generally acknowledged that it was only the second-job system, which supplemented income through temporary or entrepreneurial activity, including that carried out within the home, that made it possible to fulfil the growing expectations of individuals and their need to maintain their hard-won standard of living at all costs, even during an economic downturn. After all these years, the fundamental behaviour patterns seem to have been confirmed. On the basis of a study carried out by Censis in 2000, 84.3% of the total number of families including people with income from employment had income from a regular job, while 15.7% had temporary or illegal jobs as their source of income (Table 8). Members of a family who make their income by illegal work have the following characteristics: they are mostly between 16 and 29 years of age (41.4%), mainly resident in southern Italy (38.9%) or in the north-west (24.6%) and female (52.9%). In addition, closer analysis of these figures shows that illegal work constitutes a faithful reflection of the solutions adopted by individuals to overcome a definite personal weakness, perceived as such by the mechanisms utilised in forming the labour demand of enterprises and organisations. In any case, if the regular labour market cannot absorb these components (especially women and young people), that does not automatically mean that they are expelled from the production system. The consequence of the adjustments made by families and individuals in order to maintain or increase their available income is temporary work – and even exploitation – rather than becoming unemployed.

**Table 7 – Structure of household by number of components earning** (percentages of households)

| Method | Number of earners | | | | | Average number of earners |
|---|---|---|---|---|---|---|
| | 1 | 2 | 3 | 4 | Total | |
| *Age bracket* | | | | | | |
| Up to 30 | 54.3 | 42.1 | 2.7 | 0.9 | 100.0 | 1.50 |
| 31 – 40 | 44.7 | 49.4 | 4.8 | 1.1 | 100.0 | 1.62 |
| 41 – 50 | 38.7 | 45.2 | 12.7 | 3.4 | 100.0 | 1.8 |
| 51 – 65 | 35.1 | 39.5 | 19.2 | 6.2 | 100.0 | 1.93 |
| over 65 | 54.2 | 37.4 | 6.8 | 1.5 | 100.0 | 1.56 |
| *Educational qualifications* | | | | | | |
| None | 53.7 | 36.9 | 7.7 | 1.7 | 100.0 | 1.53 |
| primary school certificate | 46.1 | 36.2 | 13.4 | 4.3 | 100.0 | 1.77 |
| lower secondary school certificate | 44.2 | 41.2 | 11.7 | 2.9 | 100.0 | 1.74 |
| higher secondary school certificate | 39.1 | 49.1 | 9.2 | 2.6 | 100.0 | 1.76 |
| university degree | 38.8 | 51.9 | 7.0 | 2.3 | 100.0 | 1.73 |
| *Geographical area* | | | | | | |
| North | 40.9 | 43.3 | 12.3 | 3.5 | 100.0 | 1.79 |
| Centre | 43.0 | 42.5 | 11.3 | 3.2 | 100.0 | 1.76 |
| South and islands | 49.2 | 39.7 | 8.7 | 2.5 | 100.0 | 1.55 |
| Total | 44.0 | 42.0 | 10.9 | 3.1 | 100.0 | 1.74 |

(\*) With reference to head of household

*Source*: Banca d'Italia, 2001

## Table 8 – Households with components earning income from jobs (% value)

|  | 1997 | 2000 |
|---|---|---|
| Household members with income from a regular job | 87.0 | 84.3 |
| Household members with income from a temporary or irregular job | 13.0 | 15.7 |
| Total households with components earning income from jobs | 100.0 | 100.0 |

*Source*: Censis, 2000

By the 1970s, the family was already acting as an effective social buffer, able to respond in a flexible and sophisticated way to developments in the economic context and to the conditions imposed by unfavourable circumstances. The family not only created jobs within itself, by directly engaging in entrepreneurial activity, but also became a real intermediary between the supply and demand of jobs for its own children, especially when the structural changes of the late 1970s raised the level of job demand towards professional skills requiring greater experience, thus barring the way to those who, like the younger generation – which had prolonged its stay at school and university – had not accumulated knowledge that could be of immediate use to enterprises.

Access to regular jobs, too, is often achieved by decisive intervention on the part of the family. Again on the basis of a sample of young people recently studied by Censis, about 50% of those who have tried to find a job have done so through the family and its network of connections (Table 9).

This way of seeking employment reflects an active approach on the part of the family with regard to its own members that has no equal in other societies, particularly in northern Europe where, on the contrary, individual citizens take full responsibility for their own future and professional career.

Over the last few decades, the family has not only developed a greater ability to handle problems relating to the economy and to employment: problems which are all the greater in situations where the general economic trend is affected by periodic slow-downs. It has also become increasingly shrewd in handling its own financial portfolio.

During periods of two-digit inflation, that is to say chiefly from the middle of the 1970s onward, the strategies adopted by families with regard to saving and investment have mainly been directed towards the house. This has allowed them to preserve wealth in real terms, as well as benefiting from the use of the property. In addition to the house, they have found alternative security in government bonds. The income deriving from these sources supplements the family's other revenue, from work or social security, thanks to the high rates of interest offered – even going beyond the purely monetary illusion caused by a rate of inflation which partially erodes this income.

Table 9 – Method of seeking employment (% value of total non-employed) (*)

| Type of answer | Turin area | Po Valley area | Melfi area | Total of sample |
|---|---|---|---|---|
| Putting an advertisement in the newspaper | 26.5 | 28.6 | 22.2 | 24.1 |
| Sending CV to company | 42.9 | 61.9 | 40.2 | 43.3 |
| State competition | - | 14.3 | 37.6 | 25.2 |
| Replying to newspaper advertisements | 24.5 | 19.0 | 26.5 | 25.1 |
| Contacting other offices that offer career guidance | 14.3 | 19.0 | 15.4 | 15.5 |
| Advice and contacts provided by friends, relations etc. | 51.0 | 33.3 | 51.3 | 49.2 |
| Placement schemes or other periods of voluntary work | 2.0 | - | 6.0 | 4.3 |
| Other | 2.0 | - | 4.3 | 3.3 |

(*)The figures do not total 100 because more than one answer was allowed

*Source:* Censis elaboration and estimates

Only recently has the tendency to save begun to decrease, approaching the level found in the other western countries; we might say that the inclination to save has been replaced by the inclination to hoard, beginning in the 1990s with the progressive diversification of the various forms of investment available (Table 10).

An indication of this new attitude towards the way in which the family uses its own wealth can be seen in the controversial relationship between the family and the stock market. By the second half of the 1980s, during the expansive phase of the economic cycle, which lasted from 1986 to 1990, the family's search for new forms of investment with higher yields created a new "feeling" between families and investment in shares. Today, it has been shown that this relationship, consolidated in the course of the last few years – especially with the government's decision to privatise state holdings – is still weak, subject to households' behaviour that is very often emotional and orientated towards making a profit in the short term rather than any real form of long-term investment.

But it is in the field of assistance to its own members that the family really comes into its own. In order to make up for the deficiencies of the public welfare system, the family has taken on the role of "obligatory substitute", so as to ensure that its own components in need receive assistance of sufficiently high quality. According to a study carried out by Censis in 1998, over 76% of the families interviewed were directly responsible for looking after elderly relatives who were no longer self-sufficient, while only 6.5% entrusted them to the care of strangers, in institutions or nursing homes; the remaining families combined their own efforts with those of outside operators (Table 11).

The capacity for intervention in response to a demand for assistance on the part of Italian families also involves people outside the family. The most common type of help takes the form of accompanying people or having them to stay (37.4%, Table 12), followed by looking after them or keeping them company (27.1%), helping them to obtain access to welfare services or to carry out bureaucratic procedures (23.5%), and lastly direct help in economic terms (loans or gifts, 23.2%).

**Table 10 – Composition of financial assets of households (figures for end of period)**

| Country | Year | Circulating cash and savings | Bonds | Shares and investment funds | Other assets | Pro-memoria | |
|---|---|---|---|---|---|---|---|
| | | | | | | Financial assets | Financial liabilities |
| | | (as percentage of total) | | | | (as proportion of GDP) | |
| France | 1995 | 36.0 | 5.1 | 34.1 | 24.8 | 1.60 | 0.41 |
| | 1999 | 25.3 | 1.8 | 48.4 | 24.5 | 2.42 | 0.44 |
| Germany | 1995 | 41.7 | 13.5 | 18.0 | 26.8 | 1.50 | 0.64 |
| | 1999 | 35.2 | 10.1 | 27.2 | 27.5 | 1.81 | 0.73 |
| Japan | 1995 | 51.7 | 7.1 | 10.9 | 30.3 | 2.45 | 0.81 |
| | 1999 | 53.8 | 4.7 | 10.7 | 30.8 | 2.71 | 0.77 |
| Italy | 1995 | 40.3 | 30.6 | 18.4 | 10.7 | 1.84 | 0.22 |
| | 1999 | 25.4 | 17.0 | 45.6 | 12.0 | 2.27 | 0.28 |
| United Kingdom | 1995 | 24.2 | 1.6 | 19.5 | 54.7 | 2.72 | 0.74 |
| | 1999 | 19.7 | 1.3 | 51.4 | 13.7 | 2.00 | 0.56 |
| Spain | 1995 | 52.0 | 3.5 | 28.5 | 16.0 | 1.37 | 0.41 |
| | 1999 | 33.1 | 1.8 | 51.4 | 13.7 | 2.00 | 0.56 |
| United States | 1995 | 15.2 | 8.9 | 45.2 | 30.7 | 2.94 | 0.69 |
| | 1999 | 11.9 | 6.5 | 50.9 | 30.7 | 3.81 | 0.75 |

*Source*: Banca d'Italia, 2001

**Table 11 – Assistance for disabled people in the household (% value)**

| Assistance provided | 1997 | 2000 |
|---|---|---|
| Entirely by the family | 76.1 | 74.3 |
| Entirely by an institution or nursing home | 6.5 | 1.3 |
| By the family with the assistance of medical and social workers | 7.6 | 14.9 |
| By family with the assistance of non-professional collaborators | 9.8 | 9.5 |

*Source*: Censis survey, 1998

**Table 12 – Type of help given by those interviewed to people outside their families (% value) (\*)**

| | |
|---|---|
| Economic aid (loans, gifts) | 23.2 |
| Medical care | 12.2 |
| Accompanying them, having them to stay (at home) | 37.4 |
| Help with paperwork (to obtain services from local health office) | 23.5 |
| Help in doing their job | 5.3 |
| Keeping them company, occasional help as necessary, assistance | 27.1 |
| Help with housework | 12.2 |

(\*)The figures do not total 100 because more than one answer was allowed.

*Source*: Censis, 2000

### Social networks as an extension of the role of the family

The development process that has marked Italy's progress over the last forty years as one of the richest and most advanced nations in the world continues to have a distinguishing feature that is fairly clear to all those who have followed the country's long-term evolution.

This distinguishing feature is easy to identify in the Italians' ability to make use of local resources and in the nature of the country's network of economic and social relations, which has often been – and still is – characterised by solidarity rather than competition.

From certain points of view, the above-mentioned ability can be taken as a reference framework for interpreting, for example, the importance of family enterprises in the production of overall wealth. Similarly, the inclination towards solidarity can be seen as the basic force that enriches the sphere of voluntary organisations and associations in Italy. Or, lastly, that particular kind of intelligence, used to obtain benefits not only in an economic sense but also from a social point of view, might provide the best explanation for the success of the district system: always able to find a margin of competitiveness with respect to the market, always able to transfer wealth to the geographical area concerned, thus consolidating the institutional and promotional role played by the local authorities.

If we want to give an explicit definition of development for a country like Italy, we might adopt the definition of *self-aware growth*, reaffirming a criterion that has inspired the studies and research carried out by Censis over the last thirty years. The development of an area cannot be reduced to a mere quantitative increase in economic indicators; on the contrary, it is a *social process* which is also, and more especially, the articulation and enrichment of a society's own awareness of itself.

A society that grows is a society that knows how to reflect on trends in its economic growth and knows how to find the right answers, creating institutions and looking for solutions suited to the problems posed by growth.

The wealth of a society therefore lies, to a large extent, in its ability to articulate, to create suitable institutions, to exploit its various components and above all to involve as many members as possible in the development process. A society like this is a society which responds to the growing complexity of economic organisations and social relations with complex answers that are not verticalised but, on the contrary, are able to draw on the brains and skills that make it possible to manage complexity horizontally, without hierarchies.

The "virtuous" component of Italy's growth as a modern industrial nation is therefore strongly dominated by models of social organisation which have allowed many areas of the country to attain a state of affluence relatively quickly, but which have above all contributed to the creation of an original and in some ways unique system as compared with the rest of the western world.

The extensive influence of the family, the historic social role traditionally played by crafts in local communities, the consolidated presence of many Italian provinces in international trade and the traditional contribution made by local authorities (especially in the northern and central regions) in creating the infrastructures necessary for the development of enterprises: these four factors have transformed a seemingly weak productive system into an original formula for growth at a local level. The most important model, from certain points of view, is that of the industrial district, which constitutes a virtuous synthesis of the above factors and still represents a form of local economic and social growth able to combine economic advantages with the involvement, and even the solidarity, of the various organisations operating in the area concerned.

Even in the last few years, the Italian model of the *industrial district* has helped to render the country's productive system extremely flexible and able to cope with the difficult situations that have arisen at a national and international level. The devaluation of the lira and the free fluctuation of the exchange rate between 1992 and 1996 were exploited to the full by small and medium-sized enterprises in Italy, particularly in the north-eastern part of the country; the enterprises in question greatly increased their ability to export

On the internal plane, there has been a tendency to adopt the district model in the southern regions, too. Some regions, such as Campania and Puglia, are hoping to establish districts uniting productive enterprises in the area which have, even informally, reached a significant level of productive integration, becoming structures able to compete on the international markets, sometimes even in sectors of a traditional kind where there is a strong presence of recently industrialised countries.

These models have therefore represented the most robust containing factors in the face of the most critical transitions that have taken place in Italy, particularly in the period most subject to changes in productive activities (the 1970s) or during the financial crisis of the first half of the 1990s, as mentioned above.

In the first case, it was thanks to the vitality of the small and medium enterprises and to the implicit adoption of this model of production, based on "flexible specialisation" (as it was effectively defined by foreign experts studying Italian development), that Italy was able to withstand the blows of an era in which the large enterprises were restructured and downsized and the economy moved towards a more complex and contradictory phase of development: a long way from the framework of security created in the second half of the last century, based on extensive welfare, mass production and state intervention in the economy.

In the second case, it was the very existence of a truly flexible organisational approach that allowed Italy, in certain areas of the country – particularly the northeast – to reap the implicit benefits of financial weakness and to adopt strategies for ceasing to operate on a purely local scale and for conquering new markets, sometimes outside the European Community.

In this same period, characterized by serious problems of political instability, the widespread diffusion of associations (particularly associations of entrepreneurs and trades unions, but also voluntary associations) and their strong capacity for mobilisation made it possible to resist the attack of organised crime and to prevent the degeneration of a difficult social context such as that found in certain parts of southern Italy.

Furthermore, even in the face of continuing problems that were hard to solve, such as the economic divide between the regions of central and northern Italy on the one hand and those of the south on the other, the effectiveness of an approach based on the exploitation of local resources has received clear confirmation – even recently – and has allowed Italy to find a way out of the embarrassing quandary deriving from its policy of intervention and support for the south, adopted at the end of the 1980s, which was too centralised and did not help to give confidence in place of useless and damaging economic subsidies. The era of *territorial pacts* for the development of the southern regions, launched when special intervention in southern Italy came to an end, currently represents the most decisive experiment for the acceptance and diffusion of an approach to economic and social growth that is not generalised but is based on stimulating an area's own ability to plan and implement economic initiatives.

The essence of the territorial pact is to launch a development project with the extensive involvement of the whole system of enterprises and intermediaries that operate at a local level (local authorities, sectorial associations, trades unions). It uses a "method" that has already been exported on a European scale and that has come to represent a sort of "best practice" in the management of economic and social development processes. The basic idea behind the territorial pacts, and in general behind concerted planning, was born of the realisation that social cohesion is both a resource and a competitive factor: social relations and underlying common values (cultural or social) frequently constitute the factors that guarantee processes of local development and determine the success or failure of a project for a given area. Finally, the tendency to launch initiatives combining the role of the public sector with that of the enterprises in the country's social and economic development processes is demonstrated by the activity undertaken by the so-called "third sector" and by the voluntary organisations in particular. The fact that neither the market nor the public structures are able to ensure an adequate response, either quantitatively or qualitatively, to certain kinds of demand from the weakest segments of society is compensated by the extensive participation of Italians in voluntary initiatives. According to an Istat survey,[3] in 1997 there were 11,700 voluntary organisations in Italy, 60% of them operating in the northern regions. There had been a 40.3% increase compared TO 1995 and the weight of the southern regions had increased. The total number of voluntary operators amounted to 591,000, corresponding to over 10 volunteers per thousand inhabitants; 35.6% of the volunteers worked in the health sector and 23.3% were involved in welfare initiatives. The main targets for voluntary activity were, in order of importance: the sick and injured (59.3%), old people (10.2%), people in difficulty (6.3%).

The volume of the resources provided by the voluntary sector does not reflect the full value of its contribution to the community, however. The social relations that radiate out from this activity and the intangible content deriving from the process of exchanging "supply and demand for quality of life" are still difficult to quantify in terms of material wealth. At the same time, it is clear that the very existence of this contribution constitutes one of the most important factors in preserving the common values that represent the foundation of a community, providing that the public structures are often unable to improve the quality of their services.

## Conclusions

The different dimensions of analysis covered by this study offer a perception of the Italian development process which is founded on several fundamental factors.

The first is connected with the essential role of *social relations* as a driving force for development.

The peculiarity of this factor in Italy derives from the fact that these relations are, for the most part, carried on through and by means of the family. This has led to consequences of at least two kinds. On the one hand, family ties have rendered such relations stronger and more intense, ensuring continuity and better future prospects for entrepreneurial initiatives and activities of a social kind. On the other hand, relations controlled by families have very often travelled along informal channels; in the worst instances, these have induced the growth of irregular forms of labour and entrepreneurial activity and, in the course of time, have increased the size of the submerged economy that is still a feature of the Italian economic system today.

The second aspect is linked to the partial *weakness* of the central state, which still persists, particularly with regard to the organisation of services for the individual, that is to say health and welfare. The family and other social safety-nets – especially in the voluntary sector – have always acted as substitutes and buffers, playing a vital role, but changes of a demographic kind, and in particular the lengthening of old age and the simultaneous reduction in the size of the family, now make this function problematic.

This last consideration leads to a third sphere of reflection, linked to the sensation that we have just come to the *end of a cycle* that has lasted for at least three decades. At present, on account of the demographic patterns mentioned above, the role played by the main protagonists in the growth of the country is under examination. The national productive structure, based on the pre-eminence of small enterprises and on the control of enterprises by the family, is now revealing various limitations, related not only to its size but also to the very role played by the family as an incubator for entrepreneurial initiatives. The difficulties encountered by enterprises with regard to their succession and to the turnover of their management are indicative of the critical nature of the current process in which responsibility and motivation are being handed down from one generation to the next. This factor also affects more complex entrepreneurial systems, such as industrial districts, which base much of their success on the consolidated exchange of relations through well-known entrepreneurial figures.

The start of a new cycle therefore appears to be conditioned by the presence of constrains, which must be countered by strengthening all the entities that have contributed to the growth of the country.

The role of the family as an economic unit that upholds the values of sharing and wider redistribution of wealth; the role of voluntary organisations, the role of the industrial district, which is able to produce an overall value far greater than the sum of the economic contributions made by its components; the function of the territorial pact, based on negotiation and agreement on strategies for local development: these are all successful types of intervention which, as far as their approach is concerned, follow in the footsteps of an all-Italian tradition that undoubtedly stems from the time when "European material civilisation" was being launched and developed and centres on the exploitation of local processes and resources.

## Notes

1. Istat – *Le strutture familiari*, 1998
2. G. De Rita, *L'impresa-famiglia* (The Family Enterprise), in *La famiglia italiana dall'Ottocento ad oggi*, edited by P. Melograni and L. Scaraffia, Rome 1988
3. Quoted in CENSIS, *34th Report on the social situation in Italy*, 2000, Franco Angeli, Milan

## References

Bank of Italy (2001), *Annual report 2001*, Roma.
CENSIS (2000), *34$^{th}$ Report on the social situation in Italy*, Franco Angeli, Milan.
CENSIS (2000), "Un secolo da non dimenticare – L'evoluzione socioeconomica che ha trasformato l'Italia (1900-2000)" in *Note & Commenti*, n. 4/2000, Roma.
G. De Rita (1988), "L'impresa-famiglia (The family enterprise)", in P. Melograni and L. Scaraffia (eds), *La famiglia italiana dall'Ottocento ad oggi*, Rome.
G. Roma (2001), *L'economia sommersa*, Ed. Laterza, Bari.
ISTAT (1998), "Le strutture familiari", in *Le famiglie negli anni '90, Indagine multiscopo sulle famiglie*, mimeo.
SVIMEZ (2001), *Economic Report 2001 on Southern Italy*, Il Mulino, Bologna.

# Comment

## Masao Kotani

In Italy, the role of the family as an effective socio-economic buffer against critical factors now seems to be radically changed, or rather endangered, owing mainly to the low birth rate and the reduction of the average number of family members. This "crisis" of the Italian family has a lot in common with the Japanese counterpart, though the adjustment strategies adopted in Italy, which are based on the values of the local community and the tradition of "associazionismo", are really unique: from family enterprises to industrial district, from assistance for disabled members almost entirely by the family to the social care-services by the "third sector" (in the Italian sense), and what is more, to the experimental practices of so-called territorial pacts.

Toma indicates the key-concept of "social and relational capital", that may have been historically developed from the network of relative. This unquantifiable value seems to be decisive, at least in Italy, for the quality of everyday life. Again, he defines the social development of Italy, not as "a mere quantitative increase in economic indicators", but as "self-aware growth", that is, a social process which is "the articulation and enrichment of a society's own awareness of itself".

To put it briefly, the distinguishing feature of Italy's process is characterised by socio-economic solidarity, or, so to speak, face to face networks, rather than by competition of free market. So it may not be worthless to explore the sphere of small medium size variegated voluntary associations as a social capital of Italy, which would not be set out within the usual framework of family-market-state nor that of public-private.

And now I would like to examine briefly the phenomenon of the recent boom of "banca del tempo" (time bank) in Italy, as it seems to me full of suggestion in this context. The idea of banca del tempo, which has been inspired also by the examples of Local Exchange Trade System (LETS) in the United Kingdom or by that of Système d'échange local (SEL) in France, could be formulated by the principal of indirect, or rather open reciprocity in the Polanyi sense (Coluccia 2001).

In fact, in this neighbourhood organization, a member who offers on one day any service free for some other member, can take another day of someone's service at the same time as he/she did. The only medium of exchange is time of offered/taken services, so the "bank" register and coordinate everyone's accounts of time. This system, then, is evidently different from the market system or the public administration services; and not so closed as the relationship in the family or intimate friends; finally, more reciprocal or bidirectional than the social services offered by either professional workers or many voluntary organizations, or charities.

It is said that nowadays there are hundreds of banca del tempo in Italy, which are authorized and promoted also by the latest legislation (Legge del 8 marzo 2000, n.53, Disposizioni per il sostegno della maternità e della paternità, per il diritto alla cure e alla formazione e per il coordinamento dei tempi delle città, art.27). This law, on the other hand, imposes every local government (comune) to make a plan of local time-tables (piano territoriale degli orari) for facilitating the temporal coordinations of city functions and the activities of social solidarities (art.24). The planning committee is supposed to be constituted by the mayor, local administration officers, representatives of local enterprises, trade unions, universities, local voluntary associations, families, and so on.

The human-scale movements of banca del tempo could be, in this Italian context of so-called "time policy", identified tentatively with one of the above-mentioned social processes for the self-aware re-socialization of local society itself, which seems to be now at the point of de-socialization.

Of course, this challenging strategy of social harmonization would not be uncontested. After all, it must be pivotal what role the social professions should and can play, not only for banca del tempo (especially at risk of amateurism), but also for the socio-economic developments of Italy. For it is my understanding that in the Mediterranean countries where the contextual interdependence seems to be much more fundamental in everyday life, the social workers would be expected to take an indispensable part in coordination of networks such as social capital and mediation between the institutions and the individuals, rather than merely in personal case-work.

All these considerations lead to the final question: re-conceptualization of "mercato" in Italy. Is the terminology of "market" in the anglo-american economics really capable of accounting for such a particular relation between "mercato" and society in Italy? If not, I believe, the concept of "mercato" needs redefining.

**References**

Paolo Coluccia (2001) La banca del tempo, Introduzione di Serge Latouche, Bollati Boringhieri.

# Chapter 15

# The Italian Welfare System Between the European Unification and the Globalization Processes: A Suggested Interpretation

Paolo Calza Bini

**Globalization, inequalities and new needs**

The changes in today's society, characterized by production processes that are as migrant as the populations, transcend and blur national boundaries and national identities. The latter, once firmly anchored to a spatial dimension unequivocally contained within the political and geographical boundaries of national States, are becoming harder to define within the institutions historically charged with the governance of such processes.

The wider range of players and space-and-time levels in the determination of social processes requires an *a priori* institutional adaptation at the various levels (local, national, continental) at which the players interact, and a new way for the players to relate, within a new, and often conflictive, context of mediation.

The wider social interaction, together with the more complex game of related economic exchanges and interests, should be matched by a different and more sophisticated system of political, economic and social governance, whose design is still unclear.

The interests of the members of the communities become more fluid and variable, and the situations at the same time present higher risks, not only within the context of the individual outcome, but also within the higher logic inherent to the cohesion of the collectivity.

This increases the difficulty of public decisions regarding the funding and allocation of resources to satisfy the increasingly more sophisticated and unpredictable needs of the population. All this requires greater insight, wider views, decisional speed, and better listening and learning capabilities, aimed at improving institutional performance through the pursuit of results that are efficient, effective and compatible with cost-saving and fairness principles.

Thus, from the point of view of national states, the constant increase in social complexity, marked also by eminently political processes of territorial decentralization (such as those that are being strongly encouraged by the European

Union, through repeated appeals to the "constitutional" importance of the "subsidiarity" principle), amplifies the needs of the population and the demand for those services, broadly defined as "welfare". Today such demand, made explicit by the growing requests of the new social classes (not only the "new poor" but also the "new middle classes"), need to find policy makers and operators who are prepared and more sensitive, becoming themselves promoters of ideas meant to match the need for regulation and innovation.

From the point of view of the social players, on the other side, the growing differentiation of activities and socializing experiences in the daily life, the increased mobility and the intensification of communication flows enabled by the new technologies, create, one way or another, a new set of risks and opportunities. From the point of view of social identity, these factors produce effects that are unifying and massifying on the one hand, and diversifying and pluralizing on the other hand, depending on the mix of relations and experiences suffered in conditions of temporary mobility in the various places and jobs (Martinotti 1993). The interactions and reactions typical of more articulated socialization processes facilitate the emergence of a complex social demand, characterized by the request of services which are differentiated in terms of cost, impact and degree of customization, but are still being mainly demanded to the State. Such demand is also accompanied by an increasing sensitivity towards the issues regarding an "eco-social" system, that is exposed to constant degradation.

All this summarily describes a process, still in an active state of differentiation in contemporary societies, characterized by the autonomy of the various areas of associative life, the disappearance of certain types of intermediation between the individual and society, and the multiplication of roles and social belonging (Touraine 1998) that underscore the affirmation of a more diversified subjective orientation: such orientation renders the social and political order more complex and less predictable, favouring the networks of relationships, and the exchange of information, investments and goods on the one hand (Castells 1996), and collective and individual cultural identification on the other.

This scenario puts to the test the old welfare systems, that oscillate between the need to respect new and more rigid compatibilities and the natural vocation to respond to the needs of the population, needs that are often new, and in large part unpredictable in the long term. In addition, they have a diversified impact on the various layers of population. The analytical tools used until now in order to identify the characteristics of this new demand have revealed themselves unsatisfactory, precisely because burdened by the difficulty of clearly identifying such needs. They are far from being exclusively tied to income, and widely differentiated among the various layers of population, territories, generations and genders.

Satisfying these needs – whose essentiality for the individual and collective existence cannot be summarily judged with simple, rational criteria, of the kind of the utilitarian schemes prevailing at the time of strong standardization such as the "Fordist" industrial era – poses a serious problem of reorganization of the Social State. Moreover, these changes, as a whole, require a profound rethinking of the philosophy, the preferences and the principles of choice to be set as the basis of the collective and institutional action, which go well beyond criteria of a mere economic gain or market competitiveness. It has been amply demonstrated that the latter do not take into account the costs to the communities of the patterns of development, for example from the "eco-social" point of view.[1]

The often unquantifiable damages (poverty, exclusion, discomfort, undervaluation and waste of human resources), could imply a complete revision of the notions of a long-term collective interest. Avoiding and foreseeing such risks requires political farsightedness and consistent investments aimed at the public social good. The problem lies in the fact that the social subjects involved often do not have political influence and power, because they are part of an "excluded" population, or they have little "voice", because they have not gained a group consciousness as such; as is the case of the newer generations, not yet tempered by the direct and material experience, nor sufficiently socialised by an implicit knowledge of the problems.

In substance, the current social change, driven by the modernization and globalisation processes briefly outlined, while bringing a more sophisticated demand for social services, unveils at the same time primary needs of poverty and exclusion which were thought to have been eradicated and which require a quick response on part of the welfare system.

As already noted in a previous occasion (Calza Bini 2000), three main aspects in this changing environment may be underlined:

The progressive segmentation of the social system into molecular groups that represent heterogeneous needs greatly extending the range of services demanded;

The growth of areas of new poverty next to the areas of traditional material poverty: a poverty typical of the industrial and post-industrial societies that often implies difficulty in social participation, a crisis of moral values, social isolation, and diminishing quality of social and interpersonal relationships (Castel 1994);

The transformation of health, welfare and instruction demands, implying strong individual and collective requests towards the appropriation of tangible and intangible goods.

From the mid-eighties, in Italy more than in other parts of Europe, several critical factors have contributed to casting doubt over the advantages and validity of the choices adopted in the previous historical period, revealing its sometimes unfair aspects in the current social contexts. As a consequence, the Welfare State itself has become less recognizable, which has thus been often interpreted as a signal of its crisis; this has fuelled the consciousness that something had somehow to be changed. Proposals, though, sometimes paid not enough thought to the possible consequences of changes, relatively to the problems of protection in particular of the weaker members of the community.

In this perspective, globalisation presents new problems for social policy: in its triple meaning of competition and mediation among the different social realities, of definition and implementation of strategies and of measures of protection, and lastly, in a Weberian manner, of critical analysis of the first two issues.

Next to the renewed problems of welfare reform, stand new important aspects to which research should direct its attention:

The changes of the world population and the social composition of single countries relative to their demographic, social and economic characteristics;

The renewed expansion, on a large scale, of social inequalities and the distance between the two extremes, even in the more developed societies;

The continuous transformation of economic systems assailed by waves of technological and organizational innovation;

The redefinition of the political and institutional frames of the debate, channelled by the crisis and the deep restructuring of the forms of political governance of the Fordist era.

The points just made strongly indicate the need of re-examining the very foundations of equity and justice, of political and social citizenship, of government levels and the organization of the institutions designed to govern and to supply social protection, at global and local scale, in all their various relations. The emergence of the European identity, accelerated by monetary unification and by progresses in the extension of the Union's competences, needs, in such a framework, to be carefully taken into account.

## Aspects of the welfare systems in Europe: a brief overview

The history of the Social State in Europe has been marked by a recurring motif alternating two initial options: the Danish universalistic model and the particularistic, insurance-based German model. The prevalence of universalistic or particularistic elements has resulted, in each instance, into different patterns of a recognizable reality – the welfare state – corresponding to the different positions achieved, in the various national examples, along the axis of what we could define the democracy of the system, generally expressed through a series of mechanisms that can to a smaller or greater extent be traced back to the principle of redistribution (Esping-Andersen 1990). Different equilibrium points were each perceived at any given time as the most adequate expression of the principle of social solidarity and as the most acceptable base around which to build consensus.

In the period following World War II, the sustained economic development that has characterized the European industrial societies pivoted fundamentally on a sizeable expansion of the social protection systems promoted or supported one way or another by the national States. Indeed, the combination of common goals and national specificities has produced different models of welfare capitalism.

The result has been a clear differentiation in the models of welfare capitalism in connection with the path-dependent adaptive processes that have stressed one or another aspect of the welfare mix. As an example, the intervention of the universalistic welfare state in the Scandinavian countries, the combination of private income and the selective expansion of services in the United Kingdom, or the complementarities between social security and the persistence of family responsibilities and of public services in the central European countries, are substantially different from both the (income and services) welfare system typical of the United States and the welfare system of the Mediterranean-European countries, where the qualitative and adaptive role of the family, the community and the family networks has remained strong but sustained by a non marginal system of public support.

The equilibrium of the various welfare regimes that have been achieved within the strong industrial expansion of the post-war period – according to Mingione – have been greatly weakened by several processes of change starting with the oil crisis of the seventies and the consequent restructuring of the economic and social organisation. "Globalisation, labour flexibility, de-industrialization, vertical disintegration of economic organizations, second demographic transition and the spreading of new forms of individualism have contributed to redesigning the welfare picture around emerging institutions and regimes, but again with different characteristics in the various countries" (Benassi-Mingione 2002).

In the EU countries the process of welfare adaptation has been intertwined with both the issue of the constraints placed by Maastricht treaty onto the management of public finances, in view of the introduction of the single currency, and the ever-increasing pressures towards the homogenisation and coordination of social policies.

As maintained by the European Commission at the opening of the social action programme 1998-2000, the renewal of the European social policy constitutes a solid foundation on which to found a different approach to social problems issues and from which to plan subsequent intervention policies, beginning with the ample debate set off in 1993 with the "Green Book" and the "White Book", and followed by the 1995-1997 medium term social action plan, the 1998-2000 social action programme and the year 2000 agenda for social policy. These documents gather and translate into precise political directives much of what research, surveys and the scientific debate have been developing and anticipating in the last few decades about issues of labour markets, unemployment, and social inclusion and exclusion; it is also possible to trace the community organisms' dawning perception of (and concern for) a phenomenon of incumbent change with a much wider reach, one that actually presents new challenges and needs additional attention and public intervention centred around the interests of the community.

The intense transformations undergone by the structures and the dynamics of the world of labour, together with the polarisation and differentiation of social and economic behaviours,[2] are of concern at European Community top representatives' level, forcefully placing the coordination of labour policies and social protection at the centre of the Community's political action. Labour policies and social protection, using as a starting point the macroeconomic constraints designed for financial stability, are intended to strengthen structural reforms aiming at an employment growth sustained by growing "employability", enterprise creation and equal opportunity, while at the same time placing firmly at the centre-stage the common awareness that "social protection represents a production factor, at the base of economic growth and the increase in productivity, which in turn support social progress". In spite of the renewed attention, this is something that still has a way to go within the European Union, if it is true that, despite having set in motion "good policies" with some cautious successes in their implementation, social exclusion in Europe still represents a significant problem to be actively fought (European Commission 1998).

In the year 2000 the Commission and the Council have confirmed and renewed these objectives for the years 2000-2005, proposing as the primary objective, a more intense policy coordination at various levels. Thus the new agenda contemplates a significant attempt at coordinating the Community's economic policy with full employment, economic dynamism, and a greater effort towards social cohesion and justice.

## The historical construction of the welfare system in Italy

The incompleteness and defectiveness of the social legislation achieved in Italy in the first sixty years since the unification in 1861 reflect the contradictions of a country that underwent late industrialisation. The leading class was divided into an industrial bourgeoisie that lacked a predominant role, and the farmers' middle-class, with a limited culture unable to meet the new social demands and, more generally, unable to deal with modern times. Fascism was the result of this contradiction (Bartocci 1995).

The fascist period caused a break in some relevant democratisation processes (e.g. the introduction of a full universal suffrage: the Italian female population achieved the right to vote only after World War II). However, during this period the Italian welfare system assumed a more definite structure, more or less destined to remain in place during the two decades following the fall of the fascist regime, and characterized by particularism, a widespread patronage system, the fragmentation of skills, scant importance of the public social assistance sector, and relevant territorial differences in welfare services' availability and delivery.

In the post-war reconstruction period, Italy had been essentially marked by a *laissez-faire* economic policy, leaving to the State only the task of intervening in the social policies in order to protect the weaker ranks of the population, while controlling the social categories marginalised by the process of modernisation. However, social policy was orientated towards the acquisition of political-electoral consensus and towards the legitimisation of the political elite, which had gained power through the hegemony of the Christian Democrats. In this way, a model of patronage developed. In the Sixties and Seventies, in Italy as in the other European Countries, social expenditure grew considerably.

The Seventies marked a significant change in Italy's welfare state structure. In this period, some relevant reforms were launched, affecting both the welfare system (i.e. the Health Care reform, based on universalistic criteria) and the institutional structure of the State (i.e. the implementation of the constitutional principle of regionalisation).

Towards the end of the Seventies, the elements of imbalance in the social security system became evident; they were provoked by phenomena similar to those of the other Western European countries, but were rendered more dramatic by the historical anomalies typical of the Italian Welfare State.

The crisis of the Italian welfare model became increasingly evident during the Eighties, due to the contemporaneous rise of growing deficit in the State budget. In this period, it became more and more clear that some crucial problems were surfacing, and in particular: the scant sustainability of the pension system; the financial and organizational difficulties of the National Health Care Service; the ineffectiveness of the traditional labour market policies in reducing unemployment; the need for a more appropriate organisation of the social services in order to meet a rapidly changing social demand.

In the early 1990s important legislative measures brought significant changes in the institutional structure of the Italian welfare system. In particular we can mention: acts n. 142 and n. 241 of 1990, outlining the new organization of Local Autonomies, especially for the role of communes; act n. 266 of 1991, regulating voluntary associations; act n. 421 of 1992, reforming health and social security systems. Insofar as the welfare policies are concerned, the main contents of the new legislative framework can be summarized as follows:

a) Local Autonomies Act

Municipalities and provinces are defined as "self-governing local communities", and their sphere of autonomy includes statutory and financial matters. Provisions for citizens' participation to the administration of communities are established.

The functions pertaining to social services, previously shared between communes and provinces, are assigned to municipalities.

b) Voluntary Associations Act

The social value of voluntary activity is recognised and its development is promoted in order to achieve goals of public interest in the social, civic, and cultural fields. A national Observatory of voluntary associations is established. State, regions, provinces, municipalities, and other public institutions can sign agreements with these associations. Detailed regulations of voluntary activity are to be established by the Regions.

c) Reform of the health-care system

Health policy guidelines are established by the National Health Plan, which has a three-year term but can be modified before expiry if deemed necessary. The Plan sets out targets of health service and measures for compensating territorial unbalances. "Uniform levels of health assistance" (services to which all are entitled) are determined taking into account available resources and epidemiological data. The Plan establishes the "project objectives" and sets guidelines for professional training and biomedical and health research.

The Regions define Regional Health Plans in accordance with the National Health Plan, in order to tailor service organisation standards to region-specific needs and resources.

"Local Health Units" become enterprises with public legal status, endowed with organisational, administrative, managerial, and technical autonomy. A director-general is appointed to head each local health unit, on a private, five-year appointment with full managing powers.

The total number of local health units is reduced, extending their territorial competence to roughly coincide with the provinces. Each unit is further divided into districts. National, highly specialised hospitals become autonomous enterprises similar to the health units. All other hospitals remain dependent from the local health units.

In all hospitals a space is reserved for the professional practice of doctors, and 6-12% of the beds are assignable to paying patients. For general practitioners, a three-year contract under private ruling is instituted. From 1994 onwards, existing agreements between the National Health Service and the private operators will be replaced by new contracts, founded on the payment of a stipulated fee for each type of service rendered on behalf of the NHS. From 1995 onwards, regions are authorised to experiment with alternative schemes of health assistance delivery. In particular, voluntary health insurance schemes may be devised, and assistance conditions for their members may be negotiated with the Health Service; in this case members will have to renounce the services offered directly by the National Service (uniform, minimal levels of health assistance excepted).

d) Reform of the pension system

A compulsory, progressive rise of the retirement age is introduced, bringing it to 60 years for women and to 65 years for men (i.e. there is a 5-year increase for private-sector workers, while there are no changes for the other categories).

The minimum contribution period for old-age pension is progressively raised to 20 years (from 15 years).

A progressive lengthening in the pay and contribution period used to determine the pension amount is introduced, which in the future shall comprise the entire work-life for all categories of workers (former regulations were significantly differentiated and the computation was effected on the last ten years, on the last five years, or even on the last monthly pay).

Regulations on early retirement and cumulation of pensions and other earned income are standardised on the basis of more restrictive criteria.

Pensions are linked only to price index movements (formerly linked also to wage dynamics).

A revision and standardization of regulations affecting voluntary supplementary pensions is devised.

The Pension system was reformed again a few years later. January 1, 1993 and January 1, 1996 represent two important steps for the Italian pension system. "After twenty years of discussion and three years after the Amato reform the Dini reform was approved" (Ciocia 1995).

The main objectives of the pension system reforms launched in the 1990s are: "to bring the social security model in line with the insurance model and to give other welfare organisations the responsibility for social services; to build up a social security based on a three-tier system – the basic public system, a general supplementary system and a personal private pension; to include all workers in the social security system" (Ciocia 1998).

We can add that "at the centre of the Dini reform was the goal of broadening the system of a guaranteed pension to all categories of "atypical" workers who, until then, were not included. A second goal of the reform was to expand the base for the calculation of the pension amount to the entire work span. The third aim was to progressively abandon the culture of assistance eliminating, among other things, early retirement and, in the end, to introduce pension funds" (Ciocia 1995). One of the main innovations is related to the calculation used to determine the amount of the pension, moving from a re-distributive system towards a contributive system. However, the reform does not yet concern all workers, but applies fully only to those entering their first job. Workers who have already paid contributions up to 18 years are partially included, and workers who have already paid contributions for more then 18 years are excluded, and will continue to be entitled to previous conditions and regulations.

The Italian welfare state model presents, both historically and in its current structure, peculiarities that make a considerable strain to classify into a general typology. It is a mixed model, which can be placed in an intermediate position relative to the main classifications. This is apparent, for instance, in the Esping-Andersen (1990) classification, where Italy is positioned at the edge of the conservative-corporative cluster, with a score very near those of Ireland and the United Kingdom, which belong to the liberal cluster. According to a different classification suggested by Ferrera (1992) – which exploits as taxonomical criterion the degree of coverage offered by welfare systems, organised in two models (the employment-based and the universalistic models) and four classes (depending on the pure or mixed character of the models) – the Italian system has been described as a mixed employment-based system, though the author himself underlines the sharp contrast between the pension system (employment-based) and the health system (universalistic, at least since 1978).

In fact – as remarked by Ugo Ascoli (1984) – the distinctive feature of the Italian Welfare State, as shaped in the republican period, is probably due, at least in part, to its being the result of neither an equalitarian and universalistic project worked out by a strong labour movement, nor the clever planning of a ruling class striving for legitimacy, but of a process of evolution, with substantial continuity, since the post-unitary and the fascist periods, still founded on criteria of particularism and patronage.

The particularism of measures, ending up in a policy of subsidies differentiated by professional condition, social group, and territorial area, together with the overall logic of patronage – which in turn brings about a complex web of institutional forms of social intervention favouring "clientele" and social categories and giving in fact welfare agencies a mediating role aimed at the organisation and furtherance of patronage – appear as typical attributes of the Italian model. Both are strictly related to a third attribute that somehow summarises them, namely the prevalence of expenditure for social transfers over that for public consumption, a tendency that can be seen in the large share of expenditure for pensions or in the widespread use of financial transfers, as in the case of the support measures for Southern Italy ("Mezzogiorno").

**Towards a transformation of the welfare system in Italy**

The current innovations in assistance policies are examples of a more general transformation of the welfare systems, motivated by the need to respond to the changes in the composition of the social protection deficit (Esping-Andersen, 2000; Ferrera, 1998), aimed on one hand to a reduction and sustainability of social security costs and on the other hand at re-establishing a balance between social security, health care and assistance, providing more universal, fair and effective services to the citizens.

The construction of a regime of welfare capitalism in Italy, more than in other European countries, has definitely been based on the family component, which has had to adapt the quality of its own solidarity circuits to the needs related to the division of tasks between the State and the market.

In Italy the protection against the risk of poverty has been characterized by the subsidiarity of public assistance relative to the protection guaranteed by the family and by the family network, by a structural deficit of public operators' professional and coordination capabilities.[3]

Moreover, in Italy all this has happened in a framework of strong persistence of autonomous work and of small family-driven enterprises, a marked economic dualism between the North and the South, and a historical difficulty on the part of the State to govern the social dynamics.[4] Unlike other European countries, the "de-familiarization" of the protection and care systems has only happened in part. Instead, the modernisation of life styles and of the family organizational models have not fundamentally changed the care-giving role of women within the family, the family network and the formal and informal support institutions (from community and neighbourhood networks to charity organizations) (Mingione, 2002). The Italian welfare, both in its public and its private components, has developed in a complementary manner relative to this order.

Thus, the public welfare has matured peripheral characteristics with respect to the more central solidarity relationships based on the family: the creation of a universalistic health system, the weakness of policies that interfere with family responsibilities,[5] the prevalence of income integration programmes, the atrophy of the system of services to individuals and families, the territorial and category fragmentation of programmes, the tolerance of informal relationships, etc. (Negri e Saraceno, 1996; Ferrera, 1998; Benassi, 2000).

However, after a long period of immobility, the Italian welfare system is undergoing a season of changes, marked by two major events: the experimental introduction of the minimum inclusion income level (RMI) and the approval of the bill on Welfare Reform Outline, both experienced at the end of 2000.

In EU countries the welfare system adaptation process has been conditioned upon the issue of constraints imposed on the public financial management by the Maastricht treaty, in view of the introduction of a single currency, and with the ever-increasing pressures towards the homogeneity and coordination of social policies. For Italy this process has facilitated a strategy of financial adjustment with significant consequences for the organization and financing of welfare, in a moment which was particularly delicate due to profound social, demographic and occupational changes and to the chronic crisis of the Mezzogiorno.

The interdependence of public accounts and the need to deal with the organization of welfare in Italy has been explicitly raised by the work of the specifically appointed Parliamentary Commission, composed by a group of experts in 1997 to suggest cuts in public spending that would allow the adjustment of the public accounts needed to respect the Maastricht parameters.[6] The commission did not limit itself to suggesting cuts in social security spending (the only chapter where substantial savings could be realistically obtained, and were partially implemented by the Dini pension reform) but also pointed to the weakness of the welfare intervention and explicitly recommended the introduction of a national subsistence level programme. This recommendation was followed by the Government, which in 1998-1999 introduced an experimental programme, subsequently extended to other municipalities in which the experimentation is still ongoing.

Thus in Italy, in the last decade, on the wave of what has taken place albeit under different shapes in the rest of Europe, an intense activity aimed at implementing a season of reforms has occurred. The explicit objective was to establish, in a more adequate perspective of European integration – social as well as political, economic and monetary – the new order of the National Welfare System. During these years Italy has been hit by a wave of activity, long overdue but perhaps anomalous in the intensity of the economic and institutional reorganization processes, in almost all sectors of welfare: instruction and training, university and scientific research, labour and employment services, assistance and health care, social security and protection.

Social policies have suffered for some time from the processes of change in act, and many of the principles inspiring the reforms have internalised, consciously or unconsciously, the cultural aspects of change. These latter, however, often proceeds with a greater intensity, speed and impact than it could be rationally foreseen. Thus, even if the public action is alert and careful, it has to proceed in contexts of ever increasing uncertainty, that require not once for all solutions but also a constant and careful evaluation of their effects and impact, which imply continuous adjustments and a correction of the targets.

In this context, how can errors, negligence, arbitrariness, incompetence and exclusion be avoided, as the process descends from the upper to the operating levels (of the various phases of decentralization)? How can we prevent the players, deprived of the necessary information to make rigorously rational decisions, despite the abundance of information available today, from making choices and taking actions that are contrary to the collective development and civic interest, setting in motion perverse effects and/or unexpected involution processes?

This is the terrain where a great number of the unknowns reside today, not only within the "game among the players involved", but also in the effective implementation of (generally shared) social policy actions and the new order of the social protection system. If the participation of the social parts, the intensification of the institutional coordination, and the innovative imitation of good practices at decentralized levels are certainly the basis on which to lay the foundations of synergic actions and the exchange of experiences, it is however well known that all of this is hard to implement even with the best of intentions (and this is not always the case).

Another important problem in policy implementation lies in the difficulty of matching and assigning the right weight to fair general coordination guidelines on a large scale (continental, national, regional), respecting and allowing the autonomous evolution of the socio-territorial and identity differences, while reducing the inequalities (see Calza Bini 2000). The crisis of the old welfare systems has been followed by a wide debate on reforms that has induced, particularly in the development of European construction, an impulse to reformulating the social protection system also within national States.

As has been effectively argued by Ferrera (1999), the difficulties in redefining the Italian welfare system, initially hindered by the many traps inherent to the system itself, have been later removed partly thanks to the need to adapt to the construction of a common European framework.

The last decade has seen, also at local level, a renewed attention towards social policies, historically regarded as the "tail end" of policies or the "consolation price" to be awarded in order to obtain social consensus. This new attitude has undoubtedly been stimulated, on the one hand, by an alert European agenda orientated by research and programming action in social policies, and on the other hand by the (especially qualitative) growth of social demand, supported with increasing awareness, in particular at the local level (thanks also to the stimulus of *ad hoc* local projects in the services sector, born out of the possibilities opened by European financing).

Thes new political commitments taken on by the centre-left governments at the end of the second millennium runs the risk of being blockaded by the new centre-right government, but even if this were not the case, it will have to find an adequate implementation at all levels of sectoral and territorial decentralization, given the guidelines defined at European level and by the previous national governments which have indicated the prevailing direction to be followed and the character of the good practices to bring into being. A decisive point, but also the biggest unknown, lies then, in my opinion, in the way that such processes will be implemented and on how growing decentralization and federalist development will be integrated with the already consolidated practices of local welfare systems, while respecting the objective of a fairer and more equitable global social system. In this perspective, the greatest obstacle is the real difficulty of combining the larger interest of the community at macro level with the particularities typical of local social diversity found at the micro level.

**Starting the reform processes: points of view of the analysis**

Beyond the internal differences of welfare systems over time (see Esping-Andersen "universalism and families", Ferrera's "models combining private income–public utility services", or Mingione's "complementarities between social security, the persistence of family responsibilities and public services"), Europe has built social protection systems that are bigger and have a larger public-collective responsibility base than in the USA. Social sciences have long taught us that the forms of social construction can be analysed from multiple points of view. Among these, the better known ones are "top down" and "bottom up". In a systemic framework analysis of welfare from the point of view of comparative political science, this means reconstructing the structure of tutelage and protection systems built by the Social State of the various countries.

In the case of countries where political, social and economic stability has lasted over time and space, the analysis can focus on the characteristics through which the institutional welfare framework has been outlined and built, and on how it operates (top down), evaluating the real tutelage accruing to the citizens, their satisfaction, the presence/absence of quotas of population excluded from citizenship rights and the degree of levels of exclusion in each country.

The social science analysis becomes more complex when the welfare systems are observed and analysed in a diachronic and/or dynamic context, as is the case of countries characterized by an absence of political and administrative stability, intense social dynamics and economic uncertainty.

A study of the decisions and the Institutional changes of State systems, in this case, will also require a bottom up analysis of the participation of citizens, and/or of their systems of representation in the decisional processes. Here the interpretative results and the explanation of the phenomena become widely different, depending on the points of view. In order to understand phenomena (i.e. to interpret them and to try to explain them at scientific level) the socio-economic analysis needs to move at both micro and macro level in order to understand the micro-macro links and interactive connections that appear in the social construction. Indeed, in some (and only in some) occasions, they can be examined and understood with a combination of micro bottom up approach and a macro top down approach. The social analysis requires a study of the interactive connections between these levels and consequently a study of the relational systems of the active players. All of this must be carried out while observing the phenomenology from wider points of view. To adopt this research methodology is not always easy, and often the analyses cannot go beyond the application, more or less consciously, of only some viewpoints. The analytical game of adopting multiple perspectives (or changing the observation point) almost always has a limited heuristic value and creates elements of confusion in the debate of the various analyses. As a complete analysis of this type cannot be developed within the scope of this work, I will limit myself to highlighting some aspects that the game of viewpoints seems to bring to the surface in the Italian case.[7]

In Italy as in other countries, the debate on the crisis of the welfare system makes its appearance in the scientific world approximately thirty years ago. It is evident primarily at macroeconomic level in the consistently increasing public spending indicators and the budget deficit. The accumulation of public debt, threatening to cause a fiscal crisis of the State, leads to the implementation of policies aimed at reducing public spending in general and welfare spending in particular. At that time a debate at political and institutional level began, concerning the need to adapt the formal system to the new reality that was coming into being. The real process of change, however, begins to develop only after the stability constraints imposed at Maastricht by the constitution of the Monetary Union and will proceed with greater intensity under the pressure of the EU consolidation.

In the socio-economic sphere, the processes and interactions developed between the players acting both at micro and at macro levels are numerous and intense, with both top down and bottom up pressures. The contradictions and the logic driving the players' actions do not move in the same direction or with the same intensity; nonetheless, they promote a general change in cultural climate and in the awareness of the need to adapt rules and institutions to the new order of the welfare system, shaped for an European context. This gives birth to a greater attention towards the general principles of universality of citizenship, fairness, and sustainability of public spending in the definition and the practices of the national welfare systems.

This cultural maturity has brought in political pressure for the determination of institutional reforms and new social policies (both in Italy and in Europe). Implementation, however, is far from easy because of: (a) a diversity of interests, opinions and relative power of the actors involved; (b) real contradictions (such as the inevitable cost of investing in good reform operations, the sustainability of spending or even the need to reduce it, perhaps through rationalization processes, and the need to extend citizenship and social protection rights to those who were excluded by previous orders, with the inevitable risks of additional spending needs and (c) constraints or veritable traps, such as institutional and bureaucratic slowness and difficulties which are a further obstacle in a structurally rigid and not particularly efficient administration like Italy's.

This notwithstanding, the process of political participation of citizens and their social representatives, through bottom up pressure for a significant political and institutional change of the Italian welfare system, has been intense and widespread (if at times contradictory), especially because of the pressure of new social players and/or their new identities.[8] This can be seen from the original reform proposals. Among these we may remind the intense discussion on the role of subsidies to the Third sector (families, voluntary associations, non-profit organizations, etc.), which has brought about a new attention on the part of local entities, the national State and the EU vis-à-vis the Third Sector.

This has become a pillar of subsidiarity to the public action, informal at first and then increasingly more recognized and institutionalised. Thus it is difficult to tell whether the change that has so intensely marked the Italian and the European institutional order during the last years of the twentieth century and the first years of the new millennium is more the result of bottom up or top down pressures. There is no doubt that in Italy changes have run against a decade-old resistance to the institutional change of state welfare regulatory systems (Ferrera) and that the season of institutional reform has been set off by macroeconomic needs inspired by considerations of non sustainability of public spending trends.

These reforms have come to life thanks to the obligations imposed on national states by the need to conform to the EU constitution: all of this can be placed under the top down category. It is equally certain, however, that the philosophies of change coming from social pressure and from bottom up experimentation have been in a sense strongly influenced by the concrete definition of EU reform policies, in the case of services against social exclusion. The Italian and the French experience have been in great part responsible for the definition of the principles of reform. They were based on the typology of participative involvement and forms of equality capable of respecting and recognizing social differences (of gender, generation, ethnic, etc.) and socio-territorial diversity (economic structure, culture, local institutions).

In this field (especially in welfare policies in its strictest meaning), even if with the difficulties due to the many legal and bureaucratic constraints, the proliferation of social policy experiments for projects sponsored and financed by the European Commission, have often resulted in the last decade in experimentations that have anticipated more general reform. Local government entities, playing on their autonomy, have taken on the burden of opening the way for the governance of new local welfare systems. The more active regions, with regional and local service development plans, have set off and socialized the best practices resulting from the participation of citizens, voluntary associations, social science and research. This is how the processes of structural and cultural innovation in the Public Administration have begun to take hold. The more sensitive among social operators and social workers interacting with the sector of voluntary associations, have also resulted in administrative learning processes and institutional change (Ota de Leonardis and L. Bifulco).

Thus, in a sense, in some cases the reform process in a sector started spontaneously with the practices of voluntary associations, and passed into the local level through the processes of experimentation and of governance rationalization, attracting Community funding. Hence comes the impulse towards local and regional planning. This has brought the rationalization of the existing system, in a much hoped direction for national regulatory legislation for the welfare (in its strict sense) that has taken a long time to be formalized. Today, however, the problems that arise are those of extending the "happy islands" of experimentation and best practices to the entire country.

This is the challenge posed, albeit somewhat late, by the recent national legislation on welfare. It has also been underlined, however, that today in this conscious top down action (though justly recognizing ample autonomy for bottom up local governance actions) there is again a high risk that the structural and cultural diversity of the players at the local and regional levels may affect the general result and balances because of the substantial diversity in skills and bureaucratic and political competence present in the individual contexts. Indeed, if it is true that autonomy has proved favourable to the expression of conscious, competent local operators, it is equally true that it can become an additional handicap in areas where economic, social and cultural delays have until now implied the worst choices and worst practices. The general risk lies in the intensification of internal unbalances that already are a burden for our country (the historical divide between the North and the South is but an example).

In the field of social security, on the contrary, an age-old centralized regulation on the part of the central government has always had to come to terms with the social demands expressed through labour conflicts and the intermediation of the organized representations of sectoral Unions. Thus, while on the one hand there has been a high degree of universal tutelage for the working population, on the other hand an extreme particularism has taken hold by virtue of the mediation of interest groups, determining a jungle of pensions in which obvious and strident inequities appear, showing strong variances between poor and rich pensioners even at the same level of seniority at work, contribution periods, professional qualifications, etc.

The attempts at tidying up and rationalizing the Italian social security system, having to cope at the same time with the need to contain the excessive pension public spending, have met for long periods with ample resistance and obstacles to top down action. Given that they affected acquired rights and privileges, they have given rise to social conflict and strong institutional resistance that have significantly delayed and hampered the implementation of reforms. The social security reform has evolved top down thanks to the constraints on public spending imposed on the Italian government by the EU. At the same time, nevertheless, it was possible to bring about a top down institutional change thanks to the favourable political conditions created by the government's actions, after the coming into power of the left parties in 1997. So, changes were made possible by the fact that, thanks to a more general political consensus, the experts could act without bottom up opposition. They had the possibility of acting according to rational technical choices. By virtue of these conditions, the Dini and Amato governments were able to benefit from a political climate where the social conflict was relatively contained.

## Conclusions

After a long delay due to the diffuculties of legislative implementations and the removal of bureaucratic and economic obstacles, a season of reforms is now entering the operational phase. However, it runs the risk of finding three new obstacles at inception: 1) the intensification of new needs and costs induced by globalisation processes; 2) the change in the political climate and power from the centre-left to centre-right government; 3) the socio-territorial differentiation of the quality of skills and cultural and political endowments of the operators and of the human resources.

Here a number of new conflicts or simply a lack of coordination of the reform actions may take place. The rationality of the players may be limited by various factors, and with changing situations that bear unquantifiable consequences, there may be episodes of dynamic inefficiency in the institutional adaptation to social innovation that in turn can negatively affect the social well-being of the entire community.

## Notes

[1] The Delors plan, the analyses of the Lisbon group (Petrella 1995), the Copenhagen and Peking conferences and the action of humanitarian, eco-social and environmental institutions have underlined and documented the irreversible eco-social damages implied in the philosophy of competitiveness (or in any case the high social costs in the long term).

[2] In the sense of a renewed and marked polarisation at the extremes of a continuum where, more than in the past, social inequalities represent the persistence and re-emergence of the most extreme type of social exclusion.

[3] Until recently Italy was one of the few European countries that did not have a universalistic programme to fight social exclusion. In any case, the very transformation of its assistance system finds its origins in a historically fragmented and divided situation (Negri and Saraceno, 1996).

[4] This deals with structural aspects of the Italian society that are too wide and complex to be dealt with in this occasion. As far as the administrative structures are concerned, let it be said that the clientelistic use made by some institutions in order to sustain income – as has happened in the case of invalidity pensions granted to non disabled people residing in the less developed areas – indicate how the welfare tools can be used to obtain political consensus (Ascoli, 1984).

[5] E.g. the scarcity of child care institutions, the significant absence of national policies for the young, the absence of support for the non bread-winner unemployed, the absence of national regulatory frameworks for the health care services for the elderly and other weak categories.

[6] This is evident from the name of the Commission: "Commission for the analysis of the macroeconomic compatibilities of public spending."

[7] For an analysis of the game of different view points see P. Calza Bini, La disoccupazione: interpretazioni e punti di vista in Sociologia e lavoro, n 59/60, 1995.

[8] Emerging from the experience and skills developed in the social Italian sphere but also out of the pervasive globalization of social life.

## References

Ascoli, U., *Il Sistema italiano di Welfare*, in *Welfare State all'Italiana*, a cura di U. Ascoli, Laterza, Bari.
Bartocci (ed), *Lo stato sociale in Italia 1995*, Rapporto Iridiss-Cnr, Centauri/Welfare books.
Benassi, D. (2000), *Le politiche nazionali contro la povertà in Italia*, Commissione di indagine sull'esclusione sociale, Roma.
Benassi, D., Mingione E. (2002), "Welfare locale, lotta all'esclusione sociale e riforme dell'assistenza in Italia", *Economia e lavoro*, anno 35, pp 65-81.
Bifulco, L., De Leonardis, O. (1997), *L'innovazione difficile. Studi sul cambiamento organizzativo nella pubblica amministrazione*, Franco Angeli, Milano.
Calza Bini, P. (1995), "La disoccupazione: interpretazioni e punti di vista", *Sociologia e lavoro*, n 59/60.
Calza Bini, P. (1999), "I Sistemi di Welfare alla fine del secondo millennio", in *Lo Stato sociale in Italia*. Rapporto annuale Iridiss-CNR 1999, Donzelli, Roma.
Castel, R. (1994), *Les métamorphoses de la question sociale. Une cronique du salariat*, Gallimard, Paris.
Castells, M. (1996), *The Age of Information. The rise of Network Society*, Blackwell, London.
Ciocia A., in E. Bartocci (ed) *Lo stato sociale in Italia 1995*, Rapporto Iridiss-Cnr, Centauri/Welfare books.
Esping, Andersen, G. (1999), *The Tree Worlds of Welfare Capitalism*, Polity Press, Cambridge.

Esping, Andersen, G. (1990), *Social Foundation of Postindustrial Economics*, Oxford: Oxford University Press.
European Commission, Social Action Programme, 1998–2000.
Ferrera M. (1993), *Modelli di solidarietà. Politiche e riforme Sociali nelle democrazie*, Il Mulino, Bologna.
Ferrera, M. (1997), *Le trappole del Welfare. Uno Stato Sociale sostenibile per l'Europa del XXI secolo*, Il Mulino, Bologna.
Ferrera, M., Gualmini, E. (1999), *Salvati dall'Europa?*, Il Mulino, Bologna.
Martinotti, G. (1993), *Metropoli la nuova morfologia sociale della città*, Il Mulino, Bologna.
Negri, N., Saraceno, C. (1996), *Le politiche contro la povertà in Italia*, Il Mulino, Bologna.
Touraine, A. (1998), *Libertà, uguaglianza, diversità*, Il Saggiatore, Milano.

# Comment
## Nobuhiro Hiwatari

## Introduction

This is a very comprehensive, ambitious and often thought provoking paper. Maybe it is overly comprehensive, ambitions and provoking. As a result, the reader might find it a bit disjointed or disorganized. In fact the paper seems to bridge and incorporate diverse epistemologies (sociological vs. economic), fields of research (the use of welfare state typology literature, globalization and the welfare state literature, policy implementation literature), and purposes (empirical and normative analyses). In what follows, I will try to entangle the topics of this paper in such a way as to suggest the missing links of the argument and at the same time enhance the potential of this paper for future research. The article is structured in order to explain (1) the challenges faced by the (Italian) welfare state in the face of European unification and globalization, (2) the characteristics of the Italian welfare state and its recent changes, (3) the problems of current reforms. Therefore I will organize my comments in the same order as the paper.

## The challenges of globalization

The author enlists the idealistic as well as the materialistic challenges imposed by European unification and the processes of globalization and enumerates "important aspects to which research should direct its attention." The argument would have been easier to follow if the paper had clarified the following points.

(a) To what extent can the welfare state be expected to respond to the idealistic needs of the people?

The author stresses that the welfare state needs to respond to the changing idealistic needs not just the materialistic needs of the people. However, standard accounts of the War on Poverty period of the United States tend to indicate that empowering the destitute and dispossessed failed to work as social policy, which led to the return of cash benefits and economic incentives.[1] Thus, the paper could benefit greatly from a short and careful notion of how welfare policies are supposed to address idealistic changes caused by globalization.

(b) In what specific ways do the changing idealistic needs challenge the different types of welfare states in general and the Italian welfare state in particular?

Gøsta Esping-Andersen's renowned typology of the welfare state, as well as other similar typologies such as universalism vs. insurance, is embedded in the materialistic notion of "decommodification of labor." The welfare systems of countries differ in the way labor is decommodified. According to this logical construct, once we determine the critical materialistic feature of globalization or European unity we can hypothesize on the specific ways different welfare states are challenged. This logic is missing from the discussion on the idealistic challenges to the welfare state, since the paper only elaborates on existing materialistic typologies of the welfare state.

## The Italian welfare state and its changes

Although the article has an informative list of welfare policy reforms in the 1990s, the comprehensive account of the challenges of globalization makes it difficult to understand the process through which such challenges entailed actual reforms. In short, the paper could have benefited greatly from a short description of the political process of welfare reform. Without such a description, the reader is lost as to why the challenges were reflected or neglected in the reform. Unfortunately, the paper does not mention some of the recent literature on the impact of globalization on the welfare state.[2] Even a critical review of the existing arguments would have made the paper easier to follow and accentuated its contribution to the field. In a similar vein, if recent literature on the role of non-state actors and voluntary associations in welfare provision (with which I am not very familiar) had been mentioned, the implications of Italy's Local Autonomy Act and the Voluntary Association Act of 1992 would have been clarified.

## The problems of current reforms

The paper is persuasive in arguing that the current reforms are hampered in achieving their goals by the (local) political situation in Italy as well as by the top down nature of reform. However, if the article had a succinct notion of Italian local politics, in which the reforms are embedded, it would have done a great favor to the layman to understand to what extent current reforms are problematic. It would allow us to answer the following question. Is the uniqueness of the Italian welfare state being reinforced or has it changed? Regardless of whether it has changed or not, was that fact because of or in spite of the 1990 reforms? I realize that the requests I have made in this short commentary go well beyond what can be addressed in a short article. Proof of a good thought-provoking piece, this article makes the reader ask questions. Such questions should be the foundation of further work that would greatly increase our understanding of the recent changes in the Italian welfare state within a broader context.

## Notes

[1] See for instance, James T. Patterson, *America's Struggle Against Poverty* (Cambridge Ma: Harvard University Press, 1986), Edward D. Berkowitz, *America's Welfare State: From Roosevelt to Reagan* (Baltimore, Md: The Johns Hopkins University Press, 1991).

[2] For instance, Geoffery Garrett, *Partisan Politics in the Global* Economy (Cambridge, Cambridge University Press, 1998), Fritz W. Sharpf and Vivien A. Schmidt eds, *Welfare and Work in the Open Economy*, vols. 1 and 2 (Oxford: Oxford University Press, 2000), Paul Pierson ed., *The New Politics of the Welfare State* (Oxford: Oxford University Press, 2001), Evelyne Huber and John D. Stephens, *Development and Crisis of the Welfare State* (Chicago, Il: Chicago University Press, 2001), Duane Swank, *Global Capital, Political Institutions, and Policy Change in Developed Welfare States* (Cambridge: Cambridge University Press, 2002).

# Index

aggregate demand
   dynamics 6-9
   and economic growth 11
agriculture sector
   EU 49
   France 49
   Germany 49
   Italy 5, 49
   Spain 49
Austria, non-profit sector 295, 301

Belgium, non-profit sector 295, 301
business structure
   and firm size 57-9
   institutional shocks theory 180-7

Calabria, Lombardia, comparison 104
capitalism, and organizational equilibria 187-9
Cassa per il Mezzogiorno
   corruption 117
   demise 121
   establishment 7, 116
   and infrastructures 117
Central & Eastern Europe, non-profit sector 295
Centre-North
   crime 110
   employment, data 152
   employment rates
      by age 85
      by gender 107
   GDP growth rate 105
   household types 83
   informal economy 111
   infrastructures 109
   job creation, data 152
   migration 5, 8
   poverty 112

   productivity 108
   unemployment 87
      data 152
   *see also* Mezzogiorno
crime
   Centre-North 110
   Italy 110
   Mezzogiorno 110-11

demand, and growth 3-4
demographic indicators
   EU 38
   France 38
   Germany 38
   Italy 38, 316
   Japan 38
   Spain 38
   UK 38
   USA 38
   *see also* population
dualism, Italian economy 8, 9, 81-2, 157, 172-3, 212, 248

economic growth, and aggregate demand 11
employment
   educated
      EU 50
      France 50
      Germany 50
      Italy 50
      Japan 50
      Spain 50
      UK 50
      USA 50
   female
      EU 50
      France 50
      Germany 50
      Italy 50

Japan 50
labour supply 48
Spain 50
UK 50
USA 50
employment structure
  EU 50
  France 50
  Germany 50
  Italy 50
  Japan 50
  Spain 50
  UK 50
  US 50
EU (European Union)
  agriculture sector 49
  demographic indicators 38
  employment
    educated 50
    female 50
    and growth 39
  employment rates, by gender 107
  employment structure 50
  labour market, key indicators 46
  R & D expenditure 31
  self-employment 50
  structural funds, Mezzogiorno 131, 162
  technological indicators 40
  unemployment rates 48
  welfare system 337-9
European Common Market, establishment 7, 8

Falck company
  control-ownership 196
  main shareholders 198
FIAT
  control-ownership 196
  family capitalism 178-80
  main shareholders 198
Fordism 16, 27, 28
  definition 34 n.5
France
  agriculture sector 49
  demographic indicators 38

employment
  educated 50
  female 50
  and growth 39
employment structure 50
labour market, key indicators 46
non-profit sector 295, 301
R & D expenditure 31
self-employment 50
technological indicators 40
unemployment rates 48

G7 countries, service sector 42
GDP (Gross Domestic Product)
  growth
    employment elasticity
      France 43
      Germany 43
      Italy 43
      UK 43
  growth rate
    Centre-North 105
    Italy 6, 43, 105
    Mezzogiorno 105, 114
Germany
  agriculture sector 49
  demographic indicators 38
  employment
    educated 50
    female 50
    and growth 39
  employment structure 50
  labour market, key indicators 46
  non-profit sector 295, 301
  R & D expenditure 31
  self-employment 50
  technological indicators 40
  unemployment rates 48
globalization, and inequality 334-7, 351-2
growth
  and demand 3-4
  favourable conditions 8-9
  process 3, 5-6, 9-10
  theory 11
  *see also* aggregate demand

# Index

inequality, and globalization 334-7, 351-2
institutional shocks theory, and business structure 180-7
Ireland, non-profit sector 295, 301
IRI (Institute for Industrial Reconstruction) 7, 191, 194
Italy
  agriculture sector
    employment
      decline 7
      share 5, 49
  balance of payments 17-18
    technology 31
  banking system 248-9
    income & assets ratio 252
    loans 253
      and deposits 251
    and the Mezzogiorno 249-52
    territorial activities 250
  birth rate 314-15
  capitalism
    family, FIAT 178-80
    types 205
  central government
    inefficiencies 265-6
    and local governments 262
  construction sector
    investment in 6
    and labour mobility 7
    share of GDP 7
  corporate governance
    1990s 199-204
    inter-war 189-92
    post-war 192-9
  crime 110
  currency fluctuations 21, 22
  decentralisation 266-73
  demographic indicators 38, 316
    see also under population
  development, and the family 320-6
  disinflation (1980-1993) 14, 20-1
  economic activity
    indicators
      exporting 74
      industry sector 73
      services sector 73

"economic miracle"
  (1952-1971) x, 4-10, 8, 14
  (1990s) 23-7
economy
  dualism 8, 9, 81-2, 157, 172-3, 212, 248, 283
  liberalisation
    domestic 26
    external 7-8
  restructuring 27-32
employment
  agriculture sector
    decline 7
    share 7
  composition 84-5
  data 152
  educated 50
  female 50
  and growth 39
  and labour demand 49-56
  protection 88-93
  rates, age groups 85
  regions 152
  sectoral 49
employment rates
  by gender 107
    Centre-North 107
    Mezzogiorno 107
employment structure 50
and EMU 24
enterprises
  numbers employed 317-18
  see also under firms
Eurozone integration (1993-2001) 15, 22-3
exchange rates 18-19
exports
  growth 7, 9
  industrial districts 238-43
  specialisation 236-8
family
  and change 317-20
  and development 320-6
  economic role 177
  profile 314-17
  and social networks 326-9

federalism 266
financial reforms 266-73
firms
   exports 60-1
   information decentralisation 222-9
   large, outsourcing 218-20
   number 72
   performance indicators 59-63
   profits 60
   R & D 61, 63
   size 56-7
      and business structure 57-9
      manufacturing employment 213
      and productivity 59-60
   small, outsourcing 221-2
   state-owned 7
   subcontracting 214-18
fiscal decentralization, and local government 261-86, 290-1
foundations 303-5
GDP
   construction sector, share 7
   growth rate 6, 8, 10, 43, 105
government expenditure, and revenue 22
growth, and employment 39
health services, finance 267, 274-5
households
   disabled persons, assistance 326
   earners, by age 322
   employment seeking, means 324
   external help, types 326
   financial assets 325
   and population, statistics 315
   regular/irregular jobs 323
   types
      Centre-North 83
      Mezzogiorno 83
housing, demand for 6-7
industrial districts 63-4, 75
   specialisation 236-8
   and trade 238-43
industrial policies, and regulatory reforms 65-6
industrial relations, and labour market policies 51-6

inflation
   and unemployment 15, 21, 23
   and wages 53
informal economy 111
information decentralisation, firms 222-9
infrastructures 109
interest rates 19
investment
   construction sector 6
   utilities 7
job creation, data 152
labour costs, by sector 55
labour demand, and employment 49-56
labour force, distribution 29
labour market
   characteristics 81-3
   irregular 94-7
   key indicators 46
   policies, and industrial relations 51-6
   women 319-20
labour mobility 5
   and the construction sector 7
labour supply 47-9
   female employment 47-8
local governments
   and central government 262
   efficiency 264
   financial accountability 263-4
   fiscal decentralization 261-86, 290-1
machinery sector 44
manufacturing sector
   comparative advantages 236-7
   employment, by firm size 213
   production outsourcing 212-29, 233-4
   specialisation 43-4, 237-8
      export share 45
marriages, first 6-7
non-profit sector 296-302
   by main activity sector
      and employment bracket 299
      and legal form 298
      and revenue 300
   data 295, 296
   foundations 303-5
   international comparisons 300-2
   and market failures 293-4

# Index

ONLUS (Socially Useful Non-Profit Organisations) 305-6
   and participation demand 294
   prospects 306-8
   social co-operatives 303
   volunteerism 302-3
performance indicators, firms 59-63
population 38
   cities, population 319
   and households, statistics 315
   increase 7
   major cities 319
   and professional activity 318
poverty 112
privatization 25, 29, 200
   data 202-3
production outsourcing
   changing patterns 218-22
   extent 213-18
   manufacturing sector 212-29
productivity 108
public debt 20, 22
R & D expenditure 31
self-employment 50
service sector 42, 49
SMEs (Small & Medium Enterprises) 16, 28-32, 56
   trade balance, contribution 30
social networks, and the family 326-9
social-co-operatives 303
stagflation (1971-1980) 14, 16-19
state aid 66
technological indicators 40
unemployment
   1951-1970 5
   Centre-North 87, 107
   data 152
   head of family 91
   and inflation 15, 21, 23
   Mezzogiorno 87, 107
   rates 48, 86, 107-8
   Regions 152
urbanisation 319
utilities, investment 7
wage bargaining 53

wages
   by sector 54
   and inflation 53
welfare system
   development 339-42
   innovations 342-5, 352
   reforms 345-9, 352-3
women
   labour market 319-20
   professional work 320
   *see also* Centre-North; Mezzogiorno; Regions

Japan
   balance of payments, technology 31
   decentralization 289
   demographic indicators 38
   employment
      educated 50
      female 50
      and growth 39
   employment structure 50
   growth rate 76
   labour market, key indicators 46
   non-profit sector 295, 301
   public finance reforms 289-90
   R & D expenditure 31
   self-employment 50
   technological indicators 40

Keynesism 16, 27, 28
   definition 34 n.5

labour market
   irregular
      Italy 94-7
      Japan 101-3
Latin America, non-profit sector 295
local government, and fiscal decentralization 261-86
Lombardia, Calabria, comparison 104

Mezzogiorno
   and the banking system 249-52
   credit markets 109
   crime 110-11

development 115-16
development plan (2000-2006) 130-3
  lessons 146-7
  local partnerships 144-6
development policies 116-22
  lessons 122-4
employment, data 152
employment rates 107
  by age 85
  by gender 107
EU structural funds 131, 162
GDP growth rate 105, 114
household types 83
income per head 106, 113
informal economy 111
infrastructures 109-10
job creation, data 152
migration 5, 8, 114
  and NEG theory 134-5
  and NPM theory 142
poverty 112
productivity 108-9
  and TCPs 133-44
unemployment 87
  data 152
unemployment rate 107-8
see also Cassa per il Mezzogiorno;
  Centre-North
migration
  Centre-North 5, 8
  Mezzogiorno 5, 8, 114

NEG (New Economic Geography), and
  the Mezzogiorno 134-5
Netherlands, non-profit sector 295, 301
"New Planning", features 150, 163
non-profit sector
  Austria 295, 301
  Belgium 295, 301
  Central & Eastern Europe 295
  France 295, 301
  Germany 295, 301
  Ireland 295, 301
  Italy 296-302
  Japan 295, 301
  Latin America 295

Netherlands 295, 301
Spain 295, 301
UK 295, 301
USA 295, 301
NPM (New Public Management), and the
  Mezzogiorno 142

OECD countries
  employment, data 152
  job creation, data 152
  unemployment, data 152
organizational equilibria, and capitalism
  187-9

Pirelli
  control-ownership 196
  main shareholders 198
privatization
  Europe 26
  Italy 25, 29, 200, 202-3

R & D expenditure
  EU 31
  France 31
  Germany 31
  Italy 31
  Japan 31
  USA 31
Regions
  employment, data 152
  fiscal autonomy 266-73, 280-2
  institutions, and production 156-8
  labour demand 154, 156
  modelling 166-9
  policy
    scenarios 162-3, 166-72
    strategies, impact 158-61
    suggestions 161-3
  resources distribution 264-5
  revenue
    distribution 272-3
    equalisation 283-6
    per capita 276
    total 277
  tax policies 278-80
  unemployment, data 152

variations
   data 151-3
   production functions 153-6

self-employment
   EU 50
   France 50
   Germany 50
   Italy 50
   Japan 50
   Spain 50
   UK 50
service sector
   G7 countries 42
   Italy 42, 49
social networks, and family 326-9
Spain
   agriculture sector 49
   demographic indicators 38
   employment
      educated 50
      female 50
      and growth 39
   employment structure 50
   labour market, key indicators 46
   non-profit sector 295
   self-employment 50
   technological indicators 40
   unemployment rates 48

TCPs (Territorial Competitiveness Policies) 129-30
   and the Mezzogiorno 133-44
technological indicators
   EU 40
   France 40
   Germany 40
   Italy 40
   Japan 40
   Spain 40
   UK 40
   USA 40
TFP (Total Factor Productivity) 3

UK
   balance of payments, technology 31
   demographic indicators 38
   employment
      educated 50
      female 50
      and growth 39
   employment structure 50
   labour market, key indicators 46
   non-profit sector 295, 301
   self-employment 50
   technological indicators 40
   unemployment rates 48
unemployment rates
   EU 48
   France 48
   Germany 48
   Italy 48
   Spain 48
   UK 48
USA
   balance of payments, technological 31
   demographic indicators 38
   employment
      educated 50
      female 50
      and growth 39
   employment structure 50
   labour market, key indicators 46
   non-profit sector 295, 301
   R & D expenditure 31
   stock exchange crash (1987) 20
   technological indicators 40

welfare system, EU 337-9